NORTH CAROLINA
STATE BOARD OF COMMUNITY COLLEGES
LIBRARIES
SAMPSON COMMUNITY COLLEGE

P9-BVM-796

The Early Window

(PGPS-34)

Pergamon Titles of Related Interest

Apter/Goldstein YOUTH VIOLENCE: Programs and Prospects
Feindler/Ecton ADOLESCENT ANGER CONTROL.
Cognitive-Behavioral Techniques
Forgas INTERPERSONAL BEHAVIOR:
The Psychology of Social Interaction
Goldstein/Keller AGGRESSIVE BEHAVIOR:
Assessment and Intervention
Van Hasselt/Hersen HANDBOOK OF ADOLESCENT PSYCHOLOGY

Related Journals*

CHILD ABUSE AND NEGLECT
CHILDREN AND YOUTH SERVICES REVIEW
JOURNAL OF CHILD PSYCHOLOGY AND PSYCHIATRY

*Free sample copies available upon request.

PERGAMON GENERAL PSYCHOLOGY SERIES
EDITORS
Arnold P. Goldstein, *Syracuse University*
Leonard Krasner, *Stanford University & SUNY at Stony Brook*

The Early Window
Effects of Television on Children and Youth

Third Edition

Robert M. Liebert
Joyce Sprafkin

State University of New York at Stony Brook

PERGAMON PRESS
New York ● Oxford ● Beijing ● Frankfurt
São Paulo ● Sydney ● Tokyo ● Toronto

U.S.A.	Pergamon Press, Maxwell House, Fairview Park, Elmsford, New York 10523, U.S.A.
U.K.	Pergamon Press, Headington Hill Hall, Oxford OX3 OBW, England
PEOPLE'S REPUBLIC OF CHINA	Pergamon Press, Room 4037, Qianmen Hotel, Beijing, People's Republic of China
FEDERAL REPUBLIC OF GERMANY	Pergamon Press, Hammerweg 6, D-6242 Kronberg, Federal Republic of Germany
BRAZIL	Pergamon Editora, Rue Eça de Queiros, 346, CEP 04011, Paraiso, São Paulo, Brazil
AUSTRALIA	Pergamon Press, Australia, P.O. Box 544, Potts Point, N.S.W. 2011, Australia
JAPAN	Pergamon Press, 8th Floor, Matsuoka Central Building, 1-7-1 Nishishinjuku, Shinjuku-ku, Tokyo 160, Japan
CANADA	Pergamon Press Canada, Suite No. 271, 253 College Street, Toronto, Ontario, Canada M5T 1R5

Copyright © 1988 Pergamon Books Inc.

All Rights Reserved. No part of this publication may be reproduced, stored in a retrieval system or transmitted in any form or by any means: electronic, electrostatic, magnetic tape, mechanical, photocopying, recording or otherwise, without permission in writing from the publishers.

First edition 1973

Second edition 1982

Third edition 1988

Second printing, 1989

Library of Congress Cataloging in Publication Data
Liebert, Robert M., 1942-
The early window.
(Pergamon general psychology series; 34)
Bibliography: p.
Includes index.
1. Television and children — United States.
I. Sprafkin, Joyce N., 1949- . II. Title. III. Series.
HQ784.T4L48   1988   305.2'3   87-25701

ISBN 0-08-034680-4 (Hard cover)
ISBN 0-08-034679-0 (Flexi cover)

Printed in the United States of America

For Minnie and Harry Liebert
and Toby and Isaac Sprafkin

Contents

Preface

It has been estimated that by the age of 18 a child born today will have spent more time watching television than in any other single activity besides sleep. What are, and will be, the effects of this cumulative exposure?

The question is not a new one. It has been posed repeatedly since the advent of television sets as a common home fixture over four decades ago. Suggested answers, based both on simple opinion and research, have ranged from confident statements that the medium's influence is uniformly undesirable to equally glib assertions that merely watching television entertainment fare can do little to shape children's attitudes and behavior.

By the turn of this decade literally thousands of studies had been done on various aspects of children's exposure to, comprehension of, and reactions to television. Moreover, the issue of television's effects on children has raised significant social questions about possible censorship, and as a result, found its way into several important courtroom battles. After an initial focus on the possible effects of TV violence, investigators turned their attention to using television in more constructive ways, but this effort also turned out to have its tricky side and subtle issues.

The purpose of this book is to provide an account of the theory and research which now bears on television and children's attitudes, development, and behavior, and to explore the social, political, and economic factors that surround these issues. We have tried to write for those most likely to be concerned with television and its role in the future of our society: students, parents, professionals concerned with children's welfare, and men and women in the broadcasting industry or in public office who influence broadcasting policies and practices. Where methodologically complex issues seem to deserve mention, we have tried to explain them in relatively simple, nontechnical terms. We have also provided an appendix to explain briefly the essence of the correlational and experimental methods of social science research as they have been applied to the question of children and television.

The interplay of social science and social policy is both complex and difficult on many counts; we have tried to explain rather than ignore these complexities so as to provide a more complete understanding of our present state of knowledge and of the difficult road that must be followed by anyone who would influence television.

In preparing this volume we received invaluable help from many sources. We are especially grateful to Jerry Frank of Pergamon Press for his wise counsel in the development of this edition. We have benefited from the editorial suggestions of Dale Kunkel, Lynn Langenbach, L. Theresa Watkins, Rochelle Anderson, and Charlene Tyson. We also thank Gretchen Daly for her assistance in the preparation of the manuscript, Debra Martin, Virginia Calder, Donal Conway, and Bernadette Irizarry for technical assistance, and Leslie Slocum (of the Television Information Office) for providing us with valuable resource materials.

ROBERT M. LIEBERT
JOYCE SPRAFKIN

1
Background and Issues

OVERVIEW

Television, virtually unknown 50 years ago, is now present in almost every home in the United States and has spread rapidly to all corners of the world. Today the average child spends more time watching television than going to school. As a result, it is understandable that thoughtful people everywhere have asked about the effects of all this television viewing on children. In trying to assess television's possible effects, six questions continue to be raised:

1. Does TV violence instigate aggressive or antisocial behavior or "toughen" children in their acceptance of such behavior in others?

2. Do TV portrayals of minorities and women cultivate social attitudes and stereotypes?

3. Do television commercials take unfair advantage of children?

4. Does commercial broadcast television fulfill its responsibility to "serve the public interest," which it assumes by accepting a license to use the public airwaves?

5. In what ways and under what circumstances (if any) should the TV programming or advertising content that children see be subjected to censorship by government or private groups?

6. To what extent can, or should, television be used for educating and/or socializing children?

The purpose of this book is to shed light on each of these issues by describing and analyzing the social science research, politics, and legal considerations surrounding them.

OUTLINE

Imagine that we could hurl ourselves back in time to 1945, stop an average 7-year-old child on the street and ask: "What's an *airplane*?" The youngster would surely know what an airplane is and would probably be puzzled by our easy question. But suppose we had asked instead: "What's a *television*?" We can be almost certain that our young subject would *not* have been able to answer this question in 1945 even though virtually every 7-year-old in the United States could answer it today. It is easy to forget that at the end of World War II airplanes, telephones, and movie theaters were all commonplace, but most children had never seen or heard of television. Figure 1.1 shows the percentage of U.S. households with television sets for every 5-year period from 1940 to 1985.

When television was first introduced, it was little more than a luxury for the wealthy. But it was a luxury with great appeal, especially for children. Children whose families had a television set quickly became popular; groups of neighborhood youngsters swarmed to the nearest TV-equipped home to soak up early cartoon and adventure offerings. Given this response, it is not surprising that within two decades virtually every American home had a TV and many had two or more. (Despite inflation, the cost of TV sets has decreased over the years. While the average cost of a black and white receiver was $279 in 1947, by 1987 the cost had dropped to $69!) Today 92% of all households have a color receiver (Steinberg, 1985).

The United States is by no means unique in its acceptance of television. A recent analysis of the penetration of television in 10 other free-world countries reveals that television's popularity is universal. (see Table 1.1).

Table 1.1 Percentage of Homes with Television
in
10 Free-World Countries

COUNTRY	HOMES WITH BROADCAST TV (Percentage)
Belgium/Luxembourg	97
Canada	98
France	93
Ireland	90
Italy	90
Japan	99
Sweden	97
Switzerland	96
United Kingdom	98
West Germany	97

Note. Based on data reported in *Channels: 1986 Field Guide to the Electronic Media* by the Media Commentary Council, Inc., 1986, New York, Author.

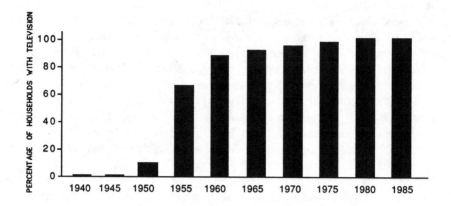

Figure 1.1 Percentage of U.S. households with television 1940–1985.
Based on data reported in *The Mass Media: Aspen Institute Guide to Communication Industry Trends* by C.H. Sterling and T.R. Haight, 1978, New York: Praeger. Also from data reported in *ABC's of Radio and Television* by the Television Information Office, 1981, New York: Author. Also from data reported in *TV Facts* by C. Steinberg, 1985, New York: Facts on File Publications.

TELEVISION USE

Television use in the United States quickly cut out its own substantial niche of time in our daily lives. As early as 1960, when television was still quite "new," the average television set in the United States was on more than 5 hours a day. Television use has steadily increased since then, so that now the average set is on more than 7 hours a day (see Table 1.2). Of course, the average person does not watch this much television. Sometimes the set is watched only by the adults or only by the children in a household—occasionally it is on but not being watched by anyone at all.

Table 1.2 Average Amount of Time a Television was *ON* in U.S. Households, 1960–1984

YEAR	AVERAGE AMOUNT OF TIME
1960	5 hrs. + 6 min.
1964	5 hrs. + 13 min.
1968	5 hrs. + 46 min.
1972	6 hrs. + 2 min.
1976	6 hrs. + 7 min.
1980	6 hrs. + 36 min.
1984	7 hrs. + 8 min.

Note. Based on data reported in *TV Facts* by C. Steinberg, 1985, New York: Facts on File Publications.

Still, there is a good deal of actual television viewing. The typical adult watches television between 2 and 3 hours per day. Most children are exposed to television almost from the time they are born. A typical 6-month-old is in front of a TV almost 1½ hours per day (Hollenbeck & Slaby, 1979). By 3 years the great majority of children have become purposeful viewers with favorite shows.

Viewing time increases and peaks at about 2½ hours per day just before a child enters elementary school. At first, the onset of school seems to diminish available TV time slightly. However, from about age 8 viewing increases steadily to an average of almost 4 hours per day during early adolescence. Viewing then levels off in the later teens at 2 to 3 hours per day. This same basic pattern, found in several studies over the past 20 years, is shown in Figure 1.2.*

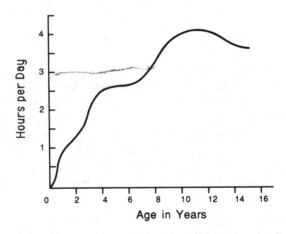

Figure 1.2 Estimated average hours of TV viewing by age in the United States in 1987.

A similar pattern holds outside the United States. In a review of international TV use, Murray (1980) found that the same basic developmental pattern—increasing viewing time to a peak in early adolescence followed by a decline— held across a number of European countries, Canada, and Australia. Variations in TV use between countries

---

*It should be noted that estimates of "average" use do not reflect the tremendous variations in usage. For example, in one study (Lyle & Hoffman, 1972), 25% of the 6th and 10th graders participating watched 8½ hours on Sunday and 5½ hours on school days! More than one third of the first graders in the same study watched 4 or more hours on a typical school day, while 10% reported no viewing at all. Some (but by no means all) of this variability is related to family background. Children from the lower social class and minority backgrounds watch more television than middle and upper middle class white children, brighter children tend to watch less than other children, and a child's viewing habits are quite similar to those of the child's parents.

was to a great extent determined by the amount of programming available and the hours of broadcast. Averaged over all ages, children in countries with large amounts of television available (e.g., Australia, Canada, Japan, United Kingdom, and United States) watch about 2 to 3 hours per day, whereas those in countries with more limited broadcasts (e.g., Germany, Austria, Italy, Sweden, Norway) watch about 1 to 2 hours daily.

HOW TELEVISION HAS CHANGED FAMILY LIFE

The appearance of television and its meteoric rise in the 1950s had a significant impact on the structuring of family life. Johnson (1967) reported that 60% of families changed their sleeping patterns because of TV, 55% altered meal times, and 78% used TV as an "electronic babysitter." He also documented that engineers in some large metropolitan areas had to redesign city water systems to accommodate the drop in pressure caused by heavy lavatory use during prime time commercials.

Robinson (1972) investigated the impact of television by comparing daily activities of set owners and nonowners in 15 locations in 11 countries.* Noting that previous research had not adequately considered all the activities which might have been affected by television, he employed the technique of *time budgets*; he asked people to fill out diaries concerning all of their activities throughout a full 24-hour day. Activities that decreased were sleep, social gatherings away from home, other leisure activities (e.g., correspondence and knitting), conversation, and household care. A later study replicated these same findings and also found that the introduction of television was associated with a decline in newspaper reading (Robinson, 1981). Robinson observed:

> It is of considerable interest to compare television with other innovations of the twentieth century. Comparing the amount of travel by owners of automobiles with that of nonowners, we were especially surprised that cross-nationally automobile owners on the average spent only six percent more time in transit than nonowners. While automobile owners were undoubtedly able to cover far more territory in the time they spent travelling, the overall shift is pale indeed compared with the 58 percent increase in media usage apparently occasioned by the influence of television. Cross-national data also indicate that time spent on housework is not grossly affected by the acquisition of home appliances like washing machines and dryers. Rather, it appears that time saved on these basic chores as a result of labor-saving devices is quickly channeled into other activities designed to improve the appearance of the home. Thus, at least in the temporal sense, television appears to have had a greater influence on the structure of daily life than any other innovation in this century. (1972, p. 428)

---

*Belgium, Bulgaria, Czechoslovakia, East Germany, France, Hungary, Peru, Poland, United States, West Germany, and Yugoslavia.

As a concrete illustration, consider a recent study done in Canada. Williams and Handford (1986) found that involvement in community activities was greatest in a Canadian town that had no television reception. After television arrived in this town, young people's participation in community activities dropped markedly. As an example, Figure 1.3 shows the number of sports activities participated in by junior high and high school students in Canadian towns with either no television, one channel, or many channels.

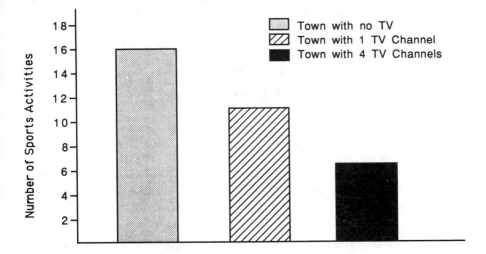

Figure 1.3 Average number of sports activities participated in by youths (Grades 7–12) in three Canadian towns. From data reported in "Television and Other Leisure Activities" by T.H. Williams and A.G. Handford, in *The Impact of Television: A Natural Experiment in Three Communities* (pp. 143–213) edited by T.H. Williams, 1986, Orlando, FL: Academic Press, Inc. Copyright 1986 by Academic Press, Inc. Reprinted by Permission.

Besides replacing some activities, the presence of television seems to alter others. Sheehan (1983) reported that more than half of all elementary school children watched TV while eating their evening meals. An even larger percentage watched while doing their homework!

TELEVISION'S SOCIAL EFFECTS ON CHILDREN

We can see that television made a spectacular appearance and now has a permanent place in our lives. What effect does all this viewing have on us? It is hard to know how to even begin to answer this question, except to state the well-established fact that we have spent our time very differently since TV's arrival.

Is exposure to television entertainment making us think or act differently? Does it change our attitudes and shape our feelings and reactions? Most adults believe television entertainment does not have an important social influence on them (see Steiner, 1963). It is, after all, only entertainment. But children are seen as more susceptible than adults, and concerns about the effects of other media on children's social and personality development were voiced long before the appearance of television. In face, sex and brutal violence were taken out of comic books and movies by the forces of censorship groups, created by those concerned about children's social and moral development (Cowan, 1978).

Today's children are getting a far heavier dose of television entertainment than their grandparents got out of comic books, movies, and phonograph records combined. A certain amount of what children see on television is considered to be "children's programming" (or kidvid), mostly Saturday and Sunday morning shows. However, *most* of the programs children watch are designed for adult or family audiences.

RECURRING ISSUES

Because television is so widespread and children watch it so much, many people have been concerned about what television is "doing" to children. There are six basic recurring issues, each with its parallel concern in movies, comic books, and popular music.

Instigation of violent, aggressive, or antisocial behavior

The possibility that certain television content stimulates unwanted or disapproved attitudes or behavior has received more attention than any other issue.

Dramatic instances of antisocial behavior

The first major study done in the United States, Schramm, Lyle and Parker's *Television in the Lives of Our Children* (1961), presented a collection of documented instances in which TV was implicated in the aggressive or antisocial behavior of otherwise innocent youth. Here are four instances reported by Schramm and his associates:

> In a Boston suburb, a nine-year-old boy reluctantly showed his father a report card heavily decorated with red marks, then proposed one way of getting at the heart of the matter; they could give the teacher a box of poisoned chocolates for Christmas. "It's easy, Dad, they did it on television last week. A man wanted to kill his wife, so he gave her candy with poison in it and she didn't know who did it". (p. 161)

> In Brooklyn, New York, a six-year-old son of a policeman asked his father for real bullets because his little sister "doesn't die for real when I shoot her like they do when Hopalong Cassidy kills 'em". (p. 161)

In Los Angeles, a housemaid caught a seven-year-old boy in the act of sprinkling ground glass into the family's lamb stew. There was no malice behind the act. It was purely experimental, having been inspired by curiosity to learn whether it would really work as well as it did on television. (p. 161)

A 13-year-old Oakville [California] boy, who said he received his inspiration from a television program, admitted to police . . . that he sent threatening notes to a . . . school teacher. His inspiration for the first letter came while he was helping the pastor of his church write some letters. When the minister left the office for an hour, the boy wrote his first poison pen letter. "I got the idea when I saw it happen on TV," he told Juvenile Sgt. George Rathouser. "I saw it on the 'Lineup' program." (p. 164)

Equally compelling instances were reported at about the same time in testimony before the United States Senate Subcommittee to investigate juvenile delinquency. Below is a sample of the documented instances provided to the subcommittee (U.S. Senate, 1961).

On July 9, 1959, the *New York Journal-American* reported that four young boys desiring a human skull for their club activities, broke into a Jersey City mausoleum, pried open a coffin and took one. They brought the skull to their clubroom where they desecrated it by sticking a lighted candle in it. Astonished police said the club members—seven boys, whose ages ranged from 11 to 14—got the idea from a television horror show.

The Chicago Tribune reported on November 22, 1959, that two Chicago boys had been arrested for attempting to extort $500 from a firm through a bomb threat. They threatened the owners and members of their families if police were notified. The boys . . . stated they got their idea from television.

According to the *Reading Eagle*, Reading, Pa., of March 2, 1960, a 16-year-old boy was arrested after neighbors spotted him entering the cellar of a home. He was wearing gloves and said he learned the trick of wearing gloves so that he did not leave fingerprints from television shows which he had watched.

A college athlete was arrested in Grand Junction, Colo., in April, 1960, after he had mailed letters threatening to kill the wife of a bank president unless he was paid $5,000. At the time of his arrest, he stated he got his idea from television shows.

The *New York Journal-American* reported on December 22, 1960, that police arrested an 11-year-old who admitted having burglarized Long Island homes for more than $1,000 in cash and valuables. His accomplice was identified as a 7-year-old friend. The boy said he learned the technique of burglary by seeing how it was done on television. (pp.1923–1924)

As a result of the foregoing reports, entertainment television came to be seen by social scientists in the early 1960s as potentially exerting a great influence on the young. Inspired by his own studies confirming that even young children can learn specific novel aggressive behaviors from television, Stanford psychologist Albert Bandura published an article in *Look* magazine in 1963 entitled, "What TV Violence Can Do To Your Child."

The first paragraph of the article read:

> If parents could buy packaged psychological influences to administer in
> regular doses to their children, I doubt that many would deliberately select
> Western gun slingers, hopped-up psychopaths, deranged sadists, slap-stick
> buffoons and the like, unless they entertained rather peculiar ambitions for
> their growing offspring. Yet such examples of behavior are delivered in
> quantity, with no direct charge, to millions of households daily. Harried
> parents can easily turn off demanding children by turning on a television set;
> as a result, today's youth is being raised on a heavy dosage of televised
> aggression and violence. (p. 46)

Bandura's article popularized the term *TV violence*. As can be seen from
the foregoing extract, he equated TV violence with almost all objectionable
behavior.

These concerns, expressed from academia, were paralleled by Congressional hearings. Senator Thomas Dodd, who between 1961 and 1964 headed
a Senate subcommittee on children's television, said:

> Glued to the TV set from the time they can walk, our children are getting an
> intensive training in all phases of crime from the ever-increasing array of
> Westerns and crime-detective programs available to them. The past decade has
> seen TV come of age. However, the same decade has witnessed the violence
> content in programs skyrocket and delinquency in real life grow almost two
> hundred percent. (cited in Merriam, 1968, p. 43)

Dramatic instances of suicide

In the past decade TV has also been linked with some dramatic instances of
juvenile suicide. For example, a 1982 article in *Family Circle* described in
detail the tragic case of 6-year-old Jeremy Nezworski, who innocently took
his own life when trying to imitate the hangman scene from a cartoon
(Remsberg, 1982). Cases like Jeremy's are not limited to very young
children. Consider the case of 18-year-old Timothy Jones, who watched an
episode of "Hill Street Blues" in which a convict tried to hang himself in a
prison cell. Later that night Jones was arrested for car theft and drunk
driving. He hung himself in his cell early the following morning (Newsday,
1982).* Even the loss of television has been accused of provoking suicide. In
California, Genaro Garcia, age 13, purposely shot himself after his father
removed the television set from his room. In his suicide note he wrote, "I
can't stand another minute without television" (*"Dad confiscates television,"*
1983, p. 3).

---

*Television's influence on suicide is further documented in two recent articles that
were published in *The New England Journal of Medicine*. Teenage suicides have been
shown to increase following the broadcast of either fictional movies (Gould &
Shaffer, 1986) or news/feature stories (Phillips & Carstensen, 1986) about suicide.

TV violence and the "toughening" of values
Instigation to violent and antisocial acts is only one of the concerns raised by TV violence. An equally important question is whether exposure to such entertainment thickens children's skins to real-life violence and aggression committed by others. Eve Merriam captured the essence of this concern as early as 1964, in an article in *Ladies Home Journal*:

> The violent entertainment forms affect children in other ways. If they are not becoming actively delinquent—our "good" middle-class children, yours and mine—they are becoming passively jaded. As a kind of self-protection, they develop thick skins to avoid being upset by the gougings, smashings and stompings they see on TV. As the voice of reason is shown to be a swift uppercut to the chin, child viewers cannot afford to get involved, for if they did, their emotions would be shredded. So they keep "cool," distantly unaffected. Boredom sets in, and the whole cycle starts over again. Bring on another show with even more bone-crushing and teeth-smashing so the viewers will react. (p. 45)

Stereotyping and the cultivation of attitudes

The concept that television is a teacher extends far beyond the issue of TV violence. If television can teach by providing examples, then children and perhaps adults may be influenced in a host of ways by the roles, relationships, and values that are implicit in the TV entertainment they see.

Racial stereotyping
On these grounds, the National Association for the Advancement of Colored People (NAACP) demanded in 1951 that CBS stop broadcasting its only series featuring black characters, "Amos and Andy." The NAACP described the deleterious effect they felt the series was having and provided a "content analysis" of the series as justification for their concern:

> ["Amos and Andy"] tends to strengthen the conclusion among uninformed and prejudiced people that Negroes are inferior, lazy, dumb and dishonest . . . Negro doctors are shown as quacks and thieves. Negro lawyers are shown as slippery cowards, ignorant of their profession and without ethics. Negro women are shown as cackling, screaming shrews, in big-mouth close-ups, using street slang, just short of vulgarity. All Negroes are shown as dodging work of any kind. Millions of white Americans see this Amos 'n' Andy picture and think the entire race is the same. (*News from NAACP*, 1951, pp. 4–5)

Sex stereotyping
Racial stereotypes are only one of several disapproved attitudes that might be transmitted by television. In 1970, Marya Mannes, a feminist spokesperson, charged television with sustaining many cultural stereotypes about women's roles. She especially targeted television commercials which

reinforce, like an insistent drill, the assumption that a woman's only valid function is that of wife, mother, and servant of men: the inevitable sequel to her earlier function as sex object and swinger.

[Mannes went on to suggest that only four types of women appear in TV ads]: the gorgeous teen-age swinger with bouncing locks; the young mother teaching her baby girl the right soap for skin care; the middle-aged housewife with a voice like a power saw; and the old lady with dentures and irregularity. . . . Only one woman on a commercial . . . has a job; a comic plumber pushing *Comet.* (pp. 66–67)

Commercialism

As we will explain in chapter 2, because U.S. commercial television is corporate, it is responsible to stockholders. Its profit derives from advertising revenues, and this ultimately creates pressure to show advertisements that sell as effectively as possible. Moreover, advertisements directed to children use a variety of sophisticated techniques to appeal to young viewers. Parents claim that children are unable to understand the commercials and that advertising to children over television is unfair. In the words of Peggy Charren (1974), president and founder of Action for Children's Television:

> The ultimate goal of the thirty seconds worth of information contained in the message must be to manipulate the child to desire, want and need the product. No industry will invest forty million to convince these two- to eleven-year olds that they do *not* need a lot of these products to be happy, healthy, wealthy and wise. . . .

> Ads for the Lone Ranger show that famous Mr. Fix-it with his sidekick Tonto, with the Bad Guy, and with adventure kits. Each of them is "sold separately" and priced separately, but they are all shown in the same commercial, because it's no fun to play with one part without the others. The prices of these and other combined sets (G.I. Joe and his accoutrements, Kung Fu and his friends) is enough to make even an affluent parent shudder. (p. 4)

In addition, there are concerns about *what* is advertised on television. Because of pricing and other considerations it makes more sense to advertise manufactured treats than fresh farm items. As a result,

> A child watching television programs for children sees ads for sugared cereals, candy, snack foods and sugared drinks in an unceasing barrage and learns nothing of the essentials for a balanced diet. On a typical Saturday morning a child will see no ads for fruit, vegetables, cheese, eggs or other valuable nutritional foods but instead will be cajoled to buy a new sugared cereal with a toy premium or to put syrup into his milk to make it "fun." (ACT, 1972, pp. 2–3)

Serving the public interest

Traditionally, two forms of mass media have been distinguished. *Print media* are those providing access to information by producing and distributing copies. Thus books, newspapers, magazines, phonograph records, stereo tapes, photographs, movies and videotapes are all print media. Printing invites competition. Anyone can, for example, go into the newspaper business without interfering with anyone else. By contrast, the *broadcast media*, radio and television, must use specific public airwaves to transmit their signals to individual receivers. Regulation, which is rare for print media because of the concept of freedom of the press (guaranteed in the United States by the First Amendment), is necessary at least up to a point in broadcasting. This is because similar or identical broadcast signals interfere with one another. (Consider, for example, how television reception is sometimes interfered with by operating an electrical appliance on the same circuit.) To avoid chaos, the "right to broadcast" is restricted to those with licenses and, of course, only one licensee is given the right to broadcast on the particular station or channel in a particular area. The government must assign public air waves, raising the question of what the public can expect from the license holder. As we will see in chapter 3 this is a very complicated issue. The licensee has a responsibility to "serve the public interest," monitored by the Federal Communications Commission (FCC), but the scope and nature of this responsibility have proven difficult to define.

Nonetheless, television's critics have long complained that TV broadcasters are delinquent in meeting their responsibility to the public. The most famous expression of this indictment was advanced in 1964 in the first public address of newly appointed FCC Commissioner Newton Minow to the National Association of Broadcasters. Minow (1964) admonished the broadcasters:

> Your license lets you use the public's airwaves as trustees for 180 million Americans. The public is your beneficiary. If you want to stay on as trustees, you must deliver a decent return to the public—not only to your stockholders. So, as a representative of the public, your health and your product are among my chief concerns. As to your health: let's talk only of television today. In 1960 gross broadcast revenues of the television industry were over $1,268,000,000; profit before taxes was $243,900,000—an average return on revenue of 19.2 percent . . . I have confidence in your health. But not in your product . . . when television is bad, nothing is worse. I invite you to sit down in front of your television set when your station goes on the air and stay there without a book, magazine, newspaper, profit-and-loss sheet or rating book to distract you—and keep your eyes glued to that set until the station signs off. I can assure you that you will observe a vast wasteland. . . . Gentlemen, your trust accounting with your beneficiaries is overdue. Never have so few owed so much to so many. (pp. 49–53)

Censorship

The First Amendment to the U.S. Constitution guarantees freedom of speech and of the press. This freedom has never been absolute, however. It is unlawful to speak or write so as to incite others to illegal acts, and communities may censor communications that are obscene or profane by their own standards. Those concerned about the effects of television on children have often threatened to use legal means (such as withholding a TV license renewal) to censor what they consider to be unacceptable content. Boycotting of advertisers, which has also been suggested at one time or another, may also be considered a form of censorship. Others, however, have expressed grave concern about placing *any* censoring function in the hands of a government agency or ideological group. These individuals say that the idea of generating lists of "approved" television programming for children frightens them more than anything they have seen so far on entertainment television.

Such questions have a legal as well as a moral component. As we will see, both TV violence and advertising have been involved in fascinating and important courtroom battles that dealt with both psychological and Constitutional issues and raised the question of whether or not any part of children's television should be "controlled" by government restraint.

Television and Education

From the earliest days of the medium, parents, educators, and social philosophers have noted the possible impact of television on educationally relevant concerns. The discussion has been a two-sided coin. On the one hand, critics have been concerned that standard commercial television may have an adverse effect on children's academic skills (such as reading) or on aspects of their cognitive functioning (for example, their imagination and creativity). On the other hand, advocates have insisted that television could be used to facilitate the development of academic and cognitive skills, if "appropriate" programming were available.

Possible adverse effects

In our discussion of how TV has changed family life, we mentioned the Canadian study in which children living in otherwise comparable towns with no television (Notel), one channel (Unitel), or many channels (Multitel) were compared. The same study provided data relevant to the question of whether television has any influence on children's reading skills (Corteen & Williams, 1986). Second-grade children in Notel scored higher on a test of reading fluency than did their peers in the towns where TV was present. But 4 years later, when TV was available in all three towns, there was no longer any difference among second graders in reading fluency. The investigators concluded that television viewing impedes the acquisition of reading skills.

They suggest that the underlying mechanism is probably one of displacement. That is, time spent with television is likely to usurp time that would otherwise be spent on reading practice.

Based on the same Canadian three-town study, Harrison and Williams (1986) also found that children in Notel initially had higher scores on a measure of creativity than children in either of the TV towns. However, once television was introduced the creativity scores of the Notel children dropped down to the levels found in Unitel and Multitel. (See Figure 1.4). Taken together with the findings of other researchers (Singer, 1982), these data suggest that heavy exposure to standard commercial television programming may inhibit children's imaginative and creative abilities.

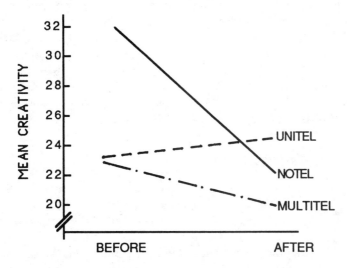

Figure 1.4 Mean creativity scores in Notel, Unitel, and Multitel before and after the introduction of TV in Notel. Based on data reported in Harrison and Williams (1986).

Using television as a teacher

Although standard TV fare may have an adverse effect on children's academic and social development, it is equally plausible that creating and exposing children to specially designed or "appropriate" programming might have beneficial effects. In fact, inasmuch as television can be found in virtually every home and is so popular among children, putting it to good use seems an obvious thing to do. It is in this context that programs such as "Sesame Street" were developed and funded.

However, as efforts have actually been made to harness television's social and educational potential, it has become apparent that purposely using television as a teacher is a tricky enterprise that can often lead to surprising controversy. In the matter of educational television, for example, researchers have found that instructional programming will be selectively watched.

2002075 1

Children who are already interested in academic topics or whose parents actively encourage them to watch educational programs are likely to choose these shows over empty, slapstick cartoons. On the other hand, children from less academically oriented or less advantaged backgrounds are likely to shun educational programming and stick to cartoon fare. As a result, social problems such as the educational gap between advantaged and disadvantaged children may ironically be *increased* by efforts to use television as an educator (Cook, et al., 1975).

The controversy is even more acute when it comes to using television to socialize children. Though generosity, cooperation, and friendliness appear to be pure virtues in the abstract, concrete examples can backfire. Most of us want our children to be generous, but it is unwise to be generous to a fault (for example, by simply giving away one's lunch money). Likewise, though friendliness is generally considered to be a desirable characteristic, most parents do not want their children to be receptive to the friendly overtures of strangers.

It is clear that television *can* be used as a teacher. Whether it *should* be used in this way continues to be the subject of heated debate, as we shall see when we return to this question in chapter 10.

THE ROLE OF SOCIAL SCIENCE

Social science, especially psychology, began to make its first major impact on society after World War II. Theory and research in the natural sciences had paid off handsomely in terms of technical innovation and accomplishment, and people began to turn to the social sciences for answers to questions concerning the forces that shape their personal and social lives. By the late 1950s, research teams and groups in technologically advanced countries everywhere were beginning to study the role of various factors in children's social and personality development. At the same time, several highly influential theories of children's psychological development were being promulgated. These theories allowed conceptual links to be formed between basic socialization processes (of prime interest to academic psychologists) and the specific effects that television viewing might have on the young.

The demand for research evidence

The demand for research appears repeatedly throughout disputes on every aspect of children's television. A major purpose of this book is to summarize and explain the considerable body of research now available on television's effects on the young.

We must make clear at the outset that questions raised about the effects of television have proven tricky for social science researchers. Many issues are phrased in global or ambiguous language, as when terms such as *TV violence* and *aggression* are used to cover a broad but unspecified array of possible instances. There is also the problem of research design. Often research apparently supports one conclusion, but on closer examination admits of alternative explanations.

Questions about *effects* are always questions about *causes*. In the real flow of events, possible causes are intermingled into a subtle and complex fabric. Trying to unravel this complexity and find the specific effects of television is an enormously difficult undertaking, and many of the studies we shall discuss turn out to be quite ambiguous when it comes to answering questions of practical concern to society.*

Then, too, there is the matter of what questions to ask. The first major studies of the effects of television tried to determine the effects of introducing the television medium (Himmelweit, Oppenheim & Vince 1958; Schramm et al., 1961). Later it became apparent that the important social questions revolved around television's specific content, because virtually everyone had a television, and television was here to stay (recall Figure 1.1).

PLAN OF THIS BOOK

We have seen in this chapter that in a few decades television has become a central fixture in the lives of children. Whereas in 1945 television viewing did not occupy any of children's time and the average child spent no more time than a couple of hours a week at movies, by 1970 children were spending more time watching television than going to school. Today the only thing children between 2 and 15 do more than watch television is sleep. This is a profound change in children's experience, and means that for the first time in human history children are exposed to more fictional characters than real people during their formative years. It is understandable that various concerns about all of this television viewing have been raised.

The purpose of this book is to review the question of what effects television has on children and youth from the point of view of both social science and social policy. Despite all the changes that have transpired in the television industry and in the social/political climate and all the objective evidence that has amassed over the years, the issues of concern about television remain largely the same. In this book, we discuss the history of

---

*Readers unfamiliar with the basic methods and terminology used in social science research should consult Appendix A.

each of these continuing concerns about the medium and the relevant scientific evidence and social issues surrounding each concern. As the reader will see, the research evidence is complex and so are the social issues. Each issue ultimately involves a myriad of forces and ideas coming from child psychology, economics, law, and politics.

Commercial television intends to be a business rather than a social force—indeed "American" television has become one of the most profitable and significant industries in the country and has successfully spread itself all over the world. How, then, does television operate as a business and how are decisions about TV program content actually made? These are the questions with which we begin chapter 2.

2

Television as a Business

OVERVIEW

Most television in the United States is a commercial enterprise, generating operating costs and profits by selling advertising time within and between its entertainment offerings. Decisions about production and program content are made for the most part by the three major networks, which distribute the programs to local affiliated stations. The prime-time and children's programming developed by the networks are both highly profitable, but the profitability of any particular offering is dependent upon the ratings it receives.

Because the advertising revenue generated by a program is determined by its ability to attract an audience, programs are developed with an eye toward maximizing their appeal to the targeted group. The overall situation conspires to produce high-action, simple, formularized entertainment.

The expansion of cable TV and the availability of videocassette recorders (VCRs) have acted to erode some of the networks' audience. These new technologies have increased the overall use of television. They have also made material available to children and youth for television viewing that would never have been broadcast over the airwaves.

OUTLINE

The programs shown on TV must be paid for by someone. Someone must decide what to broadcast. And when television uses the open airwaves—a valuable public resource—the right to broadcast must be allocated through licensing and then monitored. Understanding the way in which television is operated, financed, and controlled as a business is essential to understanding the medium and its messages.

BROADCASTING AND THE THREE U.S. COMMERCIAL NETWORKS

The major television broadcasters in the United States are the three commercial networks: American Broadcasting Company (ABC), Columbia Broadcasting System (CBS), and the National Broadcasting Company (NBC). Simply, a television network is an organization that supplies programs to local stations which broadcast them to the homes in their area.

Each of the three networks directly own several licensed stations. These stations are in the largest cities, so that each of the three networks reaches about 20% of all TV homes through their own stations. In addition, each network has more than 200 affiliated stations. Of the roughly 900 commercial television stations in the United States, about 85% are affiliated with one of the three networks.* Every day these affiliated stations broadcast 12 to 14 hours of programming and advertisements provided by the networks, including 3 hours during the lucrative prime time period (from 8:00 p.m. to 11:00 p.m. on the East and West Coasts and from 7:00 p.m. to 10:00 p.m. in the Rocky Mountain and Midwest states). Another way of looking at the reach of the networks is that a full 60% of the programming shown by network affiliated stations is supplied by the networks (who buy the programming from production companies). Later we will discuss how the networks decide which programs to air.

The networks make their profits by selling air time to advertisers who are interested in securing audiences for their advertisements. The network affiliates receive payment from the network for the use of the station's time. In addition, they have several minutes each hour to sell advertising time on their own.

SELLING TIME

Television is called *commercial* when the costs of production and broadcasting as well as all profits are derived from advertising revenue.

---

*It should be noted that although independent or unaffiliated stations are fewer in number and attract smaller audiences than the networks or their affiliates, the number of independent stations has grown enormously, from 73 in 1972 to 230 in 1985.

Manufacturers of products and providers of services wish to persuade the consuming public to use their goods and services or support their causes. To do so, they create messages cast as television messages. Obviously, most people would not buy television sets simply to watch commercials. Therefore, interesting or entertaining programs are also created and made available "free," so that the commercials will be seen by those drawn to the set by the entertainment. Thus, as William Melody (1973) astutely observed, the programs are the bait used to lure the viewers into a position where they can be exposed to persuasive messages.

Commercial television is designed to make money and has succeeded admirably well. In 1985 the networks enjoyed revenues of $8.3 billion and profits of $2.5 billion through advertising (Paskowski, 1986). Television's success as a business mirrors its success as an entertainment medium (recall Figure 1.1). For example, in 1948 NBC was losing $13,000 a day on its TV operation. But within 2 years its revenues more than tripled, and by 1951 it was in the black, where it has remained ever since. In fact, NBC, like the other networks, enjoyed an enviable growth pattern in TV advertising revenues during its formative years (see Figure 2.1). When it comes to national advertising, no other medium comes close to television, which has captured almost 50% of the market (see Table 2.1).

Table 2.1 TV's Share of the American National Advertising Dollar

ADVERTISING METHOD	PERCENTAGE OF TOTAL
Television	49.1
Magazines	18.7
Newspapers	14.4
Business paper	9.7
Radio	5.9
Other	2.2

Note. Based on data reported in *TV Facts* by C. Steinberg, 1985, New York: Facts on File Publications.

How the transaction works

The transaction underlying the TV business involves selling time—"minutes" in the industry jargon—either to advertising agencies or directly to potential sponsors. When the networks sell time, they do not simply offer a spot to a prospective buyer. Rather, a package is sold, with minutes on shows of varying quality and attractiveness and at a package price which is negotiated according to time, network and, of course, the acumen of the bargainers. But even if they fluctuate, prices are not wholly arbitrary. As Les Brown (1971) succinctly stated, "advertisers buy audiences, not programs" (p. 58).

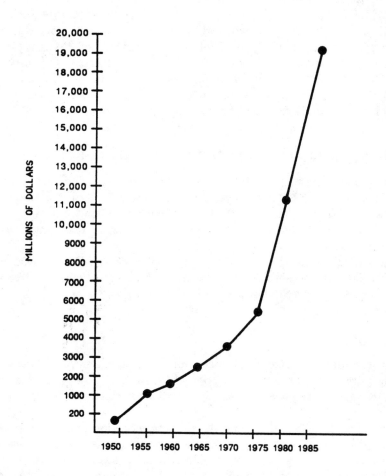

Figure 2.1 Total advertiser expenditures on U.S. television.

The Nielsen ratings are used to determine the number of homes in which a particular show ostensibly is seen. Then advertisers compute their cost for reaching each thousand homes. By this logic, a show that reaches 10 million families with spots at $40,000 per minute and one that reaches 8 million families at $32,000 per minute are equal in cost: $4 per thousand homes. In 1985, the cost of a 30-second spot on a prime-time network TV program averaged $100,000; but top-rated programs such as NBC's "Cosby Show" earned closer to $400,000 per spot. Still more expensive are spots within special programming. In 1983, the 2½-hour final episode of "M*A*S*H" drew the largest audience in TV history (77% of the audience), and earned CBS up to $450,000 for each 30-second commercial and $14 million in revenues ("S*M*A*S*H," 1983). During the 1987 season, CBS charged $600,000 per 30-second spot during its broadcast of the Super Bowl.

Advertising revenues from children's programming

Advertising on children's programs accounts for about 3% of the networks' total billings or about $250 million yearly ("Webs focus," 1986). The leading network children's advertisers in 1984 were General Mills ($28.8 million), Mattel ($26.2 million), Kellogg ($17.5 million), McDonald's ($14.5 million), Quaker Oats ($13.5 million), Hasbro Bradley ($12.2 million), Tomy ($9.8 million), General Foods ($9.1 million), and Nabisco ($9 million) ("Syndies hit," 1985). The price to air a 30-second commercial on a network children's program is now between $18,000 and $20,000.

The ratings

We have seen that the value of any particular commercial minute depends upon the popularity, or presumed popularity, of the show on which it appears. Ratings thus play a vital role in the commercial enterprise of television.

The rating system virtually came in with the television set; a group of advertisers formed an organization to telephone people to ask them what they had watched the night before. The technique was a questionable one, so the phone call was soon supplanted by the diary, which then became the preferred mode of obtaining a family's self-report of viewing patterns. Then came Nielsen.

The Nielsen Ratings

Among inveterate TV viewers, Nielsen is almost a household word. For network shows, it is these evaluations that determine which offerings will be dropped and which will continue.

The Nielsen evaluations come from machines—the patented Audimeters of the A.C. Nielsen Company. About 1,200 households selected to represent a cross section of American homes are paid $25 when the Audimeter is installed, $2 a month thereafter, and reimbursed for half their TV repair bills so that the company's device can record the activity of their television sets. The Audimeter records the minute-by-minute impulses of channel changes and stores them in an electronic memory. The unit, which is connected to both the television set and a special phone line, relays the stored information at least twice daily to a central office computer. Approximately 20% of the sample is replaced each year so that no household is monitored for more than 5 years.

Nielsen provides two important figures to those who buy the service. First is the "rating," which is the percentage of the total possible audience that a program attracts. A rating of 20 means that 20% of the homes with television are tuned to the program. The second is the "share," which reflects how a program is doing opposite other programs aired at the same time; it is a competitive score, indicating percentage of viewership out of the actual number of sets in use. In a three-network system, a program needs a one-third share to be maintained.

The Nielsen system and a similar one used by Britain's commercial network, the Independent Television Authority, can only indicate whether the set is on or off and the location of the channel selector. Whether anyone is in the room (much less watching the show or commercial message) is ignored. The real question of interest to advertisers, "How much watching actually occurs?" is not actually measured by the Nielsen ratings. This was dramatically shown in a 1972 study by Robert Bechtel and his associates in which videotape cameras were placed in the homes of 20 families, so that as the family watched television, the television watched the family. This permitted careful, complete, and reliable comparisons of diary reports and simple measures of when the set was on (the Nielsen method) with what and how much was actually viewed. The results were startling. Both the Nielsen and the diary techniques consistently overestimated by a factor of 30% to 50% the actual viewing of television. Second, the amount of viewing that occurred when the set was on varied substantially with type of program: movies, for example, were watched 76% of the time while on, sporting events less than 60%, and commercials, literally at the bottom of Bechtel's list of 11 types of program events, 54.8% of the time (see Table 2.2).

In a study of children's time spent with television, Anderson and his colleagues (Anderson, Field, Collins, Lorch, & Nathan, 1985) used time-lapsed video recording equipment to monitor the viewing behavior of 5-year-olds from 106 different families over 10 days. The youngsters looked at the television screen 67% of the time they were in the TV viewing area. In a subsequent analysis of the other family members (Anderson, Lorch, Field,

**Table 2.2 Program Categories Ranked by Percentage of Time
Watched while Program Was on**

PROGRAM TYPE	PERCENTAGE OF TIME WATCHED WHILE PROGRAM WAS ON
Movies	76.0
Children's	71.4
Suspense	68.1
Religious	66.7
Family	66.4
Game show	65.9
Talk show	63.7
Melodrama	59.3
Sports events	58.7
News	55.2
Commercial	54.8

Note. From "Correlates Between Observed Behavior and Questionnaire Responses on Television Viewing" by R.B. Bechtel, C. Achelpohl, & R. Akers, in Television and Social Behavior, Vol. 4, Television in Day-to-Day Life: Patterns of Use (pp. 274–344) edited by E.A. Rubinstein, G.A. Comstock, & J.P. Murray, 1972, Washington D.C: Government Printing Office.

Collins, & Nathan, 1986), it was found that the TV viewing room contained no viewers at all about 15% of the time that the TV was on.

Nielsen supplements its Audimeter service with information obtained from diaries to provide the broadcasters with some information about the age and sex of the viewers.* This supplementary information is critical to advertisers who want to reach the right audience with their commercials; for example, a lipstick manufacturer would want its ad placed within a program that drew a large adult female audience. Each quarter hour, 2,300 families record the program watched, channel, the number of persons viewing, and the age and sex of each viewer. Thus 1,200 Audimeter families and 2,300 diary families determine the TV offerings for 250 million American viewers.

Nielsen dominates the national ratings market. However, for local TV audiences, the American Research Bureau's rating service, *Arbitron*, has been estimating TV audiences since 1949. Arbitron is a diary method much like Nielsen's, with participants mailing in weekly diaries of programs viewed and viewers' age and sex breakdowns. To supplement the diary, Arbitron also uses telephone surveys, personal interviews, and electronic meters in selected markets.

---

*In late 1987 Nielsen began to replace the diary with a hand-held device that resembles a television remote control unit to record demographic information about the viewers.

The diary method has proven to be fallible. For example, the respondent is supposed to fill them out daily but according to Mayer (1972):

> One suspicious investigator distributed a hundred diaries, telling recipients he would be back to pick them up in seven days—and then returned in five days instead. He found a number of diaries still blank, the householder having put off till tomorrow what he forgot to do today—and an almost equally large number already complete for all seven days, the helpful respondent having gone through *TV Guide* at once and written in the shows the family "always" sees. (p. 37)

Nevertheless, the ratings figures collected by Nielsen and Arbitron determine the TV advertising rates. When are these rates derived? Four times a year, Nielsen and Arbitron conduct their ratings over "sweeps" of 200 individual TV markets, and most stations use only the ratings during the sweeps to calculate their advertising rates for the season.* Many stations substitute specials and audience-drawing movies over the sweep periods during February, May, July, and November to inflate the audience size figures which would in turn increase their revenues. (This explains much of the variability in the quality of program offerings throughout the year.)

There has been some recent experimentation with program quality rating systems. For example, the National Citizens Committee for Broadcasting conducted a study in which 200 households in Washington, DC kept TV diaries for 1 week, ranking each program viewed according to its importance and entertainment value. As one would expect, there were considerable discrepancies between the quality ratings and the Nielsens. While "I, Claudius" was ranked 46th by the Nielsens, it was ranked first by the quality index (Steinberg, 1985). Because the bottom line for the networks is audience size, not program quality, broadcasters have little interest in quality ratings.

PROGRAM DEVELOPMENT AND PRODUCTION

Television production is a complex business, dependent on artistic, political, and economic factors. The process of producing a series is lengthy and risky, as the increasingly rapid turnover indicates. Most important, it is expensive. In 1983–84, the cost of a single episode of an hour prime-time network series averaged more than $650,000 and a half-hour situation comedy averaged $350,000. Even more expensive are special events such as the ABC production of "The Winds of War," which cost $40 million for the 18-hour miniseries (Steinberg, 1985). Because TV programs are so expensive to

---

*The networks need the daily ratings to monitor the popularity of series, individual episodes, and various specials on a continuous basis.

produce, a very large audience is required to obtain the advertising revenue to cover the costs. Locally produced programs could not draw sufficient advertising revenue to offset production costs for most types of programs. It is for this reason that only three networks in the United States system supply most of the TV fare (more than three fourths of all evening prime-time programming and about 60% of all of their affiliates' programming). The independent stations (not network affiliated) do not produce much of their own programming and rely instead on syndicated shows, often old network series and old movies. This type of fare is also shown by the network affiliates when they are not showing network programming.

One recent development has challenged, on a small scale, the networks' monopoly over prime-time program acquisition. A program cooperative, called Operation Prime-Time, evolved in 1977 as a fourth network for producing alternatives to network dramatic programming. Over 100 stations, both network affiliates and non-affiliates, belong to the cooperative. The stations that carried the first miniseries production, Taylor Caldwell's "Testimony of Two Men," made a larger profit than they would have with a network program. Many of the large production companies (e.g., MCA/Universal, Paramount, Hanna-Barbera) supply programs to Operation Prime-Time (Cantor, 1982).

Operation Prime-Time is still in business and coming out with new programming. The miniseries, "Ford: The Man and the Machine," was one of their recent productions. Despite this new competition, the networks are still the primary buyers of television programs.

With the exception of daytime soap operas and game shows, the programs seen on U.S. commercial television were almost all developed either as prime-time series and specials or as children's programmings. Prime-time series and specials are designed to be seen by audiences of all ages and backgrounds and are "targeted" at those between 18 and 49. Children's programming is targeted at those under 12 and usually enjoys its first run on either Saturday or Sunday morning. These same program types are rerun by independent stations and at non-prime times. The pattern of production and revenue expectations differ for the two types in a number of interesting ways, as we shall see.

Development of prime-time programming

The cost of program development for the three networks in one year averages $250 to $300 million, a figure that does not include the hefty salaries of the executives in the programming departments (Lewine, Eastman, & Adams, 1985). Prime-time programs generate the largest chunk of advertising revenues, between 40% and 50% ("Financial figures," 1986). It is not surprising, therefore, that decisions about program concepts are made at the highest level of management and with the upmost seriousness. The motivation to avoid flops is more pronounced than that of selecting winners. Nevertheless, about 65% of new programs are cancelled by the end of their first season (Lewine et al., 1985).

A variety of ideas and even scripts are bandied around during early phases of a program's development, but the critical test comes when network executives decide whether to foot the bill for a pilot. An average 1-hour pilot costs $1.5 to $2 million to produce. In reaction to the mounting expense of developing pilots, there has been a recent trend toward trying out new program ideas in the made-for-TV movie format, a format which usually generates high advertising revenues. If the pilot is judged successful on the basis of its ratings and the reactions of network decision-makers, the series goes into full-scale production. The producer handles the day-to-day work necessary to get a program on the air every week and determines the content of the series under the network's supervision. The producer selects the writers and often provides the story line.

Once the script is written, rarely anyone but the producer changes it. Directors are under too much time pressure to interfere with content decisions, and actors rarely exert their potential power. Muriel Cantor (1982) remarked, "Even if a worker is employed in a creative task, for example as a writer, on-line producer, director, or actor, most of the important decisions about what to produce are made by others, either the program supplier or the networks" (p. 356).

Each network has a programming department that supervises the entire production process with an eye toward securing the largest possible audience of 18- to 49-year-olds—the group that spends the most money and, therefore, is most likely to appeal to potential advertisers. Network censors work through the programming department and try to protect the network from public outcry and government regulation.

Assumptions about the prime-time audience

The networks make certain assumptions that influence what gets on the air. First, although 99% of the households in the United States have TV sets, one third of that potential audience does two thirds of the daily viewing. It is on this group of steady TV viewers that the programming decisions are based. These viewers watch television, not programs, and they tend to watch during certain hours regardless of what is offered. Given this audience's predominance, the ratings are heavily weighted by their "votes," and it is the ratings that virtually determine what is aired.

Based on the ratings and on the network executives' conception of the steady TV viewer, certain informal rules have evolved for the development of new programs. New programs should: (1) be visually pleasing, (2) have a formula, so endless scripts can be written, (3) have appealing elements that carry over from show to show, (4) draw 30% of the audience, preferably a young audience, (5) win an audience early, (6) contain likeable characters, (7) not be so complex that viewers go elsewhere for light entertainment, (8) have a hint of newness without being alien to the viewer, because totally novel ideas would make viewers insecure, and (9) avoid controversy, because advertisers don't want negative feelings associated with their products (Brown, 1971). Thus:

> The character of television programs is determined by the three networks' notions of what will appeal to large numbers of people, sell products or services for advertisers, and not jeopardize the valuable licenses or the good will of affiliates by creating a negative audience response. (Baldwin & Lewis, 1972, p. 294)

The fear of controversy and preference for sticking to familiar themes and tried and true methods has kept much of television programming predictable and formularized. Another factor restricting the diversity of programs is the limited number of professionals who actually create them. Only a handful of studios in Hollywood and a few independent production companies provide all the network programming.

Children's series

Unlike prime-time shows, there are no pilots for children's series. The animation format, which represents the bulk of children's programming, is far too expensive to produce for pilot purposes. A half-hour of animation costs about $220,000. The idea for the series, including its characters, is spelled out in an outline, and artwork is drawn up that depicts the main characters in several poses and situations. If it is a live program, a casting tape of suggested actors for the roles replaces the artwork. Then children may be interviewed about these visual displays to determine the potential appeal of the program. A script may be ordered. On the basis of these materials, the network decides whether it wants to foot the bill for the series, which averages $3 million for 13 episodes (Rushnell, 1985).

In adult fare, the producer sells 11 episodes for half a season, and then another 11 for the second half if the series is retained. These episodes may be rerun, but usually not more than once during the summer. (A few highly successful series may be syndicated and shown again.) In contrast, when a network buys a children's series from a producer it signs a contract including provision for reruns and guarantees that each episode will be shown as many as four times in a year. This incredible rerun practice, which would draw cries of outrage from adult viewers, is feasible because the audiences for children's shows change quickly. This year's audience is replaced by younger brothers and sisters next year. Although the profit margin on children's programming is smaller than on adult series, once the series is sold it will almost never fail, and the programs become more profitable with repeated airings. Children's programs are also more likely to be syndicated; after being used by the network, they may be shown for years. If a series is popular, the characters will also be used in merchandising and the music may be made into a record. Both practices make more money. A trade magazine reports, "A hit Saturday morning series is an edge over any competitor—practically guaranteeing a [toy's] placement with manufacturers, retailers and, most important, consumers" ("Saturday morning," 1983). So the overall profits that can result from children's programming are considerable. The financial rewards are even greater for programs that are developed around toy/doll characters. These "program-length commercials" will be discussed in chapter 8.

The network must approve every show before it goes on the air. Therefore, producers must always consider the network and work closely with its programming department from the outset, remembering that although children will watch the show, only adults can buy it. Once the network buys the series, the producer remains responsive to network requests; the aim is to please the buying customer—the network. Those who cannot accept the system quit. Based on her extensive confidential interviews with producers, Muriel Cantor (1972) wrote:

> Those producers who are committed to particular artistic and ethical values have trouble remaining in the commercial field. One well-known producer of a series presently on the air left the field of children's programming because he could not reconcile what he considered the networks' lack of social conscience with his own ideas of good craftmanship and content. (p. 266)

Assumptions about the child audience

Just as with adult and family programming, producers of children's series have some ideas about the nature of their audience. For example, they feel that a child's attention span is limited, so that quick movement and loud noises are necessary. Further, because the ultimate goal of the programming is to attract the largest possible child audience, the programming is geared to appeal to the target age range of 2- to 11-year-olds. Obviously, it is not judged to be financially sound to tailor the programming to the needs of any specific age group. Accordingly, formats and themes are selected that have the widest appeal.* In an analysis of children's programs, Barcus (1978a) found that the most widely used format was animation (particularly cartoon comedy), and the most frequently used themes involved crimes, domestic affairs, love and romance, and science and technology.

---

*Producing programs for more restricted age ranges becomes possible with cable technology. For example, "Nickelodeon," a cable channel featuring only children's programs, offers age-specific programs such as "Pinwheel" (for pre-schoolers), "Dusty's Treehouse" (for 4- to 7-year-olds), "Mr. Wizard's World" (for 6- to 12-year-olds), and "Livewire" (for teenagers).

THE EMERGENCE OF NEW TECHNOLOGIES: CABLE AND VCRs

Despite the three networks' dominance, the expansion of cable has unquestionably eroded their share of the TV audience. While the networks' share of the prime-time audience has long been about 91%, that figure has dropped to 84% to 85% with the losses going both to cable and independent stations (Schaer, 1982). The home videocassette recorder (VCR) market has grown astoundingly fast in the early 1980s and has also had an increasing impact on our television viewing patterns.

Cable

Virtually every TV set sold in the United States today is advertised as "cable ready," meaning that it has been designed and manufactured with the expectation that it will be hooked-up to a cable system. The successful wiring of America for cable in the 1970s and 1980s has played an important role in the availability of a wide range of televised material to children.

History

Cable television had a humble start, conceived of as a way to sell TV sets! An appliance store owner in Mahanoy City, Pennsylvania, John Walson, Sr., was frustrated because when TV sets were first mass marketed in 1947 he couldn't even demonstrate the new technology to his customers. The town was surrounded by the Appalachian Mountains, which entirely blocked TV reception. Later that year, Walson erected a large antenna on a nearby mountain and strung wire down the mountain, using amplifiers to boost the signal, to a television set in a warehouse in town. He was successful in selling several TV sets to townspeople who also paid Walson $100 for a cable connection plus $2 monthly fees. In a short time, other cities that couldn't receive TV signals adopted Walson's methods.

Thus cable television was born in 1948. It was named Community Antenna Television (CATV) because it provided households with limited or nonexistent TV reception with a connection (via cables) to a "master" antenna that could pick up distant TV signals. Early cable TV merely extended the reach of commercial TV by enabling small communities access to broadcasts from major cities and by improving the quality of TV reception. By the 1960s, however, cable companies hoping to attract additional subscribers started plans to offer more than the re-transmission of local broadcasts—such as the transmission of distant broadcasts, first-run films, and special sports events. After all, cable systems could handle at least 60 channels, while broadcasting was limited to seven VHF stations per city. In the late 1960s the promise of expanded programming was temporarily stunted when the FCC imposed stiff regulations on cable operators. Clearly designed to protect the broadcasting industry, the regulations limited the transmission of distant stations that might compete with the local broadcasters. These regulations were eased somewhat in 1972 when the FCC released a new set of rules for the industry. Nevertheless, the new regulations stipulated that a cable system had to retransmit the broadcasts of all TV stations within 35 miles of its home base, be able to carry at least 20 channels, and set aside several channels for public access, educational, and local government use. In addition, there were restrictions on the number of distant signals that could be carried and on what kinds of programs and sports events could be offered. In the *Home Box Office* decision (1977), the court stated that the FCC "has in no way justified its position that cable television must be a supplement to, rather than an equal of, broadcast television." Gradually, the FCC modified or overturned many of its previous restrictions on the cable industry and in fact encouraged competition between it and the broadcasting industry. In 1985 the U.S. Court of Appeals completely eliminated the FCC's "must carry" rules. Cable systems are no longer required to carry any local broadcast stations.

Satellite communication systems have also expanded the horizons of cable operators. Aside from being able to relay TV signals over oceans, domestic satellite operators provide instant transmission of programs over vast distances. By relaying signals to a satellite transponder (device which receives and then re-transmits TV signals), a program can be received anywhere in the country by anyone with a receive-only earth station.

The far-reaching capacities permitted by satellite transmission led to the term *superstation*, pioneered by Ted Turner, owner of a VHF station in Atlanta, WTBS. In 1976, Turner started relaying his station's programming by satellite. He kept his charges low to cable operators by relying mostly on sports and movies and counted on the cable operators being hungry for additional program sources. The cable systems only had to provide a satellite receiving station and could offer another channel to their subscribers. Turner's profits come mostly in the form of increased revenues he receives from advertisers who are able to reach bigger audiences.

The second pioneer with the new satellite technology was Home Box Office (HBO). Unlike WTBS, which cable operators offer to their subscribers without additional cost, HBO became the first pay cable programming service. Beginning on a small scale in 1972, HBO became the leading pay cable system in the industry by 1975 when it solved the distribution problem. In that year, HBO leased a satellite transponder that enabled its transmissions to reach cable systems across the country. HBO dominated the pay cable industry and had literally no competition until 1978 when Showtime, another pay cable system using satellite distribution, entered the scene. To date, HBO still commands the majority of the pay TV market. In addition to unedited first-run films, both pay cable systems offer celebrity-featured concerts, cultural and theatrical productions, and special sporting events.

How Cable Systems Work

How cable television works is explained simply as follows:

> Think of a cable system as the video equivalent of a supermarket. Each one of these systems serves as a distributor of programs that it receives from a variety of sources. The supermarket then delivers through a cable the programs ordered by individual subscribers. ("How cable works," 1981)

It is the individual cable system owner who decides what to offer subscribers. The subscribers pay a monthly fee for the cable hook-up and equipment and receive a package of programs that includes all the programs from the local television stations and often those from nearby cities. Most cable systems also have satellite receivers, which enable them to offer programs from distant stations (both regular stations and superstations such as WTBS) and networks. If those networks accept advertising, generally subscribers do not have to pay extra to receive such offerings. To receive other networks, subscribers must pay an additional fee. The services that cost extra are generally movie-oriented, such as HBO and Showtime. The satellite-distributed cable program services that reach the most subscribers are presented in Table 2.3.

Estimates of audience size for cable networks are provided by the Nielsen and Arbitron Services. However, the ratings for cable are much more limited than they are for broadcast television. Only about one third of the metered families have cable, and audience figures are available for only the larger cable networks. Audience estimates of the smaller cable networks are often based on subscriber figures, sometimes supplemented by survey questionnaire data collected by the cable company. This lack of precision has limited advertisers' enthusiasm for cable commercials (Wimmer & Popowski, 1985).

The Growth of Cable

As can be seen in Table 2.4, cable television had a slow start. In 1960, less than 2% of U.S. households with TV had cable. As we discussed earlier, FCC restrictions discouraged cable expansion until the late 1970s, after which the number of cable operating systems and subscribers increased substantially. By 1985, almost 40% of all TV households in the United States had cable.

VCRs

Just as cable TV stole part of the network audience, VCRs have limited the pay cable market. VCRs and prerecorded cassettes offer the consumer what pay TV cannot: the convenience of renting and watching a movie at any time.

Table 2.3 Most Widely Received Satellite Distributed Cable Television Programming Services

PROGRAMMING SERVICE	SUBSCRIBERS (MILLIONS)	CONTENT
Basic Channels:		
1. Entertainment & Sports Programming Network (ESPN)	36.5	Sports
2. Turner Broadcasting System (WTBS)	34.8	Network reruns, sports, movies
3. Cable News Network (CNN)	33.1	News
4. USA Network (USA)	30.6	Sports, news, children's, health, comedy, movies
5. Christian Broadcasting Network (CBN)	29.7	Family programming; films, comedies, westerns, children's shows
6. Music Television (MTV)	27.3	Rock videos, concerts, interviews
7. Nickelodeon	25.7	Children's programming
8. Nashville Network	25.0	Country-oriented programming; sitcoms, music videos and concerts
9. Lifetime	23.8	Nutrition and fitness shows, network reruns, talk shows, movies
10. Cable Satellite Public Affairs Network (C-Span)	21.5	Live coverage of U.S. House of Representatives proceedings; congressional hearings
Pay Channels:		
1. Home Box Office (HBO)	14.5	Movies, specials, sports, miniseries
2. Showtime	5.4	Movies, Broadway shows, concerts, comedy and dramatic series
3. Cinemax	3.3	Movies, miniseries, comedy, music
4. The Movie Channel	3.1	Movies

Note. Based on information reported in *Channels: 1986 Field Guide to Electronic Media* (pp. 57–65), 1986, New York: Media Commentary Council Inc.

History and Growth

In 1975, Sony introduced its Betamax home videocassette machine for $1,300. The revolutionary idea was that viewers could choose when to view something and what to view among the alternatives of broadcast TV or prerecorded shows. In 1977, a competing system that was incompatible with Betamax, the VHS system, was introduced and ultimately dominated the VCR market. (By the early 1980s about 70% of all blank cassettes sold were for VHS systems.) Videodisc systems were also developed, but remained far behind VCR competitors, mainly due to their playback-only limitation. Table 2.5 shows the rapid growth of home video hardware and software since 1979. By the end of 1985, about 30% of U.S. TV households had a

VCR system. The growth has been even more dramatic in European (Hellman & Soramäki, 1985) and Third World countries (Boyd & Straubhaar, 1985).

Table 2.4 The Growth of Cable Television

YEAR	AV. MONTHLY BASIC RATE	OPERATING SYSTEMS	TOTAL SUBSCRIBERS	% OF TV HOUSEHOLDS
1960	5.00	640	650,000	1.4
1965	5.00	1,325	1,275,000	2.4
1970	5.50	2,490	4,500,000	7.6
1975	6.50	3,450	9,800,000	14.3
1976	6.75	3,651	10,800,000	15.5
1977	7.00	3,801	11,900,000	16.7
1978	7.25	4,030	12,900,000	17.7
1979	7.50	3,997	14,100,000	19.1
1980	7.75	4,048	15,200,000	20.5
1981	7.95	4,300	17,000,000	22.0
1982	8.25	4,300	21,000,000	25.8
1983	8.74	5,600	25,000,000	30.0
1984	8.92	6,200	30,000,000	36.0
1985	9.28	6,600	32,000,000	37.7

Note. Based on data reported in *TV Facts* by C. Steinberg, 1985, New York: Facts on File Publications. Data also from *Statistical Abstract of the United States—1986* by the U.S. Bureau of Census, 1985, Washington DC: U.S. Department of Commerce.

Table 2.5 Growth of Home Video Hardware and Software (in millions)

HARD & SOFTWARE	YEAR				
	1970	1980	1981	1982	1983
VCRs	0.5	0.8	1.4	2.0	4.1
Blank cassettes	10.0	15.0	23.0	34.0	57.0
Prerecorded cassettes	2.6	3.8	5.0	5.5	9.5
Videodiscs	—	—	—	5.0	8.0

Note. Based on data reported in "Prerecorded Home Video and the Distribution of Theatrical Feature Films" by D. Waterman, in *Video Media Competition: Regulation, Economics, and Technology* (pp. 221–243) edited by E.M. Noam, 1985, New York: Columbia University Press.

The major consumer use of VCRs is *time-shift viewing*—the recording of programs from broadcast and cable or pay cable television for viewing at a later time (Waterman, 1985). This practice was considered "fair use" of copyrighted material by the Supreme Court in 1984. One study (Levy, 1983), based on 1-week diaries kept by 249 households, found that VCR households recorded 3.31 programs per week, 52.7% of which were played back that same week. Dramatic series and soap operas were more likely than movies and cultural programs to be viewed the week they were recorded, suggesting that the latter may be used to develop a home library of movies and concerts. A.C. Nielsen (1986) reported that in 1986 most recording was done during prime-time (45%) and weekday daytime (23%) periods. Almost 75% of all recordings were of programs on network affiliated stations.

Prerecorded videocassettes

The purchase and rental of precorded programming is fast becoming a major industry, now totaling over $3 billion annually. In 1984, about 6,000 programs were available for VCRs, the majority of which were theatrical films. Renting cassettes has become far more popular than buying, representing 80% to 99% of cassette transactions, because rentals are so much cheaper ($1 to $5 for a 1- or 2-day rental) than purchases ($25 to $80) (Waterman, 1985). In 1985 there were 24,000 video stores in the United States (twice the number from the year before), and these stores offered an average of 1,900 different titles or 3,300 total cassettes (*Channels*, 1986). Table 2.6 presents the types of prerecorded videocassettes rented and purchased in 1985. Industry observers have commented that videocassettes for the child audience promise to be extremely marketable products. Children view the same videocassettes repeatedly and the cassettes can become part of the family's "library" to be shared with younger siblings ("Growing avenues," 1985).

Table 2.6 Types of Prerecorded Videocassettes Rented and Purchased

	PERCENTAGE	
VIDEOCASSETE	RENTED	PURCHASED
Hit movies	60	45
Classic movies	18	20
Children's movies	10	10
Music videos	6	10
Adult movies	4	9
How-to and other	2	6

Note. Based on data reported in *1986 Field Guide to Electronic Media* (p. 76), 1986, New York: Media Commentary Council Inc.

3
Regulation and Control of Content

OVERVIEW

Television stations use the public airwaves, and are therefore subject to control by the Federal Communications Commission (FCC). Television advertising, like other advertising, is also subject to control by the Federal Trade Commission (FTC). Once actively concerned about the content of children's television, both the FCC and the FTC have now become staunch adherents of deregulation. A variety of public interest organizations, most notably Action for Children's Television (ACT), attempt to influence broadcasters and advertisers in the interest of children. Such groups can influence television content either through direct pressure or by prodding government agencies to regulate the industry more stringently.

Broadcasters have several means of countering efforts to control them. The First Amendment to the United States Constitution prohibits regulatory agencies from censoring content, thus limiting their power to the creation of appropriate guidelines for the industry. The National Association of Broadcasters (NAB), the networks, and individual stations are also continuously engaged in legal and public relations efforts to protect their interests and maximize their freedom.

OUTLINE

No individual, organization, or business can operate without some constraints. The exact nature and extent of external regulation required, however, depends on the nature of the entity being considered. The print media are subject to relatively few constraints because they can operate in a highly competitive market and without the use of any public resources. The regulation of broadcast television turns out to be a good deal more complex. Broadcast television uses a public resource—the airwaves—and is thus subject to technical controls (e.g., determining the strength and nature of signals that may be broadcast), business and economic controls (e.g., prohibitions against clearly deceptive or inaccurate advertising claims), and social controls (e.g., it is unlawful to incite others to illegal acts, and this prohibition is applied to television content).

In the United States, there are two federal agencies responsible for regulating broadcast television, the Federal Communications Commission (FCC) and the Federal Trade Commission (FTC). Commercial broadcast television is also subject to extra-legal control. Public interest groups may apply pressure on advertisers and broadcasters to edit and censor certain content, and they may do so either through boycotts and economic sanctions or by advocating and demanding action from one of the regulatory agencies.

Commercial enterprises seem invariably to resist regulation, and the U.S. broadcasting industry is no exception. "Self-regulation" plays an important role in the overall countercontrol effort. As we will see both in this chapter and throughout the remainder of the book, the complex and often dramatic interplay of these forces has left some classic battle stories in its wake. But first it is necessary to further identify each of the players in the regulation game.

THE FCC

Broadcast regulation in the United States has its roots in the Radio Act of 1927, in which Congress created the Federal Radio Commission (FRC) to assign radio broadcast wavelengths and to determine the power and location of transmitters. The FRC granted 3-year licenses, and broadcasters had to prove that they would serve the "public interest, convenience, and necessity." In 1934, by an act of Congress, the FRC became the Federal Communications Commission (FCC), which extended its authority over telecommunications as well. As of October 1, 1981, the term of television station license renewals was lengthened from 3 to 5 years.

The FCC is now composed of five* commissioners who serve 7-year terms. They are nominated by the President and confirmed by the Senate.

---

*Originally there were seven members; on July 1, 1983 the size of the commission was reduced to five members.

One of the commissioners is designated by the President as chairperson. No more than three commissioners may be members of the same political party and none may have a financial interest in any FCC-related business.

The Federal Communications Act (1934) empowered the FCC with licensing responsibilities:

> the Commission shall determine that public interest, convenience, and necessity would be served by the granting of a license to a broadcast . . . any station license may be revoked because of conditions . . . which would warrant the Commission in refusing to grant a license on an original application. (Public Law No. 416. The Communications Act of 1934)

Unfortunately, there are no clear standards for what constitutes "serving the public interest." More important, perhaps, is that the Federal Communications Act of 1934 also specifically denies the FCC the authority to "interfere with the right of free speech" or to intervene in program content. Written originally for radio but extending to telecommunications, the Act states:

> Nothing in this Act shall be understood or construed to give the Commission the power of censorship over the radio communications or signals transmitted by any radio station, and no regulation or condition shall be promulgated or fixed by the Commission which shall interfere with the right of free speech by means of radio communication. (The Communication Act of 1934, sec. 326)

The effect of the FCC's imbalanced authority is captured by Les Brown (1977):

> The FCCs contradictory mandates—that of looking after the public interest and that of refraining from any involvement with programming which might constitute censorship—have kept the agency under constant criticism from Congress and citizens for failing to exert stricter program controls and for in effect "rubber stamping" license renewals. It has been called weak, bureaucratic and overly protective of the industry it regulates. (p. 146)

Some members of the FCC express frustration with the agency's inability to act on objectionable content, but support strict adherence to the First Amendment. Margita White (1978), a former FCC Commissioner, criticized the medium for sexual exploitation of women, but then opposed any censorship measures by government:

> I'm not sure whether I'm more outraged because the medium has missed the message of the antiviolence campaign, or more offended because women are to be battered through a new low in sexploitation. . . . But please, please don't turn to the Commission, which is precluded by the First Amendment and statute from censorship of program content. Even if it were not, it would make no sense to have seven government officials in Washington set standards of morals, taste, and creativity. This simply would shift influence from one powerful elite to another, with frightening implications for the future of free expression. (White, 1978)

Other factors also conspire to limit the FCC's interest in program content. One is that licensing TV stations is only one of the many functions of the FCC. Cole and Oettinger (1978) point out:

> On the face of it, a commissioner's job is overwhelming. He is called upon to decide questions involving radio and television programming and technical matters, telephone and telegraph rates, international communications by satellite and undersea cable, emission standards for microwave ovens and garage-door openers, citizens band radio, amateur radio, maritime communications, police and fire department communications, cable television, pay-television on air or by cable, data transmission services, educational broadcasting, antitrust considerations, and consumer electronics standards. (pp. 4–5)

Also, the FCC has a long precedent of *not* denying renewal applications, and such precedents turn out, practically speaking, to be almost unshakable.* Moreover, the FCC can enforce its rules and policies in less severe ways than denying licensee renewals. Based on inquiries and investigations of alleged violations, the FCC can fine stations up to $20,000.

Until quite recently, some content control was exercised by the FCC. The commission used to "recommend" *categories* of programming to broadcasters (e.g., news and public affairs) to create a balance of content. However, in 1984 the FCC abdicated its previous power in this area (FCC, 1984):

> This proceeding eliminates existing programming requirements which require the presentation of specified amounts of informational (news and public affairs), local and overall non-entertainment programming. (p. 33588)

> We believe that licensees should be given this flexibility to respond to the realities of the marketplace by allowing them to alter the mix of their programming consistent with market demand. (p. 33592)

Likewise, until 1984 the FCC had guidelines that limited the amount of time that stations could devote to commercials. Stations that exceeded 16 minutes of commercial matter per hour could not have their licenses perfunctorily renewed by the FCC staff; instead, their application and justification for exceeding the commercial limit had to be reviewed by the full FCC. In 1984, the FCC used the marketplace argument to justify the abdication of this guideline too (FCC, 1984):

> marketplace forces can better determine appropriate commercial levels than our own rules. In addition, such reliance provides a significantly less intrusive

---

*The practice of virtual automatic license renewals goes back to the early days of television in the 1940s–1950s when the government wanted the new broadcast industry to succeed. Investments in TV stations had to be substantial, and it was quite risky; so to encourage investments, the FCC didn't require high performance (Brown, 1971).

and less expensive alternative than our current regulatory scheme . . . the Commission will no longer consider levels of commercialization in the processing of license applications. Furthermore, we will no longer entertain petitions to deny based on allegations of overcommercialization. (p. 33598)

Despite its general propensity to deregulate, the commission is still exercising its power in one arena: assuring diversification in the media and avoiding concentration of control. It is out of this concern that the commission prohibits the same individual or group from (a) operating more than one station in the same service (AM, FM, or TV) in the same geographic market, or (b) operating more than 12 TV stations reaching more than 25% of American television households. NBC owns five VHF stations reaching 19.8% of American television households, CBS own five VHF stations reaching 20.6%, and Capital Cities/ABC own seven VHF and one UHF stations reaching 24.4% (*Channels*, 1986).

Three Case Histories

A sample of brief case histories reveals much about the FCC in action.

The WLBT case

In the context of the civil rights movement of the early 1960s, the local United Church of Christ charged that a TV station in Jackson, Mississippi (WLBT) had been presenting biased news coverage of the civil rights movement. Everett Parker, director of the United Church of Christ's National Office of Communications, tried to influence the station to change its coverage and failed. He then tried to get the FCC to conduct a hearing on the station's renewal application and failed again. Up to this point, the public was denied entry into the FCC license renewal proceedings. Parker then brought the case before the U.S. Court of Appeals. In 1966, Judge Warren Burger ruled that the FCC had to hold a hearing on the WLBT license and permit public participation. The FCC hearing was held but the FCC ruled in favor of granting a license renewal to WLBT. Parker appealed the decision to the U.S. Court of Appeals, and the court ruled against WLBT. This was a hard slap in the commission's face, inasmuch as the Court of Appeals may only overturn an FCC decision if judged to be "arbitrary, capricious or unreasonable."

The great cigarette war

The demise of cigarette advertising on television is a clear instance of the FCC's involvement in restricting content (censorship) in the public interest, though with advertising rather than programming content. Thomas Whiteside (1970), writing for *The New Yorker*, provides a brief history of a long debate.

Television had been enormously effective for the cigarette advertiser. Sales of Benson & Hedges 100's rose from less than 2 billion cigarettes in 1966 to over 14 billion in 1970, following an amusing and sophisticated television campaign. The television industry was pleased with its highly lucrative arrangement with cigarette manufacturers. It took in over 200 million dollars each year in revenues, accounting for 8% to 10% of the commercials ("The last drag," 1971). Not surprisingly, neither the advertisers nor the networks were particularly interested in any move that might damage the relationship.

The first blow against cigarette advertising on TV was struck in June 1967, when the FCC ruled that the "Fairness Doctrine" (that both sides of a controversial issue be given equal time) applied to cigarette advertising. The FCC suggested that a ratio of three cigarette commercials to one antismoking commercial was fair. During the summer, about a dozen petitions were filed with the commission on behalf of ABC, NBC, CBS, the National Association of Broadcasters, over 100 individual radio and television stations, six major tobacco companies, the Tobacco Institute, and Federal Communications Bar Association, each asking for revocation of the regulation. Activist John Banzhaf III, who had originally requested that antismoking commercials be aired, asked various health organizations to assist in preparing a reply to these petitions. According to Banzhaf, one official remarked, "Let me tell you the economic facts of life. My organization depends on free broadcasting time for our fund-raising drives. We are not going to jeopardize that time by getting involved in this move" (Whiteside, 1970, p. 48). So Banzhaf prepared the brief personally, and was successful. The FCC upheld its ruling in September 1967.

But enforcement was another matter. The FCC had a staff of only four persons to monitor about 1,000 TV and 7,000 radio stations. Since the commission clearly could not handle the load, Banzhaf again decided to do it himself. With the help of friends, he watched prime-time television for 2 weeks on one large station, WNBC-TV in New York. His monitoring revealed a ratio of cigarette commercials to antismoking commercials of 10 to 1; the station said the ratio was 3 or 4 to 1. The discrepancy was due to the fact that WNBC counted two cigarette commercials, one right after another, as one, and did not count simple announcements ("This show is brought to you by Marlboro") at all. Also, the antismoking ads were aired at what might be considered by most standards rather odd hours—2:30 a.m., 6:30 a.m. (WNBC-TV defended the 6:30 a.m. ads, explaining that it wanted to reach the kids before they left for school.) Banzhaf's work resulted in the FCC requiring more antismoking ads.

Then in 1969, the FCC signaled its intention to call for a total ban on cigarette ads, which required an Act of Congress. Congress opened special hearings to consider such a bill. Testimony revealed contradictions in the NAB Television Code and its practices. (The TV code called for cigarette ads that do not present smoking as an activity to be imitated, but a private study by the NAB indicated that many commercials did just that, making smoking appear attractive and socially desirable.) In 1968, the Director of NAB said, "Network [affiliates] . . . see in the area of cigarette copy nothing to be achieved by Code Authority involvement and in fact [see] potential injury to cigarette-advertising revenue if the Code Authority persues such a course" (Whiteside, 1970, p.70). In the end, after vigorous lobbying by both the tobacco and the broadcasting industries, the House passed a bill that would prevent federal and state intervention for 6 years.

Chances for the bill's passage in the Senate did not appear favorable, so both the networks and the tobacco industry began to offer compromise plans. The networks offered to gradually fade out advertising of brands with the highest tar and nicotine content; this plan was rejected. The broadcasters then suggested that they would phase out advertising over a 3-year period, beginning in January 1970. The tobacco industry offered another plan; a promise to end all radio and television advertising by September 1970. In return, it hoped to win legislation that would prevent the Federal Trade Commission from requiring health warnings in all ads. This plan rather annoyed the broadcasters (who would lose an additional 3 years of advertising revenue), and one commented:

> The thing that irks us is that the tobacco people couldn't have got the bill through the House without our help. We really lobbied for that. It would never have passed the House without us, because we have more muscle than the tobacco people have. . . . In every congressman's district, there is at least one broadcaster. These congressmen all get exposure on the local TV and radio stations. . . . I know how hard we worked through our local broadcasters on this bill, pointing out to congressmen how unfair it was to bar advertising for a product legally sold. (Whiteside, 1970, p. 78)

The tobacco industry had advertising contracts with the stations; they asked that the contracts be broken. The networks refused. Finally, a bill was proposed to ban cigarette ads on TV after January 1, 1971, giving the networks the ad revenues from the lucrative football season. The Public Health Cigarette Smoking Act was passed by both the House and Senate and signed into law by President Nixon on April 1, 1970. The last cigarette commercial was shown on January 1, 1971.

This incident in the history of broadcasting points out clearly the array of political influences that underlies regulation of television programming. More specifically, it demonstrates that while the FCC is capable of initiating censorship, it requires great impetus from the outside (e.g., Banzhaf's group).

The Prime-Time Access Rule

Another way in which the FCC felt it could legitimately respond to the public interest regarding content was through the Prime-Time Access Rule of 1970, which limited stations to showing network fare for no more than 3 hours per night (8 to 11 p.m.), which meant that the period between 7:30 and 8:00 p.m. was left for local station use. The intent of this ruling was to encourage the stations to serve local community needs in this half-hour with public service programming, to break the network monopoly in prime time, to provide independent producers with a new market outside of the three networks, and to encourage the production and airing of new program formats (Brown, 1977). In retrospect it seems that these were idealistic rather than realistic expectations. The stations themselves responded with characteristic practical business sense. Rather than producing their own local public service programming, they aired game shows and syndicated films which limited expenditures and maximized profit while honoring the letter but hardly the spirit of the Prime-Time Access Rule.

In contrast to many of its earlier positions, the current mission of the FCC is to *de*regulate the television industry. Because this posture is most apparent when it is challenged by pro-regulation forces, we will discuss issues bearing on deregulation in the section on public interest organizations.

The FTC

The Federal Trade Commission (FTC) is the government agency that regulates interstate commerce. In 1938 it was given the power to protect both consumer interest and private competition by prohibiting "false advertisements" and "unfair or deceptive acts or practices." It has the power to act on individual commercials and to issue broad trade rules and regulations that restrict or require specific advertising practices. The FTC can take into account not only what is presented in an advertisement, but also what is *not* revealed, especially in the case of information about the possible consequences of using the product. The FTC has not set forth a code of standards that specifies what it considers to be appropriate or inappropriate advertising practices. One can only surmise that from examining the past rulings of the FTC. Thus, within not entirely clear guidelines, the FTC has the power to censor content that appears on television as commercial advertisements. According to the commission's own statement:

> The Federal Trade Commission is primarily a law enforcement agency charged by Congress with protecting the general public—consumers and business people alike—against anticompetitive behavior and unfair and deceptive business practices. (FTC, 1981a, p. 3)

The FTC is composed of five commissioners who serve staggered terms of 7 years each. The commissioners may not engage in any other business during their term of office. They are nominated by the President and confirmed by the Senate. No more than three commissioners may be from the same political party. The President chooses the chairperson, who has management responsibilities.

If a company is thought to be violating an FTC regulation, the commission can:

- investigate the alleged violation.
- then, if appropriate, take legal action against the company by filing a formal charge known as a complaint and sometimes by asking the court to forbid immediately the alleged activity by issuing an injunction.
- then, either negotiate a consent order, in which the company agrees to stop the disputed practice but usually does not admit to having violated the law.
- or hold formal hearings called adjudicative proceedings, the result of which is, if the company is found to have violated the law:
- to issue a cease-and-desist order.
- or to seek civil penalties, which are like fines, and/or an injunction against a violator by suing the company in federal court. (FTC, 1981a, p. 5)

Based upon letters it receives from individuals, organizations, or businesses about allegedly unfair or deceptive practices, the FTC decides whether it should investigate a particular company, industry, or business practice. The FTC also conducts its own monitoring of commercials, especially during the pre-Christmas season, to identify any deceptive advertising practices.

The commission staff gathers information about any practice thought to be questionable. If the FTC staff member and the company agree that the company will end the disputed practice without a formal FTC hearing and without an admission that the company has done anything wrong, they draw up a "consent agreement" specifying that the FTC prohibits the practice in question and that the company will take certain actions. This agreement is then submitted to the FTC for approval. If it is approved, the complaint and proposed order are put on public record in the *Federal Register* and in the FTC headquarters. The public is given 60 days to comment on the agreement, after which time the FTC either issues the order, modifies it with the cooperation of the company, or rejects it. If the company violates its agreement to stop a practice, the FTC can fine the company $10,000 per day for each violation.

An example of an FTC consent agreement issued in final form is the case of AMF. The complaint alleged that two AMF TV commercials portrayed children following unsafe bicycle/tricycle riding habits that child viewers could imitate. AMF agreed to stop broadcasting these commercials and to produce two public service announcements on safe bicycle riding and submit them to TV stations that reach substantial child audiences.

If the FTC staff member and the company cannot come to an agreement, the staff member submits a report including its recommendations to the commission. The FTC reviews the evidence and if it appears the law has been violated, it issues a formal complaint and a hearing is held. The administrative judge presiding over the proceedings (which resemble a court trial) issues a decision. If either of the parties disagrees with it, that party can appeal to the full FTC, which then functions as an appeal court. If the FTC decision is contested, the case can be brought before the U.S. Court of Appeals and then to the U.S. Supreme Court.

The most recent FTC action against a company for its use of unfair and deceptive advertising practices in child-oriented commercials occurred in 1981. Action for Children's Television filed a formal complaint with the FTC against Tomy Corporation for advertising its dollhouse, Smaller Home and Garden Deluxe Set, in such a way as to lead children to believe that it came with an extensive array of accessories, which in fact were sold separately and for a handsome price. ACT argued that the actual cost of the dollhouse as it was portrayed in the ad was about $150. Following an FTC inquiry, the Tomy Corporation signed a consent order which stipulated that it would no longer run the existing ad and that it would use a "sold separately" disclaimer in future ads for the dollhouse.

The FTC sometimes holds hearings in response to complaints about deceptive ads. These investigations have revealed some interesting information about the deception prevalent in many advertisements. One ad for a major shaving cream demonstrated that its product gives a cleaner shave; the commercial showed the shaving cream being spread on sandpaper, and then being whisked off perfectly. The FTC claimed that this could not be accomplished unless the sandpaper was soaked for an hour; in fact, it was done even more neatly, by "shaving" sand off a pane of glass! Other examples include the case of an advertiser who substituted oil for coffee to make the coffee product look richer and darker, and the one who put marbles in a bowl of vegetable soup to force the vegetables to rise to the top and make the contents look more appealing (Brown, 1977).

Rule-making

In addition to its power to act on individual commercials, the Magnuson-Moss Act (passed by Congress in 1975) gave the FTC the power to set industry-wide standards in the form of trade-regulation rules which specify what are "unfair* or deceptive practices" in particular industries. These rules have the force of law. Table 3.1 presents the step-by-step procedures

---

*In 1980 Congress passed a bill that rescinded the power of the FTC to issue general trade regulation rules concerning "unfair" advertising practices, thus confining its powers to those that are "deceptive." For individual commercials, however, the FTC still has the power to rule on unfair practices.

the FTC follows to establish trade-regulation rules. As we will see in chapter 8 special rules for advertising directed at children triggered one of the most impassioned legal and political battles in FTC history.

Table 3.1 The FTC Rulemaking Proceeding

Step	1.	A proposal for a trade-regulation rule is published in the *Federal Register*.
	2.	A presiding officer is chosen to conduct the proceeding.
	3.	The commission accepts written comments on the proposed regulation and the issues involved (until 45 days before the start of hearings).
	4.	The commission accepts written proposals of issues for possible cross-examination during public hearings (up to 60 days after publication of the initial notice).
	5.	A "final notice of proposed rulemaking" is published in the *Federal Register*.
	6.	Persons who want to cross-examine witnesses during the hearings notify the presiding officer (within 20 days after publication of the final notice).
	7.	Informal hearings are held (approximately 90 days after the final notice is published).
	8.	The commission accepts written rebuttals of issues raised during the hearings.
	9.	The FTC staff prepares its own report making its own recommendations.
	10.	The presiding officer prepares a report summarizing the record and listing his or her findings.
	11.	The public is given a chance to comment on both the presiding officer's report and the staff report (up to 60 days after Step 10).
	12.	The commission reviews the rulemaking record and takes final action.

Note. From *Citizen's Guide to the Federal Trade Commission* (p. 17), February, 1981, Washington, DC: Federal Trade Commission.

PUBLIC INTEREST ORGANIZATIONS

A major force that has influenced the actions of both the FCC and FTC in recent years has been public interest or advocacy groups.

Action for Children's Television (ACT)

Founded in 1968 by a group of mothers in Boston, ACT has developed into a national nonprofit consumer organization devoted to improving broadcasting practices related to children. ACT's efforts include filing petitions to the FCC and FTC and testifying before the U.S. Congress. Unsuccessful at obtaining cooperation from the networks directly, ACT turned to the FCC in 1970 with a petition proposing rulemaking that would:

1. Abolish commercials on children's programs.
2. Abolish the practice of having performers on children's programs promote products or services.
3. Require TV stations to provide age-specific programming for children totaling at least 14 hours weekly.

In response to the ACT petition and growing concerns over TV violence, the FCC initiated proceedings in 1971 to examine children's programming and advertising practices and created a permanent children's unit within the FCC. In 1974 the FCC issued the Children's Television Report and Policy Statement, which emphasized that broadcasters have a "special obligation" to serve children as a "substantial and important" audience but allowed the industry to meet these obligations through self-regulation.

In 1978 ACT petitioned the FCC to conduct an inquiry to determine the degree to which the broadcasting industry complied with the 1974 Policy Statement and to adopt rules where self-regulation proved ineffective. The FCC then established a task force which in 1979 reported that the broadcasters had failed to meet their obligations to improve children's programming and recommended that the FCC take regulatory action to achieve the goal of sufficient age-specific programming for children. The FCC responded by having panel hearings about children's television programming. However, in December 1980 FCC Chairman Charles D. Ferris announced that the agency would be unable to consider the controversial proposal to require more children's television programs before Ronald Reagan took office and appointed another chairman ("FCC delays," 1980).

Mark Fowler was appointed as the new FCC Chairman. Formerly a Washington broadcasting lawyer who represented radio stations, he has been an advocate of government deregulation of broadcasting. He has said, "My conviction leads me to seek an end to content regulation of broadcasting in general" (Fowler, 1982). Instead of regulations, Fowler placed his faith in marketplace competition. His theory: "If you don't like it, just don't let your kids watch it." Competition and free choice, according to this view, will assure that the audience will always get what it wants.

In 1982, ACT filed a petition in the U.S. Court of Appeals for the District of Columbia, seeking review of the FCC's failure to issue a final decision in the rulemaking proceeding initiated over 12 years before. On December 22, 1983, the FCC ruled against making mandatory requirements for increased children's programming and closed the docket. The FCC's justification was that "the amount and variety of childen's programming available from commercial and public broadcast licensees and nonbroadcast television sources is substantial and diverse" (FCC, 1983). The one dissenting Commissioner, Henry Rivera, stated that this action "writes the epitaph of the FCC's involvement in children's television" (FCC, 1983). ACT subsequently challenged the FCC's decision, charging that the FCC had "acted arbitrarily and capriciously," but the U.S. Court of Appeals upheld the FCC ruling. During this time, ACT also filed a complaint with the FCC concerning a number of children's programs that were in effect commercials for toys. In 1985 the FCC rejected ACT's petition to hold inquiries into such product-based programming.

ACT's goals of increasing the availability of quality programming for children may be met through another government mechanism. In 1985,

Timothy Wirth (Democrat from Colorado) of the House of Representatives and Frank Lautenberg (Democrat from New Jersey) of the Senate introduced the Children's Television Education Act. If passed, it would require each broadcaster to provide a minimum of 7 hours per week (at least 5 of which must be during weekdays) of age-specific educational and informational programming for children. Compliance would be ensured through the broadcaster's license renewal procedure which puts the burden of proof on the broadcaster. The bill would also require the FCC to conduct an inquiry into the issues raised by programs designed to promote products to children, referred to as program-length commercials. Because the broadcaster frequently shares in the profits gained from the toy and related product sales, this raises questions about the broadcasters' conflict of interest concerning their quality control of children's programs. The FCC had earlier rejected ACT's request for a rulemaking aimed at prohibiting broadcasters from entering into such profit-sharing arrangements.

Whether the Children's Television Education Act is ever passed or not, the FCC's deregulatory posture bodes poorly for improvements in children's programming or advertising practices. Kunkel and Watkins (1986) observe:

> Previously, the Congress and FCC stood closer together in pursuit of programming reform. Presently, the FCC's deregulatory posture renders it a political ally to the broadcasters in this area, in effect helping them resist Congressional efforts to influence programming decisions. The industry also recognizes that even though Congress has much broader powers than the FCC, its more complex structure and politics makes the actual implementation of any regulatory proposal much more difficult and therefore more unlikely than would be the case at the Commission.

What is the likelihood that this deregulatory policy will continue? Some media commentators have forecasted a shift toward more regulation in light of the 1986 election, which puts the Democrats in control of the Senate and House of Representatives. For example, one analyst observed,

> The new Congress is not likely to continue approving a Fowler deregulation agenda that turned the communications business into a multibillion-dollar flea market . . . and across-the-board, denied the obligation of media companies to perform up to the highest standards of public service and social responsibility. (Crook, 1986, p. 1)

Indeed, in mid-January 1987, Mark Fowler resigned as chairman of the FCC. But only time will tell whether there will be a renewed interest in regulating children's programming or commercials.

Other Organizations

In addition to ACT, a number of other organizations have tried to influence the content of television entertainment and advertising.

The NABB

The first public interest media group in the United States was the National Association for Better Broadcasting (NABB) which was founded in 1949. The NABB's objectives are primarily educational, making the public aware of the broadcasters' responsibility to serve the public interest. It has published newsletters and other printed materials for use by the public. Currently it has about 300 members nationally and is most active in the area of opposing the deregulation stance of the FCC.

Small activist organizations

A host of other, less well-known activist groups have come into being (and occasionally disappeared) over the past 10 or 15 years. For example, the Media Action Research Center (MARC) was incorporated in 1974 with funds from the United Methodist Church and other Protestant denominations to undertake research on children and television. More recently, MARC has redirected its efforts toward stirring consumer action about television by means of a training program it developed called Television Awareness Training (TAT). Making use of prepared workbooks and films, the series of workshops has been used throughout the United States and Canada to sensitize people to how television influences them (Logan & Moody, 1979). MARC also publishes a quarterly newsletter, *Media & Values*, in cooperation with more than 15 religious denominations and national organizations to inform the public about media-related issues.

Other media reform groups also emerged in the 1970s to represent the interests of minority and women's groups that are poorly served by television: Gray Panther Media Task Force (representing the elderly), National Organization for Women Media Committee, and National Black Media Coalition (Branscomb & Savage, 1978). All three groups are still active. In the early 1980s, opposition to advertisements for beer and wine on television, cable systems, and radio led to the formation of a coalition of citizen groups, Project SMART (Stop Marketing Alcohol on Radio and Television). The group has called for an end to such ads and has also demanded equal time for counter-advertising to discourage young people from drinking. At stake for the broadcasting and cable industries is almost $900 million in national spot and network beer and wine advertising ("Beer and wine," 1985).

Educating the public about the influences of the media, particularly violent content, has been one of the primary goals of the National Coalition on Television Violence (NCTV). Founded and headed by Thomas Radecki, an Illinois psychiatrist, NCTV publishes regular newsletters and bibliographies that focus on TV violence and often advocate viewer, government, and broadcaster action to curb such content.

One of the most controversial media reform groups was the Coalition for Better TV (CBTV) which was headed by the Reverend Donald Wildmon.

Wildmon has also been the leader of the National Federation for Decency, which has monitored the amount of TV sex since 1977 and has published lists of the sexiest programs and their sponsors. Corporate executives from targeted companies have met with Wildmon in an attempt to be deleted from "the list," promising policy changes in sponsorship practices. For example, Proctor and Gamble, TV's largest advertiser, announced that it had and would continue to withdraw advertising support from several of the listed programs. Dissatisfied with the overall response of the industry, however, the CBTV threatened a boycott of products sold by the guilty sponsors early in July 1981 that was later cancelled, presumably to give the sponsors a chance to execute their promises for change ("Another Kind," 1981; "Fizzled boycott," 1981; "P & G's move," 1981). Soon after, the boycott was on again. It is interesting that ACT opposed the tactics of CBTV and started a campaign of its own to alert the public to the dangers of censorship. By 1983 the CBTV was disbanded, but Donald Wildmon has continued his work through the NFD to employ boycotts to pressure the sponsors of programs containing sexual themes. Although it is difficult to estimate the impact of a boycott, it does not appear that the sponsorship or ratings of the targeted programs have been influenced in any appreciable way from this practice.

Media reform groups have been somewhat effective in stimulating changes in broadcasting practices—either directly on the television/advertising industry (e.g., NFD) or indirectly through actions of the FCC or FTC (e.g., ACT). But there are strong forces within the system that oppose such efforts to regulate broadcasting. These counter-control influences, each with its own ideological, legal, and economic roots, will be discussed next.

COUNTER-CONTROLS ON THE TV BUSINESS

As we saw in the last section, the FCC and FTC regulate some aspects of the TV business. The FCC grants and renews licenses to television stations. However, the FCC generally has not interfered with the content of television. Likewise, the FTC has intervened in TV advertising that has been unfair or deceptive, but has otherwise stayed clear of regulating the content of commercials.

First Amendment

The factor limiting these government agencies from regulating television content is the First Amendment of the United States Constitution, which is explicitly upheld in the Federal Communications Act of 1934. The First Amendment states that "Congress shall make no law . . . abridging the freedom of speech or of the press."

While the First Amendment has been used as the automatic attack on almost any broadcast regulation, it is important to keep in mind the many situations outlined by Victor Cline (1974a) in which free speech is limited in the interest of society:

1. False advertising. . . .
2. Speaking a prayer, reading from the Bible, or giving instruction in religious matters . . . in public schools. . . .
3. Libel, slander, defamation of character. . . .
4. Saying words which amount to a conspiracy or an obstruction of justice.
5. Sedition . . . plan for the violent overthrow of our grovernment. . . .
6. Words that tend to create a "clear and present danger."
7. Using words that constitute offering a bribe. . . .
8. Words that threaten social harm because they advocate illegal acts.
9. Words (from a loudspeaker) at 3:00 a.m. in a residential neighborhood, disturbing the peace.
10. A public address in the middle of Main Street at high noon, which as a consequence interferes with the orderly movement of traffic.
11. Being in contempt of court. The judge may send you to jail if either your behavior or your speech is inappropriate.
12. Committing perjury under oath.
13. Television cigarette advertisements.
14. Saying words or giving information which have been classified (e.g., secret) by the government.
15. *Obscenity. While the Supreme Court has repeatedly affirmed that obscenity is not a protected form of speech, it has permitted local communities to form their own criteria of what is and is not permitted as long as these criteria include appeal to prurient interest and lack of redeeming artistic, scientific or literary value.*
16. Copyright violations.
17. Pretrial publicity which might interfere with a defendant's opportunity to secure a fair trial by his peers.
18. U.S. Government employees engaging in political speech or activity. (pp. 7–9, emphasis in original)

Clearly, restricting certain types of content on television, whether it be violence or sex, is in a gray area. Some people would argue that such content threatens the health and safety of society. But others argue that it is more important to uphold the First Amendment principle.

Self-regulation

From 1952 until quite recently the television industry, embodied in the National Association of Broadcasters (NAB), had a television code that set forth programming and advertising guidelines. The NAB was born in 1922 as a trade organization that would represent the broadcasting industry before Congress, the courts, regulatory agencies, and the public. The development of a code was a clever way for the industry to regulate itself in the face of potential government regulation. All three major networks and about two thirds of the nation's stations subscribed to it. The programming guidelines (NAB, 1981) were vague and emphasized the responsibility of broadcasters to offer programs that were innovative, creative, informative, enlightening, entertaining, and socially significant. There were sections addressing the presentation of violence and sex and broadcasters' special responsibility to children. The advertising guidelines set forth restrictions on the amount of time that commercials could be shown (9.5 minutes per hour during prime time and 16 minutes per hour during other times; for children's programs, 9.5 minutes per hour on Saturday and Sunday and 12 minutes per hour on weekdays), the number of times that programs could be interrupted by commercials (e.g., 4 times hourly during prime time with a maximum of five announcements per interruption), and the number of products that could be advertised in commercials less than 60 seconds long (i.e., one). In addition, the NAB Television Code contained very specific guidelines for all advertisements intended for children. The NAB Code Authority reviewed all nationally advertised children's toy advertisements and the premium segments of non-toy ads to help assure compliance with the code standards. The major weakness in the system was the NAB's resistance to enforce its own code. In 1963 Newton Minow, then FCC Commissioner, proposed that public hearings be held on the problem of over-commercialism. FCC spot checks revealed that a high percentage of license renewal applicants exceeded the commercial limits set forth in the NAB Code. The FCC debated between regulating on a case by case basis or formulating a general rule. It finally decided to take the latter course, and announced that stations would have to adhere to rules stated in the Television Code of the National Association of Broadcasters. This seemed like a reasonable procedure, inasmuch as the government would thereby impose only those standards formulated by the industry itself. But the NAB opposed the plan and actually organized committees in each state to lobby against it. Such a move, the broadcasters felt, would have set a dangerous precedent, leading to enforcement of a public relations document never intended to guide actual practices.

Before the FCC could hold hearings on the NAB's system, the Subcommittee on Communications and Power of the House Committee on Interstate and Foreign Commerce approved a bill prohibiting FCC control. By that time (February 1964), the FCC had gained a new member who also opposed the plan and cast the deciding vote against it.

Later, as a result of two separate and independent legal actions, the NAB Code's programming and advertising guidelines were finally eliminated altogether. The programming guidelines were eliminated in 1976 as an ironic result of the inclusion of a "family viewing" time guideline in a 1975 revision of the code. Briefly, the family viewing time provision was intended to make the 7:00 to 9:00 p.m. broadcasting period suitable for viewing by the entire family (i.e., no sex or violence). The family viewing time restriction was quickly judged to be a violation of the First Amendment. In response, the NAB quietly suspended *all* the code's programming standards.

The final blow to the advertising guidelines in the NAB Code came on March 3, 1982 when a federal court judge ruled that parts of the NAB Code were a restraint of trade. In particular, U.S. District Court Judge Harold Greene ruled that the television code's multiple product standard violated antitrust laws. The standard prohibited the advertising of more than one product in commercials of less than 60 seconds. Judge Greene concluded that this standard "raises both the price of time and the revenues of the broadcasters, to the detriment of the users of the broadcast medium [advertising] and the consumers of their products." In response, the NAB now suspended the entire code, closed the code offices, and let 24 employees go. The NAB is probably happy to be freed from code responsibilities, which had cost the organization 14% of its annual budget to administrate (Maddox & Zanot, 1984).

As one would expect, by the end of 1986 all three networks started to air 15-second ads. Only a careful analysis of current advertising practices— number, length, and content of commercials—can reveal the other effects of the NAB Code suspension. One outcome is clear, however. The suspension of the code and deregulation by the FCC and the FTC have left the networks with the freedom to broadcast almost anything they choose. Their only constraint is not to offend the public or the politicians so much that they bring regulation back.

Broadcast standards and practices—network self-regulation
Each network has a *standards and practices* department with several standards editors (or "censors") and a director who reports to a vice president for broadcast standards, who in turn reports to the network president. The standards and practices department clears the advertisements that the network airs. For example, three quarters of ABC's department of 73 employees are concerned with advertising review and clearance (Maddox & Zanot, 1984). The complete absence of regulation has led to the situation in which advertisers can argue to one network that another network will accept certain commercials if they don't. Further pressure to accept all ads comes from the network sales department, which is responsible for "selling" advertising slots.

Maintaining standards for program content also has its problems. Baldwin and Lewis (1972) interviewed 48 producers, writers, directors, and network censors involved in the production of network television series. They learned that the censors see themselves as agents of the licensee who makes sure that the programs meet network standards. On the other hand, the producers and writers described the censor as serving as "a buffer between the public, the FCC, and Congress on the one hand and the network and corporate executives on the other . . . to protect the executives from troublesome and costly criticism" (p. 324).

The censors become involved in the production process from the earliest stages, approving or suggesting changes in presentation at each stage—from the story outline, to script drafts, rough cuts, and final film cuts. According to Baldwin and Lewis, censors tend to cover themselves by issuing warnings about every conceivable aspect of programming that could be objectionable in the final film. Not all censor recommendations are followed, however. Suggestions that require reshooting are extremely costly. The ultimate decisions for changes are made by the standards and practices director whose decisions often involve compromising with producers. One producer said of the network censors:

> We fight them as hard as we can in regard to their absolutely asinine decisions. You can get away from the rules by going to the top . . . I call the boss and say, "Would you like to hear what your people are doing? Isn't that asinine?" And he's likely to agree. (p. 325)

No one envies the censors. Baldwin and Lewis described the network censors' plight:

> They're trying to pacify federal agencies, religious groups, educational groups, moral critics of all kinds who are coming at them—and still put together entertainment which people will enjoy enough to keep them in business. (p. 330)

How do the network censors make their decisions? Both NBC and ABC have created their own manuals, but these are loaded with public relations talk and could rarely be used in making actual decisions. More likely, both of these networks follow the strategy that is openly used at CBS, namely an "oral tradition" in which the old timers in the department recount the history of the decisions made about various types of content in the past. Factors such as broadcast year, season, day, hour, type of show, and character are essential descriptors that influence decisions. For example, censors tend to be more stringent with weekly series, especially those scheduled before 9 p.m., than with specials, made-for-TV movies, and miniseries (Lewine et al., 1985). Aside from considering these types of factors, the editor has to be sensitive to a much larger context:

> In the absence of a rigid code, the editor's personal sensitivity becomes the essential litmus. There are a number of things they are trying to be sensitive to, including the image of CBS, the libel and slander laws, the concerns of pressure groups, congressmen, CBS's affiliated stations, Hollywood writers and producers, and the ethical, cultural milieu of the American living room. (Levin, 1981, p. 326)

Recent staff cutbacks have lowered standards further. The reduction from 80 to less than 50 staff members in the program practices department at CBS, for example, has forced programming vice presidents to do some of the actual censoring. The first 10 episodes of all new series, all children's shows, docudramas, game shows, and theatrical films continue to be reviewed by Program Practices, whereas long-running programs are reviewed by programming executives. Several observers note a relaxation of standards regarding the portrayal of violence ("Networks lose," 1986). The standards for the presentation of sexual behavior on the programs of all three networks have also been relaxed in recent years, partially as a function of staff reductions in the standards and practices departments (Cray, 1986).

Children's Advertising Review Unit (CARU)

CARU was established by the National Advertising Division of the Council of Better Business Bureaus in 1974 as a self-regulatory agency within the advertising industry to "promote responsible children's advertising and to respond to public concerns" (CARU, 1983, p.10). The basic activity of CARU is the review and evaluation of advertising directed to children under the age of 12. CARU monitors broadcast and cable television and radio as well as print media and investigates potentially problematic ads. In addition to its own monitoring, CARU responds to inquiries by individual consumers, consumer groups, government agencies, and other advertisers. Following the suspension of the NAB Code, there was an increase in the number of discussions with advertisers regarding presentations within children's advertisements and in the number of requests by advertisers to pre-screen commercials, but there was no obvious increase in the number of investigations of ads that were aired at the time (Maddox & Zanot, 1984; "Absence of NAB," 1983). CARU also established guidelines for children's advertising which will be discussed in chapter 8. It is important to note that as a self-regulatory agency, CARU relies on the *voluntary* cooperation of advertisers.

4

TV Violence: Early Politics, Theories and Research

OVERVIEW

The effect of TV violence on children has been hotly debated for more than three decades. Senate hearings in 1954 and 1961, a Senate report in 1964, and the report of the National Commission on the Causes and Prevention of Violence in 1968 all concluded that there was a great deal of violence on television and that such content probably had an adverse effect on the young. But it was recognized that the laboratory studies available at that time bore only indirectly on the question of the relationship between viewing of TV violence and committing real acts of aggression.

As public concern about TV violence mounted, academic psychologists developed theories of how such material might influence young viewers. Bandura and Walters' social learning theory emphasized that TV provided instructional models for behavior (as suggested by the famous Bobo doll studies). Berkowitz, Tannenbaum, and others emphasized the immediate arousing and instigating effects of viewing television violence. Finally, Feshbach and Singer, financed by CBS, published a unique experimental field study that seemed to support their catharsis hypothesis. Youngsters exposed to a steady diet of TV violence were found to be less aggressive than those exposed to a nonaggressive television diet.

The clear implication was that more definitive research on the nature and effects of TV violence was needed, and this recognition paved the way for the Surgeon General's Report.

OUTLINE

We mentioned in chapter 1 that there are many parallels between concerns expressed about television and concerns expressed about movies in an earlier period. One difference between the two media is that while violent content was one of many issues for the movies, it was for TV *the* issue for over a decade. In this chapter we will tell the story of early investigations into the effects of TV violence. These studies are important because they laid the foundation for later work by defining the issues and setting forth the basic theories of exactly how TV violence might work its effects. Equally important are the first government hearings into TV violence, which set the tone for politicizing the possible effects of television on children and for threatening possible censorship.

GOVERNMENT HEARINGS AND INDUSTRY RESEARCH

As we will see in chapter 5, a variety of political, social, and scientific developments converged to instigate a major inquiry into the effects of TV violence on the young, the Surgeon General's Report. In this section we will examine the political and commercial backdrop out of which the Surgeon General's Report grew. The next section is devoted to scientific and academic developments that also played an important role in shaping the Report.

1954—The Kefauver Committee on Juvenile Delinquency

As early as 1954, Senator Estes Kefauver, then Chairman of the Senate Sub-committee on Juvenile Delinquency, questioned the need for violent content in television entertainment. Network representatives claimed at that time that research on the effects of violence viewing upon children was inconclusive, although they admitted that some risk existed (United States Senate, 1956). In addition, Harold E. Fellows, President and Chairman of the Board of the National Association of Broadcasters, promised that the NAB would soon undertake research on the impact of television programming on children.

1961—The Dodd Hearings

In 1961 Senator Thomas Dodd, who had now become chairman of the juvenile delinquency subcommittee, again inquired about violence on children's television. Testimony during hearings revealed that violence had remained a staple in the networks' TV diet.

Industry spokesmen again promised more research:

> We are moving significantly in this area [of research on effects of television on children] now. At a meeting of our joint radio and television board of

directors last week approval was given to proceed with the initial planning of an NAB research and training center in association with one of the leading universities in the nation. (cited in Baker, 1969, p. 594)

Testimony at the same hearings also revealed that the previously promised research had yet to be carried out. Leroy Collins, the new president of the NAB explained:

> Soon [after Mr. Fellows' testimony] the television code review board undertook a pilot study of "viewer attitudes" to determine the feasibility of a broader study, but about that time the Columbia Broadcasting System announced that it was engaged in sponsoring a survey which, while broader, would cover essentially the same ground. In view of this overlapping inquiry, NAB deferred to CBS in order that the larger survey could go ahead in preference to the narrower inquiry which the NAB had initiated. It is anticipated that the CBS project will be completed by the end of this summer [1961] and that a final report will be published before the end of this year. (cited in Baker, 1969, pp. 593–594]

1962–1964—The Fruits of Industry Research

In 1962, the industry, along with the United States Department of Health, Education and Welfare, co-sponsored the Joint Committee for Research on Television and Children. This committee, which consisted almost entirely of network personnel, solicited research proposals from various members of the scientific community. Unfortunately, it became clear in 1964 that few of these proposals were being carried out. In fact, only three papers were even begun as a result of the work of the joint committee. The first, by Ruth Hartley (1964), constituted a criticism and analysis of the inadequacies of previous academic research. The second was conducted by Seymour Feshbach, a psychologist who had gone on record as saying that TV violence was not harmful and might in some cases even help to drain off aggressive impulses (Feshbach & Singer, 1971). The third study was not even completed.

In 1963, the long awaited CBS report (which had superseded the research promised by the Kefauver Commission in 1954) was published by Gary Steiner. The title, *The People Look at Television*, indicates clearly the subject matter of the volume: the attitudes and beliefs of parents and other viewers about the effects of television on children, not the actual effects as determined by scientific investigation.

But the earlier hearings did have an impact, which one observer described this way:

> [The subcommittee staff for the 1961 Dodd hearings] noted that many network series mentioned in early testimony as especially violent were being syndicated, and shown on independent stations throughout the country. One committee aide observed: "It's as if they used our 1961 hearings as a shopping

list!" Many of the programs were scheduled at earlier hours than before, and were reaching younger audiences. (cited in Barnouw, 1972, p. 203)

In 1964, as Senator Dodd's hearings continued, network executives again promised to do more research. By this time the excuses had become rather pathetic. When asked by Dodd what had been done, NBC Executive Vice President Walter D. Scott replied this way:

I have asked the same question, Senator, because I have wondered why there has not been more in the way of results up to this point. I have been reminded by our people who are working very actively and closely with the Committee that it is appropriate to bear in mind that the work of scholars frequently sets its own pace and that time may be the price we must pay for meaningful results. As I understand it, they have had work done by a very large number of competent scholars in the field of social sciences. I understand that there have been something like one hundred separate projects that have been studied, that these have been narrowed down, that they are now at the stage of being ready to go ahead with, I believe, either five or six specific projects out of which they hope to get some meaningful answers. (cited in Baker, 1969, p. 595)

No new research was ever published or reported by the Committee. Scott went on to become NBC's board chairman.

1964—The Senate Subcommittee on Juvenile Delinquency

On October 27, 1964 the Senate Subcommittee on Juvenile Delinquency issued a report that was very critical of the networks.

The extent to which violence and crime are currently portrayed on the nation's television screens is clearly excessive. And in the face of repeated warnings from officials directly concerned with coping with juvenile delinquency and from competent researchers that this kind of television fare can be harmful to the young viewer, the television industry generally has shown little disposition to substantially reduce the degree of violence to which it exposes the American public. (cited in Larsen, 1968, p. 210)

With regard to the effects of this type of content, the report indicated:

It is clear that television, whose impact on the public mind is equal to or greater than that of any other medium, is a factor in molding the character, attitudes and behavior patterns of America's young people. (p. 211)

The report went on to say that industry self-regulation through the NAB Code has been largely ineffective:

The industry's claim that this Code is an effective vehicle cannot be substantiated in light of the evidence of chronic violation. Network programming policies which deliberately call for the insertion of violence, crime and brutality are hardly conducive to building respect for any central authority within the industry. (p. 211)

Finally, in the absence of an effective self-regulatory system, the report hinted at government intervention:

> Effective self-policing is the desirable approach to this problem which poses so clear a threat to our present and our future.

> But the patience of Congress, though considerable, is not endless. The public's demand for concrete results grows more intense, and indeed it should [p. 213].

1968—The National Commission on the Causes and Prevention of Violence

In 1968, the National Commission on the Causes and Prevention of Violence held hearings on the role of the mass media. Once again, network executives were questioned about the promised research; once again, it was not forthcoming. By this time, the networks were arguing that *they* should not be doing research anyway. One ABC executive stated:

> Research should be done from an objective standpoint and one that the public would be satisfied with as being done objectively, rather than that which is directly financed by our particular company. (Baker, 1969, p. 598)

Network executives also suggested that research was impossible due to the lack of adequate research design. Frank Stanton, then president of CBS and himself a PhD psychologist, remarked:

> It isn't unwillingness on the part of the industry to underwrite the research. It is that no one in the thirty-odd yeas I have been in the business has come up with a technique or methodology that would let you get a fix on this impact. . . . These people from the outside [of the industry] have been given every encouragement, every funding they have asked for to come up with methodology, and this is the field that is very illusive [sic] and it doesn't do any good to spend a lot of money and come up with facts somebody can punch his fingers through. (Baker, 1969, p. 598)

But the commission staff report did not share Stanton's know-nothing view. The report stated unequivocally that

> there is sufficient evidence that mass media presentations, especially portrayals of violence, have negative effects upon audiences . . . [and] that the burden of research and proof should be placed squarely on the mass media, especially commercial television, to carry out meaningful research on the psychological and social effects of mass media portrayals of violence. (Baker & Ball, 1969, p. 381)

In all, the commission concluded:

> We believe it is reasonable to conclude that a constant diet of violent behavior on television has an adverse effect on human character and attitudes. Violence on television encourages violent forms of behavior, and fosters moral and social values about violence in daily life which are unacceptable in a civilized

society . . . it is a matter for grave concern that at a time when the values and the influence of traditional institutions such as family, church, and school are in question, television is emphasizing violent, antisocial styles of life. (National Commission on the Causes and Prevention of Violence, 1969, p. 199)

It is interesting to note that the National Commission on the Causes and Prevention of Violence based its hearings on a series of review articles. With the exception of an analysis of how much violence is presented on television (to be discussed in the next chapter), no new research was commissioned. It was not until the end of these hearings in 1968 that Congress appropriated the funds for new studies to be conducted. This was the Surgeon General's Report, which is the focus of the next chapter.

THEORIES AND ACADEMIC RESEARCH

Three basic theories were brought to bear on the issue of TV violence in the 1960s by academic psychologists. These were social learning theory, instigation theory, and catharsis theory. Each of these viewpoints was still in a relatively early stage of development in the 1960s and, as we shall see, each theory matured concurrently with further developments in our understanding of the effects of television on children.

Social learning theory

In chapter 1, we mentioned Stanford psychologist Albert Bandura, whose 1963 *Look* magazine article, "What TV Violence Can Do to Your Child," made the TV violence issue vivid for a popular audience. Bandura has become eminent in academic psychology for his development of *social learning theory*. In fact, the history of social learning theory is intertwined with the history of exploring the effects of television on children. A closer look at the nature of social learning theory reveals the reason for the partnership.

The principles of social learning theory were first stated in Bandura's monograph with his student Richard Walters, *Social Learning and Personality Development* (1963). This small book, addressed to an academic audience (mainly psychologists), took issue with the prevailing psychoanalytic view of the child's personality development as a result of sexually tinged conflicts with parents. Bandura and Walters suggested instead that children *learn* their personalities from experiences and interactions with culture, subculture, family, and peers. Acknowledging the role of rewards and punishments in shaping children's development, Bandura and Walters nonetheless insisted that *modeling* played a uniquely important role in the child's social development. The best and most effective way to teach children novel ways of acting and their consequences is to show them the behavior you wish them to learn and display. Declaring that "models are utilized in all cultures to promote the acquisition of socially sanctioned behavior patterns" Bandura and Walters provided simple but compelling examples to make their point:

> The manner in which complex adult-role behavior may sometimes be acquired almost entirely through imitation is illustrated in an account given by Nash (1958) of the social training of children in a Cantelense subculture of Guatemala. The young Cantelense girl is provided with a water jar, a broom, and a grinding stone, which are miniature versions of those used by her mother. Through constantly observing and imitating the domestic activities of the mother, who provides little or no direct tuition, the child readily acquires a repertory of sex-appropriate responses. Similarly, small Cantalense boys accompany their fathers while the latter are engaged in occupational activities and reproduce their fathers' actions with the aid of smaller versions of adult implements.
>
> North American parents do not provide female children with miniature functioning replicas of the complex appliances that are customarily found in their households, since these would be prohibitively costly, readily damaged, and dangerous for children to operate. They frequently, however, supply their young daughters with a varied array of play materials—toy kitchen ensembles, dolls with complete nursery equipment and wardrobes, cooking utensils, and other junior-size homemaker kits—which foster imitative adult-role behavior. Play materials for male children in our culture are, generally speaking, less likely to be of direct relevance for the acquisition of sex-appropriate, everyday adult-role activities (partly, perhaps, a result, in middle-class families, of the relatively abstract nature of the occupational activities of the adult male), but they nevertheless frequently include building and other construction kits and mechanical gadgets that are associated with male occupational roles. While playing with toys that stimulate imitation of adults, children frequently reproduce not only the appropriate adult-role behavior patterns but also characteristic or idiosyncratic parental patterns of response, including attitudes, mannerisms, gestures, and even voice inflections, which the parents have certainly never attempted directly to teach. As the example taken from the Cantelense society most clearly indicated, children frequently acquire, in the course of imitative role-playing, numerous classes of interrelated responses *in toto*, apparently without proceeding through a gradual and laborious process of response differentiation and extinction or requiring a lengthy period of discrimination training. (pp. 47–48)

Bandura and Walters were in the tradition of post–World War II, academic psychologists who tried to extend theories of learning which had been developed in the 1930s based on research with laboratory animals into useful tools for social application with human beings. They also wanted their claims to stand on a research base that was reputable in the eyes of their academic colleagues. (Psychoanalysis was not considered reputable because it was not built on a base of objective research.) In order to demonstrate the importance of modeling objectively and vividly, Bandura and Walters had conducted a series of controlled laboratory experiments on the modeling of play aggression. The most famous and important of these were the Bobo doll studies of the early 1960s. (Appendix A provides an explanation of the experimental method.)

Direct imitation of play aggression: The Bobo doll studies

A major purpose of the Bobo doll studies was to demonstrate that there are two distinct effects of exposing young children to aggressive models: a *teaching effect* and a *motivating effect*. The series of studies was also designed to explore variations in each of these effects.

Although in principle there would be an enormous number of ways of displaying and measuring aggression, in practice the range of choices was sharply limited by ethical and practical considerations. The Bobo doll studies were designed to probe whether and under what circumstances novel aggressive acts will be learned and copied by young children. This question was clearly related to the concerns raised by politicians and parents that children might copy what they saw on TV, as mentioned in our earlier discussion.

Bandura selected a plastic Bobo doll as the "target" for aggression in his experiments. Though the individual Bobo doll studies differed in many particulars, all shared the feature that a child was shown another individual displaying a series of novel and distinctive assaults against an inflated plastic clown designed as a young child's punching bag (with a sand base so that it bounced back when punched and a nose that squeaked when struck with sufficient force). After exposure to such a display of behavior, the child was watched at play with the Bobo doll and other toys while his or her acts of imitative aggression were counted by trained observers. (See Figure 4.1.) Within this framework Bandura and his colleagues demonstrated several principles of their social learning theory as applied to aggression.

Vicarious consequences and the acquisition-performance distinction

Bandura and Walters (1963) declared that to understand modeling it was critical to distinguish between the child's *acquisition* of novel responses and the actual *performance* of these responses. The clearest demonstration of this fact was in a classic Bobo doll experiment, described by Bandura and Walters (1963) and subsequently published by Bandura (1965).

The children who participated as subjects were nursery school boys and girls, and the modeling sequence they saw was filmed and then projected on a simulated television set referred to when speaking to the children as a "TV show."* As Bandura (1965) described it:

> The film began with a scene in which [an adult male] model walked up to an adult-size plastic Bobo doll and ordered him to clear the way. After glaring for a moment at the noncompliant antagonist the model exhibited four novel aggressive responses each accompanied by a distinctive verbalization.

---

*Videotaping equipment was not yet widely available.

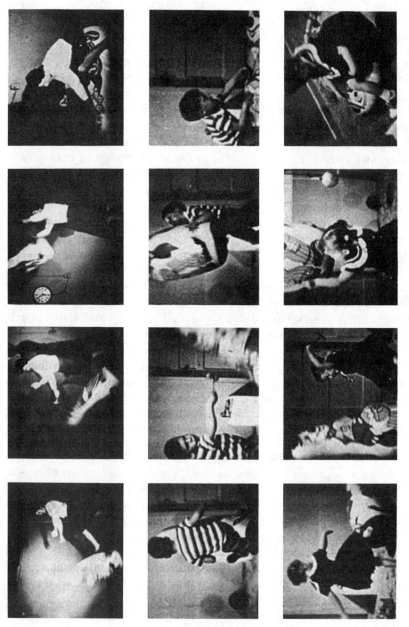

Figure 4.1 Photographs from the film *Social Learning of Aggression Through Imitation of Aggressive Models*, illustrating children's acquisition of aggressive responses through observational learning. Figure appears courtesy of Dr. Albert Bandura.

First, the model laid the Bobo doll on its side, sat on it, and punched it in the nose while remarking, "Pow, right in the nose, boom, boom." The model then raised the doll and pommeled it on the head with a mallet. Each response was accompanied by the verbalization, "Sockeroo . . . stay down." Following the mallet aggression, the model kicked the doll about the room, and these responses were interspersed with the comment, "Fly away." Finally, the model threw rubber balls at the Bobo doll, each strike punctuated with "Bang." This sequence of physically and verbally aggressive behavior was repeated twice. (pp. 590–591)

One group of the children in this experiment saw a sequence that ended at this point. Children in two other groups saw the same sequence, but with an additional scene showing consequences to the aggressive model. Returning to Bandura's vivid description:

For children in the *model-rewarded* condition, a second adult appeared with an abundant supply of candies and soft drinks. He informed the model that he was a "strong champion" and that his superb aggressive performance clearly deserved a generous treat. He then poured him a large glass of 7-Up, and readily supplies additional energy-building nourishment including chocolate bars, Cracker Jack popcorn, and an assortment of candies. While the model was rapidly consuming the delectable treats, his admirer symbolically reinstated the modeled aggressive responses and engaged in considerable positive social reinforcement. (p. 591; italics added)

The final group saw the model receive a quite different kind of consequence for his assaults against the clown:

For children in the *model-punished* condition the reinforcing agent appeared on the scene shaking his finger menacingly and commenting reprovingly, "Hey there, you big bully. You quit picking on that clown. I won't tolerate it." As the model drew back he tripped and fell, the other adult sat on the model and spanked him with a rolled-up magazine while reminding him of his aggressive behavior. As the model ran off cowering, the agent forewarned him, "If I catch you doing that again, you big bully, I'll give you a hard spanking. You quit acting that way." (p. 591; italics added)

So much for the modeling. Next came the tests of its effects. First was a test of *performance*, designed to see how much spontaneous copying occurred under each of the three conditions. Thus, after viewing the film to which they had been assigned, children were brought individually into an experimental room which contained a plastic Bobo doll just like the one in the film, three balls, a mallet, a pegboard, plastic farm animals, and a doll house which was equipped with furniture and a miniature doll family. This array of toys permitted the child to engage either in imitative aggressive responses (i.e., the model's responses) or in alternative nonaggressive and nonimitative forms of behavior.

The child was subsequently left alone with this assortment of equipment for 10 minutes, while judges made periodic observations from behind a one-way vision screen. The results of this test showed quite a bit of spontaneous imitation for children who had seen the model either rewarded or receive no consequences, but the children showed little tendency to spontaneously imitate the acts of the model whom they had seen punished. Boys also displayed considerably more imitative aggression than girls in this situation.

Social learning theory predicted that although the children in the model-punished condition had not spontaneously performed the novel aggressive acts of the model, they had nonetheless learned or *acquired* these responses and could perform them if the circumstances were made inviting. The purpose of the second test in Bandura's experiment was to see whether such acquisition had in fact occurred. The experimenter now reentered the room well supplied with sticker pictures and an attractive juice dispenser. The experimenter gave the child a small treat of fruit juice and told the child that, for each imitative response he or she could now reproduce, an additional treat would be given. These incentives led to very high rates of reproduction of the model's responses in all groups, including those who had seen the model punished. In the language of social learning theory, consequences to a model (such as those in Bandura's experiment described above) are referred to as *vicarious consequences*.

Other Bobo doll studies

Other Bobo doll studies also linked social learning theory to what children commonly see on television. For example, in one study some children saw the sort of aggressive display we have already described perpetrated by an adult while other children saw the same display perpetrated by a cartoon-like figure, Herman the Cat. The results showed that learning occurred almost as readily when the model was Herman the Cat as when it was an adult, and thus seemed to implicate cartoon as well as live formats as potential means by which children could learn aggressive responses from television (Bandura, Ross & Ross, 1963).

Later in the decade, additional Bobo doll studies were conducted by other investigators. Hicks (1965, 1968), for example, showed that many children exposed to films such as those used by Bandura (1965) could still reproduce the novel aggressive responses on request 6 to 8 months later.* In a series of studies, Hanratty and her associates (Hanratty, Liebert, Morris, & Fernandez, 1969; Hanratty, O'Neal, & Sulzer, 1972; Savitsky, Rogers, Izard, & Liebert, 1971) showed that preschool children would spontaneously

---

*It should be noted, though, that the children in Hicks' studies had been asked to give a demonstration of the modeled violence immediately after seeing it, and this experience might well have riveted their attention to the situation by signaling its importance.

imitate aggression against a human adult dressed as a clown, which took the results out of the realm of completely harmless play. Equally important, many children in these studies directly copied aggressive acts they had seen, even when the model did not receive vicarious rewards and when the children were not provoked or frustrated in any way.

Studies of disinhibitory effects

Bandura and Walters' (1963) theory recognized that direct learning and copying were only two of the many effects that could result from exposure to models. Equally important were *disinhibitory effects*, in which the observation of a response of a particular class (for example, an aggressive response) leads to an increased likelihood of displaying other, different responses that also belong to the same class. The earliest demonstrations of the disinhibitory effects of observing aggression, like the earliest Bobo doll studies, involved aggressive play as their critical measure.

Lovaas (1961) showed that nursery school children's aggressive play increased after viewing an aggressive film. Half the children saw one cartoon figure aggress against another by hitting, biting, and so on, for virtually the entire duration of the film. The remaining children saw a film of a mother bear and three babies playing together. Each child was then given two toys and was observed playing with them. On one of the toys, pushing a lever caused a doll to hit another doll over the head with a stick. On the other toy, lever pushing caused a wooden ball inside a cage to jump through obstacles. The toys were presented side by side; the child could operate either or both at once if he wished. Children who were exposed to the aggressive film used the hitting doll toy more often than those who watched the nonaggressive film. Thus, at least at the level of play, disinhibition occurred.

In view of the fact that most television programs appeared to depict aggression as a potent technique for power and achievement, investigations that focused upon the inhibiting and disinhibiting effects of consequences accruing to a model for aggression are of particular importance. In one such study, Bandura, Ross, and Ross (1961) exposed one group of nursery school boys and girls to a simulated television program in which one character, Johnny, refused another, Rocky, the opportunity to play with some toys. The program goes on to show a series of aggressive responses by Rocky, including hitting Johnny with a rubber ball, shooting darts at Johnny's cars, hitting Johnny with a baton, lassoing him with a hula-hoop, and so on. At the end of this sequence, Rocky, the aggressor, is playing with all of Johnny's toys, treating himself to sweet beverages and cookies, and finally departs with Johnny's hobby horse under his arm and a sack of Johnny's toys over his shoulder. At this point, a commentator announces that Rocky was victorious. In a second group, the program was rearranged so that after Rocky's initial aggression, Johnny retaliated in kind by administering a sound thrashing to the aggressor.

Two other groups served as controls; in one, a nonaggressive but highly expressive television program was observed, and in the second no television program was seen. Children's subsequent aggressive responses while playing for 20 minutes in a special test room constituted the primary dependent measure. The results clearly showed that those who observed a rewarded aggressor showed far more aggression themselves than children in the other groups. Moreover, at the conclusion of the experiment the children were asked to state which of the characters, Rocky or Johnny, they would prefer to emulate. Sixty percent of those who observed Rocky rewarded for his behavior indicated that they would select him as a model; only 20% of those who saw him punished indicated that they would choose to emulate him. Additionally, the authors described a classic example of how socially reprehensible but successful modeled aggressive acts may influence children. One of the girls, who had expressed marked disapproval of Rocky's aggressive behavior as it occurred, later exhibited many of his aggressive responses. Finally, in an apparent effort to make her emulation of the ruthless but successful Rocky complete, she turned to the experimenter and inquired, "Do you have a sack here?"

A number of other studies by other investigators in the 1960s also used aggressive play as a measure of aggression; all found that subjects who viewed an aggressive film model engaged in more aggressive play than children who were not so exposed (Hartmann & Gelfand, 1969; Nelson, Gelfand, & Hartmann, 1969; Rosenkrans & Hartup, 1967; Walters & Willows, 1968).

The important limitation of all these studies, of course, is that they are measuring *play*. Beating on plastic dolls that are designed to be punched and kicked around does not seem shocking or antisocial behavior, and critics of these studies were quick to note that very few parents would be upset to learn that their children had punched a Bobo doll which, after all, is a toy that is made to be hit.

What about "real" aggression? The question is obviously an important one, but it has proven difficult to design studies that can pass as both ethically responsible and scientifically compelling.

The aggression machine

A number of early studies employed a method that measured how much a person was willing to inflict pain on others. Originally devised by psychologist Arnold Buss and referred to as "the aggression machine," the method involved giving participants a pretext for giving another person electric shocks. For example, in one version participants are told that the effects of punishment on learning are being tested and that they are to serve in the role of "teacher." The participant is free to choose the intensity of the shock given for each wrong answer by the other person (the "learner"), and, thus shock intensity becomes the measure of interest. (The learner is always a confederate of the experimenter in these studies, and does not really receive any electric shock.)

In one early study using the aggression machine (Walters & Thomas, 1963), hospital attendants, high school boys, and young women viewed either the knife-fight scene from *Rebel Without a Cause* or a film of adolescents engaging in constructive activities. Both before and after viewing the film, everyone participated in an experiment which ostensibly required shocking another person for making errors on a learning test. The critical measure was the difference in the intensity of shocks given during the two sessions. In all three groups, those who saw the aggressive film gave stronger shocks in the second session than did those who saw the constructive film.

The aggression machine was subsequently used in many other investigations which demonstrate both that viewing violence increases aggression and that laboratory shock is related to real-life violence (Berkowitz & Geen, 1966, 1967; Geen & Berkowitz, 1966, 1967). In one study (Hartmann, 1969), delinquent adolescent boys were either angered or treated neutrally and then shown one of three films, two of which were aggressive in content. Regardless of whether they were angered or not, seeing an aggressive film produced more subsequent aggression (ostensible electric shocks to another person) than did the neutral film. At the same time, boys with a past history of aggressive behavior were more aggressive than other boys.

Clearly, by the end of the 1960s there was a great deal of theoretical rationale and laboratory evidence showing that televised aggression can disinhibit young viewers, at least in some contrived circumstances, so that they become more likely to behave aggressively. But the TV programs seen were often either simulated or taken out of context, which greatly limits the conclusions that can be drawn. Nor was there agreement as to precisely *how* TV violence worked its influence.

Thus, although social learning theory has played an unusually important role in analyzing TV's posisble effects on children, other theoretical viewpoints also played important parts in early discussions of TV violence.

Instigation theories

There is an alternative to the social learning analysis of the effects of TV violence. One could take the view that exposure to the violent content in these studies somehow *instigated* an immediate aggressive response (Berkowitz, 1962, 1969; Tannenbaum, 1971). In addition to various properties of the modeling sequence, the emotional state of the subject would presumably influence the likelihood that instigation to increased aggression would actually occur.

Tannenbaum and Zillmann advanced an arousal model of how TV violence instigates aggression. The theory contends that many communication messages can evoke varying degrees of generalized emotional arousal and that this can influence any behavior an individual is engaged in while the arousal persists. Increased aggression following TV violence would be interpreted as a result of the level of arousal elicited by the story, rather than a result of the modeling of aggression. One of the propositions of the theory is that nonaggressive but arousing TV content can instigate increased aggressive behavior. This proposition has been supported by experiments showing that an erotic film which was more arousing than an aggressive film produced more aggressive responses in viewers (Tannenbaum, 1971; Zillmann, 1969).

Justification as a factor

A significant contribution of the instigation theories of the 1960s was their attention to justification as a factor in the impact of modeling cues. These theories claimed that modeled aggression in a television or movie sequence would be more likely to make observers feel and act aggressively if the aggresson they had seen appeared justified than if it appeared unjustified. The reasoning behind this claim is straightforward: In real life it is considered more appropriate to act aggressively when one is justified than when one is not. Thus, observing justified aggression is more closely associated with actual aggression, and when justified aggression is observed, it therefore tends to instigate (i.e., "trigger") aggression in observers.

An experiment by Berkowitz (1965) is typical of the research. In this experiment, male college students were individually exposed to a confederate secretly following a script. The confederate insulted half of the subjects during the course of his interaction with them. Then half of the insulted and half of the noninsulted subjects viewed a film showing justified aggression, while the other half saw a film showing unjustified aggression. Finally, they had an opportunity to shock the experimental confederate—the very one who had insulted them. The young men who were most likely to give a large number of longer duration shocks were those who had been angered and then seen entertainment in which justified aggression was depicted.

A later investigation within the same theoretical framework (Hoyt, 1970) examined some of the factors that influence justification. College men were angered, not by being insulted, but by receiving a large number of electric shocks from an experimental confederate in a learning experiment. The young men next saw a film clip of a fight scene. In one condition, the justification was based on vengeance; the victor was seen as avenging an unfair beating that he had previously received. In a second condition, justification was based on self-defense. In a third situation, the introduction to the film combined both vengeance and self-defense motives. In the fourth condition, there was no introduction and thus no justification was provided at all. Then the roles were reversed: the students had the opportunity to shock the experimental confederate. In terms of number and duration of shocks given to the confederate, those in the no justification condition were lowest in level of aggression; those in the vengeance and self-defense condition were the highest.

Other studies involved trying to show the importance of a link between the film and cues in the observer's actual situation in order for a sequence to trigger aggression. A description of one of these studies (Berkowitz & Geen, 1966), entitled "Film Violence and the Cue Properties of Available Targets," will serve to illustrate the nature of the research. Berkowitz and Geen predicted that a violent film would be most likely to trigger aggression when the observers were angry *and* the available target for their own aggression was in some way related to the violent film. The groups in their experiment represented all possible combinations of seeing the vicious fight scene from the film *Champion* or an exciting but nonviolent track meet, being angered or not by an experimental confederate, and whether or not there was a link between the person beaten up in the movie (a character played by actor *Kirk* Douglas) and their own potential victim.

The experiment was introduced as a study of problem solving, conducted by a research assistant introduced as either Bob Anderson or as *Kirk* Anderson. The research assistant could apparently choose the number of shocks to give the subject as "feedback" in the first part of the problem-solving task. To half of the subjects he gave one shock; to anger the other half, he gave seven. Then the subjects saw the film sequence to which they had been assigned, under the pretext that the effects of such "diversions" were being studied. Finally, the roles were reversed and the subject decided how many shocks to give the research assistant. In addition to the unsurprising fact that those who received more shocks gave more shocks back, the study provided support for the subtler hypothesis it was designed to test. Subjects who saw Kirk Douglas beaten up and were then angered by a man also named Kirk gave more shocks than those in any other group.

The catharsis hypothesis

Many centuries before TV violence became a subject for public concern and controversy, Aristotle speculated about the psychological effects of drama, suggesting that by witnessing dramatic offerings the audience "purges" its feelings of grief, fear, and pity. Since then the same idea has been extended to feelings of aggression and anger. The notion that aggressive impulses can be drained off by exposure to fantasy aggression has its roots in psychoanalytic and drive theories, which assume that mental as well as physical energies can (and must) be released in various ways. This is what is meant by catharsis. The idea is very much what people have in mind when they talk of "letting off steam." The basic assumption is that frustration (for example, not getting one's way), being insulted, and the like, produce an increase in aggressive drive. Increased drive is unpleasant, and the individual seeks to reduce it either by engaging in aggressive acts or by engaging in fantasy aggression. One way to induce aggressive fantasy is by exposing someone to fictional aggression of the sort often found in action/adventure movies and TV programs. Catharsis theory therefore predicts that exposure to TV violence will reduce aggression in the observer (Feshbach, 1955).

The catharsis hypothesis has generally failed to receive support in studies with children. In a study by Alberta Siegel (1956), for example, pairs of nursery school children were taken to an experimental room where they saw a film. Then the experimenter left the room, and the children played and were observed for 15 minutes. Play with aggressive toys (e.g., toy daggers) as well as outright assault on each other were recorded. Each pair of children saw both an aggressive film (a Woody Woodpecker cartoon) and a nonaggressive film (about the Little Red Hen) about 1 week apart. If the catharsis hypothesis were correct, the children should have been *less* aggressive after viewing the violent cartoon; in fact, they were actually somewhat *more* aggressive after viewing it. This has been the usual result, but the catharsis hypothesis was not discarded entirely.

Feshbach and Singer's Television and Aggression

Seymour Feshbach and Robert Singer (1971) presented a modified formulation of the catharsis hypothesis. They suggest that the mass media serve to stimulate fantasy, and that the fantasy thus provided must satisfy some sort of need. In this view, fantasies can be seen as "substitutes for overt behavior that are partly rewarding in themselves [and] which may [also] reduce arousal [and serve] as coping or adaptive mechanisms" (1971, p. 11).

According to Feshbach and Singer, fantasy may reduce the likelihood of real aggression in two ways. First, it may reduce the arousal level of an angry individual. If he can sufficiently punish his nagging mother-in-law or demanding boss in his thoughts, he will feel less desire to punish them in his actions. Or if the individual is rewarded often enough for fantasy aggression (he pushes his boss off a bridge in thought and feels better afterward), he gets into the habit of using fantasy aggression to "cathart" (drain off) his aggressive feelings. The result is that he is *less* likely to actually behave aggressively. Television, according to this view, can provide fantasy material usable for catharsis, especially if viewers perceive the characters and circumstances in the fantasy material as similar to themselves and their own circumstances.

Second, television violence may reduce a person's potential for aggression through *inhibition*. According to Feshbach and Singer:

It may frighten the viewer of violence and its possible consequences; it may create anxiety over aggressive impulses and the eventuality that they may be acted out. The viewer consequently avoids aggressive behavior in order to reduce his fear of what he may do or what may be done to him. (p. 15)

In the late 1960s Feshbach and Singer performed an ambitious test of their revised catharsis hypothesis, investigating the effects of television violence on a large number of boys in the natural environment (Feshbach & Singer, 1971). The subjects were approximately 400 adolescent and pre-adolescent boys in institutional settings in New York and California. Three of the institutions were private schools, drawing on upper middle-class youngsters. The remaining four were homes for boys who lacked adequate home care or were experiencing social and personal adjustment difficulties. These latter youngsters were of predominantly lower-class background; 35% were black and an additional 10% were Chicano or Puerto Rican.

The boys were divided into two groups, according to whether they watched aggressive or nonaggressive television. Each boy was required to watch at least 6 hours of television per week for 6 weeks; he could watch more if he wished, but all programs had to be from a designated list. The aggressive diet consisted of about 75 programs, of which 20 were seen most frequently (e.g., "Bonanza," "I Spy," "Rifleman," and "The Untouchables"). The nonaggressive diet consisted of about 150 programs, with about 50 being viewed relatively frequently (e.g., "Andy Williams," "Gomer Pyle," "Petticoat Junction," and "Wide World of Sports").

A number of measures of aggression were employed, including projective tests and attitude questionnaires. The most important measure concerning the effects of television violence on aggressive behavior was the Behavior Rating Scale. This scale consisted of 26 items, 19 of which pertained to aggression. Some of these referred to physical aggression toward other people, oneself, or property. Other items referred to nonphysical aggression including grumbling, being bossy, sullen, or disobedient, as well as cursing or arguing angrily. Each behavior was rated once a day according to whether it was directed toward authority or toward peers, whether it was provoked or unprovoked, and whether it was mild or moderately strong. The raters were house parents, supervisors, teachers, and proctors.

Feshbach and Singer found that on the Behavior Rating Scale, boys in the nonaggressive TV group were more aggressive than boys in the aggressive content group, both in aggression toward peers and in aggression toward authority. When the data were analyzed by institutions, this difference was found to be due solely to three of the seven institutions—all boys' homes. Here, then, aggression was less frequent among those on the aggressive TV diet, as predicted by the catharsis hypothesis. On a week-by-week basis, aggression in boys in the nonaggressive TV group increased over the 7 weeks in which data were gathered; that of boys in the aggressive TV group declined over the same period.

In the private schools, the reverse pattern appeared; boys in the nonaggressive TV groups declined significantly in aggression, and boys in the aggressive television group tended to increase. This suggested that disinhibition was at work, with violence viewing making some boys more aggressive; but when the two groups were compared, the differences were not significant.

While these findings appear consistent with the catharsis hypothesis, the study is subject to a number of technical criticisms (Liebert, Sobol, & Davidson, 1972). A particularly important problem concerns differential liking of the programs viewed by control and experimental subjects. Based on the data presented by Feshbach and Singer, Chaffee and McLeod (1971) showed that boys in the nonaggressive TV group liked their assigned programs significantly *less* than boys in the aggressive television group. Thus, an important alternative explanation—or rival hypothesis—for the fact that some control subjects were more aggressive is that they resented being restricted to nonaggressive programs, and this resentment was expressed in an increase in aggression.

Another difficulty encountered by Feshbach and Singer relates to the experimental results themselves. A crucial requirement of experimental studies is that all groups be treated identically except for the manipulation of the independent variable (in this case, the different TV diets). Unfortunately, the Feshbach and Singer study did not meet this requirement. Boys in the nonaggressive TV group in institutions where the catharsis effect appeared had objected strongly to not being permitted to watch "Batman" (a highly aggressive program); the investigators then permitted them to include "Batman" in their list. This procedure constitutes an important difference in the treatment of the groups. Yielding to "a very strong objection" could have encouraged such related actions as grumbling, complaining, breaking rules, becoming sullen, refusing tasks, or acting bossy in other matters (all of which were scored as aggressive behaviors on the rating scale). Thus, another possibility is that experimental differences may have resulted from subjects having won an unreasonable demand from experimenters in one group and not in the other, rather than from differences in the television diet *per se*.

This does not finish our discussion of TV violence research, but we can only do so in the light of the Surgeon General's Report.

5

The Surgeon General's Report

OVERVIEW

Stimulated by a request from Senator John O. Pastore, the United States Department of Health, Education, and Welfare directed the Surgeon General (Chief Government Health Officer in the United States) to undertake an investigation of the effects of television violence on children and youth. The effort was quickly mired down by "politics" as it was learned that the committee appointed to actually guide the investigation— the Surgeon General's Scientific Advisory Committee on Television and Social Behavior—had been selected in a highly biased way. The industry had been allowed to secretly blackball seven possible committee members (including Bandura, Berkowitz, and Tannenbaum), and had also been able to load the 12-person committee with five of its own officers and consultants.

Operating under this cloud, and led by government health official Dr. Eli A. Rubinstein, the committee agreed to let the National Institute of Mental Health (NIMH) solicit and fund $1 million worth of research. Forty projects were selected in this way, touching on diverse aspects of television and children's social behavior. The project themes pertinent to our inquiry include measuring the level of violent content on TV (which was found to be high), establishing the level of viewing by U.S. children (which was discussed in chapter 1), and determining the effects of TV violence through both correlational and experimental studies. While each of the projects had its limitations, researchers consistently found some significant relationship between TV violence and aggressive and other objectionable behavior by children and adolescents. The research made it equally obvious that the occurrence of such behavior always involves many factors. In almost all of the studies, viewing TV violence affected some youngsters more than others.

When the projects were completed, the technical reports were sent to the committee which then had to interpret the findings and submit its own report to the Surgeon General. At Dr. Rubinstein's urging, the committee hammered out a unanimous report, but it was so complex, hedged, and ambiguous that one reporter concluded that TV violence was really not a factor in children's aggressiveness at all.

OUTLINE

As we have seen, as late as the 1960s surprisingly little of practical importance had been established about the real, practical effects of television violence on children. Meanwhile, the medium was continually being accused of cultivating "undesirable" attitudes and behavior. And the industry, for its part, continually promised research that was either never completed or turned out to be irrelevant to the general question of television's effects on the aggressive or antisocial behavior of children. Finally, everyone thought increased government regulation of content was possible. By the end of the decade, TV violence was ripe to become a public issue. It was against this backdrop that Senator John O. Pastore, Chairman of the Subcommittee on Communications of the Senate Commerce Committee sent a letter to Health, Education, and Welfare Secretary Robert Finch, which said in part (Cisin et al., 1972):

> I am exceedingly troubled by the lack of any definite information which would help resolve the question of whether there is a causal connection between televised crime and violence and antisocial behavior of individuals, especially children. . . . I am respectfully requesting that you direct the Surgeon General to appoint a committee comprised of distinguished men and women from whatever professions and disciplines deemed appropriate to devise techniques and to conduct a study under his supervision using those techniques which will establish scientifically insofar as possible what harmful effects, if any, these programs have on children. (p. 1)

Pastore apparently envisioned a definitive report such as the then famous Surgeon General's Report of 1964, *Smoking and Health*, which concluded rather unambiguously that there existed a causal relationship between cigarette smoking and lung cancer and led to the currently required warning on all cigarette packages sold in the United States.

THE SURGEON GENERAL'S SCIENTIFIC ADVISORY COMMITTEE

Secretary Finch directed Surgeon General William H. Stewart to select a committee to authorize and examine research relevant to questions about the effects of television on children. The Surgeon General, announcing that he would appoint an advisory panel of scientists respected by the scientific community, the broadcasting industry, and the general public, requested nominations from various academic and professional associations (including the American Sociological Association, the American Anthropological Association, the American Psychiatric Association, and the American Psychological Association), distinguished social scientists, the NAB and the three major networks.

The blackball procedure

From the 200 names suggested, the office of the Surgeon General drew up a list of 40 and sent it to the presidents of the National Association of Broadcasters and of the three national commercial broadcast networks. The broadcasters were asked to indicate "which individuals, if any, you would believe would *not* be appropriate for an impartial scientific investigation of this nature." They responded with a list of seven names,* including three prominent social scientists whose work was mentioned in chapter 3—Albert Bandura, Leonard Berkowitz, and Percy Tannenbaum. The secretly blackballed seven were:

> Albert Bandura, Professor of Psychology at Stanford University, and an internationally acknowledged expert on children's imitative learning. Bandura had published numerous research articles which suggested that children might learn to be more aggressive from watching TV.

> Leo Bogart, Executive Vice President and General Manager of the Bureau of Advertising of the American Newspaper Publishers Association. Dr. Bogart had previously published a book on television.

> Leonard Berkowitz, Vilas Professor of Psychology at the University of Wisconsin, principal investigator of an extensive series of studies showing that watching aggression can stimulate aggressive behavior, author of two books on aggression and consultant to the 1969 Task Force on Mass Media and Violence.

> Leon Eisenberg, Professor and Chairman of the Department of Psychiatry at Harvard University.

> Ralph Garry, Professor of Educational Psychology at Boston University, author of a book on children's television, and a principal consultant to the U.S. Senate Subcommittee on Juvenile Delinquency.

> Otto Larsen, Professor of Sociology at the University of Washington and editor of *Violence and the Mass Media*.

> Percy H. Tannenbaum, Professor of Psychology and Communication at the University of Pennsylvania and prominent for his theoretical analyses of the arousing effects of media entertainment depicting violence and sex.

The names of all these people were thereupon removed from the list of possible committee members in deference to the wishes of the industry whose product was under scrutiny.†

---

*It should be noted that CBS did not eliminate any names from the list.

†There was a somewhat parallel precedent for this blackball procedure—the Surgeon General's Advisory Committee on Smoking and Health—whereby the tobacco industry had been given the opportunity to review the names of the proposed committee members. The reasoning for this practice was that it prevented the tobacco industry from weakening the impact of the committee report by claiming that the committee was prejudiced against it.

Another significant fact added insult to injury, and that was that the industry had submitted the names of some of its own officers and permanent consultants as possible committee members. These people were not blackballed by the industry, and no public interest or professional society was ever sent the list of names for comment. So, when the 12-person committee was selected (and given the name, "The Surgeon General's Scientific Advisory Committee on Television and Social Behavior"), five industry executives and consultants were among those appointed. They were:

- Thomas E. Coffin, PhD, Vice President of NBC
- Ira H. Cisin, PhD, CBS Consultant
- Joseph T. Klapper, PhD, Director of CBS Social Research
- Harold Mendelsohn, PhD, CBS Consultant
- Gerhart D. Wiebe, PhD, former CBS Executive

The remaining seven individuals appointed were:

- Irving L. Janis, PhD, Professor of Psychology, Yale University
- Eveline Omwake, MA., Professor of Child Development, Connecticut College
- Charles A. Pinderhughes, MD, Associate Clinical Professor of Psychiatry, Tufts University
- Ithiel de Sola Pool, PhD, Professor of Political Science, Massachusetts Institute of Technology
- Alberta E. Siegel, PhD, Professor of Psychology, Stanford University Medical School
- Anthony F.C. Wallace, PhD, Professor of Anthropology, University of Pennsylvania
- Andrew S. Watson, MD, Professor of Psychiatry and Professor of Law, University of Michigan

Disclosure

This biased selection procedure of systematic inclusion and exclusion was not intended to be a matter of the public record. Even the nonnetwork members of the committee, all of whom are well respected by the scientific community, were not told anything about it. However, on May 22, 1970, six months after the committee was formed, the blackball procedure was publicized in a *Science* article entitled, "Seven Top Researchers Blackballed from Panel" (Boffey & Walsh, 1970). HEW Secretary Robert Finch tried to explain away the travesty as handily as he could, saying that the selection was designed to assure impartiality. James J. Jenkins, then chairman of the American Psychological Association's board of professional affairs, took a different view. He described the procedure as deplorable and analogized (Boffey & Walsh, 1970):

It looks like an exemplar of the old story of the "regulatees" running the "regulators" or the fox passing on the adequacy of the eyesight of the man assigned to guard the chicken coop. (pp. 951–952)

The committee takes shape

The committee was now under the shadow of a dark cloud. Its composition appeared "rigged," but disbanding the committee would be tantamount to a confession of guilt by the politicians and government officials who had set up the dubious appointment and blackballing procedure. The urgent political need in Washington was to keep the committee "clean" and quiet after that. (As we shall see later, this effort was not entirely successful.)

A new figure now emerged as central on the stage, Eli A. Rubinstein. Rubinstein, a psychologist who had served as Assistant Director of Extramural Programs at the National Institute of Mental Health, was appointed in 1969 as vice chairman of the Surgeon General's Scientific Advisory Committee on Television and Social Behavior and was given the task of guiding the committee through its work.

Decision to forego a coordinated research approach in favor of individual projects

Many options were theoretically available to the committee, but the built-in antagonism between industry-linked and independent members, together with practical considerations, sharply limited the options that could be seriously considered. The committee rejected the possibility of developing any sort of research plan on its own and purposely decided to support many small, uncoordinated studies by different investigators with different goals. Scientists were simply invited, through the government's usual advertising channels, to submit proposals that might be pertinent to the interests of a "scientific advisory committee on television and social behavior." The proposals were evaluated by small review panels of prominent academic researchers who judged each proposal on its scientific merit. The budget allocation for the research itself, $1 million, was a fraction of the amount put into research on cigarette smoking and cancer. Nonetheless, the project was described as generously funded by politicians and even by the researchers.

The freedom and independence of the review panels was stressed both to the panels and the press (whose members sensed, quite rightly, that more headline material would come out of the committee). Albert Bandura, though blackballed from the committee, reviewed some proposals, and Percy Tannenbaum, also blackballed, received a substantial piece of the $1 million for his research. (Remarkably, Tannenbaum was funded for a project that he announced would not be completed until after the committee had submitted its report and been disbanded.)

Altogether, about 40 formal proposals were submitted, which is a sizable number given the short notice and the complicated bureaucratic steps involved in applying for a grant or contract from the National Institute of Mental Health to do social science research. Twenty-three projects were selected and funded in this way;* the investigators were free to proceed with their contracted research without interference and to prepare technical research reports of their findings and offer any conclusions they deemed appropriate. The committee was, however, to receive interim reports and enjoyed the prerogative of finally writing the official report to the Surgeon General. Individual investigators were asked not to discuss or disclose their findings until the official report had been published.

The role of overview writers

An additional effect of disclosures about the political nature of the committee appointments was to influence the form of the final report. Publication plans were made for (a) an official report of the committee to the Surgeon General and (b) a series of simultaneously published technical volumes written by the principal investigators with little or no editorial interference from the committee or anyone else.

In anticipation of the published volumes, the projects were grouped into five categories, and one of the principal investigators from each category was invited to "overview" the projects in his category as they were conducted (see Table 5.1). The overview writers had no authority, but during a period of almost 2 years they visited each research team and exchanged progress reports of their research. The overview writers' most important task was to write an overview summary of the work done in their category, to be the lead chapter of each of the anticipated technical volumes.

Table 5.1 The Five Categories of Projects Composing the Technical Volumes of the Surgeon General's Report

TOPIC	OVERVIEWER
Media Content and Control	George A. Comstock
Television and Social Learning	Robert M. Liebert
Television and Adolescent Aggressiveness	Steven H. Chaffee
Television in Day-to-Day Life: Patterns of Use	Jack Lyle
Television's Effects: Further Explorations	Bradley S. Greenberg

*It should be noted that many of the projects served as umbrellas for several individual studies, and thus sometimes a project had several aims or resulted in several different chapters within one of the technical volumes.

PROJECT THEMES

Despite the lack of coordination or integration, the projects did fall into meaningful groupings. The most frequent questions posed were about the relationship between exposure to TV violence and subsequent aggression by the viewer. But the individual projects differed enormously in the conceptions, procedures, and methods, which were largely chosen on the basis of the independent predilections of each of the principal investigators.

In addition to studies of TV violence and aggression, there were studies designed to determine the current level of exposure to TV among children and the degree to which TV entertainment was, in fact, violent. There were also studies of advertising, of producers' perceptions of television, and even one on the difference in children's reactions to color and black-and-white TV. (Appendix B briefly describes all the studies conducted for the Surgeon General's Report.)

Level of violent content

A persistent accusation about television since the 1950s is that it was too violent. To examine this claim, academic researchers and public interest groups performed simple content analyses in which the number of aggressive or violent acts were counted. (Other information was also gathered from these content analyses and will be discussed in later chapters.)

Although it may not seem so at first, useful content analyses can only result when careful, systematic, "scientific" procedures are followed. There are three matters that must be considered in evaluating any content analysis.

Problems of definition
Definition is extremely important for content analyses. For example, what is a violent act? Almost everyone would agree that purposeful stabbing and shooting are violent. But what about verbal insults? What about threats of violence? If a sequence is ongoing (a fist fight or a shoot-out) would it count as one act of violence or several? Many other problems and issues of this sort can easily be raised.

Sampling
The aim of content analysis is usually to provide a characterization of television content in general (e.g., to answer the question, "How much violence are children actually exposed to on TV?"). This raises the issue of which programs to sample. Does one look only at prime time or at other times as well? Should only new network programs be included, or should one also include independent stations and reruns? Again, this is a very brief example of the types of problems that invariably arise and must be addressed.

Reliability

A final issue concerns reliability. This technical term refers to the degree to which a measurement procedure (whether it is a standard psychological test or a procedure for observers to use in noting and recording violent acts on television) produces consistent results. Reliability is often determined by asking two or more people to use a procedure (for example, in counting the number of violent acts on a TV show) to see if they come up with the same results.

Early content analyses of TV violence

The first content analyses of television were conducted in the early 1950s. Two researchers, Smythe (1954) and Head (1954), independently analyzed a large sample of television programming. The results of both studies were quite similar and together provide a picture of TV's portrayal of violence during the early days of television. First, crime and violence were prevalent TV themes. During one television week in 1953, there were 3,421 violent acts and threats (Smythe, 1954). More aggression appeared in children's programs (7.6 acts per program) than in general dramas (1.8 acts), situation comedies (0.8 acts), or even crime-detection programs (5.1 acts) (Head, 1954). While interesting, the results of these early analyses should be regarded cautiously. It is unclear in either study what was used as a definition of violence or aggression. Further, Smythe did not report the reliability of his coding procedure.

Gerbner's work

The person to provide the most systematic method of analyzing television for violent content was George Gerbner, long-time Dean of the Annenberg School of Communications at the University of Pennsylvania. Gerbner proposed a definition of TV violence that raters (college students) could be trained to use through apprenticeship and by following a manual, and he video-recorded a large sample of programs (requiring many videotape recorders and a substantial library of tapes). In 1968 Gerbner conducted a study of violence in television drama for the Mass Media Task Force of the National Commission of the Causes and Prevention of Violence (Lange, Baker, & Ball, 1969). His analysis on the 1967 and 1968 TV seasons formed the basis of his report to the Commission (Gerbner, 1969). This information, along with what he collected in 1969, played a critical role in shaping the Surgeon General's Report.

Gerbner (1972) first established the representativeness of programming for 1 week in October by comparing it to that of other times during the year. Then trained teams of observers watched each dramatic program shown during a week in October selected in 1967, 1968, and 1969, recording the number of violent episodes. For the purposes of this study, violence was defined as:

The overt expression of physical force against others or self, or the compelling of action against one's will on pain of being hurt or killed. The expression of injurious or lethal force had to be credible and real in the symbolic terms of the drama. Humorous and even farcical violence can be credible and real, even if it has a presumable comic effect. But idle threats, verbal abuse, or comic gestures with no real consequences were not to be considered violent. (p. 31)

Gerbner used two units of analysis: the play or skit and the program hour. Although in most prime-time programs these units are equivalent, many children's programs present several plays per hour (e.g., as in a half-hour cartoon program). Investigating more than the amount of violence, he also examined what types of programs contained the most violence, who acts violently, who is victimized by violence, and what happens to the participants.

Gerbner's report was striking. In 1969 "about eight in ten plays still contained violence, and the frequency of violent episodes was still about five per play and nearly eight per hour" (p. 33). Further, the most violent programs were those designed exclusively for children—cartoons:

The average cartoon hour in 1967 contained more than three times as many violent episodes as the average adult dramatic hour. The trend toward shorter plays sandwiched between frequent commercials on fast-moving cartoon programs further increased the saturation. By 1969, with a violent episode at least every two minutes in all Saturday morning cartoon programming (including the least violent and including commercial time), and with adult drama becoming less saturated with violence, the average cartoon hour had nearly six times the violence rate of the average adult television drama hour, and nearly 12 times the violence rate of the average movie hour. (p. 36)

In fact, according to Gerbner, in 1967 and 1968 only two cartoons were nonviolent, and only one was nonviolent in 1969. The overall situation had not changed since Smythe and Head found that children's programming contained about three times as much violence as adult drama.

The claim that TV content was highly violent was considered to be scientifically validated by Gerbner's report. The violence index and related analyses have been conducted every year from the mid-1960s to the present. Over the years, critics have objected to various aspects of Gerbner's method, some of which will be discussed in the next chapter. Nevertheless, Gerbner's periodic analyses remain the most frequently cited source for the level of violence on prime-time and Saturday morning TV.

Level of viewing

Advertisers have had estimates of audience size available since they began to employ television for commercial purposes in the late 1940s. However only one major public report of TV use by children had been done, as part of Schramm et al's. (1961) *Television in the Lives of Our Children* (see chapter

1). Lyle and Hoffman (1972) were funded to update the earlier report. Based on interviews, self-administered questionnaires, and viewing diaries from 274 first graders, 800 sixth graders, and 500 tenth graders from a town in Los Angeles, the researchers found that television viewing continued to be a very time-consuming activity, surpassing all other activities except sleep and school. Indeed, over one quarter of the sixth graders and only a slightly smaller proportion of the tenth graders watched at least $5\frac{1}{2}$ hours on a given school day, and over one third of the first graders watched 4 or more hours daily.

Perceived reality

One would expect from social learning theory and from much research in developmental psychology that the impact of TV violence (and other TV content) would depend on how it is perceived. The presumption is that children, like adults, are more likely to act on what they perceive as real than on what they consider to be only "make-believe."

The issue is somewhat more complicated than it first appears, however, because TV fare can be real in some ways and make-believe in others. Only the youngest children believe that TV dramas are actual life events occurring in real time inside the television box. Most preschoolers know that animated shows are make-believe, and many first graders will agree quickly that a TV crime drama story is only a story. But fictional stories about fictional characters can portray life as it is and thus be quite realistic in suggesting appropriate ways of solving problems or dealing with others. (One can get the message of honesty in the story of Pinocchio without believing that wooden boys can become alive or that anyone's nose literally grows lie by lie.) So, questions about how real TV seems to children are about the social attitudes and beliefs portrayed, rather than whether the stories themselves are true.

Two studies done for the Surgeon General's Report pertain directly to how youngsters perceive television. Other studies to be described when we discuss TV violence later in the chapter also bear on children's perceptions of the reality of television.

Lyle and Hoffman (1972) asked the youngsters in their study how realistically TV portrayed life. About half the first graders felt that people on TV were like those they knew. The sixth and tenth graders were more skeptical, but large percentages believed that TV characters and real people were alike most of the time. Lyle and Hoffman also found that Mexican American and black children were less skeptical than Caucasian youngsters.

The perceived reality of television was addressed in a slightly different way by Greenberg and Gordon (1972a). They showed 325 fifth-grade boys and 263 eighth-grade boys a series of violent and nonviolent scenes from television dramas and then asked them questions about their perceptions. They found that the children from the lower socioeconomic class, both black and white, rated the violent behavior shown as more acceptable, more lifelike, and more enjoyable to watch than those from more economically advantaged families.

Possible effects of TV violence: Correlational studies*

If TV violence stimulates aggressive behavior, then those who watch large amounts of it should be more aggressive than those who do not. Does such a correlation in fact exist? A number of studies funded for the Surgeon General's Report asked this question, and all found the answer to be yes.

McIntyre and Teevan (1972) examined the relationship between viewing habits and deviant behavior in 2,300 junior and senior high school boys and girls in Maryland. About 300 of the youngsters were black, and the overall sample represented a wide range of socioeconomic backgrounds.

To obtain information, McIntyre and Teevan asked each youngster to list his/her four favorite programs—"the ones you watch every time they are on the air." A violence rating was assigned to each program, and then an average violence score was computed for every subject. These scores were then correlated with a measure of deviance—a self-report checklist with five scales. The first scale measured engaging in aggressive or violent acts, such as having serious fights at school, hurting someone badly enough that he or she needed a bandage, and participating in gang fights. The other scales measured petty delinquency (including trespassing and vandalism), defiance of parents, political activism, and involvement with legal officials (representing the more serious forms of delinquency). Answers on all five scales were scored for frequency. The relationship between the various types of deviance and objective violence ratings of the four favorite programs were small but most were *statistically significant*.† In general, the greater the deviance on any scale or on the combined scales, the more violent the programs that the youngsters called favorites.

McIntyre and Teevan considered not only the influence of television on deviant behavior per se, but also on attitudes toward deviance, especially aggression. Consistently, those whose favorite programs were violent were significantly more likely to approve of both adult and teenage violence. They concluded that:

---

*See Appendix A for an explanation of the correlational method.

†In social science research a *statistically significant* result is one that has a low likelihood (usually less than 1 in 20) of having occurred in a particular sample by chance.

Certainly television can be no more than one among many factors in influencing behavior and attitudes. However, there is consistently a significant relationship between the violence rating of four favorite programs and the five measures of deviance, three of approval of violence and one of beliefs about crime in the society. Furthermore, these relationships remain when variables expected to decrease the likelihood of deviance are introduced. The regularity with which these relationships appear suggests that they should not be overlooked. (1972, p. 430)

In another major correlational study, Robinson and Bachman (1972) questioned more than 1,500 older adolescents concerning their television viewing habits. The subjects were asked how many hours of television they watched in an average day and what their four favorite programs were. For those who were able to list favorites, a violence-viewing index was computed based on the total amount of rated violence for their favorites. This sample was divided into four groups ranging from none to high preference for violence. The measure of aggression was a self-report checklist that included eight items about serious physical aggression.

When a total score was computed based on all eight items, adolescents in the three groups who reported at least some preference for violent programs were significantly more aggressive than those who did not list violent programs among their favorites. The same pattern was found for individual items; for example, in response to an item about getting into a serious fight at school, 50% more subjects in the high violence-viewing group than in the low violence viewing group responded yes. The tendency for those who preferred violent television to be more aggressive themselves held for most of the eight items; of particular interest is that there was a steady increase in aggression across the four groups. Certain other variables, such as mother's education, race, and previous level of reported aggression also were related to present levels of aggression, but in all subgroups those who reported a preference for (and presumably watched) a high level of violence were always the most aggressive. Robinson and Bachman concluded that television violence probably served a reinforcing or a facilitating function for adolescents who were already high in aggression.

Dominick and Greenberg (1972) determined the amount of exposure to television violence for each of 434 fourth, fifth, and sixth grade boys enrolled in Michigan public schools during the spring of 1970. Exposure to violence was then related to each youngster's approval of violence and willingness to use it himself. Measures were also obtained of the degree to which the boys both perceived violence as effective and suggested it as a solution to conflict situations. Higher exposure to television violence in entertainment was associated with greater approval of violence and greater willingness to use it in real life. The investigators concluded:

> For relatively average children from average environments . . . continued
> exposure to violence is positively related to acceptance of aggression as a mode
> of behavior. When the home environment also tends to ignore the child's
> development of aggressive attitudes, this relationship is even more substantial
> and perhaps more critical. (pp. 332–333)

When Dominick and Greenberg repeated their research with girls, they found a pattern that closely followed that seen for boys, and reported that for girls exposure to TV violence makes a "consistent independent contribution to the child's notions about violence. The greater the level of exposure to television violence, the more the child was willing to use violence, to suggest it as a solution to conflict, and to perceive it as effective" (p.329).

McLeod, Atkin, and Chaffee (1972a,b) questioned 473 adolescents in Maryland and 151 in Wisconsin about aggressive behavior, television viewing, social characteristics of their families, and reactions to television violence. The subjects were mostly white and middle class, although about 15% of the Maryland sample was black.

Violence viewing was indexed by giving each subject a list of 65 prime-time programs, which had been rated for violent content, and requesting information on frequency of viewing. For each subject, the frequency score of each of the 65 programs was multiplied by its violence rating. These scores were then summed to give a measure of overall violence viewing.

Self-report measures of aggression included an overall aggression score, based on: (a) a 17-item scale in which the respondent was asked to judge how much each statement applied to him (e.g., "When I lose my temper at someone, once in a while I actually hit them"); (b) a behavioral delinquency scale, in which the subject was asked how often he had been in school fights, gang fights, or achieved revenge by physical aggression; (c) a self-report scale of generalized aggression; and (d) a four-item test that presented hypothetical conflict situations and asked the subject to choose his most likely response among several alternatives (e.g., "Suppose someone played a real dirty trick on you, what would you do? Hit, yell, ignore, or laugh at them"). In addition to the overall aggression score, subjects were also asked about how well they control their tempers and the degree to which they approve of aggressive behavior.

Reactions to television violence were assessed, including perceived learning of aggression (e.g., "Some programs give me ideas on how to get away with something without getting caught"), linkage of television violence to real life (e.g., "Action and adventure shows tell about life the way it really is"), and involvement in violent programming (e.g., "I sometimes forget that characters in these shows are just actors"). Additionally, identification with violent characters (each subject picked the TV star he would most like to resemble, and the violence of that person's typical role was then rated), and the perceived efficacy of such characters were measured (e.g., "The guy who gets rough gets his way"). Finally, family environment data were gathered. The various indices included perceptions of parental control over television, parental emphasis on nonaggression, parental interpretation of television violence, parental punishment and affection, and social class. Again, the results from this extensive study showed that violence viewing was significantly related to self-reported aggressive behavior.

For the 151 adolescents in their Wisconsin sample, McLeod et al. (1972b) also reported data gathered from questioning others about the subjects. They queried mothers on a number of items (including a comparison of her own child's fighting to fighting by other children, how often her child did mean things or was aggressive when younger, and how her child would handle an argument). They asked peers for ratings on irritability, physical aggression, and verbal aggression and obtained teacher ratings on a four-point overall aggression scale for the sixth graders. The mothers also estimated viewing habits for themselves and their children, and each filled out a questionnaire on family environment.

As with self-reports, correlations between others' reports of aggression and violence viewing were significant. Additionally, the correlations between past violence viewing and present aggressive behavior were very similar to those for present violence viewing; past violence viewing was actually somewhat more strongly related to aggression than present viewing. This latter finding suggests that aggressive habits are indeed built over time by exposure to aggressive TV content.

Process-oriented correlational studies

So far we have described what are technically called "synchronous correlational studies." That is, these studies correlated one measure (some index of exposure to TV violence) with another measure (of aggressiveness or willingness to act in a disapproved fashion) with both measures capturing the same slice of time (which is what is meant by "synchronous"). Correlations observed under these conditions are often ambiguous with respect to cause and effect. The fact that watching more TV violence goes with being more aggressive does not, by itself, show that viewing TV violence *causes* aggressiveness.

There are two logical problems with interpreting synchronous correlations as reflecting cause and effect relationships, the third variable problem and the directionality problem. Each of these is explained below in the context of studies done for the Surgeon General's Report.

The third variable problem
The problem is that some "third variable" may be responsible for producing the correlation between TV violence viewing and aggression, although neither

is causing the other. For example, parents who emphasize nonaggression may cause their children to be relatively nonaggressive and to watch relatively little violent television. Contrarily, parents who emphasize aggression may cause their children to be aggressive and watch a lot of violent television.

It is possible, however, to assess the influence of a third variable with a procedure called the *partial correlational technique*. Conceptually, we want to "subtract out" the third variable's influence and see what is "left over." If the relationship (previously strong in either direction) is now reduced to insignificance, then the third variable remains a very likely candidate as a plausible cause for the relationship. If, however, the relationship that remains after "partialing" is as strong or nearly as strong as it was before, then the third variable is a poor rival hypothesis for explaining the relationship. Such a result lends support to our original hypothesis.

McLeod et al. (1972a) used partialing to analyze their findings. For their first set of data (self-reported aggression and viewing violence), they found that subtracting out the influence of total viewing time, socioeconomic status, and school performance left the relationship unchanged. Similarly, when the effects of various types of parental punishment practices, parental affection, and perceived learning of aggression were partialed out, the relationship between violence viewing and adolescent aggressiveness continued to be significant.

For the second set of data (others' reported aggression and viewing violence), partialing out the effects of total television viewing time, socioeconomic status, and school performance, again left the relationship essentially unchanged. Partialing other variables, such as parental punishment practices, parental affection, and perceived learning of aggression, reduced the correlation somewhat, but still showed that aggression based on both others' and self-reports was associated with violence viewing (McLeod et al., 1972b). The researchers concluded:

> Our research shows that among both boys and girls at two grade levels [junior high and senior high], the more the child watches violent television fare, the more aggressive he is likely to be as measured by a variety of self-report measures. . . . Partialing out [total] viewing time slightly reduces the . . . correlations of violence viewing and aggressive behavior in most cases, but the basic result is the same as for the raw correlations. . . . Similarly, the partialing out of socioeconomic status and school performance does not alter the basic pattern of raw correlations. . . . We may conclude, then, that adolescents viewing high levels of violent content on television tend to have high levels of aggressive behavior regardless of television viewing time, socioeconomic status, or school performance. (McLeod et al., 1972a, pp. 187–191)

The directionality problem

The partial correlational technique attempts to solve one of the problems correlational research is subject to, that of the possible influence of third variables. An additional problem remains—directionality. If we know that A and B are directly related, we still do not know whether A causes B or vice versa. Procedures can be employed in an attempt to solve the directionality problem. One involves examining data on the various theoretical rationales that underlie each of the competing causal hypotheses.

Chaffee and McLeod (1971) performed such a process analysis on the data presented above. The two rival causal hypotheses are that viewing television violence increases aggressive behavior (H1), and that aggressiveness increases television violence viewing (H2). Each of these hypotheses assumes that some process is acting to produce the observed relationship; in other words, that there are secondary hypotheses underlying each of the primary ones. Chaffee and McLeod suggested the process analysis presented in Table 5.2.

Table 5.2 Two Hypotheses about Violence Viewing and Adolescent Aggressiveness, Showing Secondary Hypotheses Involved in a Process Analysis

H1: Viewing television violence increases the likelihood of an adolescent behaving aggressively.

    $H1_a$: By viewing television violence, an adolescent learns aggressive forms of behavior; this increases the probability that he will behave in this fashion in subsequent social interaction.

H2: Aggressiveness causes adolescents to watch violent television programs.

    $H2_a$: Aggressiveness leads to a preference for violent programs, which in turn causes the aggressive adolescent to watch them.

Note. Adapted from "Adolescents, Parents, and Television Violence," presented by S.H. Chaffee and J.M. McLeod (1971, September) at the meeting of the American Psychological Association, Washington, DC.

The "learning hypothesis" ($H1_a$) derived from laboratory studies is considered to be the process underlying H1. Support for H1 can be provided by demonstrating that subjects do indeed learn from television violence and realize the potential use of what they learned. McLeod, Atkin, and Chaffee measured perceived learning of aggression using the following three items.

1. These programs show me how to get back at people who make me angry.

2. Sometimes I copy the things I see people do on these shows.

3. Some programs give me ideas on how to get away with something without being caught.

The process underlying H2 (aggressiveness increases television violence viewing) is presumed to involve a preference for televised violence that exists previous to observing it. Thus, support for H2 can be provided by showing that subjects who are high on measures of aggressive behavior are more likely than other youngsters to show preference for aggressive television programs. The relevant measure, then, is choice of favorite programs.

Chaffee and McLeod compared the two hypotheses as shown in Figure 5.1. The arrows indicate the time order suggested by the two hypotheses. As can be seen from the figure, viewing violence is related to learning, and learning is related to aggressive behavior. But even though preference is related to viewing,* it is *not* related to aggressive behavior. These data, then, offer relatively clear support for the hypothesis that viewing violence causes aggression, rather than the reverse.

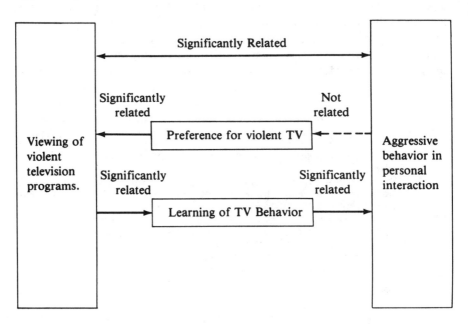

Figure 5.1 Correlations of violence viewing, aggressiveness, and two intervening processes. Entries indicate hypothesized time order. The overall relationship is clearly accounted for more adequately by the learning path (H1) than by the preference path (H2). From *Adolescents, Parents, and Television Violence* by S.H. Chaffee and J.M. McLeod (1971, September) at the meeting of the American Psychological Association, Washington, DC.

Long-term effects

But what about long-term effects? To answer, Lefkowitz, Eron, Walder, and Huesmann (1972) used the so-called *cross-lagged panel technique* to assess the relationship between television violence viewing and aggressive behavior.

---

*This relationship is perhaps not as strong as might be expected. Evidently, children's violence viewing is only relatively selective and intentional; many may watch violence even though they do not prefer it (e.g., "it may just happen to be on").

Earlier, Eron (1963) had determined the amount of violence viewing and aggression of 875 third-grade youngsters. Aggression was measured by peer ratings. Each child rated every other child in his or her class on a variety of physical and verbal aggressive behaviors. A child's aggression score was determined by the number of peers who said he or she was aggressive. A measure of television violence viewing was obtained from an interview with each child's mother. Eron found that boys who watched a great many violent programs were more likely to be rated high in aggressive behavior by their peers. This relationship did not hold for girls.

Ten years later, when the original participants were 19, Lefkowitz and his associates again obtained information about violence viewing and aggression for 460 of the original 875 subjects. The measure of aggression was peer ratings based on most recent contact, with the items essentially the same as those used in the third-grade study. The data for boys are presented in Figure 5.2. (The data collected from the girls did not reveal significant differences.)

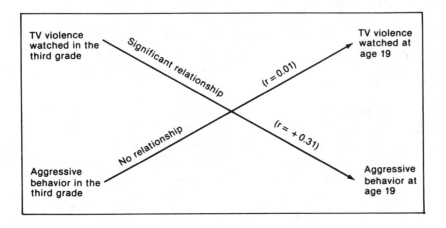

Figure 5.2 The correlations between television violence and aggression for 211 boys over a 10-year lag. From "Television Violence and Child Aggression: A Follow-up Study" (p. 49) by M.M. Lefkowitz, L.D. Eron, L.O.Walder, and L.R. Huesmann, in *Television and Social Behavior. Vol. III: Television and Adolescent Aggressiveness* edited by G.A. Comstock and E.A. Rubinstein, 1972, Washington, DC: U.S. Government Printing Office.

The relationship between viewing television violence in the third grade and aggression 10 years later is significant, while the one between aggression in the third grade and violence viewing when the boys were 19 is not. The pattern supports the hypothesis that viewing television violence is a long-term cause of aggressive behavior.*

Possible effects of TV violence: Experimental studies

However carefully designed, correlational studies always leave the possibility that some unknown additional factor or combination of factors is responsible for the observed relationship. In contrast, true experiments (that is, those in which participants are randomly assigned to different experiences or treatments) can lead to fairly unambiguous statements about cause and effect. The limitation of experiments is that they are usually restricted to weak or shallow representations of the circumstances of ultimate practical interest. For example, few parents would be willing to have their child's TV viewing (or their own) drastically altered for the next 5 years in order to determine for certain what the effects might be. Similarly, investigators cannot ethically create harm or put anyone at risk, which rules out experimental studies of physical aggression except in artificial forms. (Recall the "aggression machine" discussed in chapter 4.)

On first exposure, many of the experiments done as projects for the Surgeon General's Report seem artificial, but they were earnest and useful attempts to demonstrate a direct causal relationship between viewing of actual violent TV content and many measures of a child's willingness to hurt other children.

Stated willingness to aggress
Leifer and Roberts (1972) investigated the effects of the motivation for and consequences of televised violence on a child's willingness to aggress. Previous justification studies had usually employed college students, not young children. Additionally, earlier justification studies and the response

---

*To understand the logic behind this conclusion more fully, consider the possibility raised in our earlier discussion of correlational studies, that a relationship will appear between overt aggression and preferences for aggressive television simply because persons who are more willing to use aggression themselves are also more likely to enjoy seeing it used by others in television dramas. This is an important "rival hypothesis" to the notion that seeing aggressive television *causes* aggressive behavior. However, if the rival hypothesis was correct, preferences for aggressive television at age 19 in the Lefkowitz study should "go together" with overt aggression in the third grade as closely as preferences for aggressive programs in the third grade go with aggression at age 19. In other words, the relationships, if accounted for by a constant third variable, should go both ways in time. In contrast, if television aggression does cause aggressive behavior later, it would be plausible to find a link between earlier television watching and later aggression but not vice versa. This is exactly what was disclosed by the Lefkowitz data.

consequences studies used relatively short sequences, in which motivations and/or consequences were closely related, especially in time, to the action. But real television programs usually last a half hour or more, the motivations of the characters are less explicitly stated, and consequences to the aggressor may occur long after the aggressive acts themselves. Leifer and Roberts wished to investigate young children's understanding of these two factors in regular programming and their influence on children's attitudes toward violence. To do so, they developed a measure of aggression based on the concept of the *response hierarchy.*

When an individual has a number of responses available, his/her alternatives are arranged in a hierarchy—a steplike progression from most probable to least probable. For example, in a threatening situation a very timid individual may prefer to run away. If unable to do so, the individual's next choice may be to call for assistance. If this, too, is impossible the person may attempt to placate the threatening party. Fighting may only be a last resort. In other words, if our first response is blocked, we will then try the second, and so on, until we have exhausted our repertoire of possible responses.

Leifer and Roberts suggest that the overt behavioral tests used in many studies tap only the first response in the hierarchy, but that the influence of television violence may be to change the relative positions of other responses as well. Televised violence may raise physical aggression from, say, the sixth most probable response to the second most probable response and thus increase the likelihood that aggression will occur.

Based on interviews with youngsters, Leifer and Roberts developed six situations that were likely to anger younger children aged 4–10 and six situations appropriate to older children and adolescents aged 10–16. There were four characteristic types of responses: physical aggression, verbal aggression, escaping the situation, and positive coping (including telling an adult). A situation was presented, and then the alternative responses were shown in such a way that each response was paired with every other response, giving a total of six pairs. These were presented to young children in a booklet; the child marked the picture depicting his or her chosen response. Older children saw the pictures on slides, and marked the letter "a" or "b" on an answer sheet. An example of a complete item, including the situation and the possible responses, is shown in Figure 5.3.

One study employing this measure involved six programs that had been assessed by adults in the community for the amount of violence contained: two children's programs ("Rocket Robin Hood" and "Batman"), two westerns ("Rifleman" and "Have Gun Will Travel"), and two crime dramas ("Adam 12" and "Felony Squad"). They were asked to list the violent episodes, the aggressor and victim in each incident, the victim's response, the justifiability of each act, and the appropriateness of immediate and final

Figure 5.3 Sample of a complete response hierarchy item. From "Children's Response to Television Violence" by A.D. Leifer and D.F. Roberts, in *Television and Social Behavior, Vol. 2: Television and Social Learning* edited by J.P. Murray, E.A. Rubinstein, and G.A. Comstock, 1972, Washington, DC: U.S. Government Printing Office.

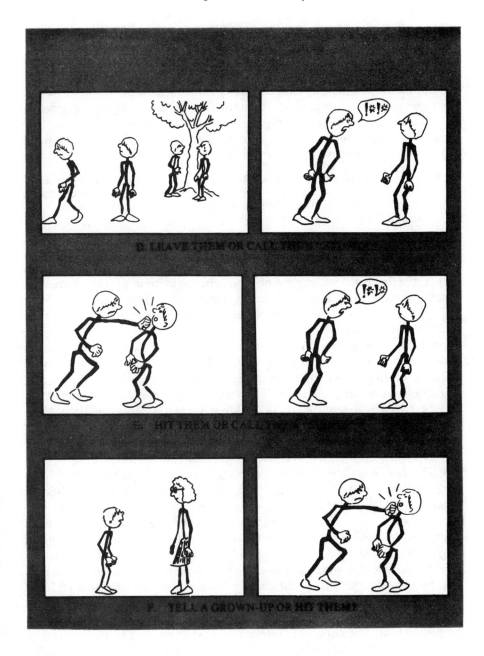

Figure 5.3 Continued

consequences. To ensure that the episodes were truly aggressive, the three most frequently listed ones were then used.

Participants were 271 youngsters in kindergarten, 3rd, 6th, 9th, and 12th grades. Each saw one of the programs, then filled out a multiple choice questionnaire and the response hierarchy instrument. Children who viewed the more aggressive programs were more likely to select physical aggression as a response. Surprisingly though, motivations, consequences, and the child's understanding of these factors were unrelated to subsequent aggressive responses. As the investigators themselves put it:

> Whatever analysis was performed, the amount of violence in the program affected the amount of aggression subsequently chosen. Nothing else about the program—the context within which violence was presented—seemed to influence subsequent aggression. (p. 89)

Increased "hurting" another child via an aggression machine

Liebert and Baron (1972) conducted an experimental laboratory study in which the measure of aggression was an adaptation of the aggression machine described in chapter 4. The participants, 136 boys and girls between the ages of 5 and 9, were taken to a room containing a television monitor and told that they could watch television for a few minutes until the experimenter was ready. The sequences they saw came from actual television shows, but had been videotaped earlier. For all the children, the first 2 minutes of film consisted of commercials selected for their humor and attention-getting characteristics. The following $3\frac{1}{2}$ minutes constituted the experimental treatment. Half the children viewed a sequence from "The Untouchables," which contained a chase, two fistfighting scenes, two shootings, and a knifing. The other children saw an exciting sports sequence. For everyone, the final minute seen was another commercial.

Each child was then escorted to another room and seated in front of a large box that had wires leading into the next room. On the box were a green button labeled HELP and a red button labeled HURT. Over the two buttons was a white light. The experimenter explained that the wires were connected to a game that another child in the adjoining room was going to play. The game involved turning a handle, and each time the child started to turn the handle the white light would come on. The experimenter explained that by pushing the buttons the subject could either help the other child by making the handle easier to turn or hurt the other child by making the handle hot. The longer the buttons were pushed, the more the other child was helped or hurt. The child was further told that he or she had to push one of the buttons every time the light came on. After insuring that the child understood which button was which, the experimenter left the room, and the light came on 20 times. After this, each child was taken to a playroom containing aggressive and nonaggressive toys, and aggressive play was assessed.

Using total duration of pushing the HURT button as their measure of aggression, the investigators found that children who viewed the aggressive program were significantly more willing to hurt another child than were those who watched the sports sequence. When average duration was computed (total duration divided by the number of HURT responses), the same results were obtained. As seen in Figure 5.4, the pattern appears for boys and girls of both ages.

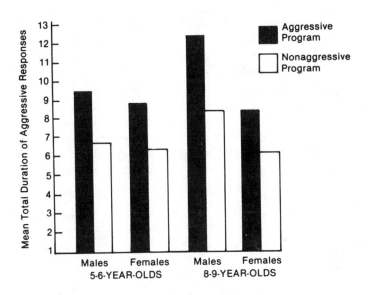

Figure 5.4 Mean total duration of aggressive responses. From "Short-term Effects of Televised Aggression on Children's Aggressive Behavior" by R.M. Liebert and R.A. Baron, in *Television and Social Behavior. Vol. 2: Television and Social Learning* edited by J.P. Murray, E.A. Rubinstein, and G.A. Comstock, Washington, DC: U.S. Government Printing Office.

It was possible that children who viewed the violent television scene pushed the HURT button longer because they were more excited or aroused. If this line of reasoning is correct, *any* response of this group would be of higher intensity; therefore, they also should have pushed the HELP button longer. They did not. The programs used made no difference in total duration, average duration, or number of HELP responses. Consistent with previous research, children in the aggressive film condition also were more aggressive in the play situation, with the effects much stronger for younger boys than for any of the other groups. What this study suggests is that, at least in the short term, children will be less kind and more cruel to peers as a result of watching TV violence.

Blunting of sensitivity to violence

Rabinovitch, McLean, Markham, and Talbott (1972) conducted a laboratory experiment that addressed the question: Can TV violence blunt children's sensitivity? Sixth-grade children saw either a violent program (an episode of "Peter Gunn") or a nonviolent one (an episode from "Green Acres"). Then each child was tested using a stereoscopic projector which simultaneously presented different images to each eye for such a brief exposure that only one is seen. The two images were very similar, but one was violent and one nonviolent (see Table 5.3). For example, one slide showed a man hitting another over the head with a gun; the corresponding nonviolent slide showed a man helping another pound a pole into the ground with a gun butt. Another pair contrasted hitting someone with a book and showing the book to him (see Figure 5.5). After each slide pair was presented, the child wrote down a description of what he or she had seen. Those who had seen the episode from "Peter Gunn" were less likely to report violence, suggesting that they had become at least temporarily less sensitive to it.

Table 5.3 Description of Pairs of Slides Used in Free Response Measure of Violence Perception

NUMBER	VIOLENT SLIDE	NONVIOLENT SLIDE
1	One man hits the other over the head with a gun.	One man helps the other pound a pole in the ground with a gun butt.
2	One man shoots the other with a rifle.	Both men walk. One carried a rifle.
3	One man pushes the other off a bridge.	Both men walk on the bridge.
4	One man kicks the other off a merry-go-round.	Both men ride on a merry-go-round.
5	One man hits the other over the head with a book.	One man shows the other something in a book.
6	One man, tied up, tries to hit the other man.	One man holds a rope. The other looks at the rope.
7	One man hits the other over the head with a car jack.	One man helps the other take a car jack out of the car trunk.
8	One man hits the other over the head with a rock.	Both men help to lift a rock.
9	One man holds the other and takes money at gunpoint.	One man gives the other man money from his wallet.

Note. From "Children's Violence Perception as a Function of Television Violence" (p. 239) by M.S. Rabinovitch, M.S. McLean, Jr., J.W. Markham, and A.D. Talbott, in Television and Social Behavior, Vol. 5, Television's Effects: Further Explorations edited by G.A. Comstock, E.A. Rubinstein, and J.P. Murray, 1972, Washington, DC: U.S. Government Printing Office.

Figure 5.5 Sample slide pair from Rabinovitch's study of the perception of violence. Courtesy of Martin Rabinovitch.

Aggressive and prosocial play among preschoolers

Stein and Friedrich (1972) compared the effect of "prosocial" or socially desirable programs, aggressive programs, and neutral films on preschool viewers' behavior. This was the first study to examine the potential positive effects of television on children's naturally occurring social behavior. (Many studies followed it, as will be seen in chapter 10.)

Stein and Friedrich studied 97 preschool children, ranging in age from 3 years 10 months to 5 years 6 months. They were enrolled in a special summer nursery school program established for the study. The range of social class backgrounds was relatively wide, because special efforts were made to recruit children from poorer as well as middle class homes. The children were divided into four classes of about 25 children each and met for 2½ hours in either the morning or afternoon three times a week.

The experiment took 9 weeks to complete: 3 weeks of baseline observation. 4 weeks of controlled television viewing (the period of experimental manipulation), and 2 weeks of postviewing observation. During the period of television viewing, children were randomly assigned to one of three groups according to type of programs seen: aggressive, neutral, and prosocial. Aggressive programs consisted of six "Batman" and six "Superman" cartoons, each containing several episodes of verbal and physical aggression. Prosocial programs were 12 episodes of "Mister Rogers' Neighborhood," which emphasized cooperation, sharing, delay of gratification, persistence at tasks, control of aggression, and similar prosocial themes. Neutral programs were children's films of diverse content, emphasizing neither aggression nor prosocial behavior. Almost no aggression occurred in these films, but some prosocial behavior was present. Each program lasted between 20 and 30 minutes; children in all groups saw one program a day, 3 days a week.

The most important measure was observations of the children either during free play or in the classroom. Each child's behavior was observed and recorded for three 5-minute periods each day. Behaviors were scored in five general categories: aggression, prosocial interpersonal behavior, persistence, self-control, and regression. Each category was further divided into more specific behaviors; for example, self-control included rule obedience and delay of gratification, regression included crying or pouting and withdrawal. Observers were "blind" to experimental conditions; that is, they did not know to which treatment the child they were observing had been exposed. Before analyzing their data, Stein and Friedrich further categorized their subjects by dividing them at the median (midpoint) on the basis of their scores on three variables: IQ, socioeconomic status, and initial (pre-experimental) level of aggressive behavior.

The results of this study showed that children who viewed aggressive programming were more likely to be aggressive in interpersonal situations than those who viewed neutral or prosocial television. However, the effect had a clear limitation: it held only for those children who were in the upper half of the sample (above the median) in initial level of aggression.

Socioeconomic status and IQ, previously assessed by the investigators, influenced which prosocial lessons were learned. Self-control was influenced in the predicted ways: children in the prosocial condition increased, while those in the aggressive condition decreased. On the prosocial interpersonal measure, only the children in lower socioeconomic classes responded as might be expected by increasing in prosocial behavior.

CREATING THE REPORT

It is desirable at this point to describe the to-be-published report from the vantage point of the committee in mid-1971. In addition to some ancillary documents (such as an annotated bibliography of studies done prior to the report), all of the technical papers submitted to the committee would be published in the five technical volumes we mentioned before. Much more important than these complex and weighty reports (which ran to more than 2,000 pages when printed) was the official report of the committee to the Surgeon General. The committee had to read, study, and discuss all the technical reports, consider their implications, and offer interpretations and conclusions in a report of their own. What conclusions were reached in this official report and exactly how they were worded would doubtless be extremely important in how the press and public interpreted the overall inquiry.

A general understanding prevailed among the principal investigators, staff, and the committee that no statements about the science *or* politics of their work would be made to the press or public until the technical reports had been completed, read, discussed by the committee, and the official statement had been completed.

A very important issue was at stake until the last minute: whether or not the committee (composed as it was of industry people and the independent academics with varying views on the issues among them) would agree on a single report. The alternative, a commonplace result of blue-ribbon government inquiries, was to produce several conflicting reports. In such circumstances the industry people would likely collaborate on one report and the independents on one or two others. The press and administration critics would have a field day, and the whole thing would be dismissed cynically as a predictable failure. Eli Rubinstein, as the government's representative, was adamant in his pursuit of a single report, and applying a hand both skilled and subtle, he and his staff managed to hammer out a document everyone would sign on December 31, 1971, the deadline that

Rubinstein had insisted from the outset was absolute. (Federal funds ran out, technically at least, at midnight on the 31st.)

All committee meetings were behind closed doors at this point. The private goings on were surely not dull. According to John P. Murray, research co-ordinator for the project and one of the few non-committee members who was present during the deliberations (Paisley, 1972):

> There was a big move by Government officials to get a consensus report. There was a lot of anger, the meetings were extremely tense with the warring factions sitting at either end of the table, glaring at each other, particularly toward the end. (p. 28)

The result was undoubtedly a compromise, with the "network five" scoring its share in the battle. According to *Newsweek* ("Violence revisited," 1972):

> At one point during the committee meetings . . . former CBS consultant Wiebe raised his eyes from a particularly damning piece of evidence and grumbled: "This looks like it was written by someone who hates television." But the most ardent defender of the industry was CBS research director Joseph Klapper, who lobbied for the inclusion, among other things, of a plethora of "howevers" in the final report. (p. 55)

The committee did sign a unanimous report just before the deadline and, of course, it took time to print, bind, and duplicate the document. During this waiting time, committee members were concerned that each hard-bargained subtlety they had won actually appeared in the published wording. Everyone was sensitive to the possibility of intrigue.

Television and growing up: The impact of televised violence was the title the committee gave its official report. Though manageable compared to the thousands of pages of technical reports, this 169-page work did not make for light reading either. So an 11-page summary of the report was published, both separately and as the first chapter of *Television and growing up: The impact of televised violence.*

Except for the committee members and staff, this brief but all-important 11-page statement by the committee was not seen by the researchers until a summary of the summary was published by Jack Gould in the *New York Times* on January 11, 1972, under the headline: "TV VIOLENCE HELD UNHARMFUL TO YOUTH."

6

Aftermath of the Report

OVERVIEW

Sufficient controversy surrounded publication of the Surgeon General's Report to warrant follow-up hearings, which were held in March 1972. The hearings led to a "new consensus" among social scientists and government officials that TV violence had been shown to be one of several significant contributors to aggressive and antisocial attitudes and behavior, and that a time for action had come. As a result, in the mid-1970s efforts were made to curb the amount of violence on TV. A major commitment was also made to obtain periodic measures of TV violence and Gerbner's Violence Index became the tool for doing so. Soon the medical establishment, the Parent Teacher Association (PTA), the American Psychological Association, and even a major advertising agency came out for a reduction in TV violence. In three major court cases the possible effects of TV violence have been pitted against broadcasters' First Amendment rights. In each case, First Amendment considerations prevailed.

Ten years after the appearance of the Surgeon General's Report, the National Institute of Mental Health (NIMH) undertook an update of the report based on recent research findings. The Ten-Year Update's conclusions about TV violence were clear. TV violence was implicated as a *cause* of aggressive behavior.

OUTLINE

The first public disclosure of the conclusions recorded in the Surgeon General's Report was written by a newspaper reporter, Jack Gould of the *New York Times*. Gould had somehow managed to get his hands on a copy of the 11-page summary of the Surgeon General's Report, and on January 11, 1972, published a front page story in the *Times* under the headline, "TV VIOLENCE HELD UNHARMFUL TO YOUTH." The first paragraph of the article states:

> The office of the United States Surgeon General has found that violence in television programming does not have an adverse effect on the majority of the nation's youth but may influence small groups of youngsters predisposed by many factors to aggressive behavior.

Speaking more clearly and explicitly than social scientists ever do, Gould claimed that only children already inclined toward aggression would be affected by TV violence and that their number was small. These claims were, of course, arguable. In fact, Gould's article produced an enormous furor and accusations that the Surgeon General's Report had been an industry "whitewash." As a result, more public attention was focused on TV violence in the spring of 1972 than ever before.

It is appropriate to step back for a moment to examine the problems reporter Gould faced. First, he was reading a summary of a summary, inasmuch as he had seen a summary of the Surgeon General's Report which itself was largely an effort to integrate and interpret a set of technical reports.

One thing the technical reports to the committee made clear was that TV violence did not have a uniform effect on all children. In many ways this is unsurprising, because very few factors do have uniform effects. Thus, the technical project reports revealed differences in aggressive attitudes and behavior on the basis of gender, age, social and economic background; moreover, many of these factors influenced the degree to which TV violence had an effect in experimental studies. In the official committee report, factors associated with increased aggression were lumped together as "predispositions" and thus it could be said that TV violence had its greatest impact on those who were "predisposed" to respond to violent content in the medium. "Predisposition" turns out to be quite a subtle word, and one way to read the committee's report was that TV violence was entirely harmless except for possible effects on rare and troubled children. Presumably this is the way Jack Gould interpreted the 11-page summary.

The Gould story greatly upset a number of the social scientists who had authored the technical reports, and many contacted one another and local newspapers in order to rectify what seemed like a gross misrepresentation of their efforts. Articles on the subject of TV violence and children appeared in most of the nation's major newspapers and news magazines. Conclusions varied widely. Norman Mark (1972), writing in the *Birmingham News*, announced:

> Dynamite is hidden in the Surgeon General's Report on children and television violence, for the report reveals that most children are definitely and adversely affected by television mayhem.

Many of the researchers associated with the project felt that their work had been represented inaccurately, and at the least minimized what seemed a clear relationship between viewing of TV violence and youngsters' aggressive behavior. Monroe Lefkowitz, Principal Research Scientist at the New York State Department of Mental Hygiene wrote in a letter to Senator Pastore:

> The Surgeon General's Scientific Advisory Committee on Television and Social Behavior in my opinion ignores, dilutes, and distorts the research findings in their report, "Television and Growing Up: the Impact of Televised Violence." As a contributor of one of the technical reports whose study dealt with television violence and aggressive behavior . . . I feel that the Committee's conclusions about the causal nature of television violence in producing aggressive behavior are hedged by erroneous statements, are overqualified, and are potentially damaging to children and society.

Lefkowitz' response is strong, but by no means unique. Matilda Paisley, in a report of Stanford University's Institute for Communication Research entitled "Social policy research and the realities of the system: Violence done to TV research," indicated that fully half of the researchers who replied to her questionnaire stated that the results of their own research had *not* been adequately reported by the committee (Paisley, 1972). Some typical replies, with letters substituted for respondents' names, appear below:

> Respondent B commented that, "In fact, they went too deep on some of our extraneous findings, in order to obscure the main conclusion." Respondents G, L, and P spoke of "strange emphases," "misleading focus," and "selective emphases," respectively. Respondents E and F spoke of errors in reporting their research. Respondent T stated that "the conclusions are diluted and overqualified." (Appendix III, p. 4)

One item on the Paisley questionnaire read: Whatever the findings of your own research suggest, which of the following relationships of violence viewing to aggressiveness do you feel is now the most plausible?*

(a) viewing television violence increases aggressiveness;
(b) viewing television violence decreases aggressiveness;
(c) viewing television violence has no effect on aggressiveness;
(d) the relationship between violence viewing and aggressiveness depends on a third variable or set of variables;
(e) other, please specify

---

*Almost half of the investigators were involved in projects that did not bear directly on this question.

None of the 20 investigators who responded to this question selected answer (b) or selected (c). Clearly, then, these researchers felt that there was a relationship between TV violence and aggressiveness, and that the catharsis hypothesis was untenable. Seventy percent of the respondents simply selected response (a)—viewing television violence increases aggressiveness. All of the remainder qualified their replies with some version of alternative (d) or (e).

Two passages from the committee's official report will exemplify the cautious flavor of its tone and give the reader a sense of why it stimulated such controversy.

In sum. The experimental studies bearing on the effects of aggressive television entertainment content on children support certain conclusions. First, violence depicted on television can immediately or shortly thereafter induce mimicking or copying by children. Second, under certain circumstances television violence can instigate an increase in aggressive acts. The accumulated evidence, however, does not warrant the conclusion that television violence has a uniformly adverse effect nor the conclusion that it has an adverse effect on the majority of children. It cannot even be said that the majority of the children in the various studies we have reviewed showed an increase in aggressive behavior in response to the violent fare to which they were exposed. The evidence does indicate that televised violence may lead to increased aggressive behavior in certain subgroups of children, who might constitute a small portion or a substantial proportion of the total population of young television viewers. We cannot estimate the size of the fraction, however, since the available evidence does not come from cross-section samples of the entire American population of children. (p. 7)

Thus, the two sets of findings [correlational and experimental studies] converge in three respects: A preliminary and tentative indication of a causal relationship between viewing violence on television and aggressive behaviors; an indication that any such causal relation operates only on some children (who are predisposed to be aggressive); and an indication that it operates only in some environmental contexts. Such tentative and limited conclusions are not very satisfying. They represent substantially more knowledge than we had two years ago, but they leave many questions unanswered. (p. 11)

THE PASTORE HEARINGS

In March 1972 shortly after the publication of the technical reports, Senator Pastore held further hearings to clarify the situation (U.S. Senate, 1972). When questioned by Senator Pastore and members of his subcommittee, Ithiel de Sola Pool, a member of the Surgeon General's Advisory Committee, commented:

Twelve scientists of widely different views unanimously agreed that scientific evidence indicated that the viewing of television violence by young people causes them to behave more aggressively. (p. 47)

Alberta Siegel, another committee member, stated:

Commercial television makes its own contribution to the set of factors that underlie aggressiveness in our society. It does so in entertainment through ceaseless repetition of the message that conflict may be resolved by aggression, that violence is a way of solving problems. (p. 63)

Pool and Siegel were among the academic members of the committee; they had pressed for a "strong" report on the basis of the data all along. But even Ira Cisin, Thomas Coffin, and the other "network" committee members agreed that the situation was sufficiently serious to warrant some action.

The networks' chief executives also testified. Julian Goodman, President of NBC, stated:

We agree with you that the time for action has come. And, of course, we are willing to cooperate in any way together with the rest of the industry. (p. 182)

Elton H. Rule of the American Broadcasting Company promised:

Now that we are reasonably certain that televised violence can increase aggressive tendencies in some children, we will have to manage our program planning accordingly. (p. 217)

Surgeon General Jesse Steinfeld made the unequivocal statement that:

Certainly my interpretation is that there is a causative relationship between televised violence and subsequent antisocial behavior, and that the evidence is strong enough that it requires some action on the part of responsible authorities, the TV industry, the Government, the citizens. (p. 28)

Although few social scientists would put the seal "Absolutely Proven" on this or any other body of research, the weight of the evidence and the outcry of the news media did become sufficient to produce a belated recognition of the implications of the research.* Testimony and documentation at the Hearings of the Subcommittee on Communications, U.S. Senate, were overwhelming. Senator Pastore now had his answer. It is captured entirely in the following interchange, late in the 1972 hearings, between Pastore and Dr. Eli Rubinstein. (Recall that Rubinstein was Vice-Chairman of the Surgeon General's Committee and monitored the research and refereed the Committee in Dr. Steinfeld's absence.)

---

*Cater and Strickland (1975) have noted that it was not until after the report that social scientists and government officials reached a "new consensus" on what the data meant.

Senator Pastore: And are you convinced, like the Surgeon General, that we have enough data now [about the effects of television on children] to take action?

Dr. Rubinstein: I am, sir.

Senator Pastore: Without a re-review. It will only substantiate the facts we already know. Irrespective of how one or another individual feels, the fact still remains that you are convinced, as the Surgeon General is convinced, that there is a causal relationship between violence on television and social behavior on the part of children?

Dr. Rubinstein: I am. sir.

Senator Pastore: I think we ought to take it from there. (p. 152)

EMERGING REACTIONS TO THE REPORT

The wake of the Surgeon General's Report ran wide and deep. We have already seen that there was a great deal of controversy over the report itself, especially regarding the validity of the committee's interpretations of the technical data. This led to additional hearings and then to a number of significant government and industry responses. What the Surgeon General's Report did stimulate was public interest. At the same time, social scientists were actively encouraged to explore the issue of television's effects on children in depth and from many vantage points, with financial support readily available from government agencies and private foundations. The 10-year period from 1970 to 1979 was the golden age of television for social science, if not for the medium itself. We shall discuss the results of many of these efforts in the remainder of the book. All of the major developments reflected their origins in the Surgeon General's Report.

For now, though, we will restrict ourselves mainly to the TV violence issue. The scientific evidence focused attention on the issue and helped to convince the public and Congress that TV violence should be reduced. The pressures generated by these groups actually resulted in industry action. Anticipating external controls, the broadcasting industry adopted self-regulatory measures in response to clear pressures from Congress, the public, and advertisers.*

The report also stimulated research and funding in the area. In 1975, the Ford Foundation, National Science Foundation, and Markle Foundation sponsored a major conference in Reston, Virginia, to establish research priorities and increase funding on television and human behavior. In 1976, the National Science Foundation announced its support of a $1.5 million grant program entitled "Policy Related Research on the Social Effects of

---

*As we will see shortly, in the long-run these measures were *not* effective in reducing the level of TV violence.

Broadcast Television." Also in 1976, the American Broadcasting Company provided modest funding for university research on television effects.

The sheer quantity of research on television and social behavior demonstrates the incredible growth of interest in the area. As Murray (1980) points out, a 1972 bibliography (Atkin, Murray, & Nayman, 1971) contained 285 core citations, and his own in 1980 contained 2,886 citations, 60% of which had been published over the preceding 5 years.

AFFIRMATIVE ACTION

Affirmative action was a banner phrase in the earlier part of the 1970s, and its spirit is reflected in much of the aftermath of the TV violence issue. In 1973, Jessie Steinfeld, recently retired from his official capacity as Surgeon General, wrote an article for *Readers Digest* entitled "TV Violence *Is* Harmful," in which he declared: "It is time to be blunt. We can no longer tolerate the high level of violence that saturates children's television" (p. 37).

The violence index

In Senator Pastore's March 1972 hearings, in which it might be said that the new consensus emerged, one specific idea was heavily promoted by foundation officials, government officers, and social scientists: a regular violence index.

Lloyd Morrisett, President of the Markle Foundation, which had a long interest in children and television, said at the hearings:

> We are impressed by the need for techniques to monitor on a continuing basis the amount and quality of violence on television as a means of informing the public and allowing a more complete understanding of the problem. In suggesting an attack on this problem we fully understand the complexity of the issue. It will be difficult to design sound measures of violence on television and the first ones will undoubtedly be imperfect and need to be improved over time. Despite this and other problems we believe the issue is important enough to warrant immediate action. (cited by Cater & Strickland, 1975, p. 93)

Such a violence index was established, and not surprisingly the investigator to take on the task was George Gerbner. Every year since 1967 George Gerbner and his colleagues have continued to monitor the amount of violence on prime-time and weekend daytime (children's) shows. Using the same procedures over time (described in chapter 5), this work represents the longest running record of TV violence portrayals.

Table 6.1 shows the percentage of programs containing violence over the 18-year period from 1967 to 1985. Perhaps the most remarkable thing about these data are their consistency. Violence is the stock and trade of entertainment television and this is no less true 2 years ago than it was 20 years ago. Equally clear is the fact that virtually all cartoons are based on violence; in no year has the percentage of cartoons containing violence been lower than 90%.

Table 6.1 Percentage of Programs Containing Violence

YEAR	ALL PROGRAMS (%)	PROGRAMS AIRED 8–9 p.m. E.S.T. (%)	PROGRAMS AIRED 9–11 p.m. E.S.T. (%)	CARTOONS (%)
1967	81.3	78.9	69.2	93.8
1968	81.6	75.0	76.2	96.0
1969	83.5	63.2	80.8	98.1
1970	77.5	57.1	69.2	96.0
1971	80.6	75.0	76.5	93.9
1972	79.0	74.1	69.7	91.9
1973	72.7	56.3	63.3	96.9
1974	83.3	69.0	86.2	90.6
1975	78.4	51.6	85.7	91.4
1976	89.1	72.0	86.1	100.0
1977	76.9	65.6	66.7	93.3
1978	84.7	59.3	86.1	97.8
1979	81.0	71.0	69.7	98.4
1980	85.4	72.4	74.3	97.1
1981	85.8	80.8	79.5	91.3
1982	76.0	71.4	57.1	95.9
1983	82.1	72.0	73.7	92.5
1984	87.5	82.1	75.7	98.1
1985	85.0	78.6	79.5	92.1
Total	81.8	69.5	75.0	95.1

Note. Based on data reported in Television's Mean World: Violence Profile No. 14–15 by G. Gerbner, L. Gross, N. Signorielli, and M. Morgan, 1986, Philadelphia, PA: University of Pennsylvania, Annenberg School of Communications.

The emphasis on violence in U.S. children's cartoons is even more striking when we turn to Table 6.2, which shows the number of violent acts per program hour. The typical cartoon has a violent act every 3 minutes, a violence rate that is four or five times greater than for prime-time or family programming. Again, except for minor fluctuations, the figures have really not changed at all over the years. What all this suggests, of course, is that despite promises to the contrary, the Surgeon General's Report had no real effect on the degree of TV violence offered by commercial television.

Also consistent over the years has been the social groups that tend to be the victims of violence. The groups that are most likely to be the victim rather than the perpetrator of violence include women (of all ages, but especially young adult and elderly women), young boys, nonwhites, foreigners, and members of the extreme upper and lower classes.

Table 6.2 Number of Violent Acts per Program Hour

YEAR	ALL PROGRAMS (%)	PROGRAMS AIRED 8–9 p.m. E.S.T. (%)	PROGRAMS AIRED 9–11 p.m. E.S.T. (%)	CARTOONS (%)
1967	7.7	8.0	3.5	21.6
1968	6.7	4.5	4.1	22.9
1969	8.8	4.5	3.6	28.4
1970	7.4	3.3	4.1	22.4
1971	6.9	4.4	4.3	16.3
1972	7.5	5.2	5.2	15.8
1973	7.0	5.1	4.7	13.2
1974	6.9	4.0	6.7	12.1
1975	8.1	3.6	7.2	16.3
1976	9.5	4.7	6.8	22.4
1977	8.0	6.0	5.9	15.6
1978	8.3	4.0	4.8	25.0
1979	8.1	6.3	5.2	17.2
1980	10.0	6.4	5.2	26.9
1981	10.7	5.5	6.1	30.9
1982	8.3	5.4	4.1	30.3
1983	8.7	6.0	4.2	25.5
1984	10.9	7.6	6.5	27.3
1985	9.7	7.6	6.4	21.3
Total	8.4	5.4	5.3	21.1

Note. Based on data reported in *Television's Mean World: Violence Profile No. 14–15* by G. Gerbner, L. Gross, N. Signorielli, and M. Morgan, 1986, Philadelphia, PA: University of Pennsylvania, Annenberg School of Communications.

Critics have found Gerbner's work vulnerable on several counts. Most important, perhaps, is that his violence scoring system includes humorous acts and accidents. As a result, Gerbner's analyses are often at odds with those of other studies using the more conventional definition of "acts intended to harm or threaten people or property." For example, a contrast between Gerbner's classification and one done by the *Christian Science Monitor* revealed that Gerbner made light-hearted but innocent sitcoms such as "The Flying Nun" and "That Girl," appear quite violent, whereas the *Monitor* study characterized them as nonviolent (Coffin & Tuchman, 1973).

The Reston Conference

As we mentioned earlier in this chapter, in 1975 three foundations (Ford Foundation, National Science Foundation, and Markle Foundation) held a conference on television and human behavior. The conference had two objectives: (a) to organize a broad range of people (including representatives of academia, private and public foundations, media advocacy groups, the broadcasting industries, advertising, and government regulatory agencies) to develop a set of guidelines for future TV research, and (b) to frame the guidelines to maximize the utility of social science research for television policymakers within the government and the broadcasting and advertising industries. Relatively little consensus on specific issues was reached at the conference, but it became plain that all the researchers were quite interested in the role of television in the socialization of young persons. There also seemed to be some agreement that a causal link between TV violence and aggressive behavior had already been established, and that little more could be learned given the ethical and practical limitations of research. Thus, many researchers were inclined to try to harness TV's potential for various goals of society, an effort which we shall discuss in detail in the last chapter of this book.

The new activists

The new consensus also spurred a new set of activists, with a variety of ambitions for television. Many of these efforts, as we will see in chapter 10 were designed to harness television's potential, but a few were trying to see TV violence curbed by more direct means.

The Medical Establishment

In December 1975, the publication of an article by a Seattle physician in the *Journal of the American Medical Association* marked the beginning of a national movement by the AMA to curb TV violence. Dr. Michael Rothenberg, a pediatrician, had given a few lectures on the effects of TV violence on children. He then used the materials he collected for his talks to write a review article for the prestigious medical journal. The article was accepted immediately and made the lead article, cover picture and all. His conclusions, printed in bold type on the first page of the article stated:

> One hundred and forty-six articles in behavioral science journals, representing 50 studies involving 10,000 children and adolescents from every conceivable background, all showed that violence viewing produces increased aggressive behavior in the young and that immediate remedial action in terms of television programming is warranted. . . .

> The time is long past due for a major, organized cry of protest from the medical profession in relation to what, in political terms, I consider a national scandal. (p. 1043)

Rothenberg's concerns and suggestions that remedial action be taken were soon after echoed by another pediatrician, Dr. Anne Somers, in the April 1976 edition of the *New England Journal of Medicine*. After documenting the dramatic rise in violent crimes by youthful offenders and reviewing the research evidence linking TV violence to aggressive behavior in children, Somers spelled out the role that she felt the American Medical Association should take to reduce TV violence:

The essential first step is general professional acceptance of the role of television violence as a risk factor threatening the health and welfare of American children and youth and official organizational commitment to remedial action. Recent publication of Dr. Rothenberg's brilliant "call to arms" on this subject was an important beginning.

Next, it is essential that the American Medical Association and other organizational spokesmen for the profession make their views known to the industry—both to the networks and local stations, to the FCC, and to federal and state legislators, especially the two responsible committees of Congress. The approach should be twofold: a reduction of violence in general entertaining programming and support for the concept of the Family Viewing Hour.* The primary argument for the latter is not that it will save children from exposure to violence; it will not. But its very existence commits the industry to values other than commercialism and may force them, and the rest of us, to come up with some positive guidelines for realizing television's enormous positive cultural and educational potential. (p. 816)

Aside from organizational action, Somers urged individual practitioners dealing with children and adolescents to make available to parents the guides to children's television published by media/child advocacy groups such as Action for Children's Television.

Perhaps the most emotional statement voiced by the medical profession against TV violence came from another physician, Dr. F.J. Ingelfinger (1976), who published an editorial called, "Violence on TV: An Unchecked Environmental Hazard" in the *New England Journal of Medicine*. Only his exact words can capture the sentiment expressed:

Diseases caused by the environment—for some reason called environmental rather than envirogenic—are prime public concerns. Hardly a day passes without some pesticide, industrial agent, drug or apparatus being indicted as responsible for some human disorder. These indictments, however, are not without their dilemmas, for the suspect agent is often beneficial as well as purportedly harmful. Without pesticides, nutritional crops are at risk, without drugs, illness may go unchecked and without nuclear power plants, the economy may falter. Thus, society is forced to arrive at difficult risk/benefit decisions. Ironically enough, however, while chlordane is banned and aspirin impugned, an environmental hazard of far greater magnitude and with no redeeming benefits whatsoever (except for fattening a few pocketbooks) goes unchallenged. The hazard is the exaltation of violence on television, its victims are all our children, and the disease is a distortion of values, attitudes and morality. . . .

---

*The Family Viewing Hour was a National Association of Broadcasters guideline set forth in 1975 which stated that the 8–9 p.m. broadcast period should be free from themes that would be objectionable for child viewers (i.e., sex and violence).

If the medical profession is truly interested in curtailing the environmental hazard of excessive TV violence, it must make sure that the voices of protest multiply geometrically, from one to two to four, and so on, so that eventually the swell of the chorus can no longer be ignored. But noise, even loud noise, will probably not suffice. "An organized cry of protest" requires by definition organization, which in turn requires leadership and money. Doctors and their families must act as advocates and enlist not only other doctors but patients as well. Letters, as Anne Somers suggests, must bombard our representatives in Congress. . . .

The AMA, if it is really ready to fight this environmental disease, should appoint a panel that will identify the programs most notorious for their routine and persistent portrayal of violence. Once these programs have been so identified, let the list be posted in doctors' offices. The application of the boycott is then straightforward: those who believe that violence on TV must be contained will simply pledge themselves not to purchase products promoted in association with the offending programs. Our dogs, after all, can survive even if they have to do without any canine gourmet dish that happens to underwrite a weekly gangland-police shoot-out, and our kitchens will function without electronic devices promoted between gory executions and garrottings.

Or shall we medicos and our spouses and friends sit back, as we have been doing, and fold our hands over contented bellies, while the after-dinner entertainment of our children shows that nothing can be accomplished in this world without brass knucks, kicks in the groin, switch blades or Saturday Night Specials. (pp. 837–838)

These articles were effective in summoning support. During 1976 and 1977, the AMA took several actions as a stand against TV violence. In 1976, the House of Delegates of the AMA resolved that it would:

1. Declare its recognition of the fact that TV violence is a risk factor threatening the health and welfare of young Americans, indeed our future society.
2. Commit itself to remedial action in concert with industry, government and other interested parties.
3. Encourage all physicians, their families and their patients to actively oppose TV programs containing violence, as well as products and/or services sponsoring such programs. (American Medical Association Policy, 1976)

The report of a content analysis by the National Citizens Committee for Broadcasting released in July of 1976 helped to pinpoint the sponsors of TV violence on whom the AMA would focus. The public interest organization, headed by a former FCC commissioner Nicholas Johnson, monitored TV entertainment for 6 weeks and identified the companies that advertised on the most violent programs. They found the following companies to be most often associated with violent programs: Tegrin, Burger King, Clorox, Colgate-Palmolive, and Gillette (Brown, 1976).

In February 1977 Dr. Richard E. Palmer, President of the AMA, declared TV violence a "mental health problem and an environmental issue" and asked 10 major companies to examine advertising policies that support TV programs high in violence ("Pull Plug," 1977). Further AMA action took the form of national workshops to inform physicians about TV violence effects, research to monitor the amount of TV violence, and encouragement to the National PTA to organize its own campaign.

In 1985, 10 years after his original *JAMA* article, Dr. Rothenberg was still trying to influence his medical colleagues to protest the lack of government regulation of television content that was potentially hazardous to children's health. In a pediatric care journal he reiterated his earlier concerns about TV violence and aspects of advertising and concluded (Rothenberg, 1985):

> Clearly, much of the programming and commercial message content of television programs being watched by children and youth is potentially, and often demonstrably, a mental and physical health hazard to the young. . . .
>
> Despite the scientific evidence, the United States federal government has been unwilling to take action to protect children from this hazard. Presumably, the federal government is more concerned with the political and financial aspects of the problem than it is with the health hazard. In my opinion, this is unacceptable and should be protested by all those involved in providing health care for children. (p. 149)

A variety of medical groups have recently taken stands on various aspects of television content, especially violence: The American Academy of Pediatrics organized a task force to examine television effects and in 1986 published a pamphlet, *Television and the Family*, which was distributed to its members and made available for wider distribution to their patients. The pamphlet addressed the problems of excessive TV viewing (i.e., children not participating in healthier and more developmentally important activities such as reading and socializing), the negative effects of TV violence and commercials, and recommended that parents modify the TV viewing habits within their family and take actions such as contacting local television stations, sponsors, networks, and the Better Business Bureau to report objectionable program and advertising content. The pamphlet also encouraged support of the Children's Television Education Act (see p. 51).

The American Academy of Child Psychiatry also organized a task force that focused on violence and the media. The task force concluded that "there seems to be a causal relationship between televised violence and later short- and long-term aggressive behavior" (American Academy of Child Psychiatry, 1984, p. 1) and recommended that the academy work with other professional groups to educate the public about negative and positive effects of television on the socialization of children. Similar ideas were echoed by Dr. Chester Pierce (1984), a psychiatrist who published an article in the *American Journal of Social Psychiatry* entitled, "Television and Violence: Social Psychiatric Perspectives." Pierce expressed concern about the negative impact of TV violence and urged psychiatrists to help parents promote a "TV hygiene" by modifying family viewing practices.

The American Psychological Association (APA)
The American Psychological Association, which represents more than 60,000 psychologists, has now taken a stand against TV violence. In 1984, the APA presented testimony on the impact of televised violence on children before the Subcommittee on Juvenile Justice of the Senate Judiciary Committee. The testimony, delivered by John Murray (1984), a respected TV researcher, clearly stated that "viewing violence does lead to increases in aggressive attitudes, values, and behaviors." In 1985, Aletha Huston (1985), another prominent TV researcher, testified on behalf of the APA before the House of Representatives Subcommittee on Telecommunications, Consumer Protection, and Finance. Concerning TV violence, she set forth the TV violence viewing–aggressive behavior link and advocated the passing of the Children's Television Education Act.

In February of 1985 the APA passed a resolution stating:

WHEREAS, the great majority of research studies have found a relationship between televised violence and behaving aggressively, and

WHEREAS, the conclusions drawn on the basis of 25 years of research and a sizable number of experimental and field investigations is that viewing televised violence may lead to increases in aggressive attitudes, values, and behavior, particularly in children, and

WHEREAS, many children's programs contain some form of violence,

BE IT RESOLVED that the American Psychological Association (1) encourages parents to monitor and to control television viewing by children; (2) requests industry representatives to take a responsible attitude in reducing direct imitatable violence in "real-life" fictional children's programming or violent incidents on cartoons and in providing more programming for children designed to mitigate possible effects of television violence, consistent with the guarantees of the First Amendment; and (3) urges industry, government and private foundations to support relevant research activities aimed at the amelioration of the effects of high levels of televised violence on children's attitudes and behaviors.

In 1986, the APA established a Task Force on Television and Society to review and integrate existing research on television effects and to make recommendations regarding how to remediate the negative and enhance the positive influences of television, and how the APA and other scholarly groups, the government, and the television industry can work together to enhance the mental health aspects of television (Abeles, 1986).

The PTA
The National PTA made an effort to deal with TV violence by doing a survey in which 3,000 parents of school-age children were asked to rate prime-time programs for 6 weeks, between October 22 and December 2,

1977. The final report (National PTA, 1978) identified the top 20 quality programs, the 10 worst-quality programs, and the 10 most violent programs. Examples of "excellent" programs (defined as "positive contribution to the quality of life in America, lack of offensive content, and high program quality") are "Little House on the Prairie," "Eight is Enough," "Waltons," "Donnie and Marie," and "World of Disney;" "poorest" programs included "Maude," "Kojak," "Three's Company," and "Welcome Back Kotter," the most violent series included "Kojak," "Charlie's Angels," "Police Woman," "Six Million Dollar Man," and "Starsky and Hutch."

J. Walter Thompson
This famous advertising agency provided economic reasons for reducing TV violence. Ten percent of the adult sample surveyed considered not buying a product because it was advertised in violent programming, and 8% said they actually had refrained from purchasing a product for that reason. The president of the Agency, Don Johnston, presented these results at a meeting of the American Advertising Federation. He stated, "We are counseling our clients to evaluate the potential negatives of placing commercials in programming perceived as violent. Our motivation is primarily social, but there are certain business considerations that confirm our recommendations" (Dougherty, 1976). He warned that public aversion to violent programs was growing and might result in protest letters and product boycotts.

The Heller manual

The industry undertakes relatively few affirmative action steps on its own and for the most part responds only when pressed. A noteworthy exception is a manual written by Dr. Melvin S. Heller, at the behest of ABC, to assist ABC Broadcast Standards personnel in their jobs. Heller wrote a 99-page manual based on his 7 years of experience consulting with the Code Authority of the NAB and then with ABC's Broadcast Standards Department and on his own research on children and television for ABC. In Heller's words, "What was needed was a way to begin applying the findings of our own research, as well as that reported by others, to the practical tasks of broadcast standards editors" (Heller, 1978, p. 2). The manual emphasizes the portrayal of violence on television but also contains sections on sexual, stereotypic, and prosocial content, as well as a special section on the child audience. While the manual is couched in psychodynamic theories and rationales (e.g., Oedipal stage, unconscious mechanisms) no longer highly regarded by many psychologists and psychiatrists, the effort as a whole is commendable and offers some excellent suggestions to editors on how to make decisions about controversial content. For example, Heller suggests these questions when evaluating content that presents mischievous or dangerous behavior:

a) Does the portrayal of the act, or a modification of it, carry with it the possibility of similar imitations of mischief, potentially dangerous or reprehensible behavior?

b) Would juveniles and other vulnerable viewers tend to think that such portrayals might be fun, or result in kicks or quick publicity?

c) If the portrayed behavior might appeal to a small group of predisposed youngsters or childish adult viewers, are the downside risks, dangers, and potential untoward consequences clearly and sufficiently elaborated in the storyline?

d) Is the result of an easily replicated deed, such as pushing someone off a crowded subway platform in the path of an oncoming train, presented as a spectacular, formidable and shocking act which might tempt a predisposed individual to imitate it? In other words, is the effort so small and the result so awesome and grotesque as to promise cheap, instant publicity or notoriety, no matter how reprehensible the act might be?

e) If the act as portrayed caused no actual harm, was this due to a lucky escape, and could a possible modification or miscalculation in imitating it be fraught with danger and risk?

f) Finally, would you knowingly allow your children to attempt this stunt, risking their own or someone else's welfare?

An unsatisfactory answer to any of the above questions readily labels it as an unacceptable or borderline portrayal. The risk quite likely outweighs any possible gain in its showing, even in an unusual dramatic vehicle of artistic merit. If high action requires high risk, the risk must be portrayed as absolutely essential to survival, and must be carefully scrutinized as to its potential for capricious imitation by impressionable viewers. (pp. 65–66)

While the manual does not take into account all of the existing research on television's effects, it does encourage a sensitive evaluation process.

LEGAL BATTLES OVER TV VIOLENCE: THE FIRST AMENDMENT PREVAILS

On three separate occasions in the 1970s various efforts to curb TV violence by one means or another collided legally with the protections guaranteed by the First Amendment to the Constitution of the United States.

Family viewing time

The early evening (7 to 9 p.m.) has long been considered the time when the family is most likely to be watching television as a unit. It is the early segment of prime time. As we noted in chapter 1, it is truly prime time for children, accounting for far more of their television viewing than does watching actual children's shows. An effort to establish a family viewing time, spearheaded by the FCC in response to a variety of pressures, was the first collision between the First Amendment and the TV violence issue.

It all began in 1970 with the Prime Time Access Rule, which stated that stations could only show 3 hours of network fare per night (8 to 11 p.m.), which meant in practice that the period between 7:30 and 8:00 p.m. was left free for local station use.* As we mentioned in chapter 3, the intent of this ruling was to encourage the station to serve local community and family needs in this half-hour with public service programming, to break the network monopoly in prime time, to provide independent producers with a new market outside of the three networks, and to encourage the production and airing of new program formats (Brown, 1977). All of this might have decreased violence on television and improved its overall quality. However, inasmuch as the rule itself did not dictate what content could be aired, local stations responded to the ruling as an opportunity to air game shows or syndicated films which are inexpensive and thus highly profitable.

A more daring step was then taken. In 1974, Congress asked that the FCC report on the "specific positive actions taken or planned by the Commission to protect children from excessive programming of violence and obscenity" ("Wiley feels," 1974). This message had clear implications for future fiscal appropriations to the FCC. The FCC chairman at the time, Richard E. Wiley, called several meetings with the three network presidents. Arthur E. Taylor, then president of CBS Television, proposed a plan in which the networks would keep the evening hours from 7:00 to 9:00 free from themes that would be objectionable for child viewers (i.e., sex and violence). Actually, this amounted to only 1 hour; the first half-hour is programmed with news, and the 7:30 to 8:00 slot had already been taken from the networks with the Prime Time Access Rule.

This period was called the "family viewing" time, and by 1975 the National Association of Broadcasters included it in its code. This was the closest that the FCC ever came to try to control TV content directly. It used the National Association of Broadcasters as an intermediary mechanism, but the pressure the FCC exerted was undeniable. A poll conducted by the Opinion Research Corporation for *TV Guide* in October 1975 showed that the public supported the family hour guidelines; 82% of adult Americans were in favor of them (Hickey, 1975).

But the family viewing hour was seen as a threat to First Amendment rights, and it was challenged in court by Hollywood's TV writers and producers. On November 4, 1976, Judge Warren G. Ferguson ruled against the FCC, the NAB and the three networks' efforts to uphold the family viewing time because (a) the government pressure violated the First Amendment, (b) the FCC proceeded in an unofficial manner, and (c) the networks were a party to restricting individual broadcasters in their First Amendment rights. The only way that the family code could be adopted was

---

*The period between 7:00–7:30 p.m. had been the long-time domain of the news.

by individual broadcasters voluntarily abiding by it. They chose to abandon it instead.

The Zamora trial

During a 2-week period in October 1977, TV violence was a codefendant in a murder trial. On June 4, 1977, Ronald Zamora, 15, killed his next-door neighbor Elinor Haggart, 82, a Miami Beach widow, in the process of burglarizing her home with a friend. Finding the boys in the midst of their burglary, she warned them that she was going to call the police, whereupon Zamora shot her to death. Four days later, Zamora confessed to the murder and 4 months later went to trial for charges of first-degree murder, burglary, robbery, and possession of a firearm while committing a felony.

Zamora's defense attorney, Ellis Rubin, pleaded that his client was temporarily insane at the time of the murder because he was "suffering from and acted under the influence of prolonged, intense, involuntary, subliminal television intoxication." Zamora's parents described their son as a "TV addict" who watched 6 hours daily and favored cops-and-robbers programs such as "Kojak," "Baretta," and "Starsky and Hutch." Kojak was his idol, and Zamora's parents testified that the boy went as far as to ask his father to shave his head so he would look more like his hero. A psychiatrist, Dr. Michael Gilbert, examined the boy and testified that Zamora had compared the situation to an episode of "Kojak:" "He recalled some program where women who had been shot got up and walked away, and he said he felt that might happen" (Buchanan, 1977a). Dr. Gilbert further asserted that Zamora's shooting Mrs. Haggart when she threatened to call the police was a "conditional response" similar to that of a dog who automatically responds to a bell to get his meals. In Gilbert's words, "The woman's statement 'I'm going to call the police' was a symbol of everything Zamora had seen on television, and he reacted to rub out the squealer" (Buchanan, 1977a). This was claimed to be the result of Zamora's "addiction" to television and his long years of watching crime shows and horror movies.

Rubin labeled television an "accessory to the crime" throughout the trial and stated: "It is inevitable that TV will be a defendant. I intend to put television on trial" ("Did TV," 1977, p. 87). In his closing remarks, Rubin said: "If you and I can be influenced by short commercials to buy products, certainly an hour 'commercial' on murder could influence this boy when he's seen them over and over" (Buchanan, 1977b). The title of a *Time* (1977) article on the trial reflects the nature of the trial: "Did TV Make Him Do It? A Young Killer—and Television—Go on Trial for Murder."

Testimony by other psychiatrists and psychologists challenged Gilbert's testimony and Rubin's defense claims. Several mental health professionals rejected Gilbert's "conditioned response" theory and the temporary insanity plea. Further, the conditioned response theory was brought into question by the testimony of a psychiatrist, Dr. Albert Jaslow, who said that Zamora's own report of the incident indicated that $1\frac{1}{2}$ hours elapsed between Mrs. Haggart's threat to call the police and the murder; such a delay is not feasible if his shooting were a conditioned or automatic response. Dr. Jaslow also reported that he asked Zamora, "Did television teach you to kill anybody?" and that the boy answered "No." Further, Jaslow said Zamora told him that the one thing he had learned on television was, "The bad guys didn't get away with it" (Buchanan, 1977b). Another psychiatrist, Dr. Charles Mutter, also testified that Zamora did not blame television for his actions but provided evidence that Zamora imitated TV characters. Zamora was reported by Mutter to have said, "Sometimes I'd be a cop and sometimes a bad guy" and that he "wished the shooting had been like a TV show where the dead get up when the show is over" (Buchanan, 1977b).

In terms of knowing right from wrong and the nature and consequences of his act (the criteria for sanity in Florida law), the weight of the mental health professionals' testimony sided with Zamora being sane. However, this is not to say that the consensus was that Zamora was a typical 15-year-old boy. Dr. Helen Ackerman, a psychologist who examined Zamora on three occasions, testified that the defendant was "emotionally disturbed, erratic and unpredictable," referring to alleged suicide attempts including "riding his bicycle into heavy traffic and standing under knives he had thrown into the air" (Buchanan, 1977a).

After nearly 2 weeks of testimony, the jury deliberated for slightly less than 2 hours and found Ronald Zamora guilty of murder, burglary, armed robbery, and possession of a firearm. The verdict resulted in Zamora facing an automatic life sentence with chance for parole after 25 years. Apparently the state had not sought the death penalty because of Zamora's age.

A bit of irony is that the 9-day trial of Zamora (and television) was broadcast on a public television station. Given television's role in the case, Judge Paul Baker banned all TV viewing by the jury members on the first day of the trial. As one would expect, the jurors complained, and the judge compromised by allowing them to watch anything but news shows and taped excerpts of the trial. The jurors then requested being allowed to watch tapes of the trial without the sound so they could see what they looked like on TV. Their request was denied ("Actor Savalas," 1977).

Niemi vs. NBC

In 1974 a 9-year-old girl, Olivia Niemi, was attacked by three older girls and a boy on a beach in San Francisco in the process of which she was artificially raped with a bottle. Four days before the incident a movie, *Born Innocent*, portraying a girl being similarly raped with a plumber's helper, was aired by an NBC San Francisco TV station, KRON-TV. Olivia's mother and her lawyer, Marvin Lewis, claimed that Olivia's assault was provoked by the movie and demanded $11 million in damages from NBC and the affiliate station due to the broadcasters' alleged negligence in showing the movie, especially during prime time when children and adolescents comprise a fair share of the audience. The following description of the movie scene in question comes from the judge of the California appeals court that considered the lawsuit: An adolescent girl, played by Linda Blair (then 15 years old), is seen taking a shower in the shower area of a girls' reform school (Daltry, 1978):

> Suddenly the water stops and a look of fear comes across her face. Four adolescent girls are standing across from her. One of the girls is carrying a plumber's helper, waving it suggestively at her side. The four girls attack and wrestle her to the floor. She is shown naked from the waist up, struggling as they force her legs apart. Then the television film shows the girl with the plumber's helper making intense thrusting motions with the handle of the plunger until one of the four says, "That's enough." The young girl is left sobbing and naked on the floor. (p. 69)

The legal term for the alleged negligence is *vicarious liability*; it is based on the presumed incitement of a criminal act if it is vividly depicted in a book, TV show, or other medium, the source of that depiction being responsible for damages to the victim. The alleged involvement of the TV broadcast in this violent act was immediately dramatized by the press with headlines such as: "Television on Trial: The Tube Made Me Do It" (Daltry, 1978, p.69), "TV on Trial" (Levering, 1978, p.5), and "Was TV Born Guilty?" (Mandel, 1978, p. 35). It is important to realize that unlike the Zamora case, TV in general was not on trial; rather, the broadcasters of a specific program were charged with negligence for presenting an explicit depiction of a violent/sexual act.

The First Amendment was the major argument of the defense lawyers of NBC. They argued that a ruling in favor of Niemi would stifle journalists, broadcasters, and publishers. The only legal basis for holding someone responsible for what he/she wrote (or showed on TV) is if the content is obscene or libelous, neither of which pertains to the case. There are other exceptions to protection by the First Amendment. For example, speech that is "directed to inciting or producing imminent lawless action and is likely to incite or produce such action" is not protected. Intent to incite is a critical component of this First Amendment exception. The head NBC defense attorney, Floyd Abrams, argued that NBC did not advocate or intend to incite rape with its broadcast. Siding with the NBC defense, several organizations filed friend-of-the-court briefs against the suit arguing about the dangers of infringing on First Amendment rights. NBC's allies included the other two networks, the Writers Guild of America, the Directors Guild

of America, the National Association of Radio and FM Stations, the
Motion Picture Association of America, the National Association of
Broadcasters, and the American Library Association. CBS argued that if
Niemi won,

> journalists and creative artists would be forced to avoid factual reporting on,
> or fictional portrayal of, violent acts for fear of incurring enormous liability if
> some jury could be convinced that some anti-social act somewhere was
> 'inspired' by the drama or the report in question. (cited in Levering, 1978, p. 5)

Concerning the First Amendment issue, Marvin Lewis argued,

> Our forefathers would roll over in their graves if they saw the use that the
> First Amendment is being put to. They did not design the First Amendment to
> allow the graphic portrayal of the gang rape of a child before a nationwide
> children's audience. (Daltry, 1978, p. 69)

Lewis also argued that NBC's promotion of the movie showed that they
were trying to attract a young audience. They scheduled the movie
immediately after "The Wonderful World of Walt Disney," and they ran an
ad in *TV Guide* promoting *Born Innocent* on the same page as *Born Free*, an
innocuous wildlife movie to be aired the night before. Lewis contended that
the similarity of names may have led people to believe that *Born Innocent*
was a sequel to *Born Free*. Further, before its broadcast there were clear
signs that the movie (or at least the rape scene) was objectionable. Lewis had
evidence that after pre-screening the movie, 15 national advertisers refused
to sponsor the movie, and NBC's broadcast standards department had
misgivings about it. The California Medical Association was the only group
to file a friend-of-the-court brief on Niemi's behalf which argued that "the
First Amendment cannot be a shield from civic responsibility for forseeable
consequences of harmful acts" (cited in Levering, 1978, p. 6).

On another level, the defense also claimed that the assailants denied ever
watching *Born Innocent*. Marvin Lewis contested that with the statement of a
National Park Service Officer who said that the attackers told him they had
seen the movie and specifically referred to the rape scene. The defense also
claimed that the girl who led the attack was an emotionally disturbed
youngster with a history of sexually deviant activities. Marvin Lewis argued
that broadcasters should not air explicit, violent, or sexual scenes such as
that in *Born Innocent* precisely because there are many disturbed people in
the audience who might be inspired to imitate what they viewed.

NBC offered to settle out of court shortly after the suit was filed. When
Olivia's mother refused, NBC retaliated by charging the mother with being
an "unfit guardian" for subjecting her daughter to the trauma of such a
legal proceeding. The judge found their charges to be unacceptable. What
followed was a series of actions in which the case was thrown out of court
(on First Amendment grounds), then appealed and put back in court, and
then challenged and again thrown out of court, all of which lasted about 3

years and involved two rulings by California's highest court and one by the United States Supreme Court.

During the summer of 1978 the case went to court in San Francisco, and on August 8, before witnesses were even heard, the negligence suit was thrown out of court because Judge Robert Dossee ruled that the plaintiff had to prove that the network intended its viewers to imitate the violent sexual attack depicted. With the case being treated by the judge as a strict First Amendment case, Marvin Lewis could not win; it was not feasible to prove that NBC intended its viewers to copy the rape scene.

Notes of interest: Ronald Zamora, who was serving his life sentence, filed a $25 million lawsuit against all three commercial networks claiming they were responsible for his murdering his neighbor in 1975. He lost. One of Olivia's attackers was sent to a federal reformatory for 3 years, and the other three were put on juvenile probation. NBC aired *Born Innocent* a second time, but at 11:30 p.m. and with most of the offensive rape scene edited out. In June 1982, the Supreme Court justices left intact earlier rulings by lower courts that the television networks and stations almost never can be held legally responsible when aggressive acts portrayed on television are imitated by viewers.

TEN-YEAR UPDATE

In early 1979, a group of researchers in the television effects field suggested to the then Surgeon General Julius Richmond the need for a review and synthesis of the literature on television and behavior that was conducted after the 1972 Surgeon General's Report. The Surgeon General agreed and encouraged the National Institute of Mental Health, which played such a significant role in this area in the past, to undertake this project. Dr. David Pearl, Chief of the Behavioral Sciences Research Branch within the Division of Extramural Research Programs of NIMH, was assigned as the project director.

The Ten Year Update, as the project came to be called, was formulated quite differently from the 1972 Surgeon General's Report. First, the impetus for the project did not come from Congress but from researchers in the field. Second, considering the amount of research conducted since 1972, it was decided that the new report would be based on a review and integration of existing research rather than on new studies. Third, it was decided to focus on a much broader spectrum of television's influences and audiences than did the earlier report, which had been restricted primarily to television violence and child and adolescent viewers.

Seven consultants assisted Pearl in the endeavor. Two were psychiatrists and the rest had PhDs either in psychology or communications. Four of the seven had contributed to the 1972 Surgeon General's Report. The advisory panel consisted of:

- Steven H. Chaffee, Director, Institute for Communication Research, Stanford University
- George Gerbner, Dean, Annenberg School of Communications, University of Pennsylvania
- Beatrix A. Hamburg, Associate Professor of Psychiatry, Harvard Medical School, and Children's Hospital Medical Center, Boston
- Chester Pierce, Professor of Psychiatry and Education, Harvard Medical School
- Eli A. Rubinstein, Adjunct Research Professor in Mass Communications, University of North Carolina
- Alberta E. Siegel, Professor of Psychology, Stanford University School of Medicine
- Jerome L. Singer, Professor of Psychology, Yale University.

These advisors made recommendations on topics to be reviewed and on scientists to prepare the reviews. They considered drafts of submitted reviews and wrote introductory comments for the major sections of the report. Two other individuals also played integral roles. Lorraine Bouthilet, PhD, formerly an NIMH staff member, assisted in the writing and editing and Joyce B. Lazar, Acting Director of the NIMH Research Advisory Group, assisted in the planning and conduct of the project.

The advisory panel commissioned 24 review chapters from scientists considered experts in their respective areas. The topics were organized into six major sections: cognitive and affective aspects of television, violence and aggression, social beliefs and social behavior, television and social relations, television and health, and television in American society. Table 6.3 presents the scientists and the titles of their review chapters. As is apparent from the titles, aside from TV violence, the reviews cover a wide range of topics that were not addressed in the 1972 Surgeon General's Report, such as television and cognitive processing, imagination, educational achievement, sexual learning, social reality, and media literacy. We will discuss the research included in these reviews within the relevant chapters of the book. There were also reviews on such diverse topics as television and the elderly, persons in institutions, American social institutions, and health portrayals. The emphasis was on entertainment television. Areas such as news programming and political socialization were not covered.

The report, entitled *Television and Behavior: Ten Years of Scientific Progress and Implications for the Eighties*, came out in two volumes. Volume 1 (Pearl, Bouthilet, & Lazar, 1982a), which was available in May 1982, was a 91-page summary report of the 24 reviews written in nontechnical language for a lay audience. Volume 2 (Pearl et al., 1982b), which came out about 5 months later, contains 362 pages of review chapters. Even though only 10% of Volume 1 and 20% of Volume 2 addressed TV violence directly,

Table 6.3 Contents of the Ten-Year Update

Cognitive and Affective Aspects of Television

    Introductory Comments—Jerome L. Singer
    Cognitive Processing in Television Viewing—W. Andrew Collins
    The Forms of Television: Effects on Children's Attention, Comprehension, and
        Social Behavior—Mabel L. Rice, Aletha C. Huston, and John C. Wright
    Television and the Developing Imagination of the Child—Dorothy G. Singer
    Television Viewing and Arousal—Dolf Zillmann
    Television and Affective Development and Functioning—Aimee Dorr
    Television and Educational Achievement and Aspiration—Michael Morgan and
        Larry Gross
    Television Literacy and Critical Television Viewing Skills—Charles R. Corder-Bolz

Violence and Aggression

    Introductory Comments—Eli A. Rubinstein
    Violence in Television Content: An Overview—George Comstock
    Television Violence and Aggressive Behavior—L. Rowell Huesmann
    Television and Aggression: Results of a Panel Study—J. Ronald Milavsky, Ronald
        Kessler, Horst Stipp, and William S. Rubens
    Violence in Television Programs: Ten Years Later—Nancy Signorielli, Larry Gross,
        and Michael Morgan

Social Beliefs and Social Behavior

    Introductory Comments—Alberta E. Siegel
    Television and Role Socialization: An Overview—Bradley S. Greenberg
    Television Advertising and Socialization to Consumer Roles—Charles K. Atkin
    Growing Old on Television and With Television—Richard H. Davis and Robert W.
        Kubey
    Television and Sexual Learning in Childhood—Elizabeth J. Roberts
    Television's Influence on Social Reality—Robert P. Hawkins and Suzanne Pingree
    Television and Prosocial Behavior—J. Philippe Rushton

Television and Social Relations

    Introductory Comments—Steven H. Chaffee
    The Family as Portrayed on Television 1946–1978—Lynda M. Glennon and Richard
        Butsch
    Television and Social Relations: Family Influences and Consequences for
        Interpersonal Behavior—Jack M. McLeod, Mary Anne Fitzpatrick, Carroll J.
        Glynn, and Susan F. Fallis

Television and Health

    Introductory Comments—Beatrix A. Hamburg and Chester M. Pierce
    Programming Health Portrayals: What Viewers See, Say, and Do—George
        Gerbner, Michael Morgan, and Nancy Signorielli
    Health Campaigns on Television—Douglas S. Solomon
    Television and Persons in Institutions—Eli A. Rubinstein and Joyce N. Sprafkin

Television in American Society

    Introductory Comments—George Gerbner
    Television and American Social Institutions—George Comstock
    The Organization and Production of Prime Time Television—Muriel G. Cantor

most of the newspaper coverage following the release of the first volume focused exclusively on the conclusions concerning the effects of such content. Just a brief sampling of headlines includes "An 'Overwhelming' Violence-TV Tie" (1982, p. C27), "Warning From Washington: Violence on Television is Harmful to Children" (1982, p. 77), and "Study Links TV, Youths' Aggression" (1982, p. 7).

One of the many conclusions of the report was about TV violence effects:

> Most of the researchers look at the totality of evidence and conclude, as did the Surgeon General's advisory committee, that the convergence of findings supports the conclusion of a causal relationship between televised violence and later aggressive behavior. The evidence now is drawn from a large body of literature. Adherents to this convergence approach agree that the conclusions reached in the Surgeon General's program have been significantly strengthened by more recent research. (Pearl et al., 1982a, p. 37)

However, the advisory panel also urged the reader to focus on the broader conclusions of the report:

> Television can no longer be considered as a casual part of daily life, as an electronic toy. Research findings have long since destroyed the illusion that television is merely innocuous entertainment. While the learning it provides is mainly incidental rather than direct and formal, it is a significant part of the total acculturation process. (Pearl et al., 1982a, p. 87)

The networks immediately criticized the report for its conclusions about TV violence. These criticisms were formalized by ABC in 1983 in a 32-page pamphlet entitled *A Research Perspective on Television and Violence*, which disputed the major conclusions of the NIMH advisory panel concerning the relationship between television violence and aggressive behavior and social attitudes. The 7-member advisory committee then responded point-by-point to the ABC report in a letter and formal critique to the new Surgeon General Dr. C. Everett Koop. It stated in part:

> The pamphlet, "A Research Perspective on Television and Violence," purports to be a rigorous and objective refutation of the NIMH report. However, the ABC statement is neither rigorous nor objective. Instead, it is a shallow attempt, ostensibly for public consumption, to focus on only one portion of the NIMH review, rehash industry attacks on independent research of the past ten years, ignore or distort both the evidence presented in the NIMH report and the consensus of the field, and present conclusions that obscure the issues and deceive the readers. It would be no exaggeration to compare this attempt by the television industry to the stubborn public position taken by the tobacco industry on the scientific evidence about smoking and health.

7

Twenty Years of TV Violence Research

OVERVIEW

In the 20 years since the publication of the Surgeon General's Report, research into the TV violence issue has burgeoned. Laboratory experiments continue to provide evidence of a causal relationship between violence viewing and aggression. The results of nonexperimental field studies and, to a lesser extent, field experiments support the same conclusion. While a few studies have produced ambiguous or negative results, the majority of new investigations suggest that viewing violent entertainment can increase aggression and cultivate the perception that the world is a mean and scary place. Several other extensive literature reviews have also arrived at the conclusion that there is causal link between TV violence and aggression or other antisocial behavior, although it is equally clear that TV violence always works in conjunction with other factors.

In sum, TV violence can provide instruction in antisocial and aggressive behavior which will sometimes lead to direct copying or disinhibition of such behaviors. These effects do not invariably occur, however, and depend upon characteristics of the viewers and the situation. In contrast, the value-shaping and cultivation effects of TV violence appear to be very widespread, suggesting that TV violence can work in subtle and insidious ways to adversely influence youth and society.

OUTLINE

Since the appearance of the Surgeon General's Report, there have been literally hundreds of publications in the scientific and popular literature dealing with the question of TV violence. In this chapter we describe and analyze all that has been said over the past 20 years on the matter of the possible antisocial effects of television upon children, concluding with our own appraisal of the current status of the TV violence issue.

It would not be possible to describe, or even mention, every report or comment that has been published. Rather, we have tried to summarize the major research studies and to capture the essence of the current consensus as well as to note and comment on the questions that are still being investigated or debated.

The research portion of the chapter is organized according to the methods of research used by the investigators (laboratory experiments, field experiments, and nonexperimental studies). Within each of these broad categories we have organized the material chronologically. In this way we hope the reader can keep track of the research just as it unfolded in the literature, and thus view it from the vantage point of a professional social scientist.

LABORATORY EXPERIMENTS

The Surgeon General's Report had made it fairly clear that TV violence reliably stimulates aggressive responses in laboratory experiments. This claim has received consistent additional support in the ensuing two decades.

The Heller and Polsky Experiments

In 1970, ABC commissioned a series of studies on TV violence effects by two consultants, a psychiatrist, Marvin Heller (who later wrote the *Broadcast Standards Editing* manual for ABC described earlier) and a lawyer, Samuel Polsky. One of Heller and Polsky's projects was a pair of laboratory experiments (Projects I and II) in which institutionalized children from various groups were shown either aggressive cartoons or noncartoon, nonaggressive material and then observed by raters using the Feshbach Behavior Rating Scale. The researchers found significant "increases in a variety of aggressive behaviors and attitudes . . . following exposure to cartoons," but dismissed the findings as "still a relatively unimpressive percentage of the potential number of incidents" (Heller & Polsky, 1976, p. 77).

The Drabman and Thomas Experiments

One of the things the Surgeon General's Report had made clear was that direct aggression was not the only antisocial effect that might result from exposure to TV violence. Another, equally troublesome possibility was that violent TV fare might "harden" youngsters, so that they would be more likely to expect and accept antisocial behavior on the part of others. It was this latter possibility that was examined by Drabman and Thomas (1974). In their experiment, 22 male and 22 female third and fourth graders viewed either an aggressive cowboy film or no film. Then the youngsters were left in charge of two younger children whom they could see via a TV monitor. What the subjects saw was actually a prepared videotape of two children playing quietly at first and then becoming progressively aggressive toward one another and destructive to property. Finally the fighting became so vigorous that the camera appeared to be knocked over. The researchers measured how long it took the subject to seek adult help after the aggressive behavior began, and whether the subject intervened before the youngsters abused each other physically. Drabman and Thomas found that relative to the no-film control group, the boys and girls who saw the aggressive cowboy film took longer to seek adult help and were much more likely to tolerate all but the violent physical aggression and destruction. Whereas 58% of the no-film children who went for help did so after the children started arguing and destroying each other's property but before the extreme forms of aggression appeared, only 17% of the children in the film group responded to these lower levels of aggression.

The same pattern of results appeared in a second study (Drabman & Thomas, 1976) in which an exciting control excerpt from a baseball game was used instead of a no-film condition. These findings, obtained with a more appropriate control group, lend further support to the claim that TV violence makes young viewers more apathetic to real-life violence.

In a third study in the series, Thomas and Drabman (1977) asked: Would TV violence affect children's expectations of other children's aggression? They showed 88 third and fifth grade children either a 15-minute aggressive excerpt from a TV detective series or a nonviolent one from a nature series. Then the children were given the Response Hierarchy measure of Leifer and Roberts (1972) in which the child is presented with a series of conflict situations and paired choices of how to handle them (physical aggression, verbal aggression, leaving the field, or positive coping). In the Thomas and Drabman study, the youngsters were asked (a) how they thought other children their age *would* act in the situation, and (b) how they thought other children their age *should* act. Relative to the control group, children who saw the aggressive excerpt were more likely to predict that other children would react aggressively to the conflict, but exposure to the aggressive excerpt did not influence the children's responses about what others should do.

The Bryant, Carveth, and Brown Cultivation Experiment

George Gerbner, who is famous for his work on the Violence Index which we discussed earlier, is also widely noted for his "cultivation analysis" of the effects of entertainment television. According to this analysis, exposure to television, especially violent television, cultivates a view of the world as a dangerous place to live, in which one runs a high likelihood of being a victim of violence. Gerbner and his associates have accumulated considerable correlational data that are consistent with this view; we will discuss these data later. The work of Bryant, Carveth, and Brown (1981) is especially convincing because they used the experimental method to demonstrate the cultivating effects of television.*

The subjects in the Bryant et. al. experiment were 90 undergraduates who viewed specially selected television programs over a 6-week period. Initially, each subject was given a test of anxiety level (the Taylor Manifest Anxiety Scale; Taylor, 1953), on the basis of which he/she was classified as being high or low in anxiety. (Potential subjects falling in the middle range on the anxiety test did not participate in the remainder of the study.) Then, within each anxiety group, subjects were assigned to one of three viewing groups, based on the television programs they were permitted to watch over the relevant 6-week period.

Those assigned to the *light viewing condition* were asked to watch very little television. Those assigned to the *heavy viewing/justice condition* watched a lot of action-adventure TV (at least 28 hours a week), with the programs chosen so that the good guy always won in the end and justice always prevailed. Finally, those in the *heavy viewing/injustice condition* watched at least 28 hours of action-adventure TV per week, but their programs were chosen to have unjust endings (e.g., with the "bad" people getting away with violent crimes, etc.).

Subjects in the heavy viewing/injustice condition showed significantly greater increases in anxiety than those in either of the other groups. In addition the perceived likelihood of being a victim of violence increased most for those who saw a heavy dose of unjustified violence, next most for those who saw a heavy dose of justified violence, and least for those who were light viewers during the 6 weeks of the experiment and therefore saw very little TV violence. The victimization results are shown in Figure 7.1. The overall pattern is quite consistent with cultivation theory, and

---

*We are discussing this work as a laboratory experiment. In fact, however, it is extensive and naturalistic enough that it actually falls on the border between laboratory and field experiments. As such, it makes an unusually important contribution to the literature on the cultivation theory of TV violence.

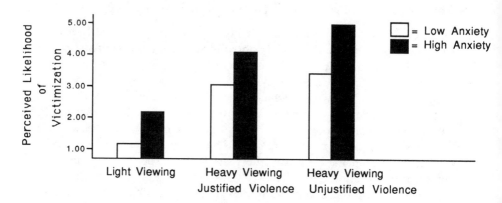

Figure 7.1 Perceived likelihood of being a victim of violence as a function of amount and type of violence viewed in the Bryant, Carveth, and Brown (1981) study. *Note.* Based on data reported in "Television Viewing and Anxiety: An Experimental Examination" by J. Bryant, R.A. Carveth and D. Brown, 1981, *Journal of Communication, 30*, pp. 106–119.

constitutes the strongest and clearest research support generated for the theory thus far. Moreover, the fact that these data converge with the correlational data to be discussed later adds further credibility to the validity of the basic cultivation hypothesis.

Atkin (1983)

One way of thinking about TV violence is that it conveys a sense of "what the world is really like." That is, children (and perhaps adults) may act aggressively to the extent that they see aggression as appropriate, expected, or typical in the world in which they live. Such an idea is consistent with Bandura's social learning theory (see chapter 4), in which TV violence is presumed to disinhibit observers to the degree that it produces the perception that violent or aggressive ways of approaching life are acceptable.

To test the hypothesis that seemingly realistic presentations of violence on TV produce higher levels of aggression than obviously fictional ones, Atkin (1983) created three versions of a 6-minute TV news program, complete with news stories and appropriate commercials, and presented them to 10- to 13-year-old boys and girls in a school setting. The "news program" was identical for all groups except for a critical 15-second scene. The critical scene showed college students arguing and then beginning to physically brawl with each other in a university classroom. In the *realistic violence condition* the critical scene was presented as an actual bit of news, with an announcer saying the following as the scene appeared on the screen:

Channel Six photographer Bob Ray was on hand this afternoon when young Congressional candidate Bill Tompkins addressed a political science class on university campus, but he didn't plan on this development. . . . The subject of amnesty turned the quiet classroom into a regular pier six brawl—two unidentified students obviously had some opposite views on the issue, and made them forcibly apparent. (p. 618)

The *fantasy violence condition* presented the identical scene, but the announcer introduced it as an advertisement for a movie rather than as an actual fight scene, saying

Saturday night at 11:30 on Cinema Six the focus is on action! Rip Torn, Natalie Wood and Robert Wagner star . . . young Americans on a narcotics trip turn the classroom into a no-holds-barred battle. . . . (p. 618)

In a *no-violence control condition*, the critical scene was a simple commercial for the movie, which did not either mention or display any violent content.

After the youngsters watched one of the three versions of the program, they completed a response scale similar to the one used by Leifer and Roberts (see p. 99), designed to assess their willingness to behave aggressively in various situations. As might be expected from previous research, those who viewed the fight scene as fictional violence from a movie were subsequently more aggressive than those who saw no violence at all. Further, as predicted, those who thought they were seeing a real fight scene taking place in a college classroom were most willing of all to behave aggressively. The basic pattern of results is shown in Figure 7.2.

FIELD EXPERIMENTS

The major limitation of laboratory experiments is that they *are* in the laboratory. Such research is well-suited to identifying and analyzing the operation of underlying mechanisms, but is not as convincing when it comes to demonstrating effects of social significance. For this reason, field experiments have continued to be seen as an important source of information on the effects of TV violence.

Steuer, Applefield, and Smith (1971)

Steuer, Applefield, and Smith (1971) investigated the effects of aggressive and neutral television programs on the aggressive behavior of 10 preschoolers in their school environment. These boys and girls comprised a racially and socioeconomically mixed group and knew each other before the study began. First, they were matched into pairs on the basis of the amount of time they spent watching television at home. Next, to establish the degree to which aggressive behavior occurred among these youngsters before any modification of their television diets, each was carefully observed in play with other children for 10 sessions, and the frequency of aggressive responses recorded. (This part of the study is referred to as the *baseline* observation phase.)

Steuer and her associates used a demanding measure of physical interpersonal aggression, including: (a) hitting or pushing another child; (b) kicking another child; (c) assaultive contact with another child which included squeezing, choking, or holding down; and (d) throwing an object at another child from a distance of at least 1 foot. The baseline established a high degree of consistency within each pair prior to the modification of the television diet.

Next, Steuer and her colleagues investigated the effects of television. On 11 different days, one child in each pair observed a single aggressive program taken directly from violent Saturday morning program offerings, while the other member of the pair observed a nonaggressive television program. Subsequent observations of the children at play provided continuous measures of interpersonal physical aggressive behavior by each child. Changes from the original measures, if any, would have to be caused by TV effects.

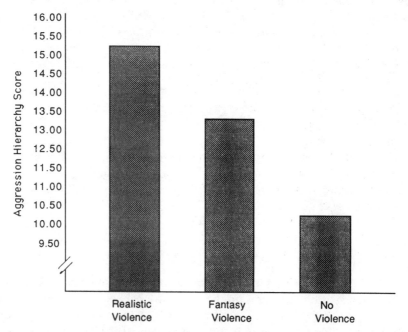

Figure 7.2 Average willingness to aggress as a function of being exposed to realistic violence, fantasy violence, or no violence in the study by Atkin (1983). *Note.* Based on data reported in "Effects of Realistic TV Violence vs. Fictional Violence on Aggression" by C. Atkin, 1983, *Journalism Quarterly, 60*(4), pp. 615–621.

By the end of the 11 sessions, the two groups had departed significantly from one another in terms of the frequency of interpersonal aggression. In fact, for every pair, the child who observed aggressive television programming had become more aggressive than his or her partner who watched neutral fare.

The Milgram and Shotland studies

Milgram and Shotland (1973) conducted a series of studies addressing the question: To what extent would viewers imitate an antisocial act seen on television in real life? The major portion of the $500,000 study focused on the antisocial act of stealing from a charity donation box. This was a unique experiment in that CBS actually produced the experimental programs. Three versions of a "Medical Center" episode were produced which modeled such stealing in varying ways. The overall plot revolved around Tom, an orderly who worked at the hospital and faced extreme economic and emotional pressures. His hardship occurred at the time when the hospital was running a charity drive. One version showed Tom stealing money from several hospital charity boxes and subsequently going to jail for it; in a second version, he stole the money and got away with it; in the third version he was shown being tempted to steal the money but then donating a coin. In the fourth condition a neutral episode was shown.

In three experiments varying in the specific versions shown, audiences viewed a "Medical Center" episode in a theater. In each experiment, several hundred participants, ranging in age from high school seniors to a heterogeneous sample of adults, were offered a free radio which was to be picked up a week later at another location. The situation was designed to be a frustrating one. When participants arrived at the location where they were to get their radios, they found only an empty office and a sign indicating that there were no more radios. The office also contained a charity box containing coins, a $10 bill, and several $1 bills, one of which was protruding from the box. Concealed cameras recorded the subject's behavior. Hence, a situation was created that paralleled key elements of the TV program—there was a frustrating situation and the temptation to take money from a charity box.

Milgram and Shotland found that overall there were trivial amounts of money taken and what little stealing occurred did not vary significantly with the episode version shown. An example of the amounts of money taken is that in one experiment 5.2% of the subjects stole all the money, 3.5% stole the protruding dollar, and 6.9% tried to break into the box but failed. Further, they tested for immediate effects in a fourth experiment which involved viewing versions of the episode in the office containing the charity box. Again, no version effects were found. A fifth experiment used a home viewing situation and the same assessment situation of being offered a gift and finding an empty room with a charity box. Again, no significant differences between episode versions were found. The authors conclude,

> First, the evidence . . . generated must be taken seriously, and serve as a constraint on discussion of television's effects. For the results of the present experiment are not that we obtained no findings, but rather that we obtained no differences in those exposed to our different stimulus programs. . . . [I]f television is on trial, the judgment of this investigation must be the Scottish verdict: Not proven.

In a critique of the Milgram and Shotland study, Comstock (1974) cogently points out its many flaws. First, the question addressed by the research reflects a narrow perspective:

> It would seem to represent a rather singular thrust—the test of the hypothesis that any specific antisocial act shown on television will have fairly immediate and quite widespread imitation. Now that's a scary proposition, but if true we'd long be well aware of it with every evening's dramatizations predicting the next few days' newspaper headlines. (p. 136)

Second, the sample was biased in that only 5% to 7% of those recruited actually showed up for the study. One wonders how representative the participants were. Third, the fact that several studies showed no results implies a corroboration of findings that is misleading because essentially the same design (with all its flaws) was used throughout. Perhaps the most basic potential problem was the use of a medical charity which, given societal values, might have been too strict a test; in other words, the pressure not to steal might have been too great, thus producing a relatively insensitive measure of willingness to steal. Then, too, it should be remembered that the subjects were all adults or older adolescents, rather than children.

The Parke-Berkowitz studies

A series of three field experiments conducted in the United States and Belgium studied the effect of full-length violent films on the aggressive behaviors of male adolescent juvenile delinquents residing in minimum security institutions (Parke, Berkowitz, Leyens, West, & Sebastian, 1977). In all three studies, the youngsters were observed in naturalistic (i.e., not contrived) situations before and after the film exposure. Film effects on aggressive behavior were apparent in all three studies.

In the first study, which was conducted in the United States, 30 boys in each of two living unit cottages participated, one group forming the aggressive film and the other the neutral film condition. In setting up the units originally, boys were randomly assigned to the cottages. For 3 weeks before and after a 1-week film treatment period, the boys' social and noninterpersonal aggressive behaviors were observed for three consecutive nights each week. During the treatment week, the boys saw a different movie every weekday evening. Those in the aggressive film group watched *The Chase, Death Rides a Horse, The Champion, Corruption,* and *Ride Beyond Vengeance.* The neutral films were *Buena Serra Mrs. Campbell, Ride the Wild Surf, Countdown, Beach Blanket Bingo,* and *A Countess from Hong Kong.* Behavioral observations were taken before, during, and after the movie viewing each evening. The investigators found that the boys who saw the aggressive films behaved more aggressively than those who viewed the neutral films on measures of general aggression (defined as the sum of physical threat, physical attack, verbal aggression, noninterpersonal physical and verbal aggression, and physical and verbal self-aggression) and physical aggression (defined as the sum of physical attack, noninterpersonal physical aggression, and physical self-aggression). There was no evidence of the prior aggression levels having an impact on magnitude of effect.

The second American study was conducted in the same institution with 120 boys who did not participate previously. Aside from minor modifications, the study was a replication of the first. The modifications included increasing the number of observations, changing a few netural films to equate more for interest level between the two film groups, and adding two conditions. To determine the effect of repeated exposures, an aggressive and a neutral film group were added in which only one film (either aggressive or neutral) was viewed. For the single exposure conditions, boys initially high in aggression became more physically aggressive after exposure to the aggressive film than to the neutral film. A similar pattern was found for the repeated exposure groups. Contrary to expectation, the aggression effects were not greater for multiple than for single exposures to film aggression; in fact, the reverse was true for general and physical aggression measures.

The third study, which was conducted in Belgium, followed essentially the same multiple exposure procedure, except the observation period before and after the film week was condensed from 3 weeks to 1, and the films used were changed to be more appropriate for Belgian audiences. (The aggressive movies were *Iwo Jima, Bonnie and Clyde, The Dirty Dozen, Zorro,* and *The Left-Handed Gun.* The neutral movies were *Lily, Alexandre le Bienheureux, Daddy's Fiancée, Sebastien Parni Les Hommes,* and *La Belle Americaine.*) The results, similar to the first two studies, indicated that the boys exposed to the aggressive films became more physically aggressive relative to those who viewed the neutral films. (See Figure 7.3.) Initial aggressiveness influenced the results for the other aggression measures; the boys initially high in aggression showed a greater increase in general and verbal aggression after exposure to the aggressive film than to the neutral film. An additional feature of the Belgian study was that it included an assessment of group membership characteristics—the boys provided rankings of each other based on dominance and popularity. The most dominant, popular, and aggressive boys showed the strongest aggression effects. Also affected to a large degreee were the *least* popular youths.

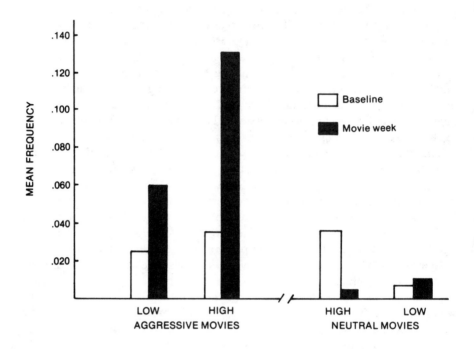

Figure 7.3 Physical aggression index (immediate effects) for initially high- and low-aggressive boys in the Parke et al., (1977) study. *Note.* Adapted from "Some Effects of Violent and Nonviolent Movies on the Behavior of Juvenile Delinquents," by R.D. Parke et al., 1977, *Advances in Experimental Social Psychology, 10,* p. 155. Copyright 1977 by Academic Press. Adapted by permission.

NONEXPERIMENTAL STUDIES

Although the "true experiment" is the ideal in science, we have explained before why it is often not chosen in practice. There are just too many aspects of the effects of TV violence (or any other major social issue) that cannot ethically or practically be studied by manipulating the relevant variables. Thus, researchers through the 1970s and 1980s have continued to make extensive and sometimes imaginative use of nonexperimental methods to explore the effects of TV violence.

Heller and Polsky (1976)

The Heller and Polsky (1976) report, mentioned previously, included two nonexperimental studies (Projects III and IV) in which juvenile offenders were interviewed and asked about the degree to which TV and other factors might have influenced their penchant for crime and violence. In the first of these studies (considered a pilot for the second), Heller and Polsky found that more than a third of the boys interviewed "indicated they had been consciously aware of acting out the techniques of a crime which they had previously seen 'demonstrated' on television!" (p. 94, exclamation in original). In their conclusions regarding this project, however, Heller and Polsky are inclined to minimize the importance of television violence for these boys because none of the youngsters attributed his own criminal propensities to television. The pattern is continued in Project IV, a study of 100 youthful violent offenders, 98 of whom were black. (One of the interesting artifacts emerging from this overwhelming racial bias in the sample is that the young men in this group said they were 12 times more likely to imitate Flip Wilson than Humphrey Bogart.) Roughly paralleling the findings of Project III, 22 of these offenders reported actually trying criminal techniques they had seen on television, and 19 of them said their television-inspired crimes were carried out successfully and without detection. Another 22 men reported contemplating crimes they had seen on television and more than half of the total sample (52%) felt that television had changed their thoughts or beliefs.

The Belson study

In a large-scale study conducted for CBS, Belson (1978) collected information about television viewing, aggressive behavior, and other personal characteristics of more than 1,500 male adolescents in London. After equating for a variety of variables related to aggressive behavior, the extent of aggressive behavior of the heavy and light TV viewers was compared. Belson concluded that the evidence "is very strongly supportive of the hypothesis that high exposure to television violence increases the degree to which boys engage in serious violence" (p. 15). (The antisocial behaviors included deeds that were serious enough to be labeled juvenile delinquency such as inflicting bodily harm to others and damage to property.) CBS chose to view the findings as inconclusive, and the study did not receive much publicity. (Just as a note of interest, this study took 8 years to complete and cost CBS $300,000.)

Singer and Singer (1981)

Jerome and Dorothy Singer (1981), a husband-and-wife team from Yale Universitiy, did a 1-year longitudinal study of the relationship between TV violence viewing and aggressive behavior among 141 preschoolers. The sample included children from almost 50 private and public kindergartens in the New Haven, Connecticut area. Information about the children's TV viewing habits was obtained through daily parental records for 2 consecutive weeks on four different occasions over 12 months. The youngsters' aggressive behavior during free-play periods in kindergarten was observed periodically throughout the year.

Like previous studies, this one revealed a significant relationship between TV violence viewing and actual aggressive behavior. The relationship held for girls as well as for boys and was particularly clear among youngsters who viewed the most TV violence. The Singers (Singer & Singer, 1981) concluded their report by stating:

> The link of heavy viewing to attacking other children or property as a consistent pattern cannot be denied. Frankly, we had not anticipated so clear a result as we obtained. (p. 153)

Gerbner's studies

In the decade since the publication of the Surgeon General's Report, Gerbner has gone a long way in developing and advancing his cultivation theory about television's influence on viewers' conceptions of social realities. The theory predicts that the more a person is exposed to television, the more likely the person's perceptions of social realities will match those represented on TV:

> the more time one spends "living" in the world of television, the more likely one is to report perceptions of social reality which can be traced to (or are congruent with) television's most persistent representations of life and society. (Gerbner, Gross, Morgan & Signorielli, 1980, p. 14)

The procedure used to test the theory involves comparing frequent TV users ("heavy viewers") and infrequent users ("light viewers") on their perceptions of various social events. The social events used reflect those areas that content analyses have shown television to represent in a distorted way. The expectation is that heavy viewers would give more "television answers" (reflecting the TV world) to social reality questions than would light viewers.

Gerbner has conducted this type of analysis on many different samples of people differing in age, income, education, and race, and has found support for his theory. Heavy viewers are more likely than light viewers to have outlooks and perceptions congruent with television portrayals—even after eliminating the influence of variables such as income and educational levels.

A study on adolescents serves to illustrate the method used (Gerbner, Gross, Signorielli, Morgan, Jackson-Beeck, 1979). A total of 587 adolescents (average age between 13 and 14 years) from New York City and New Jersey filled out questionnaires that offered two answers to each question; one based on actual facts and one based on the television portrayal ("television answer"). Table 7.1 presents the questions and the percentage of heavy and light viewers selecting the "television answer." While the differences are not dramatic, for every question a greater percentage of heavy viewers than light viewers responded with the television answer, whether the question was about the number of criminals, the fear of walking alone at night in a city or one's own neighborhood, the frequency of police violence, or general trust in people. Questions about the personal characteristics of the adolescents were also asked, including sex, socioeconomic status, achievement, experience as a victim of violence, and frequency of newspaper reading. Some of these variables influenced the differential responding of heavy and light viewers, and in some cases made the discrepancy much greater than the overall percentages reflect in Table 7.1. For example, for the question about the percentage of people who are involved in violence in any given year, of the boys, 87% of heavy viewers overestimated the violence, while only 58% of the light viewers did so. Of the adolescents who were never victimized by violence, 75% of the heavy viewers gave the TV answer compared to only 29% of the light viewers. Gerbner would say that adolescent boys who have not experienced personal violence and don't watch much TV diverge from the "mainstream" cultivated by television; otherwise similar boys who watch TV frequently share a relatively homogeneous conception of a violent, mean world. In Gerbner's own words, "The most significant and recurring conclusion of our long-range study is that one correlate of television viewing is a heightened and unequal sense of danger and risk in a mean and selfish world" (Gerbner et al., 1979, p. 196).

Additional evidence supporting Gerbner's cultivation theory is provided in a study that used Gerbner's procedures on youngsters in Australia. Pingree and Hawkins (1981) obtained responses to social reality questions (parallel to those used by Gerbner) and television viewing diaries from 1,085 2nd, 5th, 8th, and 11th graders residing in Perth, the largest city in Western Australia. As with U.S. samples, heavy viewing was associated with more TV answers. The youngsters in the sample watched TV between 2 and 4 hours daily, and during evening prime time 50% to 70% of the available commercial programming were U.S. reruns. It is interesting that the frequency with which the children viewed U.S. programs related more to the perception of Australia rather than the U.S. as a "mean world."

Although heavy viewers in general are more likely than light viewers to have the attitudes and beliefs portrayed on television, some groups seem to be more susceptible than others. For example, cultivation effects appear to be greater among adolescents who have low involvement with their parents (Gross & Morgan, 1985).

Table 7.1 Percentage of Heavy and Light Viewers Giving "Television Answer"
to Violence Questions

	VIOLENCE QUESTION	PERCENTAGE OF VIEWERS	
		HEAVY	LIGHT
1.	"Think about the number of people who are involved in some kind of violence each year. Do you think that 3% of all people are involved in some kind of violence in any given year, or is it closer to 10%*?"[a]	83	62
2.	"Think about the number of people who are involved in violence each week. Do you think 1 person out of every 100 is involved in some kind of violence in any given week, or is it closer to 10 people* out of every 100?"[b]	73	62
3.	"About what percentage of all people commit serious crimes—is it closer to 3% or 12%*?"[b]	88	77
4.	"Would you be afraid to walk alone in a city at night?"[a] (*Yes)	52	46
5.	"Are you afraid to walk alone in your own neighborhood at night?"[a] (*Yes)	32	13
6.	"Is it dangerous to walk alone in a city at night?"[b] (*Yes)	86	79
7.	"On an average day, how many times does a policeman usually pull out his gun—less than once a day or more than five times a day*?"[a]	18	6
8.	When police arrive at a scene of violence, how much of the time do they have to use force and violence—most of the time* or some of the time?[b]	56	45
9.	"Can most people be trusted, or do you think that you can't be too careful* in dealing with people?"[b]	62	52
10.	"Would you say that most of the time people try to be helpful, or that they are mostly just looking out for themselves*?"[b]	64	56

Note. Based on data reported in "The Demonstration of Power: Violence Profile No.10" by G. Gerbner, L. Gross, N. Signorielli, M. Morgan, and M. Jackson-Beeck, 1979, *Journal of Communication, 29*(3), pp. 177–195.
*"Television" answer.
[a]Based on New York City sample (*N* = 140).
[b]Based on New Jersey sample (*N* = 447).

Hennigan, Del Rosario, Heath, Cook, Wharton, and Calder (1982)

Evidence that TV may foster crime comes from a study of the relationship between the introduction of TV and crime in the United States (Hennigan et al., 1982). Using a highly sophisticated time-series design, these investigators provided a detailed statistical analysis of the crime rate (obtained from the FBI's *Uniform Crime Reports*) in 68 cities across 13 states both before and after the introduction of television. Because the FCC imposed a freeze on new licenses in the early 1950s, the cities could be divided up into 34 that received TV before 1951 and 34 that did not receive it until after 1955.

The findings were dramatic and startling. The introduction of television always brought a subsequent increase in the rate of larceny.* This was true regardless of whether TV had been introduced before 1951 or after 1955 and irrespective of whether the city or state level of analysis was employed. The authors (Hennigan et al., 1982) concluded:

> The fear that television has increased crime in the United States is indeed well-founded. For the first time, a study directly assessed how the introduction of television affected crime and strongly suggested that television increased larceny. (p. 475)

Larceny is presented considerably less often than crimes of violence on TV. Why, then, should television have produced so clear an influence on this type of crime? Hennigan and his associates (Hennigan et al., 1982) suggest that the underlying mechanism may be frustration and deprivation. They argue that:

> [During the 1950s] lower classes and modest life-styles were rarely portrayed in a positive light on TV, yet the heaviest viewers have been and are poorer, less educated people. It is possible that . . . television caused younger and poorer persons (the major perpetrators of theft) (a) to compare their life-styles and possessions with those of the wealthy television characters and (b) those portrayed in advertisements. Many of these viewers may have felt resentment and frustration over lacking the goods they could not afford, and some may have turned to crime as a way of obtaining the coveted goods. . . . (p. 474)

The NBC Longitudinal Study

In 1970, NBC began a 3-year longitudinal study of the relationship between TV violence viewing and aggressive behavior. The project changed hands at NBC several times, but was finally completed by a team led by NBC's Vice President for News and Social Research, PhD sociologist J. Ronald Milavsky (Milavsky, Kessler, Stipp, & Rubens, 1982). The actual research was conducted in two cities, Minneapolis, Minnesota and Fort Worth, Texas. Over the course of 3 years (1970–1973), the researchers collected measures of both aggressive behavior (using peer nomination and self-report methods) and exposure to TV and televised violence in particular (using a self-report method) up to six times from 2,400 elementary school children (7–12 years old) and 800 teenage boys (12–16 years old). As had been found in many prior studies, the relationship between viewing TV violence and aggressive behavior measured at the same point in time was significant. However, the authors then made a variety of statistical adjustments they felt

---

*Larceny is defined by the FBI as "any stealing of property which is not taken by force and violence or by fraud" (Hennigan et al., 1982, p. 465).

were needed, after which the results were no longer clearly interpretable. Others who have examined the Milavsky/NBC study closely have concluded that the results, when correctly viewed statistically, point to a real effect (Turner, Hesse, & Peterson-Lewis, 1986).

Singer, Singer, and Rapaczynski (1984)

Singer, Singer, and Rapaczynski (1984b) followed 63 boys and girls over a 5-year period, from the time the children were 4 years old until they were 9, obtaining data periodically on television viewing, aggressiveness, restlessness and self-restraint, and the children's beliefs about the degree to which they live in a "mean, scary world."

Children who had watched the largest amounts of TV as preschoolers were the most aggressive at age 9. This relationship remained just as strong after the effects of children's initial levels of aggression were statistically removed. As the investigators note, their finding is consistent with the great mass of other data that has been collected on the effects of TV violence over the past 20 years. In addition, children who watched the most television, especially the most violent television, were also the ones who were most restless and least able to show self-restraint at age 9. And finally, heavy TV viewers were more likely to hold the belief that the world is a mean, scary place in which to live. The authors' final conclusion (Singer et al., 1984b) is:

> We cannot avoid the implication that parents, educators, and industry representatives must take seriously the possible consequences for the early school-age child . . . of unrestrained viewing of a medium in which realistic violence continues to be so frequently displayed. (p. 88)

The Huesmann, Lagerspetz, and Eron Study

In one of the most extensive recent investigations of TV violence and aggression, Huesmann, Lagerspetz, and Eron (1984) studied 758 children in the United States and 220 children in Finland over a 3-year period. When the study began, the children were in the first, second, and third, fourth, and fifth grades. Such a study is said to use an "overlapping longitudinal design." It has the advantage of providing a wide range of data in a reasonably manageable time period.

The investigators used a method similar to the one Lefkowitz et al., (1972) had used in their study for the Surgeon General's Report, namely, they collected reports from every child's peers about the degree to which he/she was aggressive. The results showed that for boys in both countries and for girls in the United States, the more TV violence youngsters watched the more aggressive they were in dealings with their peers. Equally important were the cumulative effects over time. The more TV violence a youngster watched in any given year, the more likely he or she was to display an increase in aggression during subsequent years.

This study also revealed some interesting facts about the manner in which TV violence works its effects. For boys, the greatest effect seemed to be for those who most readily identified with violent characters. For girls, the greatest effects were upon those who preferred masculine activities. And for children of both sexes and from both countries, a vicious cycle type of relationship between TV violence viewing and aggression was observed, such that TV violence viewing seems to stimulate aggressiveness, which in turn stimulates more TV violence viewing. The authors conclude that TV violence produces aggression by providing aggressive role models, producing attitudes that favor aggression, and by suggesting that aggression is a justifiable way of dealing with others and solving interpersonal problems.

Huesmann et al.'s 22-year longitudinal analysis

Huesmann and his associates (Huesmann, 1986; Huesmann, Eron, Lefkowitz, & Walder, 1984) went back to find the youngsters in the original Lefkowitz, Eron, Walder and Huesmann study (discussed in chapter 5) when they were 30 years old. As seen in Figure 7.4, they found a clear and significant relationship between exposure to TV violence at age 8 and the seriousness of criminal acts performed by these individuals 22 years later, at age 30. Reviewing these findings, Huesmann, (1986) concludes:

> Aggressive habits seem to be learned early in life, and once established, are resistant to change and predictive of serious adult antisocial behavior. If a child's observation of media violence promotes the learning of aggressive habits, it can have harmful lifelong consequences. Consistent with this theory, early television habits are in fact correlated with adult criminality. (pp. 129–130)

The Joy, Kimball, and Zabrack Study

Joy, Kimball, and Zabrack (1986) took advantage of a unique situation to determine the effects of television on children's aggressive behavior. As part of a larger study which we described previously, the investigators identified a town in Canada in which, because of its location in the mountains, there had been no television reception available until 1974. The town was then compared to two other Canadian towns. One of these towns received a single station on the Canadian network (CBC) and the other received CBC plus the three major U.S. networks (NBC, ABC, and CBS). The researchers referred to these towns by pseudonyms: Notel was the town without television, Unitel was the town that received only CBC, and Multitel was the town that received all four networks. According to Canadian census figures,

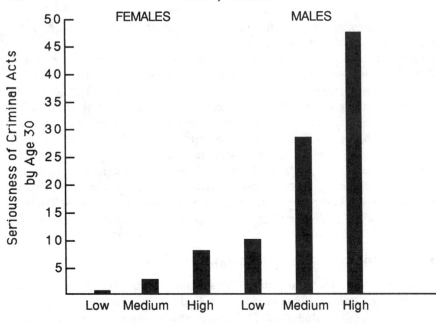

Age 8 Frequency of TV Viewing

Figure 7.4 The relation between age 8 frequency of television viewing and seriousness of criminal convictions at age 30. High and low subjects at age 8 were in the upper and lower quartiles. *Note.* From "Psychological Processes Promoting the Relation Between Exposure to Media Violence and Aggressive Behavior by the Viewer" by L.R. Huesmann, 1986, *Journal of Social Issues, 42,* p. 129. Copyright 1986 by Society for the Psychological Study of Social Issues. Reprinted by permission.

the three towns were similar in virtually all respects (e.g., population, income level, etc.), except for the degree to which television was available to them. Thus, the researchers had come upon the conditions of a "natural experiment," in which the effects of television could be examined.

The researchers began to collect data for the first phase of their research in 1973 and concluded just before CBC reception became available in Notel. In each town, they observed children's physical and verbal aggression during play periods, obtained teachers' ratings of students' aggressiveness, and had students rate the aggressiveness of other students both before and 2 years after Notel received television.

Children in Notel showed a significant increase in both physical and verbal aggression, whereas there was no such change for children in either Unitel or Multitel (see Figure 7.5). The researchers concluded:

> The finding that Notel children displayed more aggression 2 years after the introduction of television into their town further strengthens the evidence for a relationship between television and aggression demonstrated previously in laboratory, field, and naturalistic studies. Particularly striking about the

results of this study is that the effects of television were not restricted to a subset of children. Boys and girls, children initially high and low in aggression, and those watching more or less TV were equally likely to show increased aggressive behavior. (p. 339)

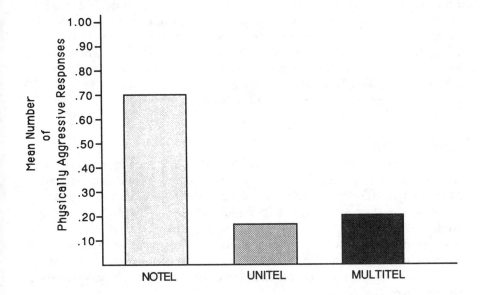

Figure 7.5 Mean increase in number of physically aggressive responses as a result of introduction of television in Notel, compared with the increases in Unitel and Multitel, which had television all along. *Note.* **Based on data reported in "Television and Children's Aggressive Behavior" by L.A. Joy et al., in** *The Impact of Television: A Natural Experiment in Three Communities* **(pp. 303–360), edited by T.M. Williams, 1986, Orlando, FL: Academic Press.**

CURRENT STATUS OF THE TV VIOLENCE ISSUE

After all these years and dozens of major studies, what can be concluded about TV violence and children?

Conclusions of Other Literature Reviews

Apart from our own review in this book, there have been three other detailed reviews of the TV violence literature.

Andison (1977)
Andison (1977) pooled the findings of 67 studies conducted between 1956 and 1976. He concluded that a relationship between TV violence viewing and aggressive behavior had been found consistently across research

methods, age of subjects, measures of aggression, and time period and country of investigation.

Dorr and Kovaric (1980)
Like Andison, Dorr and Kovaric noted the generality of the TV violence effect. "First," they wrote, "we conclude that television violence seems to be capable of affecting viewers of both sexes and varying ages, social classes, ethnicities, and levels of usual aggressiveness" (p. 193). They noted, however, that TV violence effects depend on amount of exposure and on subcultural norms. Thus, groups that are, on the average, the heaviest TV violence viewers and those most accustomed to aggressive tactics will be most affected.

Hearold (1986)
Hearold reviewed every study she could find in the literature dealing with the effects of television on behavior, using a technique called meta-analysis. Meta-analysis allows a reviewer to estimate the relative size of effects, not just whether they are statistically significant or not. Hearold found 230 studies all told in the literature. Like Andison, and Dorr and Kovaric, she concluded that the literature reveals an undeniable relationship between TV violence viewing and antisocial behavior and attitudes. Hearold reached the following additional conclusions, made possible by using the meta-analytic technique.

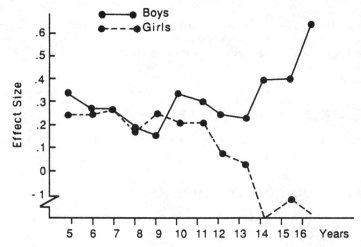

Figure 7.6 Antisocial treatments and physical aggression by age and sex. The points at each year are averages of 5 years (±2 years of the specified year). *Note.* **From "A Synthesis of 1043 Effects of Television on Social Behavior" by S. Hearold, in** *Public Communications & Behavior: Volume I* **(p. 100), edited by G. Comstock, 1986, New York: Academic Press. Copyright 1986 by Academic Press. Reprinted by permission.**

1. The effects of TV violence on physical aggression are about the same for girls and boys up until about age 10. Thereafter the effect increases for boys but decreases for girls. (See Figure 7.6). Hearold explains the pattern by noting that age 10 is about the time that the sexes are sharply differentiated in terms of social expectations, with adolescent males expected to become "manly" and forceful and adolescent females expected to become "feminine" and demure.

2. Seeing violence that appears justified and realistic has a greater aggression-instigating effect than seeing violence that appears unjustified and/or that brings negative consequences to the aggressor. This result is what would have been expected by both social learning and instigation theories (See chapter 4).

3. TV violence can have an effect even when the observer is not aroused, but either frustration of provocation will increase its aggression-producing effects. This result is consistent with arousal theory.

The question of "effect size"

Most of the studies we have discussed have asked whether or not TV violence has an effect on antisocial attitudes and behavior. The answer to this question appears to be yes. But it is equally clear that TV violence is *a* cause, not *the* cause, of aggressiveness, criminality, and so on. This raises the practical question: Just how important is TV violence as a contributing force to antisocial behavior?

The question of importance is evaluated by statisticians and research methodologists in terms of "effect size." That is, is the effect of a particular force (such as TV violence viewing) large enough to be of any practical importance? The pre-eminent authority on effect size statistics is Robert Rosenthal of Harvard University. Rosenthal (1986) reviewed the question of the effect size of TV violence viewing for the *Journal of Social Issues*. Here is Rosenthal's own summary of his paper:

> This paper shows in practical, quantitative, yet intuitive terms just what the social consequences are likely to be [of the effects] typically found in the research on media violence and social behavior. Estimates are provided for how well we can predict . . . current antisocial behavior from current exposure to media violence [and] subsequent antisocial behavior from earlier exposure to media violence, adjusting for earlier levels of antisocial behavior . . . *the practical consequences associated with [both] estimates were found to be substantial.* (p. 141, emphasis added)

What are the Specific Effects of TV Violence?

Although many discussions of TV violence focus on the general question of whether such material has adverse effects, it is useful to break down possible effects into three categories: direct instruction and copying, disinhibition of aggressive or antisocial behavior, and value-shaping and cultivation of antisocial attitudes.

Direct instruction and copying

There is little doubt that specific forms of aggressive or antisocial behavior can be learned from television. Bandura's (1965) early studies showed that young children quickly learned novel forms of aggression against a Bobo doll and Heller and Polsky (1976) found that juvenile offenders learned a variety of criminal techniques from television. But whether such acts will actually be copied (acted out in real-life) depends upon both the individual and the circumstances. Many case studies show copying of antisocial TV behaviors by unusual or troubled individuals. However, Milgram and Shotland's (1973) studies help to drive home the obvious point that TV crimes are rarely imitated on a wide scale.

Disinhibition of aggressive or antisocial behavior

In general, experimental research supports the claim that TV violence viewing can disinhibit aggression or other forms of antisocial behavior. However, such effects have not been demonstrated in all studies. Further, there is a clear trend for disinhibitory effects to be more likely to occur among individuals who are initially more aggressive. For example, in the field experiments of Stein and Friedrich (1972) and Parke and Berkowitz (1977), TV violence increased overt aggressiveness only among those who were relatively more aggressive at the beginning of the study. Although most correlational studies find a relationship between TV violence viewing and aggressiveness, the correlations are often small and are sometimes open to alternative explanations. (See our earlier discussion of the limitations of the correlational method for drawing inferences about cause and effect.)

Value-shaping/cultivation effects

The accumulated data provide strong and unambiguous support for the hypothesis that TV violence viewing can cultivate antisocial attitudes and shape viewers into acceptance of aggressive behavior as an appropriate and acceptable way of dealing with others. Laboratory experiments, field experiments, and a wide range of simple and sophisticated correlational studies all converge on this conclusion. Moreover, the value-shaping effects of TV violence appear to hold for children of both sexes and to the full age range from preschool through late adolescence and adulthood.

THE VOICE OF THE CRITICS

So far in our discussion we have emphasized the impressive degree to which the data support the conclusion that exposure to TV violence has adverse effects on children and society. Certainly it is fair to say that this has been the conclusion of the great majority of analysts. As with any important social issue, however, there is always an argument from the other side of the fence.

In the matter of TV violence, there have been two major criticisms of past research. The essence of these criticisms is summarized in the following two sections.

TV Violence Diverts Attention From More Important Matters

This argument was made quite forcefully by Robert Kaplan and Robert Singer, in reply to the Surgeon General's Report and the new activism that came in its wake (see chapter 5). Kaplan and Singer (1976) wrote:

> It is fascinating that so many hours of research and so many funding dollars have been directed at the possible effects of TV violence on aggressive behavior when it seems most likely that television is not a major cause of human aggression, an activity which considerably antedates audio-visual media. It is unlikely that war, murder, suicide, the battered child syndrome, other violent crimes, and man's inhumanity to man stem to any marked degree from television viewing. Many social scientists may have become victims of the "bearer of bad news" syndrome. Like the Persian emperor beheading messengers who brought bad news, we berate television, which, it is true, shows us ad nauseam and out of all proportion the aggression which man commits against man.
>
> Instead of castigating the networks it might be more useful to ask why the public is so fascinated by programs portraying violence. We would like to suggest investigations into the connection between violence and unemployment, racial prejudice, poor housing and lack of medical care, the prevalence of guns and the ease of obtaining alcohol, the high mobility of the population, the prevalence of broken families, the role of age, the still partly subservient role of women, the lack of public school courses in child-rearing, and a possibly declining faith in the just nature of our political and judicial system. (pp. 63–64)

Rowland (1983), in a radical book entitled *The Politics of TV Violence*, makes a related point. He claims that politicians and government officials have long delighted in the TV violence issue because it has allowed them to portray themselves as highly concerned about the welfare of children and the quality of television programming without ever running the real risk of being forced into any legislative action. The resulting game was also one the industry could play. By selectively sponsoring certain research projects that were inherently biased or flawed, the industry could create the impression of being cooperative while at the same time diverting attention from its vast profits and enormous political power.

TV Violence Research is Unconvincing

Writing in 1984 issue of *Psychological Bulletin*, Canadian psychologist Jonathan Freedman presented a review of the literature on TV violence and concluded that "there is little convincing evidence that in natural settings viewing television violence causes people to be more aggressive" (p. 227). Freedman's argument is built on two points.

Laboratory experiments are irrelevant

Freedman rejects the entire body of laboratory experiments. The rejection is based on three points. First, he challenges the validity of laboratory measures of aggression (such as punching a Bobo doll). Second, he suggests that laboratory experiments are open to what social psychologists call "demand characteristics." That is, in a laboratory experiment it is clear to the subject that a researcher has chosen what they are to see on television. If what they see is aggressive they may assume that the experimenter expects them to behave aggressively. If they actually do make this assumption, their heightened aggressiveness might be no more than compliance with what they guessed the experimenter wanted them to do. Freedman's third point concerns the televised materials themselves. He contends that experimenters may be choosing materials that are more violent than typical programming, and argues that, in any event, material presented "in isolation" is unlike material seen in the context of hours upon hours of television viewing in the home. This final point has also been made by others, including Cook, Kendzierski, and Thomas (1983) and Comstock, Chaffee, Katzman, McCombs, and Roberts (1978).

Field experiments and nonexperimental studies have not provided sufficiently "consistent" results

Freedman acknowledges that there is some consistency in the outcome of nonexperimental studies in that they generally show a relationship between TV violence viewing and aggressiveness. According to Freedman, however, this is not enough. He emphasizes that the correlational studies cannot stand alone because correlation does not, by itself, imply causation. Freedman calls the results of field experiments "inconclusive." Aside from criticizing the data analyses and/or interpretations of various studies, he points out that in some of these studies all children seem to be susceptible to TV violence effects, whereas in other studies effects have been found just for males or just for children who were relatively more aggressive at the outset. And we are reminded that the two field experiments sponsored by the industry failed to produce any evidence for the claim that TV violence has adverse effects.

Two replies

It is not surprising that researchers interested in TV violence saw fit to reply to Freedman. The two major replies were offered by Huesmann, Eron, Berkowitz, and Chaffee (1987) and by Friedrich-Cofer and Huston (1986). These authors make quite similar points, so we will combine their statements and explain how they replied to each of Freedman's complaints.

As to the validity of laboratory measures, the use of the Bobo doll measure is "picking on a straw man." Researchers realized as early as the late 1960s that aggression against toys was an inadequate measure of the effects of TV violence; many laboratory studies since then have used situations in which a child's willingness to be aggressive toward other children has been measured and/or directly observed.

Freedman's suggestion that children behave aggressively in the laboratory just to please experimenters is also something of a red herring. It's rather like saying, "they didn't really mean it." As we will see in the next chapter, young children cannot understand the motives and intentions of TV advertisers even when the advertiser uses persuasion techniques that seem transparently manipulative to adults. Is it plausible then, that these same children ferret out the subtle, unstated expectations of researchers whose aim is to avoid biasing them?

Freedman's claim that the results of field experiments are not consistent from one study to another is rather misleading. Studies using various methods have supported the proposition that TV violence can induce aggressive and/or antisocial behavior in children. Whether the effect will hold only for the most susceptible individuals (e.g., boys from disadvantaged homes) or whether it will hold for a wider range of youngsters obviously depends in part upon the measure being used. There are many more social constraints against engaging in violent rape than in approving of aggressive tactics in response to a social slight, so TV violence effects are of course more likely to show themselves with all sorts of youth if our measures are of activities in which any child might be willing to engage. Neither does anyone doubt that the occurrence of serious violent or criminal acts results from several forces at once. Researchers have said that TV violence is *a* cause of aggressiveness, not that it is *the* cause of aggressiveness. There is no *one*, single cause of any social behavior.

8

Television Advertising and Children

OVERVIEW

There is little doubt that TV advertising directed at children "works" for the advertiser by increasing product sales. But studies show that shopping conflicts between parents and children can often be linked to the child's demand for something advertised on TV. Other research reviewed in this chapter shows that young children are unable to understand the "selling intent" of TV commercials, and that misleading impressions are often created by commercials despite the disclaimers (e.g., a quick announcement stating "partial assembly required"). Advertisements for heavily sugared foods have an adverse effect on children's nutritional beliefs and diets, which are difficult to counteract with pronutrition messages.

The FTC proceeded in 1978 to hold hearings on children's TV advertising with an eye toward possible rulemaking. The record of the hearings, combined with a review published in 1977 by the National Science Foundation, left little doubt that young children are often confused, misled, and taken in by TV commercials. Thus, regulation seemed a real possibility. But the industry counterattacked successfully, for the most part through direct pressure on members of Congress. Congress, which approves the FTC's budget annually, forced the commission to abdicate its previous authority to prohibit "unfair" advertising and thus effectively quashed the FTC hearings. Deregulation is the current watchword of the new FTC.

Industry self-regulation was always rather weak (and completely voluntary), and today networks feel especially pressured to give in to the demands of advertisers to show any children's commercials they wish. In response, some researchers have begun to develop curricula for teaching children about the TV business. These curricula appear to be moderately effective, but they are not in widespread use.

OUTLINE

This chapter is devoted to the topic of TV advertising and children in all its aspects. Our discussion begins with the benefits and costs of exposing children to commercials. We then turn to the array of issues that have been studied by TV advertising researchers. The matter of regulation and the recent move toward deregulation is taken up next. And finally, we consider the new antidote to advertising directed at children: teaching them to become more sophisticated judges of advertisements and advertised products.

BENEFITS AND COSTS OF CHILDREN'S TV ADVERTISING

There is no doubt that TV is an attractive place to advertise. Graphics, camera work, and old-fashioned cleverness make TV commercials a potent way of advertising to the credulous young child. In fact, a children's TV commercial is carefully written, designed, and usually musically scored with the help of private research agencies so as to maximize its impact on the young viewer.

Correlational studies in which amount of exposure to television advertising is related to various behaviors and attitudes have shown that frequent viewers more than infrequent viewers reported liking frequently advertised foods (Atkin, Reeves, & Gibson, 1979); requesting advertised cereals and other advertised foods (Atkin, 1975c,e; Atkin et al., 1979; Clancy-Hepburn, Hickey, & Nevill, 1974); asking to go to frequently advertised fast food restaurants (Atkin, 1975c); and consuming advertised cereals, candies, and snacks (Atkin, 1975c; Atkin et al., 1979; Dussere, 1976).

The economic outcomes of TV advertising are truly impressive. Effective use of commercials has rapidly transformed some companies into major concerns. For example, in 1955 Mattel launched a TV-based advertising program that propelled it from a $500,000 company to a truly big business of $12 million almost overnight (Jennings, 1970). Advertising and broadcast industry spokesmen typically argue that the economic advantages of using TV advertising get passed on to the consumer in the form of lower prices for advertised products (see Table 8.1).

That conflicts ensue when parents refuse their child's product requests has also been reported (Atkin, 1975c,e) and observed (Atkin, 1978a). Atkin (1978a) found that 65% of all parent denials resulted in observable parent-child conflict in the form of arguments.

A study by Goldberg and Gorn (1977) suggests that negativistic attitudes toward parents are inspired by commercials. Four- and five-year old children saw a program with no commercials, two commercials for a toy, or the programs and two commercials on 2 successive days. Children were later shown photographs of a father and son and told that the child requested the

Table 8.1 Advertisers' Arguments Supporting TV Advertising

There has been little or no attention paid by critics to the benefits that proceed from our industry's advertising and merchandising system, and to the increased costs to the consumer that would inevitably occur, we feel, if toy advertising were limited or unduly restrained or proscribed.

Toys are advertised on television to the consumer—to the child and his or her parents. This creates awareness on the part of this child and parent and provides them with choices.

The mass merchants—chain, discount, variety, and department stores—who sell the overwhelming bulk of the toys in this country take advantage of the advertising-created awareness by featuring the TV toys in their newspaper price ads. The more attractive his price, the more likely the merchant is to draw the toy-shopping parent into his store.

The outcome of this system, it has been our experience, is a narrow spread between the manufacturer's price to the store and the ultimate cost of the toy to the consumer. The Marketing Sciences Institute of Harvard University has quantified these relationships in studies of marketing productivity. The evidence is powerful. Before television advertising of toys, in the mid-1950's, the distribution markup was 100 percent; that is, the price paid by the consumer was about double the price paid by the retailer to the manufacturer. Today, that 100 percent markup has shrunk to about 36 percent. To put it another way, the toy that a manufacturer sold to the trade 20 years ago for $3 cost the consumer $5.98. Today, it costs him only $4 or so because of this unique TV/mass merchandising/price-feature system. . . .

Is television advertising harmful to children? According to expert scientific opinion, toy commercials have few effects, if any, either helpful or harmful, on the mental health or emotional development of the viewing child. Further, the right kind of advertising can add some positive values to viewing. Children, like adults, enjoy good TV commercials. To be sure, there are commercials they dislike, and others they hate, but many they find interesting, and highly engaging. They develop favorites, and consider many of them delightful, irrespective of whether or not they wish to buy the product featured. Also, they often learn from them, which is why *Sesame Street* borrows so heavily from commercial TV in devising its learning messages, which attempt to teach children the alphabet, or to count. . . .

What would happen to children's television programs if commercial sponsorship were to cease or decline? Programs of particular interest to children on commercial television would be dramatically reduced, if not eliminated.

The reason for this is that television—like radio, magazines, newspapers, and other communications media—depends on advertising revenue to finance program development, production, facilities and talent. Certainly reduction or elimination of commercial sponsorship would seriously curtail the opportunities for better programming on children's television in the future. (Quote from the testimony of Aaron Locker, representing the Toy Manufacturers of America at hearings before the House of Representatives Subcommittee on Communications of the Committee on Interstate and Foreign Commerce: Locker, 1975, pp. 349–352)

advertised toy, but the father refused to buy it. Less than 40% of the commercial viewers felt the boy would still want to play with his father, while over 60% of the no-commercial group thought so. Further, the study assessed the possible materialistic effects of commercials on children's peer relations. The children were asked whether they would rather play with friends in the sandbox or with the advertised toy. Preference for the interaction with friends was shown by about twice as many children who were not exposed to the commercials. Further, they were asked if they would rather play with a "nice boy" without the toy or with a "not so nice boy" with the toy. Seventy percent of the no-commercial group selected the nice boy without the toy, while only 35% of the commercial viewers selected him.

RESEARCH ON CHILDREN'S UNDERSTANDING OF COMMERCIALS

A commercial is intended and specifically designed to produce an effect. Commercials are intended to sell particular products or services; their effectiveness is ultimately measured in sales. Adults are presumed to recognize commercials and to grasp the selling intent. We discount part of what is said when we know someone is just making a pitch or trying to sell us something. If children do not understand that commercials differ from entertainment programming in this way, then any TV advertising directed at them may be unfair. With this argument in mind, researchers have sought to establish (a) whether children perceive *any* difference between entertainment programming and commercials, and (b) whether children perceive and understand the selling intent of commercials.

Are Commercials Seen as Different from Regular Programming?

The first investigator to attempt to answer this question was Scott Ward who was awarded a contract to contribute research on children's responses to TV advertising to the Surgeon General's Report. Ward and his colleagues (Ward, Levinson, & Wackman, 1972) reasoned that if children discriminated the difference between commercials and regular programming, their attention to the TV would drop when the commercials came on. They had mothers watch their own children watching television at home, recording the children's attention to the screen for ten 1-hour periods over 10 days. Although the oldest children showed a more dramatic drop in attention when the commercials came on, the younger children also showed a noticeable decline in attention. (See Figure 8.1.) Subsequent studies have confirmed that children as young as 5 typically show a decline in attention with the onset of commercials (Winick & Winick, 1979).

Interestingly, 3- and 4-year-olds often show an *increase* in attention when commercials come on (Zuckerman, Ziegler, & Stevenson, 1978).

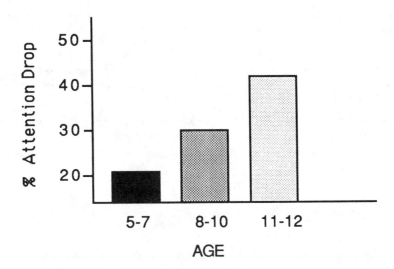

Figure 8.1 Amount of attention drop when commercials came on according to age in Ward, Levinson, and Wackman's 1972 experiment. *Note.* Based on data presented in "Children's Attention to Television Advertising" by S. Ward, D. Levinson, and D. Wackman, in *Television and Social Behavior. Vol. IV: Television in Day-to-Day Life Patterns of Use* (pp. 491–515), 1972, Washington, DC: U.S. Government Printing Office.

Interview studies are consistent with observational data. In a study in which preschoolers were asked to identify each in a series of brief television segments as a "program" or "commercial," it was found that although 5-year-olds were significantly more accurate than 4- or 3-year-olds, the percentage of correct identifications was quite high for all three groups (79%, 66%, and 64%, respectively; Levin, Petros, & Petrella, 1982). Furthermore, when one examines children's accuracy in labeling child-oriented commercials only (i.e., excluding programs and adult-oriented commercials), the average correct figure is even higher, 80%. Similarly, Gaines and Esserman (1981) found that 90% of 4- to 5-year olds and 100% of 6- to 8-year olds correctly identified a commercial as distinct from the program in which it was embedded.

However, if children know and recognize some distinctions between commercials and programs, they may still not understand the selling intent.

Children's Understanding of Selling Intent

Blatt, Spencer, and Ward (1972) were the first to ask children directly about the intent of commercials. They reported that kindergarteners appeared to think the purpose of commercials was simply to be helpful and informative to viewers, and had almost no appreciation of their self-serving nature and selling intent. A typical kindergarten child, asked "What are commercials for?" replied:

> If you want something, so you'll know about it. So people know how to buy things. So if somebody washes their clothes, they'll know what to use. They can watch what to use and buy it.*

In contrast, second graders had a clear understanding that commercials are intended to sell, and a rudimentary understanding of the profit motive behind this intention. Here is a brief dialogue between one second-grader and the interviewer:

> *Interviewer:* What are ads for?
>
> *Second grader:* To make you buy [product name].
>
> *Interviewer:* Why do they want you to buy it?
>
> *Second grader:* So they can get more money and support the factories they have.

Fourth- and sixth-graders were quite sophisticated. Most had a clear recognition of the purpose of commercials, a solid understanding of the motives of advertisers, and at least some sense that advertisers use purposeful and sometimes artful techniques to achieve their objectives. Here are some examples.

> *Fourth grader:* They put free things inside [a cereal box] so you'll buy it.
>
> *Sixth grader:* [The purpose of commercials is] to advertise the product, to make people buy it, to benefit them because then they get more money.

In a more extensive investigation by Ward, Reale, and Levinson (1972), a larger sample of children responded to similar questions. As can be seen in Table 8.2, clear age differences again emerged in children's understanding of the purpose of commercials. Most of the youngest children's responses were in the lowest category of understanding, for example, "commercials are to help and entertain you." In contrast, by age 11 to 12, most children understand the nature of the adman's mission, for example, "commercials are to make people buy things."

Several later studies also asked children of various ages about the purpose of commercials (Bever, Smith, Bengen, & Johnson, 1975; Gaines & Esserman, 1981; Robertson & Rossiter, 1974; Sheikh, Prasad, & Rao, 1974; Ward, Wackman, & Wartella, 1977). All concluded that most youngsters under age 8 cannot explain the selling intent of commercials. For example, Gaines and Esserman (1981) found that only 10% of 4- to 5-year-olds and

---

*All direct quotes are from Blatt et al., 1972, p. 457.

28% of 6- to 8-year-olds defined the purpose of commercials in terms of persuasion (i.e., "to try to make you buy things").

Table 8.2 Children's Understanding of the Purpose of Commercials by Age Group

	DEGREE OF UNDERSTANDING		
AGES IN YEARS	LOW (CONFUSED, UNAWARE OF SELLING MOTIVE; MAY SAY "COMMERCIALS ARE FOR ENTERTAINMENT.") (%)	MEDIUM (RECOGNITION OF SELLING MOTIVE, SOME AWARENESS OF PROFIT-SEEKING; "COMMERCIALS ARE TO MAKE YOU BUY THINGS.") (%)	HIGH (CLEAR RECOGNITION OF SELLING AND PROFIT-SEEKING MOTIVES; "COMMERCIALS GET PEOPLE TO BUY AND THEY PAY FOR THE SHOW.") (%)
5–7	55	35	10
8–10	38	50	12
11–12	15	60	25

Note. Adapted from "Children's Perceptions, Explanations, and Judgments of Television Advertising: A Further Exploration" by S. Ward, G. Reale, and D. Levinson, in Television and Social Behavior. Vol. IV: Television in Day-to-Day Life: Patterns of Use (p. 473) edited by E.A. Rubinstein, G.A. Comstock, and J.P. Murray, 1972, Washington, DC: U.S. Government Printing Office.

One criticism of these studies is that young children have difficulty explaining anything; therefore the results could be due to the youngsters' general lack of verbal ability. When nonverbal means of assessment are used, the age at which children show some realization of selling intent is much younger. In one study (Donohue, Henke, & Donohue, 1980), for example, 2- to 6-year-olds were shown a cereal commercial and then asked to point to the picture that showed what the commercial character wanted them to do. Eighty percent of all the youngsters (and fully 75% of the 2- to 3-year-olds) correctly selected the picture of a mother taking a box of that brand of cereal off the shelf in a supermarket over the alternative picture of a person watching television. Obviously, though, this methodology might have overestimated the percentage of children who "understood" the selling intent of the commercial.

As one might expect from the increasing comprehension of selling intent, children's trust in commercials declines with age. Ward, Reale, and Levinson (1972) asked children between the ages of 5 and 12 whether they thought commercials always tell the truth. A majority of children had already begun to lose their faith in the truth of commercials by age 5, and only 1 12-year-old in 20 still believed that commercials are always truthful. (See Figure 8.2.) Later studies confirmed that there is a growing cynicism toward the truthfulness of commercials during middle childhood (Robertson & Rossiter, 1974; Ward, Wackman, & Wartella, 1977).

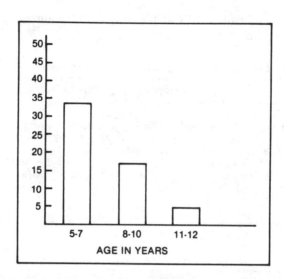

Figure 8.2 Percentage of children who believe that commercials always tell the truth, as a function of age. *Note.* Based on data presented in "Children's Perceptions, Explanations, and Judgments of Television Advertising: A Further Exploration" by S. Ward, G. Reale, and D. Levinson, in *Television and Social Behavior. Vol. IV: Television in Day-to-Day Life: Patterns of Use* (pp. 468–490), 1972, Washington, DC: U.S. Government Printing Office.

EFFECTS OF COMMON ADVERTISING TACTICS

A variety of tactics are commonly used by advertisers trying to reach child television audiences. The two questions asked about such tactics are: Are they effective sales techniques? Do they have adverse effects?

Misleading Impressions and Disclaimers

Television advertisers always try to display their products in the best possible light. A game or toy will almost inevitably be displayed in its fully assembled state, completely functional, and in a context that displays its maximum capabilities. For example, a hypothetical ad for a small train set might show the toy careening around a track with flashing signal lights, passing a large train depot, and disappearing under a tunnel while three or four youngsters respond with obvious glee to the product's capabilities. Such a presentation might imply that the product is sold assembled and operable, and that all the accouterments seen are included with the product at its basic purchase price.

To avoid the charge of fraudulent advertising, advertisers are expected to dispel these inferences. Often, the necessary information is not presented.

Atkin and Heald (1977) found that most children's commercials did not contain the information required to make an appropriate assessment of the product. (See Table 8.3.)

Table 8.3 Percentage of Children's Toy Commercials Containing Information Needed to Evaluate the Toy

TOY INFORMATION	TOY ADS (%) (N = 270)
Mention of price	0
Mention of "hard" qualities[a]	11
Mention of appropriate age	1
Mention of skill needed	32
Suggestion of difficulty to duplicate toy demonstration	27

Note. Based on data reported in "The Content of Children's Toy and Food Commercials" by C.K. Atkin and G. Heald, 1977, Journal of Communication, 27(1), 107–114.
[a]Information about materials or durability.

Many advertisers do take some action to disclaim misleading impressions. They point out that the purchaser will have to prepare the product before using it ("partial assembly required"), power its mechanical function ("batteries not included"), or acquire certain displayed features through an additional purchase ("clothes and accessories sold separately"). Does the presence of such a disclaimer in a TV ad actually have the effect of removing misleading impressions that might otherwise be conveyed to a child?

The answer is, it depends on how the disclaimer is presented. For example, a common practice is to present disclaimers visually, as written words briefly flashed on the screen just before the end of the commercial. Atkin (1975a) demonstrated that such disclaimers are not very effective unless they include an audio component as well. He showed a Mattell Vertibird® commercial to 500 preschool and grade school children. For half the children, the video disclaimer "batteries not included" was presented only visually (in a superimposed video display), and the rest were exposed to an audo-visual presentation. The children in the audio-visual group were more than twice as likely to report that batteries weren't included as were those in the video-only group.

The issue concerning disclaimers is the specific language used—whether it is understandable to young viewers. Liebert, Sprafkin, Liebert, and Rubinstein (1977) did a study in which 240 6- and 8-year-olds saw two toy commercials containing either no disclaimer, a standard audio disclaimer ("some assembly required"), or a modified audio disclaimer ("you have to put it together"). In terms of understanding the disclaimer message, children in the standard disclaimer group were no better off than those in the no disclaimer group, while the modified disclaimer resulted in significantly better comprehension for both age groups. These findings emphasize the importance of using language appropriate to the age of the intended audience.

Even when there is no concrete information missing, an ad may mislead by implying extravagant claims about what can be done with the product. Atkin (1975a) demonstrated that such practices may backfire. He showed a large sample of preschool and grade school children a commercial for a block game in which two children were shown constructing either (a) a tall elaborate structure, with the voice-over encouraging players to build "a sky-high tower so you can be the champion," or (b) a modest structure, with the voice-over emphasizing "it's fun . . . anyone can play." Then the viewers were observed playing with blocks. The children in the extravagant presentation group were more likely than those in the modest presentation group to display hostile behavior (verbal and physical aggression). Further, the extravagant version produced only half the level of brand name recall as the modest version, and the youngsters were slightly less likely to state that the blocks would be fun to play with. So the extravagant claims resulted in worse recall, less desire to play with the toy, and more aggression.

Product Endorsements

One way to increase the appeal of a product is to have it implicitly or explicitly endorsed by a popular or famous individual. Iskoe (1976) was among the first to demonstrate formally that this technique works. He found that a variety of products were seen as more appealing by children if they had been endorsed by a famous personality than if they had not. It is not surprising that some endorsers were more effective than others. For example, Mohammed Ali had a greater effect on product preferences than Lucille Ball.

More recent research provides a fuller picture of the effects of celebrity endorsements on children's product preferences and reactions to commercials. In a project funded by the Federal Trade Commission (Ross et al., 1984), over 400 children between 8 and 14 years of age viewed one of seven television commercials for toys (embedded in a program) and then answered questions about toy preferences and perceptions of the ad shown. All but one of the ads was for a model racing set (the control ad was for an electronic game) and the ads varied in the presence or absence of an endorsement by a famous racecar driver and of real racing footage. The results indicated that the celebrity endorser and real racing footage can produce preference effects across the age range studied. Children who viewed the commercials with the endorser also thought that he had expert knowledge about the toy race set. In addition, the racing footage led to exaggerated perceptions of the physical characteristics (size, speed, complexity) of the toy race car set and to a diminished awareness that the ad was staged.

A study by Kunkel (1986) examined the influence of "host-selling" by comparing children's reactions to commercials that featured characters who were also in the program surrounding them to those that did not contain such a carry-over of characters between program and commercial. Children (4- to 5- and 7- to 8-year-olds) viewed either a Fruity Pebbles Flintstones® cereal or a Smurfberry Crunch® cereal commercial. For half the Flintstones cereal group, the commercial was embedded in a cartoon segment from the Flintstones program, whereas the other half saw it within a Smurfs cartoon. Likewise, the Smurfberry Crunch commercial was embedded either in a Smurfs or Flintstones cartoon. Among the 7- to 8-year-olds, those who viewed the commercials that contained characters from the adjacent program (i.e., host selling) were more favorably influenced toward the advertised product than those in the non–host selling condition. The 4- to 5-year-olds were not differentially responsive to the two techniques with regard to attitude toward the product. However, both age groups were significantly less likely to discriminate commercial from program content when the host-selling format was used.

Premium Offers

Including special toys or other prizes inside the box has long been a favorite tactic for increasing cereal sales to children. Charles Atkin pioneered research on the effects of such offers. In an interview study, Atkin (1975e) found that about half of the mothers of 3- to 11-year-olds reported that their children requested specific cereals for the sole purpose of getting the premium inside the box. In a follow-up, he actually observed mothers and children in the cereal aisles of grocery stores. He found that 9% of all children's requests for specific cereals explicitly mentioned the premium. Although many mothers displayed obvious reluctance to buy a cereal for this reason, refusals typically resulted in open conflict between the parent and the child at the supermarket (Atkin, 1975d).

Program-Length Commercials

A recent development in children's program production is the making of programs that feature characters that are planned or existing toys. Both the toy manufacturer and program producer profit handsomely from this practice. Typically, the toy company and program producer share in the program costs and then in the toy and program revenues. The success of this method has been demonstrated by toy sales and program viewership (Boyer, 1986; "Toying with," 1985). Many of these shows are aired by the independent stations who are hungry for programming, and have been known to be given a share in the toy profits.

In what is, to date, the only study reported that examined the effects of program-length commercials, Bryant (1985) found that such "programs" do make the associated products more appealing. Eighty kindergarteners were shown a Tarzan cartoon (neutral with regard to product) plus one of four possible shows: (a) an episode of "The Transformers," which included the robot, Insecticons®; (b) two 30-second commercials for the Insecticons toy; and another animated program, "She-Ra" (neutral with regard to product); (c) The "Transformers" episode and the two ads for Insecticons; or (d) "She-Ra" (control). After viewing the television, the children were given tokens which they could exchange for 1 of 10 displayed toys, one of which was an Insecticon Transformer. A significantly greater number of Insecticons were purchased by children who had seen "The Transformers" program plus the Insecticons commercials than by those in any other condition. The least Insecticons were purchased by those in the control group. The children who viewed either the Insecticon commercials of "The Transformers" program purchased an intermediate number which did not differ from each other. As an ingenious secondary measure, all the youngsters were given discount coupons to purchase an Insecticons for half price at a local toy store. While the results were not statistically significant due to small sample size (only 16 children used the coupons), the findings were in the same direction, with the combination of program-length commercial and commercial yielding the greatest number of purchases.

CONCERNS ABOUT PRODUCTS ADVERTISED

So far our discussion has focused on children's television advertising in general. Equally important are issues that have been raised about the advertising of specific types of products. We will discuss two concerns: that sugared food ads may adversely affect children's nutritional habits, and that proprietary medicine ads may increase the use of either legal or illegal drugs.

Ads for Heavily Sugared Foods

One of the most frequently voiced concerns about children's TV advertising is that much of it offers heavily sugared products. The concern is understandable. Commercials for such products comprise about 80% of children's TV advertising. Barcus (1978b) analyzed 33 hours of children's weekend morning programming and found that on the network affiliated stations, 34% of the commercials were for sweetened cereals, 29% for candies and sweets, and 15% for fast food chains. Natural foods such as dairy products, fruits, vegetables, or meats were rarely advertised. Aside from the emphasis on highly sugared manufactured foods, the presentation techniques used in the food ads also give reason for concern. Food ads focused on taste, especially sweetness and texture (e.g., chewy) and provided little, if any, information about nutritional content or attributes, except perhaps "fortified with essential vitamins" or "part of a balanced breakfast." It is therefore not surprising that children rarely mention nutritional reasons as the basis for a particular cereal request or that they have nutritional misconceptions. For example, Atkin and Gibson (1978) found that in a study of 4- to 7-year-old children, less than half realized that presweetened cereals produced more cavities than nonsweetened cereal. They also found that the disclosure "part of a balanced breakfast" was ineffective. Two thirds of the 4- to 7-year-old sample could not recall any of the foods shown with the cereal and showed no understanding of the term "balanced breakfast." Similarly, Atkin et al., (1979) found that youngsters who are heavily exposed to food ads were twice as likely as those less frequently exposed to believe that sugared cereals and candy are highly nutritious. And finally, Ross, Campbell, Huston-Stein, and Wright (1981) found that children usually assume that ads for cereals and beverages flavored with artificial fruit flavors contain real fruit, even though these products usually contain no fruit at all. (It is understandable why children are misled. Many of the ads show real fruit next to the product or picture it on the container.)

Gorn and Goldberg (1982) undertook an extremely ambitious study that directly tested the effects of exposure to commercials for sugared snacks on children's actual food selections. The study was conducted in a summer camp setting with 288 youngsters who were between 5 and 8 years of age. During each of 14 consecutive days, the children viewed a different half-hour Saturday morning cartoon. Four experimental groups were constructed which were based on the presence and nature of the commercials embedded in the programs: (a) sweetened snack food commercials (e.g., candy bars, Crackerjacks, Kool Aid); (b) fruit commercials (e.g., orange juice, grapes), (c) public service announcements (PSAs) that emphasized the value of eating a balanced diet and restricting sugar intake, and (d) no commercials. There were 4.5 minutes of commercials (in the conditions with commercials) within each half-hour show. Snack choices were made available daily immediately after the television viewing. The daily offerings consisted of orange juice, Kool Aid, two fruits, and two candy bars, and the children were asked to individually select a glass of one of the beverages plus two of the four snack foods. The results indicated that the children were significantly influenced by the sweetened snack commercials—those exposed to the sweetened snack ads (which included Kool Aid and candies) selected the least orange juice and the least fruit of the four groups. Those in the fruit commercials group selected the most orange juice but there were no significant differences in the snack food choices between the fruit, PSA, and no commercials groups (but all selected more fruit than the sweetened snack group).

It is interesting that the absence of commercials for sweetened snacks was just as effective as the PSAs and fruit commercials in encouraging the selection of fruit over candy. It is also interesting that regardless of which commercials they had seen, the children knew that the camp doctor would like them to eat fruit. However, their likelihood of actually selecting a fruit snack was influenced by their exposure to candy commercials.

Corroborating evidence for the influence of commercials for high carbohydrate snacks comes from a smaller scale study (Jeffrey, McLellarn, & Fox, 1982) in which 96 children (ages 4–5 and 9–10 years) viewed 5 minutes of commercials embedded in a children's program. These children had their snack food consumption assessed the week before and immediately after the TV exposure. Each child saw commercials from one of three categories: low-nutrition (e.g., Pepsi, Fruit Loops), pronutrition (e.g., carrots, milk), and control (toys). The consumption measure was based on the amount of food eaten from a snack tray which held 12 small cups, 6 containing high-nutrition foods (e.g., cheese, carrots, juice) and 6 containing low-nutrition foods (e.g., chocolate, cookies, soda). For boys, exposure to the low-nutrition ads led to a significant increase in the number of calories consumed during the designated snack period; this was not the case for boys in the other two groups or girls in any group. Moreover, in terms of what they ate, the boys in the low-nutrition group tended to eat more of the low-nutrition foods and beverages offered. The pronutrition ads did not influence snack consumption.

Counter-effects of pronutrition messages

The pronutrition ads that were included in the experiments of Gorn and Goldberg (1982) and Jeffrey et al. (1982) did not produce significant increases in the selection of pro- over low-nutrition snacks. What about the efficacy of longer messages? The evidence is not much better: Peterson, Jeffrey, Bridgwater, and Dawson (1984) assessed the impact of exposing kindergarteners to a 10-day treatment of pronutritional education programs (15-min segments from commercial and PBS shows) plus pronutritional PSAs (5 min). Compared to no-treatment control classes, children in the pronutrition media condition demonstrated acquisition of the pronutrition concepts taught in the treatment; however, there were no treatment effects on food preference or behavioral eating measures.

A study by Galst (1980) suggests that adult reinforcement of pronutrition ads may be the critical variable in producing positive outcomes. After a behavioral eating pretest (i.e., snack choices), 65 children between 3.5 and 6.8 years old were assigned to one of five groups: (a) commercials for sugared products without adult commentary, (b) commercials for sugared products with adult commentary focusing on the health problems resulting from consumption of such products, (c) commercials for nonsugared products and pronutritional PSAs without adult commentary, (d) commercials for nonsugared products and pronutritional PSAs with adult commentary that reinforced the value of consuming healthy foods, and (e) no exposure control. The four television exposure groups viewed two cartoons daily plus 4.5 minutes of commercials (the content varying by condition) every day for 4 weeks. A behavioral eating test each day following the television exposure indicated that the intervention that was most effective in reducing the children's selection of sugared snacks was the presentation of commercials for nonsugared foods and pronutritional PSAs with positive evaluative comments by an adult co-viewer. Exposure to these ads without the adult commentary was *not* effective. It should be noted, however, that even with adult reinforcement of pronutrition messages, the children did not select unsugared snacks more than sugared snacks. Thus, it appears that the long-term exposure to commercials for sugared snacks cannot be easily reversed in a 4-week treatment.

Ads for Proprietary Drugs

Ads for medicines are never intentionally directed at children but, of course, children see them nonetheless. Among the concerns that have been raised in this regard are whether exposure to such ads make children excessively dependent on these legal drugs, whether they foster misconceptions about medicine and health, and whether seeing ads for legal drugs leads to illegal drug use. Fortunately, research shows that most of these concerns are *not* warranted.

A large-scale 3-year study sponsored by NBC revealed that adolescents who see many drug ads are somewhat more likely than other adolescents to use these drugs, but the relationship is a very weak one. Moreover, the evidence clearly does *not* support the idea that seeing ads for legal drugs leads to increased use of illegal ones (Milavsky, Pekowsky, & Stipp, 1975–76). In addition, a study done with fifth-, sixth-, and seventh-grade children found that high exposure to medicine commercials was only very slightly associated with the perception that people are often sick and take medicines or the belief that medicine gives quick relief (Atkin, 1978b).

Rossiter and Robertson (1980) offer further support that youngsters' usage of proprietary drugs are only to a modest extent influenced by their exposure to proprietary drug advertising on television. Collecting data from over 1,000 children from third, fifth, and seventh grades, these investigators found that exposure to such advertising was moderately related to number of requests for proprietary drugs ($r = .30$) but only slightly related to actual usage ($r = .10$), which suggests that parents mediate children's requests and control children's usage of these drugs. The relationship between drug advertising exposure and proprietary drug usage did not vary significantly based on the child's age or frequency of illness or on the parents' educational level. The study concludes with the following policy-related statement, "TV drug advertising does not seem to influence children to an extent that may be regarded as socially harmful or worthy of further legislative attention" (Rossiter & Robertson, 1980, p. 328).

REGULATION OF CHILDREN'S TV ADVERTISING

The history of efforts to regulate children's TV advertising in the United States, like the history of efforts to regulate violence and sex in TV entertainment, is an object lesson in the way in which politics, economics, and scientific research are inextricably woven together. In this section we describe what has transpired over the past 25 years.

The Growth and Demise of FTC Involvement

The FTC of the 1970s was a decidedly pro-consumer agency. It had quietly (and rather successfully) been taking up the cause of children's TV advertising on a case-by-case basis until the latter part of the decade, when a variety of factors came together in a push for more general rule-making. One of these factors was the publication of a literature review and policy recommendations on children's TV advertising by the prestigious National Science Foundation (NSF).

The NSF Report

Partly in response to pressure from ACT, in 1975 the NSF commissioned a distinguished panel to review the research on the effects of television advertising on children and to recommend areas for future research. The panel members included:

- *Richard P. Adler*, Graduate School of Education, Harvard University;
- *Bernard Z. Friedlander*, Department of Psychology, University of Hartford;
- *Gerald S. Lesser*, Graduate School of Education, Harvard University;
- *Laurene Meringoff*, Graduate School of Education, Harvard University;
- *Thomas S. Robertson*, The Wharton School, University of Pennsylvania;
- *John R. Rossiter*, The Wharton School, University of Pennsylvania;
- *Scott Ward*, Graduate School of Business, Harvard University.

The review was organized around 10 policy issues, which maximized its usefulness to policymakers (National Science Foundation, 1977):

1. Children's ability to distinguish television commercials from program material.
2. The influence of format and audio-visual techniques on children's perceptions of commercial messages.
3. Source effects and self-concept appeals in children's advertising.
4. The effects of advertising containing premium offers.
5. The effects of violence or unsafe acts in television commercials.
6. The impact on children of proprietary medicine advertising.
7. The effects on children of television food advertising.
8. The effects of volume and repetition of television commercials.
9. The impact of television advertising on consumer socialization.
10. Television advertising and parent-child relations. (p. ii)

Twenty-one relevant studies were reviewed (the majority of which were conducted after 1974), and the general conclusions of the scientific panel were:

> It is clear from the available evidence that television advertising *does* influence children. Research has demonstrated that children attend to and learn from commercials, and that advertising is at least moderately successful in creating positive attitudes toward and the desire for products advertised. The variable that emerged most clearly across numerous studies as a strong determinant of children's perception of television advertising is the child's age. Existing research clearly establishes that children become more skilled in evaluating television advertising as they grow older, and that to treat all children from 2 to 12 as a homogeneous group masks important, perhaps crucial differences. These findings suggest that both researchers and policymakers give greater attention to the problems of younger viewers, since they appear to be the most vulnerable. . . . Research can guide policy by providing concrete information on the actual impact of television advertising on children. In the long run, such research can provide essential factual guideposts for directing policy toward adequate safeguards against economic exploitation of these young viewers. (p. i–ii)

The FTC Investigation of Children's TV Advertising

In 1977, shortly after the release of the NSF report, the FTC responded to long-standing petitions from ACT and the Center for Science in the Public Interest to investigate children's TV advertising. (CSPI is a District of Columbia corporation devoted to improving domestic food policies.) Both the ACT and CSPI petitions were directed at broadcasts in which children comprise at least half the audience. ACT's petition sought a ban on televised candy commercials during these periods. CSPI's petition sought the following changes: (a) a ban on TV ads for between-meal snacks for which more than 10% of the calories are derived from added sugar, and (b) mandatory disclosures of the added sugar content of foods and the dental health risks posed by eating sugared products. In July 1977, representatives of several organizations met with then FTC Chairman Michael Pertschuk to endorse the petitions. These endorsers included the American Academy of Pediatrics, the American Parents Committee, and the Dental Health Section of the American Public Health Association.

In response to these petitions, the FTC Advisory Staff in 1978 proposed that the commission should proceed to rulemaking to determine whether it should (FTC, 1978):

> (a) Ban all televised advertising for any product which is directed to, or seen by, audiences composed of a significant proportion of children who are too young to understand the selling purpose of, or otherwise comprehend or evaluate, the advertising.
>
> (b) Ban televised advertising directed to, or seen by, audiences composed of a significant proportion of older children for sugared products, the consumption of which poses the most serious dental health risks.
>
> (c) Require that televised advertising directed to, or seen by, audiences composed of a significant proportion of older children for sugared food products not included in paragraph (b) be balanced by nutritional and/or health disclosures funded by advertisers. (pp. 10–11)

The FTC solicited public comment on the above proposals through the fall of 1978. During the winter of 1979 6 weeks of hearings on children's television advertising were held in San Francisco and Washington, DC. About 200 witnesses representing the broadcasting, food and toy industries, health and education professionals, consumer groups, and parents testified.

Following the hearings, the FTC Presiding Officer, Judge Morton Needelman, reviewed the evidence submitted and issued a statement clarifying the disputed and nondisputed issues. Needelman indicated that the issues that should be pursued are (FTC, 1979):

> 1. To what extent can children between the ages of 2 and 11 distinguish between children's commercials and children's programs, to the point that they comprehend the selling purpose of television advertising aimed at children?
> 2. To what extent can children between the ages of 2 and 11 defend against persuasive techniques used in these commercials, such as fantasy or cartoon presenters, premiums, limited information, and various associative appeals?
> 3. What health effects, actual or potential, attach to any proven lack of understanding or inability to defend against persuasive techniques? (pp. 6–7)

The issues that Needelman considered unworthy of further FTC attention included: TV advertising not specifically directed at children, TV advertising's effectiveness in getting children to ask for advertised products (proven), parent-child conflict resulting from such requests (proven to be present but not severe), and the adverse effects of overconsumption of sugar on obesity and the formation of dental caries (proven) (FTC, 1979).

Throughout these events, the broadcasters, advertisers, and targeted manufacturers launched a counterattack. In 1978 they reportedly raised a $30 million "war chest" to fight the FTC (ACT, 1980). Industry groups lobbying in Washington tried to prevent the hearings from ever taking place. They almost convinced the House and Senate Appropriations Committee members to forbid the FTC from using any funds on the children's advertising rulemaking; they sought to undermine the participation of groups such as ACT by attempting to cut their public participation funds; and they challenged Michael Pertschuk's role, accusing him of being biased.

In December 1979, the Court of Appeals ruled that while Pertschuk's participation was lawful and appropriate, he had to withdraw from further participation in the proceedings. The industry lobbyists continued their opposition during and after the hearings. By May 1980, their pressures in Washington culminated in Congress passing a bill that eliminated the power of the FTC to rule on "unfair" advertising practices, thus confining its powers to "deceptive" practices. Further, the proceeding was suspended until the FTC developed specific rules concerning deception.

In June 1980, the FTC Commissioners instructed the staff to present recommendations for the future conduct of the proceeding. On March 31, 1981 the FTC staff released its report and recommendation. The recommendation that appears on the cover page of the report succinctly states: "Recommendation: That the Commission Terminate Proceedings for the Promulgation of a Trade Regulation Rule on Children's Advertising" (Federal Trade Commission, 1981b). In its report, the staff acknowledged that there were many problems with children's advertising, but that they were not in a position to do anything about it at the time. The following is a summary statement of the bases for this rather defeatist recommendation (FTC, 1981b):

Staff recommends that the Commission terminate the children's advertising rulemaking proceeding. While the rulemaking record establishes that child-oriented television advertising is a legitimate cause for public concern, there do not appear to be, at the present time, workable solutions which the Commission can implement through rulemaking in response to the problems articulated during the course of the proceeding. . . .

The record developed during the rulemaking proceeding adequately supports the following conclusions regarding child-oriented television advertising and young children six years and under: (1) they place indiscriminate trust in televised advertising messages; (2) they do not understand the persuasive bias in television advertising; and (3) the techniques, focus and themes used in child-oriented television advertising enhance the appeal of the advertising message and the advertised product. Consequently, young children do not possess the cognitive ability to evaluate adequately child-oriented television advertising. Despite the fact that these conclusions can be drawn from the evidence, the record establishes that the only effective remedy would be a ban on all advertisements oriented toward young children, and such a ban, as a practical matter, cannot be implemented. Because of this remedial impediment, there is no need to determine whether or not advertising oriented toward young children is deceptive. Staff's recommendation for this portion of the case is that the proceeding be terminated.

Other major concerns expressed in the proceeding were that advertisements for sugared products directed to children under twelve may have adverse effects on their nutritional attitudes, and may undermine children's health because such advertisements do not warn children of the possible effects of the over-consumption of sugar on their nutritional and dental well-being. The rulemaking record established that advertising for sugared products is concentrated during children's television programming and that this advertising persuades children to ask for the advertised products. However, the evidence on the record is inconclusive as to whether this advertising adversely affects children's attitudes about nutrition. Therefore, staff recommends that rulemaking be terminated on this issue.

With regard to dental health, the rulemaking record establishes that dental caries is a major childhood disease, and that the consumption of sugar contributes to the formation of dental caries. Evidence on the record also establishes that there are a number of factors other than the sugar content of a food which are important contributors to the formation of dental caries. However, it became apparent during the course of the proceeding that there is no scientific methodology for determining the cariogenicity of individual food products which is sufficiently scientifically accepted to justify formulation of a government-mandated rule. Since such identification would be a threshold step in the implementation of any proposed rule, the lack of a methodology precludes regulation through rule-making of child-oriented advertising for food products on the ground that such products contribute to dental caries. Thus, staff recommends that the rulemaking be terminated on this issue. (pp. 2–4)

On September 30, 1981 the FTC announced that

It is not in the public interest to continue this proceeding. . . . We seriously doubt . . . whether a total ban should ever be imposed on children's advertising at the end of rulemaking proceedings. . . . We cannot justify sacrificing other important enforcement priorities to its continuation. ("FTC gets off," 1981, p. 40)

Recently the FTC has signaled even more clearly that it has no interest whatsoever in protecting children from even the greediest advertising practices. For example, in 1984 it completely rescinded its ban on program-length commercials. Shortly thereafter it hailed the profit-sharing arrangement whereby the stations get a piece of the toy profits as a laudable "innovative technique" to fund children's programming (FCC, April 12, 1985). Child advocacy groups such as ACT and the American Academy of Pediatrics are protesting strongly that this practice is unfairly exploitive of children.

Industry Self-regulation

The first industry action with regard to children's TV advertising was in 1961 when the NAB adopted its Toy Advertising Guidelines and subsequently added guidelines to cover the advertising of all products intended for children. The guidelines dictated the frequency and spacing of commercials, banned the advertising of certain products (e.g., hard liquor, gambling aids), and identified unacceptable advertising techniques (e.g., implying that a child's social status would be raised by using a product). As we explained in chapter 3, the real purpose of the NAB Code was to forestall or prevent government regulation. The code was never enforced vigorously, and the NAB gladly abandoned it altogether when government policy and judicial decisions suggested that the country was entering a period of *de*regulation.

The other industry effort at self-regulation, also mentioned in chapter 3, is the Children's Advertising Review Unit (CARU) of the Council of Better Business Bureaus. CARU is still in existence and in fact revised its guidelines on children's TV advertising as recently as 1983. The CARU guidelines are similar but not identical to the old NAB Code and adherence to them is voluntary.

CARU still raises its voice in protest to some of the most flagrant advertising offenses. For example, in 1985 it protested an advertisement for Live Wires® shoes because of a jingle that baldly stated wearing the shoes would enhance a child's popularity. The jingle went: "Hey look, there's a new kid in town. . . . She's wearing Live Wires. That's the kid we want to meet." But violations of the CARU guidelines by advertisers are common and on the increase (Kunkel, 1986).

With the government and the industry off their backs, the networks and independent stations are free to air any commercials they please. Everyone realizes, though, that if advertising practices become sufficiently offensive, external regulation could return. So, each of the networks has promulgated its own set of guidelines (Maddox & Zanot, 1983). The lack of uniform standards makes it quite difficult to maintain any standards, a problem that is exacerbated by the fact that independent stations typically wink at all but the most outrageous indiscretions (Alsop, 1985).

TRAINING YOUNG CONSUMERS

As regulation of commercials became a thing of the past, interest in finding ways to teach children about the nature and purpose of TV commercials has grown. This interest has taken two forms. One is to develop classroom curricula that teach the realities of television advertising. The other is to use the medium itself, through public service announcements and consumer information films, to increase children's sophistication as consumers of television advertisements and products.

Classroom Curricula

There have been two major efforts to develop a TV consumer education curriculum for children.

Feshbach, Feshbach, and Cohen (1982)

These investigators designed and tested two three-session curricula with second and fourth graders. One curriculum focused on the purpose or economic bases of advertising and the other on the motivational aspects (i.e., techniques by which wants for the product are created). Over 200 children were assigned to either one of the experimental training groups or a control group that received instruction in social comprehension. The children in both the commercial training groups compared to those in the control group rated advertised products as less desirable, found commercials less credible, had a better understanding of commercials and were less accepting of them, and to some extent were less apt to choose an advertised product over an unadvertised product in a simulated behavioral choice situation. Although the economic and motivational training were separated into two distinct interventions for theoretical reasons, it would seem that the optimal training procedure would combine the two components.

Donohue, Henke, and Meyer (1983)

These investigators compared the effects of two commercial awareness training programs to a control. One program (traditional instruction) examined videotaped commercials and discussed the selling intent of the advertiser and the techniques used to make the products seem appealing. In the other program (role playing) the children participated in making a cereal "commercial." Seventy-five first graders were assigned to one of the three groups. Both interventions, compared to the control, enhanced children's recognition of commercials as distinct from programs and their realization that products advertised on television are not necessarily better than those that are not advertised. However, the traditional instruction was more effective in helping children to articulate why commercials are shown on TV. As in the Feshbach et al. (1982) study, one would imagine a combination of both approaches would be most powerful.

Consumer Education Films and Public Service Announcements

The possibility of using carefully designed films to teach children about the nature of TV commercials is appealing because, unlike a classroom curriculum, once a film is made it can be distributed or shown widely at very low cost.

The Six Billion $$$ Sell and Seeing Through Commercials

The potential of consumer training films for children was first demonstrated by Donald Roberts and his colleagues (Roberts, Christenson, Gibson, Mooser, & Goldberg, 1980). These studies focused on two films, *The Six Billion $$$ Sell* (by Consumer's Union) and *Seeing Through Commercials* (by Vision Films), both designed to teach children about the selling intent of commercials and the persuasive techniques used in them. (See Table 8.4 for a summary of the content of the two films.) Both before and after viewing one of these films or a control film, children's skepticism toward commercials was measured with items such as "When someone famous tries to get you to buy something in a TV commercial, you can be pretty sure it is as good as he says it is" (agree-disagree), and "Most of the things they say on TV commercials are true" (agree-disagree). The researchers found that *The Six Billion $$$ Sell* viewers became more skeptical about commercials than the other two groups. In addition to the general questions about commercials, the youngsters were shown actual commercials containing the specific techniques described in the film and were questioned about them. Their responses provided further evidence of the film's effectiveness in increasing viewer skepticism regarding commercials. The film was particularly successful with the youngest children (second graders in one study and fourth graders in another study) and with those who watched the most television.

PSAs for Young Consumers

Christenson (1982) assessed the impact of consumer information PSAs on children's responses to commercials. The "PSAs" studied were 2-minute messages composed of a 1-minute excerpt from *The Six Billion $$$ Sell* plus two PSAs (one network and one locally produced). The media spots focused on the intent and credibility of commercials (i.e., commercials are intended to get people to buy the products advertised and they do not always tell the truth). Forty-five children in first or second grade and 45 in fifth or sixth grade saw two animated Saturday morning network programs containing commercials (cereal, gum, game), the same three commerciuals preceded by the consumer PSAs, or three PSAs irrelevant to consumer issues. The results of subsequent interview and questionnaire procedures showed that the PSAs significantly increased awareness of commercial intent by the younger group (the older group was already aware) and skepticism about the truthfulness of commercials by both age groups. However, the PSAs had a rather limited impact on children's evaluations of the qualities of the products they saw advertised during the study. Nevertheless, it is encouraging that brief televised announcements can modify children's awareness about and skepticism toward commercials; perhaps more frequent exposure to such messages is necessary to get children to incorporate the ideas into their processing of actual commercials.

Table 8.4 Summary of the Basic Contents of Two Instructional Films

THE SIX BILLION $$$ SELL	SEEING THROUGH COMMERCIALS
Announcer comments on various "tricks" used in commercials and says we will look at some.	A scene shows the making of a commercial in which the actor cannot stand the product and steps out of character to explain that commercials are "pretend."
"Selling the Star"—use of celebrity testimonials.	Shows how addition of song, happy children, play, etc., can make any product look like fun.
"Now You See It. Now You Don't"— exaggerations, irrelevant claims, tricks of camera and lighting.	Examination of how camera can be used to make product look larger than it really is.
"New! New! New!"—use of the word "new" to imply superiority.	Discussion of special effects used to make a product look exciting—sound effects, excited spectators, rapidly sequenced visuals shot from many perspectives.
"Word Games"—use of scientific-sounding words to imply superiority.	
"The Giveaway"—promoting premium offers rather than the product itself.	Discussion of special effects to make a product seem beautiful—set, dramatic lighting, filters on cameras, music and sound.
"Promises, Promises"—association of product with glamour, success, fun, and the good life.	
"Brand Loyalty"—promoting a brand rather than the product itself.	Discussion of implied messages— disclaimers, premium offers, etc. A closing "commercial" full of the "tricks" discussed above—included for discussion by viewers at the end of the film.
Children conduct a group discussion about commercials in general and come to the conclusion that people should make their own product choices and should be very careful about the claims made in commercials.	

Source. Roberts, Christenson, Gibson, Mooser, & Goldberg, 1980.
Note. From "Developing Discriminating Consumers" by D.F. Roberts et. al., 1980, Journal of Communication, 30(3), p. 97. Copyright 1980 by The Annenberg School of Communications. Reprinted by permission.

9
Race and Sex on TV

OVERVIEW

The cultivation of children's attitudes through the stories they are exposed to originated with the earliest fairy tale. Today, concern focuses on race and sex stereotyping and the portrayal of sexuality on television.

Clark (1972) observed that there are two ways in which the presentation of women and minorities can be biased: lack of recognition and lack of respect. Recognition refers to the frequency with which a group receives TV roles at all. Respect refers to how characters behave and are treated once they have roles.

Although blacks were once almost ignored on TV, this situation has changed as a result of the pressures of black and broader-based civil rights groups. Women and other minorities have not fared so well in terms of recognition. No other group on television is accorded respect even approaching that of the white male. Moreover, both correlational and experimental studies show that how groups are portrayed on TV can exert an influence on the attitudes of the young viewer. Employment practices within the television industry also favor the white male. Women and minorities account for a disproportionately small percentage of the television workforce, and hold almost none of the important jobs.

Until the mid-1970s, sexuality was considered taboo by producers and the networks. However, broadcast television has become more preoccupied with sexual themes in the past 15 years, causing critics to hiss that the networks responded to the Surgeon General's Report by trading violence for sex. There is almost no research on the effects of sexual material on children, probably because even soliciting for child participants in such studies would be a violation of deeply held values. Research suggests that adolescents who watch a lot of sexual content on TV are less satisfied with their own sexual status and hold serious misconceptions about sex and sexuality.

With the advent of cable and videocassette rentals, the opportunity to see sexually explicit material (i.e., erotica and pornography) on television has increased enormously. The initial government inquiry into pornography suggested there were no adverse effects. But more recent research and a new government inquiry suggest that aggressive pornography can increase aggressive behavior and cultivate negative attitudes toward women.

OUTLINE

We have already mentioned on several occasions Gerbner's theory that TV content "cultivates" various ideas and attitudes about the world and the people in it. Representation of racial groups, gender roles, and sexual relationships on television potentially cultivate underlying attitudes of children (and perhaps adults) who watch. In this chapter we consider race and sex stereotypes on television, both in terms of their prevalence and their effects, and then consider the highly controversial issue of sex and sexuality.

STEREOTYPING

There is enormous diversity within every subgroup of our society. For example, some men are very ambitious and others are not ambitious at all; some women are very ambitious and others are not ambitious at all. Likewise, some white people are very rich and some are very poor; some black people are very rich and some are very poor. A group is said to be stereotyped whenever it is depicted or portrayed in such a way that *all* its members appear to have the same set of characteristics, attitudes, or life conditions. In this section we raise two interrelated questions about stereotyping and television: To what extent does television stereotype various groups? To what extent do such stereotypes influence the attitudes and behavior of youthful viewers?

Our focus will be mainly on the depiction of women and minorities, because most of the research has been concerned with these two groups. However, we will also describe work on stereotyping of the elderly.

Stereotyping of Blacks and Other Minorities

In Smythe's (1954) early study, only 2% of all TV characters were black. The few blacks who did appear were presented either as minor characters or as lovable but stereotyped buffoons ("Amos and Andy"). The poor treatment of blacks by TV did not go unnoticed by the burgeoning civil rights movement, which made the portrayal of blacks on television a political and social issue of the 1960s. Concern with television's portrayal of blacks was later fueled by Cedric Clark (1972), a black Stanford social scientist. In an essay entitled "Race, Identification, and Television Violence", especially written for the Surgeon General's Report, Clark contended that "the mass media commit violence by virtue of their effects on the Black self-image" (p. 121). Further, he provided a cogent analysis of how the process worked.

For Clark, there are two issues to consider when examining the way in which any group is portrayed on television: *recognition* and *respect*.

Recognition is the degree to which a group is present at all. The very infrequent appearance of blacks on television during the 1950s and 1960s meant that they were getting no recognition. Clark emphasized the social and political importance of failing to recognize blacks on television. Recognition, Clark wrote, "can operate as a form of social (and political) control. By not recognizing somebody, we can devalue his importance and hence keep his behavior under control..." (p. 123).

Respect has to do with the status and importance accorded to members of a group. It is a necessary ingredient in the process of self-affirmation. A medium that presents a group in a way that connotes low status is depriving that group of respect. Thus, both recognition and respect are essential before we can say a minority group is receiving fair treatment.

The civil rights movement and Clark's ideas combined to produce significant changes in both the recognition and respect blacks were accorded on television. By the 1970s, blacks appeared in new prime-time television entertainment in almost the same proportion as they did in the U.S. population (Gerbner, Gross, Morgan, & Signorielli, 1982). Their formal social-occupational status also changed. Whereas they had been cast as entertainers, servants, or buffoons during their rare appearances in the 1950s and early 1960s, a decade later they were more likely to be cast as "regulators" of society, typically playing such roles as teachers or policemen (Clark, 1972; Roberts, 1970).

These seeming advances are somewhat deceptive, however. For example, although blacks appeared more often on TV than they had previously, they were largely segregated from whites. When Lemon (1977) examined the racial composition of 17 prime-time shows, she found that all of the characters in four of the series were black and that there were almost no blacks at all on the other 13 shows. Similarly, Weigel, Loomis, and Soja (1980) found that only 2% of the human appearances in drama and only 4% in comedy involved cross-racial interactions. Weigel et al. also reported that 77% of the commercials they analyzed had only white characters. Baptista-Fernandez, Greenberg, and Atkin (1980) found the same pattern of segregation on Saturday morning shows, as did Barcus (1983), who reported that in 82% of children's programs white and minority children never appear together.

Even the somewhat improved treatment of blacks on television has not spilled over to other minorities. For example, Hispanic-Americans are very under-represented on television, filling less than 2% of the roles (as compared with almost 10% in the population). Moreover, virtually all the Hispanic TV characters are men; female Hispanics are virtually *un*represented on television (Greenberg & Baptista-Fernandez, 1980). And when nonblack minorities do appear, they are usually presented in an unfavorable light. In prime-time programming, minorities and foreigners are almost invariably portrayed either as villains or as victims of violence (Gerbner, 1982; Gerbner, Gross, Signorielli, & Morgan, 1986).

Stereotyping of Women

From the earliest days of the medium women were, and still are, disadvantaged television characters in terms of both recognition and respect. The only changes over the years appear to have been that flagrant presentations of women as sex objects in commercials are less likely to occur today than 10 or 15 years ago and that now one or two "token" women may appear in prestigious roles.

Turning first to recognition, women occupy only between one quarter and one third of all roles on entertainment television. This figure has been remarkably stable for almost 20 years (Barcus, 1983; Gerbner, 1972; Gerbner et al., 1982; Signorielli, 1982, 1986; Tedesco, 1974; U.S. Commission on Civil Rights, 1977, 1979).

In terms of respect, women fare poorly in both the formal occupational roles they hold and in the personality traits they display. The majority of TV women are not employed; instead, they are mainly assigned marital, romantic, or family roles. When women on television are employed, the range of jobs is quite limited. (The most common jobs are secretary and nurse.) As with recognition, these basic facts are well-documented and have hardly changed over the past 20 years (Busby, 1974; DeFleur, 1964; Gerbner, 1972; Gerbner et al., 1986; Long & Simon, 1974; Seggar, 1975; Signorielli, 1982; Tedesco, 1974; U.S. Commission on Civil Rights, 1977, 1979).

The personalities of TV women are passive, deferential, governed by emotion, and generally weak. Men, in contrast, tend to be active, dominant, governed by reason, and generally powerful. Again, the pattern is consistent and reliable (Barcus, 1983; Donagher, Poulos, Liebert, & Davidson, 1975; Downs & Gowan, 1980; Greenberg, Richards, & Henderson, 1980; Lemon, 1977; Levinson, 1975; Signorielli, 1982, 1986; Sternglanz & Serbin, 1974).

The pattern seen in television programming is also paralleled by the presentation of women in commercials. A review of four studies on sex role portrayals on TV commercials (Courtney & Whipple, 1974) reported the consistent finding that "women are not portrayed as autonomous, independent human beings, but are primarily sex-typed" (p. 117). Analyses of commercials in subsequent years yielded similar findings (Marecek et al., 1978; O'Donnell & O'Donnell, 1978). The most recent review of research on sex stereotyping in advertising (Courtney & Whipple, 1983) concluded that TV ads still portray a woman's place as in the home where she can serve her family and defer to male authority.

And finally, ads directed specifically toward children also show the pattern. There are about twice as many male as female characters in children's ads, and the males are almost invariably the ones with the dominant, forceful, active roles (Barcus, 1971, 1977; Doolittle & Pepper, 1975; Macklin & Kolbe, 1984; Welch, Huston-Stein, Wright, & Plehal, 1979).

Even when ads are for products that seem neutral with regard to gender, elementary school children can tell whether an ad is supposed to be for boys or girls depending upon the music, action, and camera work that it uses (Huston, Greer, Wright, Welch, & Ross, 1984). So, sex-stereotyped elements pervade every aspect of children's commercials, not just the occupations or personalities of the actors.

Stereotyping of the Elderly

Persons over the age of 65 now comprise almost 15% of the population and the percentage is expected to rise over the next decade. Measured against this criterion, the elderly are markedly under-represented on television. Content analyses have consistently shown that elderly persons occupy no more than between 1.5% and 3% of all roles (Gerbner, Gross, Signorielli, & Morgan, 1980a; Greenberg, Korzenny, & Atkin, 1979; Northcott, 1975). Television is also selective in the type of programming in which the elderly appear. They are almost twice as likely to appear on talk shows or comedies as in dramatic presentations (Harris & Feinberg, 1977).

We mentioned previously that television has always under-represented women, and this is no less true of elderly women than of younger ones. Holtzman and Akiyama (1985) found that in prime-time shows preferred by children, elderly men outnumber elderly women by more than two to one. (In fact, because men tend to die younger than women, elderly women substantially outnumber elderly men in the real world.)

In terms of respect, the elderly are most often portrayed as unhappy (Aronoff, 1974; Gerbner et al., 1980a) and are rarely portrayed in romantic situations (Harris & Feinberg, 1977). The comments made by other characters about the elderly are also revealing. Bishop and Krause (1984), examining comments about the elderly on children's Saturday morning programs, found that over 90% of the statements made about the elderly by other characters were negative. Northcott (1975) found a similar trend in prime-time programs. He also noted that the elderly in these programs typically had problems that they could not solve for themselves but that were solved for them by younger adults. Thus the elderly may be considered one more minority group that is given short shrift by entertainment television.

Effects of Stereotyped Portrayals

In the mid-1970s, research reports started to appear that examined the impact of televisions's sex role and race stereotypes on child viewers.

Children's acceptance of televised stereotypic sex role portrayals was explored in a correlational study by Frueh and McGhee (1975), who reasoned that if children accept TV's sex role messages, frequent TV viewers should have more stereotypic beliefs (such as girls should play with dolls, dishes, and dresses and boys should play with trucks, guns, and tools) than infrequent TV viewers. They found that for both boys and girls in kindergarten, second, fourth, and sixth grades, frequent viewers were far more likely than infrequent viewers to identify with the sex stereotyped roles associated with their own gender. Similarly, Beuf (1974) found that 3- to 6-year-old children who were heavy TV viewers made more sex-typed occupational choices than light viewers.

An experimental study by Tan (1979) found that adolescent girls exposed to a heavy dose of beauty commercials were more likely than a control group of girls not exposed to the commercials to believe that being beautiful is an important characteristic and is necessary to attract men. Twenty-three high school girls (16–18 years of age) viewed 15 commercials that emphasized the desirability of sex appeal, beauty, or youth (e.g., ads for toothpaste or soap), and 33 girls viewed commercials that did not contain beauty messages (e.g., ads for dog food, soy sauce, or diapers). They were then asked to rank order the relative importance of 10 attributes (e.g., pretty face, intelligence, sex appeal, hard-working, youthful appearance, competence) in each of four areas (career/job, wife, to be liked by men, and desirable personal attribute). The beauty ad group ranked the importance of the sex-appeal qualities higher than the neutral group for both "to be liked by men" and "to be personally desirable."

Morgan (1982) measured the viewing habits and acceptance of sex role stereotypes of 349 6th through 10th graders across 2 years, using a time-lagged panel design. Simple correlations showed a connection between TV viewing levels at 1 year and belief in sex role stereotypes the next year for both sexes, but when IQ and social class were partialed out,* it appeared that TV had a significant effect only on girls with relatively high IQs or who were from economically advantaged backgrounds. (See Figure 9.1.) Morgan explains these results in terms of Gerbner's theory of "mainstreaming."

The idea is that television depicts the most commonly held cultural stereotypes or "mainstream views." Those who are already likely to hold the mainstream view will not be influenced much by television. For them, TV shows are just repeating "what they already know" about people. On the other hand, individuals who would not otherwise hold the mainstream view but watch a lot of television will be influenced over time, in the direction of moving toward the mainstream.

Morgan demonstrates from other data that most boys, and most lower IQ and poorer girls, are immersed in the mainstream, stereotypic view of females by parents and peers. Thus they will probably hold a sex-stereotyped view regardless of how much or how little TV they watched.

---

*That is, removed statistically. See our earlier discussion of this technique on p. 94.

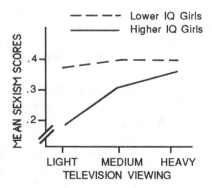

Figure 9.1 Illustration of mainstreaming: Sexism scores for higher and lower IQ girls as a function of amount of TV viewing. Based on data reported in "Television and Adolescents' Sex Role Stereotypes: A Longitudinal Study" by M. Morgan, 1982, *Journal of Personality and Social Psychology, 43*(5), 947-955.

But brighter girls or those from advantaged homes are likely to receive a somewhat less stereotyped (and less mainstream) view from their mothers and other women. As a result, they will have less stereotyped views themselves *unless they receive a large dose of television stereotypes.* This appears to be exactly what happened in Morgan's study.

Finally, Kimball (1986) used data from the Canadian "natural experiment" mentioned previously (see p. 153) to examine the impact of television on sex-role attitudes. Before the arrival of television in Notel, children there held less strongly sex-typed attitudes than did children in the towns that received TV. But the children in Notel showed a sharp increase in sex-role stereotyping following the introduction of TV in their town. The effect on girls was particularly noticeable in the area of interpersonal relationships, whereas boys were most affected in the area of their perceptions of what constituted appropriate employment for the two sexes.

In contrast to the fairly numerous studies dealing with sex stereotypes, we know of only one study that directly examined the effects of race stereotypes on children's attitudes. Graves (1975) selected eight previously broadcast cartoons that varied in the portrayal of blacks (positive or negative). The positive portrayals showed blacks as competent, trustworthy, and hard-working. The negative portrayals showed them as inept, destructive, lazy, and powerless. Graves found that there was a positive attitude change for the black children who saw either portrayal and for the white children who saw a positive portrayal. However, white children exposed to a negative portrayal changed the most and in a negative direction. Overall, these results suggest that while the mere presence of black TV characters may have a positive impact on black children, the type of characterization of blacks is critical in terms of the potential negative impact on white children. Graves' findings are particularly striking because the attitude changes occurred after only a *single* program exposure.

WOMEN AND MINORITIES IN THE TELEVISION INDUSTRY

Equal employment opportunity for women was a major goal of the feminist movement in the late 1960s, as it was for blacks and other minorities in the civil rights movement. These movements were effective in applying pressure on the television industry, which heretofore had been quite biased in its employment practices. (A characteristic, we should note, that it shared with academia and many other industries.)

Partly as a result of the pressures we have mentioned, the FCC in 1969 adopted a nondiscrimination rule prohibiting discrimination in employment by broadcast licensees on the basis of race, color, religion, or national origin. Partly in response to pressures from the National Organization for Women, in 1971 the FCC included women in its nondiscriminatory ruling, stating "It is fully appropriate, in our judgment, for the attention of broadcasters to be drawn to the task of providing equal employment opportunity for women as well as for Negroes, Orientals, American Indians, and Spanish Surnamed Americans" (FCC, 1971, p. 709). The FCC ruling required broadcast licensees with five or more full-time employees to furnish equal employment opportunity statistics with their license renewal application.

As part of its 1977 and 1979 reports, the U.S. Commission on Civil Rights conducted a study of the employment status of women and minorities in 40 television stations in major markets throughout the nation, including the 15 network owned and operated stations, 15 network affiliates, and 10 public stations. The Commission on Civil Rights wanted to determine the effectiveness of the FCC equal employment opportunity ruling. It found that the minority and female employment at the 40 stations increased between 1971 and 1975, and that the increases occurred in the upper job categories. However, the job categories were designated such that 75% of all employees were in upper level jobs. Many females and minorities were given impressive titles and salaries, but their positions in the organizational structure were relatively low, suggesting that the stations were artificially creating the impression of an equal employment situation. The most significant finding was that females and minority members were almost absent from the decision-making positions, which were the domain of white males. In the

1979 update (representing 1977 statistics), the commission did not find significant increases in the proportion of minorities and females employed as managers and officials.

The United Church of Christ's Office of Communication provided the funding for an update of television hiring practices between 1980 and 1985 (Wachtel, 1986). Based on employment statistics filed with the FCC, Wachtel examined the percentage of minorities and women in the top four categories of employment (officials and managers, professionals, technicians, and sales workers). Table 9.1 presents the figures every 5 years from 1975 along with the national workplace proportions. The report points out that the increasing proportion of females employed in these positions was due to *white* women; between 1980 and 1985 the increase in employment was less than 1% for minority women. Figure 9.2 shows the employment distribution of officials and managers by race and sex. The report concludes (Wachtel, 1986):

> The trends of the current decade are anything but hopeful. Women have continued to make inroads, but the pace of change has slackened. Minority representation in television has actually decreased from 1980 to 1985.... The philosophy of deregulation has been especially damaging to minorities as it relates to EEO policy and enforcement. (pp. 21–22)

Table 9.1 National Commercial Stations' Employment of Minorities and Women in Top Four Categories (and National Workforce Proportion)

YEAR	PERCENTAGE IN TOP FOUR CATEGORIES	
	MINORITIES	WOMEN
1975	10.0 (—)	13.0 (40.0)
1980	13.7 (17.8)	21.5 (42.5)
1985	15.2 (19.9)	26.7 (44.2)

Note: Based on data reported in *Television Hiring Practices 1980–1985: A Report on the Status of Minorities and Women* by E. Wachtel, 1986, New York: United Church of Christ.

SEX AND SEXUALITY

Human sexuality is a highly charged topic. Obscenity, one type of speech *not* protected by the First Amendment (see chapter 3), has been taken by the courts to refer to sexual material. (Occasionally, critics of TV violence have labeled such material "obscene," but the courts generally take obscene to imply a sexual component.)

How and to what extent is human sexuality displayed on TV, and what effects do these portrayals have? These are the questions with which we will be concerned in this section.

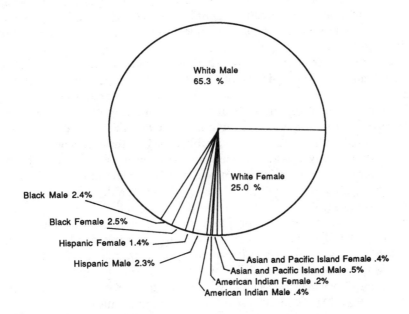

Figure 9.2 Distribution of officials and managers by race and sex, 1985. Based on data reported in *"Television Hiring Practices 1980–1985: A Report on the Status of Minorities and Women* **by E. Wachtel, 1986, New York: United Church of Christ.**

Sex on TV

Only in recent years has the issue of real sex warranted attention in a book about television. Aside from stereotypic sex-role portrayals, there wasn't much sexual content on TV. Throughout early TV history, the standards and practices departments in the broadcasting industry perpetuated and maintained a very puritanical TV world in which use of words such as *pregnant* were taboo, and all married couples apparently slept in separate beds. By the late 1960s and early 1970s, when public criticism was firmly centered on the issue of televised violence, network censors and TV producers were already engaged in behind-the-scenes battles over the limits of sexual reference (Cowan, 1978). The resulting gradual and progressive relaxation of strictly held taboos passed with little reaction from the general public until 1977 when "Soap," a sex-oriented prime-time situation comedy was aired.

"Soap" and the censors

The case of "Soap" illustrates the depth of feeling that was held a mere decade ago about the possibility of making specific reference to sex on broadcast television. It is also one more instance in which would-be censors have failed to control the medium. Despite the hew and cry, "Soap" paved the way for the not inconsiderable amount of sexual content that we find on television today.

Even before its airing, the promotional releases for "Soap" were sufficient to incite demonstrations, a deluge of complaint letters, and the withdrawal of some advertising support largely due to anti-"Soap" campaigns launched by the National Council of Churches and other religious groups (*"If the eye,"* 1977). Several of ABC's affiliates did not air the premiere episode of "Soap" and many aired it an hour later (presumably to reduce the child audience).

Although by today's standards the sexual content in "Soap" would hardly raise an eyebrow, when the program premiered on television in 1977, so too did several sexual themes. "Soap" featured two middle-aged sisters who lived in a suburban Connecticut town with their families. Some of the more controversial aspects of the program included conversations about an impotent husband, a homosexual son who was interested in a sex-change operation, a sexually promiscuous daughter, and extramarital affairs.

In fact, the appearance of "Soap" in 1977 was just the tip of an iceberg. Sprafkin and Silverman (1981) analyzed prime-time television for its sexual content in 1975, 1977, and 1978 and found that an astonishing revolution in television's sexual mores had occurred in a period of just 4 years. The frequency of kissing and hugging had increased substantially, and the frequency of sexually suggestive remarks had soared, showing almost a ten-fold increase. Table 9.2 illustrates the type of innuendo that could be heard on TV at that time and Figure 9.3 shows the increase detected by Sprafkin and Silverman.

Would-be censors soon realized that "Soap" was not the only sexy series. Soon TV was being closely scrutinized for sexual content by religious-based organizations and public interest groups. One of them, the National Federation for Decency (NFD), counted and published the number of sexual references on individual prime-time TV series along with the names and addresses of the "top sponsors of sex on television." The NFD report called for action:

> When you purchase products from a company which advertises on programs which exploit sex and make it a commercial product, you help promote such shows. Make your purchases in the marketplace in keeping with your convictions concerning sex on television. (National Federation for Decency, 1977, p. 1).

Table 9.2 Examples of Televised Sexual Innuendos

1. An attractive woman asks her boss to change his mind about something. He responds, "Once I make a decision, it takes a lot to get me to change it...and you certainly have a lot," as he leers at her ample chest.
2. A marriage counselor asks a couple "How's your love life," to which the husband replies, "I do my duty." The counselor remarks, "You must not think of it as a duty." The wife exclaims, "Don't tell him that. It's the only edge I've got."
3. Two single women caught up in a robbery scene discuss what they will miss out on if they get killed. One remarks, "Once in our lives we should have 'fo-do-de-do-doed'.... if we die now we saved it for nothing!"

Note. Courtesy of Silverman and Sprafkin.

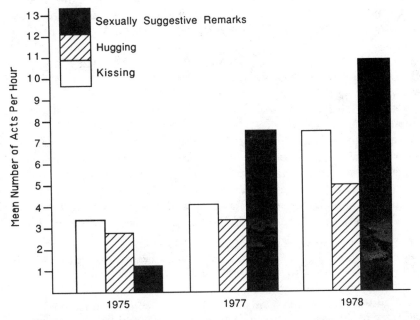

Figure 9.3 Mean number of physically intimate or suggestive behaviors per hour for three prime-time seasons. Based on data reported in "Update: Physically Intimate and Sexual Behavior on Prime-Time Television: 1978–79" by J. N. Sprafkin and L. T. Silverman, 1981, *Journal of Communication, 31*(1), 34–40.

The NFD based its findings on its own monitoring study of 15 weeks of prime-time programming. The report found 2.81 references to sex per hour of prime-time viewing, which meant, "At that rate, over a period of one year viewers would be exposed to 9,230 scenes of suggested sexual intercourse or sexually suggestive comments" (p. 2). It was also pointed out that "89% of all sex shown on prime-time television is presented outside marriage" (p. 2).

The NFD used its own findings to exert direct pressure on TV's "sex sponsors" (p. 3). In mid-1978, the NFD picketed the Sears Tower in Chicago and Sears-Roebuck stores in 34 cities to protest Sears' sponsorship of "Three's Company" and "Charlie's Angels," two programs rated as highly sexual by the NFD. Sears then withdrew its sponsorship from these shows. Other "sex sponsors" received similar treatment. However, the networks' response was to reply that their programs were "responsible popular entertainment" and to criticize the pressure/censorship tactics of the religious groups ("Sex on television", 1978). There is very little boycotting today.

Next, the print media chimed in. A spate of newspaper and magazine articles appeared in the late 1970s concerning TV's apparent obsession with sex, with headlines such as "TV is Getting Tough on Violence and Loose with Sex" (*New York Times*, September 11, 1977), "TV Tunes in Sex as Crime Fades" (*New York Times*, March 20, 1978), "The Jiggly Effect Takes Off" (*Newsday*, April 23, 1978), and "The Year TV Turned to Sex" (*TV Guide*, May 6, 1978). Perhaps most visible was *Newsweek's* February 20, 1978 feature story, "Sex and TV," which showed scantily clad Suzanne Somers on the cover.

Many of the articles were tinged with criticism about TV's new emphasis on sex. While most network officials denied it, a CBS censor admitted to a *Newsweek* reporter: "With the mix of programming today, sexuality has taken the place of violence" ("Sex and TV," 1978, p. 54).

Criticism came from public officials as well. Margita White, a member of the FCC, wrote a harsh editorial in the *New York Times* (White, 1978):

> The name of the network ratings game for the coming seasons is *sex*. There is every indication that the networks, in shifting from violent themes, will be falling all over each other to see which can expose most often the most of the female anatomy....

> I'm not sure whether I'm more outraged because the medium has missed the message of the antiviolence campaign, or more offended because women are to be battered through a new low in sexploitation. But I do know that the networks will be hearing a new chorus of "I'm mad as hell and I won't take it any more".

Current sexual content and practices

What about sex on TV in the 1980s? Recent studies (e.g., Greenberg et al., 1986) present a consistent picture.

First of all, TV is bolder about sex than it was just a few years ago. Comments about sex acts are now likely to be presented in a serious context rather than a humorous one. There is also a marked increase in the number of sex acts presented visually. (The shows of the 1970s that caused such a furor only talked about sex.) Men and women can now be seen in bed together. Moreover, these (presumably) copulating couples are typically not married to one another. According to the analysis of Greenberg and his associates, unmarried intercourse occurs five times as often as married intercourse on the prime-time series adolescents watch most often. Finally, there has also been a willingness, both verbally and visually, to present sex acts that would have been absolutely taboo just a few years ago, including homosexuality.

And, as a fit concomitant to this change in mores, there is now a new generation of critics of sex on TV, who are bringing a different message than did the failed "decency" campaigns of the 1970s. For example, Planned Parenthood recently launched a major newspaper and magazine ad campaign to pressure the networks to permit programs and advertising to discuss birth control. Using sexually suggestive illustrations to catch the eye, their ads questioned, "They did it 20,000 times on television last year. How come nobody got pregnant?" and "When JR took Mandy for a little roll in the hay, which one had the condom?"*

Nonbroadcast sources of sex on TV

With the emergence of cable channels and VCR rentals (see chapter 2), the opportunities for children and adolescents to be exposed to "R-" and "X-" rated programs has increased substantially. Particularly relevant, because its viewership is largely teenagers, is the cable station Music Television (MTV), which airs video clips of recording artists performing their current popular music hits. Critics charge that MTV is replete with sexual (and violent) content. A content analysis of a random sample of 1984 MTV videos (Baxter, De Riemer, Landini, Leslie, & Singletary, 1985) revealed that 59.7% of the videos portrayed sexual feelings or impulses, 31% presented provocative clothing, 27% showed dance movements of a sexually suggestive nature, and 21% showed nondance movements of a sexually suggestive nature. Less frequent, but undeniably present, were the more discouraged sexual activities; sadomasochism appeared in 5% of the videos and sexual bondage in 2%.

Effects of TV Sex

Although sex on prime-time TV is tolerated or approved of by most adults, they nonetheless do *not* approve of having children exposed to such material. For this reason, we have no studies that directly explore children's perceptions of TV sex or any direct measures of its effects on them. For adults and adolescents, a bit more is known. There have been several studies that give us a look at TV sex from their point of view.

---

*In response to the AIDS epidemic, some stations have broadcast public service messages urging the use of condoms to prevent AIDS.

Adult perceptions

Sprafkin, Silverman, and Rubinstein (1980) asked several hundred adults to watch a sample of 15 prime-time shows and indicate the degree to which they thought the sexual content was suitable for an adult, a teen, and a child audience. The respondents also answered a variety of questions concerning programming policy issues, the degree to which TV sex is a problem, the perceived impact of TV sex on children, and how suitably they thought TV had presented 13 specified sexual themes for the three age groups.

Overall, 63% of the respondents thought there was too much sex on TV. To varying degrees the adults read sexuality into many of the programs they were shown. For example, the respondents "saw" sexual intercourse when the scenes contained not intercourse, but affectionate touching, suggestive behavior, and kissing. Programs containing frequent displays of kissing, affectionate touching, suggestiveness, and references to prostitution or other "atypical" sexual behaviors were considered unsuitable. As might be expected, the suitability ratings became increasingly conservative as the considered audience went from adult, to teen, to child. In the general evaluations of TV's past presentations of 13 sexual themes, children were considered to be an inappropriate audience for most of the topics. Many of the respondents thought programs dealing with rape, prostitution, extramarital sex, striptease, and child molesting were unsuitable for teenagers. By contrast, the majority of respondents deemed all 13 themes suitable for an adult audience. (See Table 9.3.)

Table 9.3 Percentage of Adults Judging TV's Presentations of Various Sexual Topics to be Unsuitable for Three Audiences.

TOPIC	AVERAGE ADULT	AVERAGE TEEN	AVERAGE CHILD
Childbirth	6	12	32
Birth control	6	15	44
Abortion	13	27	58
Necking or petting	6	20	53
Premarital sex	16	39	69
Marital sex	8	21	43
Extramarital sex	17	41	69
Homosexuality	21	35	61
Prostitution	17	41	72
Striptease	19	46	65
Transsexualism	15	32	57
Rape	22	43	71
Child molesting	27	40	58

Note. From *Public Reactions to Sex on Television* (p.19) by J. N. Sprafkin, L. T. Silverman, and E. A. Rubinstein, 1979, New York: Brookdale International Institute. Reprinted by permission.

What did these adults think would be likely to happen if children were exposed to sexual themes on TV? Forty-eight percent felt the children would "ask questions about topics they were too young to understand", 41% said they would be "confused or upset", 41% said they would "use language that is unacceptable to the parents", and 35% said they would "tolerate behaviors or lifestyles in others that are unacceptable to the parents." However, 45% said the children would "initiate useful discussions with their parents", and 19% that they would "learn something positive." Consistent with these latter findings, 73% of the respondents indicated that at some time sexual content on TV had prompted a discussion in their household; of these, 51% reported that the ensuing discussion was a positive or useful experience.

Consistent with the beliefs of adults in general, many parents believe that television plays a significant role in the development of their children's attitudes and values toward sexuality. Roberts, Kline, and Gagnon (1978) reported that in a sample of 1,400 parents of 3-to 11-year-old children, 50% stated that they thought their child learned most about sexuality from television. Most parents reported that their children learned more about sexuality from television than from siblings, peers, older children, adults, school, books, magazines, or movies.

Effects on adolescents
There is evidence from a number of studies bearing on the effects of TV sex on adolescents. We know, for example, that by early adolescence most youngsters can comprehend much of the sexual talk and innuendo on prime-time television, and by mid-adolescence they understand almost all of it (Silverman-Watkins & Sprafkin, 1983).

TV sex also seems to have definite cultivation effects on youthful viewers. Baran (1976) asked whether television's glorification of sexual activity related to adolescents' disappointments with regard to sex. He found that those high school students who attributed greatest realism to televised sexual portrayals were least satisfied with their own sexual practices, regardless of whether they were virgins or already had coital experience. Buerkel-Rothfuss and Mayes (1981) found that youthful soap opera viewers estimated that divorce and abortion were significantly more common occurrences in the real world than did nonviewers.

Another way to proceed is to ask youngsters themselves how much about sex they have learned from TV. Though such a study would probably not be condoned with child subjects, Louis Harris and Associates (1986) were able to survey 1,000 adolescents and ask what they thought about TV's implicit sex lessons. These teenagers ranked entertainment TV as fourth (after friends, parents, and courses at school) as a source of sex information. About half believed that television dealt with such topics as pregnancy, the personal consequences of sex, the likelihood of contracting a sexually transmitted disease, and so on, in a realistic manner. These results lend urgency to Planned Parenthood's concern that teenagers may be the victims of serious sex *mis*information as a result of their taking the implicit facts of life as seen on television as true or accurate.

PORNOGRAPHY

So far our discussion has focused on entertainment content with a relatively modest sexual component. But, with the advent of cable and the availability of rental movies in a VCR format, many children and youth now have ready access to material that is provocative and explicit in its sexual content. As with other topics we have considered, we find social science research and government inquiries complementing one another in an effort to find and articulate the truth.

Government Inquiries

There have been two major government inquiries into the effects of pornography. They were active at different times in the nation's history and staffed with people representing almost opposite ends of the policital spectrum. Perhaps it is not surprising that they reached quite different conclusions.

National Commission on Obscenity and Pornography
Established in 1967 by Congress in response to widespread complaints by people who objected to receiving unsolicited pornography in the mail, the mission of the National Commission on Obscenity and Pornography was to analyze (a) pornography control laws, (b) the extent of pornography distribution, and (c) the effects of pornography on the public, particularly on minors and in relationship to crime and other antisocial behavior and to recommend appropriate legislative and/or administrative action.

Of the 18 members appointed to the commission by President Lyndon Johnson, there were three attorneys, three clergymen, two psychiatrists, two sociologists, a librarian, two teachers, a book publisher, a magazine and book distributor, a judge, a state's attorney general, and a TV network research director. These individuals continued in their full-time jobs while serving on the commission, meeting intermittently for 1 or 2 days at a time over a 2-year period. Support staff was hired to do tasks such as contracting for research and writing report summaries.

The "Effects" Panel, which was composed of five members, reviewed and evaluated existing research relevant to the effects of exposure to sexual stimuli and designed a program of new research in the area. The research procedures included surveys, quasi-experimental and experimental studies, and studies of national statistics of rates and incidence of sex offenses. Based on surveys and experiments with adults, the panel asserted that established patterns of sexual behavior are very stable and are not significantly modified by exposure to sexually explicit stimuli.

The commission concluded (Commission on Obscenity and Pornography; 1970):

> The Commission believes that there is no warrant for continued governmental interference with the full freedom of adults to read, obtain or view whatever such material they wish. Extensive empirical investigation, both by the Commission and by others, provides no evidence that exposure to or use of explicit sexual materials play a significant role in the causation of social or individual harms such as crime, delinquency, sexual or nonsexual deviancy or severe emotional disturbances. (p. 58)

There were many critics of the commission's report. Victor Cline (1974b) carefully reviewed the research data upon which the commission report was based and concluded that the interpretations were biased in the direction of protecting freedom of speech. Cline points out inaccuracies in the commission's report of the research, unwarranted conclusions, lack of discrimination between poor and good studies, and failure to report findings indicating a significant relationship between exposure to pornography and either sexual deviance or affiliation with criminal groups. For example, in the Tannenbaum (1971) study referred to earlier, it was found that an erotic film produced more aggressive responses in male subjects than an aggressive film and that exposure to both films elicited an even higher level of aggressive responding. Although this study was *financed* by the commission, these results were never mentioned in the report.

The report of the Pornography Commission was rejected by President Nixon and the U.S. Senate. At the root of the rejection was one of the commission's recommendations that all existing laws restraining access to explicit sex materials by consenting adults be repealed. (The commission also recommended stronger legal prohibition against distribution of such materials to minors.)

The Meese Commission on Pornography

In May 1985, U.S. Attorney General Edwin Meese appointed a new commission to examine issues of obscenity and pornography. The Attorney General's Commission on Pornography was composed of 11 members (two attorneys, three university professors, a judge, a former city mayor, a radio program producer, a magazine editor, and two child care advocates) and was provided a very modest budget. Instead of conducting research, the commission relied on past studies and testimonies from victims and law enforcement officials. In contrast to the conclusions of the 1967 commission, the Meese Commission concluded that there is a causal link between exposure to violent pornography and aggressive behavior toward women. But the commission felt that the evidence was not persuasive regarding a link between exposure to nonviolent and nondegrading sexually explicit material and acts of sexual violence. Nevertheless, the commission's recommendations applied to *all* pornography (defined as "sexually explicit and intended primarily for the purpose of sexual arousal"), calling for action by the FCC (to restrict pornographic cable television shows) and the public (to pressure law enforcement agents, monitor the media, etc.). Another controversial aspect of the report resulted in a dissenting statement by two commission members. In the absence of direct scientific evidence, the report stated that exposure to aggressive pornography would result in increases in *sexual* violence. Unlike the liberal sexual attitudes evident in the earlier commission's report, the new report is clearly conservative.

The Meese report mirrors the sexual morality of the Reagan era just as the earlier report reflected the sexual liberalism of the 1960s. A 1986 poll ("Sex busters", 1986) showed that the Meese commission accurately reflected the sexual tenor of the times. It was believed that exposure to sexually explicit movies, magazines, and books, lead people to commit acts of sexual violence (54%) and rape (56%), lead people to be more sexually promiscuous (65%), and encourage people to consider women as sex objects (61%).

Research Evidence

Although there has been no research conducted on the effects of televised sexual content on children or adolescents (due to the obvious moral constraints on such research), there has been a considerable amount of research on the impact of pornography and sexual aggression on young adults (i.e., college students).

Edward Donnerstein (1984) and his colleagues have conducted the most systematic program of research to elucidate the factors that influence the impact of pornography on aggression. Most of the studies utilize a similar design. Subjects, who are generally undergraduate men, are first angered or treated in a neutral manner by a male or female accomplice. Then the subjects are shown one of several films that vary according to sexual and aggressive content. Following exposure, subjects are given the opportunity to aggress against the accomplice with the Buss "aggression machine" described in chapter 4. Using this basic paradigm, it has been found that:

1. Aggressive pornography against female targets definitely *can* increase the willingness of a male subject to aggress against a female target. However, the response of the victim in the pornographic story and whether the potential aggressor has recently been angered combine to determine whether he *will* actually become more aggressive.

2. The film victim's reactions to aggressive sex determines the film's impact on subsequent aggression to a female victim; for nonangered subjects, only a positive victim reaction produces more aggression, whereas angered subjects become more aggressive after either positive or negative victim reactions.
3. Anger instigation is not a necessary component, but it heightens the level of aggression following exposure to aggressive pornography.
4. Aggression against male targets is not affected by exposure to aggressive pornography in which a woman is the victim.
5. There is little evidence that *non*aggressive pornography influences aggressive behavior, unless inhibitions to aggress are diminished.
6. Films presenting nonsexual aggression against women can instigate aggression toward a female target, but the effect is heightened by juxtaposing sex and aggression.

Although nonaggressive pornography does not appear to increase the willingness to aggress against women, it does cultivate undesirable attitudes toward them. Zillmann and Bryant (1982) did an experiment with under-graduate students involving exposure to *non*aggressive pornographic films. Some students watched 36 such films, others watched 18, and still others watched none over a period of 6 weeks. The major finding was that heavy exposure to this kind of pornography produced a "trivialization of rape" in the minds of both male and female viewers. This trivialization was manifested in the heavy viewer's willingness to have significantly shorter prison terms for rape than those who had watched less pornography or none of it. The massive exposure also led to an increase in sexual callousness toward women by men. This was reflected in agreement to such questionnaire items as, "Pickups should expect to put out", and "A woman doesn't mean 'no' unless she slaps you". Therefore, far from being innocuous, frequent exposure to nonaggressive pornography appears to cultivate extremely negative attitudes toward women.

10
Harnessing Television's Potential

OVERVIEW

Interest in harnessing TV's potential to benefit children and society can be traced to the earliest days of the medium. Crude educational television in the 1950s was transformed by the Corporation for Public Broadcasting (CPB) and other sophisticated organizations into a network of public television stations broadcasting "quality" television for a wide audience as well as specialized programs for children. "Sesame Street", which is exemplary of such programs, has been shown to have some instructional value, but probably has its greatest influence on advantaged children, who are the ones most likely to watch.

Research aimed at increasing TV's effectiveness and decreasing possible adverse effects has shown that young children have great difficulty in following the plot lines and implicit messages of ordinary television and thus may fail to comprehend intended messages and/or derive unintended ones. Action appears to be the prime ingredient for capturing and holding young children's attention but, ironically, high action programs may heighten aggressiveness even when they contain no violent content. Special curricula designed to teach children more about television and develop critical viewing skills appear to be quite successful.

The 1970s saw an unprecedented effort to use television as an active force in the socialization of children. Rooted in early laboratory experiments that showed that TV models could increase children's altruism and self-control, researchers looked for instances of prosocial behaviors in commercial programs and then demonstrated that exposure to shows "naturally rich" in such examples had discernible effects on child audiences. At the same time, social scientists and producers collaborated in making programs designed to have specific social effects on children's attitudes and behavior. Taken together, these efforts suggest that no one program is likely to have a lasting or dramatic influence. On the other hand, a very substantial effect would result from saturating entertainment television with models who repeatedly display cooperation, tolerance, and self-control. Whether such an effort would truly be prosocial or a chilling new form of brainwashing and what, if anything, we will do with TV's enormous potential power over the young have become the great unanswered questions.

OUTLINE

Our discussion so far has demonstrated that television is, indeed, a powerful force in the lives of our children. Virtually every child watches television for several hours every day. There are no vacations from television. It is watched *more* on the weekends and on holidays than on regular school days. It "works" in the sense of being a potent sales-promoting tool for advertisers. It is influential in shaping children's attitudes toward their gender and their sexuality. It can instigate aggression and cultivate the view that we live in a mean and scary world. Can it not also be used for good? The time has come to examine this question.

Efforts to harness television's potential fall into two distinct categories: those that have academic/educational objectives and those that have social objectives. Our discussion begins by treating educational and prosocial television separately. Later in the chapter, though, will will see that the intentional use of television to influence children raises a number of fundamental issues that transcend any specific objectives.

EDUCATIONAL TELEVISION

Since television was first put on public display, educators have been drawn to the idea that television could potentially serve as a teacher in every home, complementing the efforts of classroom teachers and supplementing school curricula. This section begins with a discussion of what happened to this dream over the past 40 years. We shall see that practical issues of technology, funding, and attracting a large child audience away from alternative programming in a competitive market have all limited the impact that educational television has actually had.

History of Educational/Public Television in the United States

From the earliest days of television, many people argued that the United States needed a public television network to air educational and cultural programs that might not be shown on commercial networks. Not surprisingly, initial attempts to designate some channels exclusively for educational programming were bitterly fought by commercial broadcasters and networks who claimed that all of television was their domain. The FCC compromised in 1952. It set aside a number of UHF channels for educational purposes. At that time very few TV sets had the capacity to receive UHF channels; most could only receive the VHF stations 2 through 13. So, the public had an outlet for educational television but the commercial interests didn't feel seriously threatened.

Progress was slow, but by 1959 there were 45 educational stations. All were low-key, tight budget operations. Some were community operated, others were operated by universities or local school systems. Almost 90% of the programs were adult education courses, some of which permitted viewers to obtain high school or college credit by watching lectures over television and then arranging to take examinations. An occasional, low-budget program for children was also included.

Supporters of educational television began an intense lobbying effort. They told congressional leaders that educational television was on a financial precipice and urged government to contribute money. As a result, in 1962 Congress passed legislation authorizing funds for the construction and equipping of educational television stations. In 1967 the Carnegie Commission on Educational Television called for the establishment of a public network in the United States, structured like Britain's BBC, but carrying only educational programming. The method of funding proposed by the commission was a trust fund established by putting a special tax on all new television receivers.* The commission called for a funding level of about $100 million a year.

The Congress agreed to fund public educational television, but rejected the television tax. Instead, it created the Corporation for Public Broadcasting (CPB) as a means of channeling federal tax money into public television. The CPB is an autonomous board of 15 members appointed by the President, on advice and consent of the Senate. The board elects its own chairperson annually. No more than eight members may belong to the same political party. Board members serve 6-year terms and the appointments are staggered so that every 2 years there is a turnover of five members.

Through the 1960s educational television had gradually evolved into a broader enterprise called *public television*. The transformation was completed in 1970, when CPB created a new network, the Public Broadcasting Service (PBS) to develop and manage national program services in the public interest. The offerings of PBS today are wide and varied (see Table 10.1) and almost every American family with a television has access to its programs.

The Audience for Educational/Public Television

In 1959, educational television had a *potential* audience of about 25 million viewers, but only about 2 million people watched even a single educational television program in a given week (Schramm, 1960). As the quality and quantity of available programming rose, so did the size of the audience. As seen in Figure 10.1, during 1974 PBS network programs were seen in over 33 million households. By 1984, this figure had almost doubled, to 63.8 million households. Put in slightly different terms, during the 1980s U.S. public television is attracting approximately 90 million viewers weekly, with each viewer watching an average of about $3\frac{1}{2}$ hours per week (Fuller, 1985).

---

*In Britain there is a yearly tax on *all* television sets.

Table 10.1 Percentage Distribution of Public Television Broadcast Hours by Type of
Program, Producer, and Distribution

	PERCENTAGE OF ALL BROADCAST HOURS
Type of Program	
Information/Skills	24.5
Cultural	22.8
Children's/Other	26.0
Instructional television	14.3
News/Public affairs	12.4
Producer	
Public television station	48.2
Children's Television Workshop & other independents	27.1
Foreign/Co-Production	10.1
Local	6.7
Other	7.9
Distributor	
PBS	67.1
Local	6.2
Regional network	10.8
Other	15.9

Note. Based on data reported in *Statistics in Brief* (p. 6) by Corporation for Public Broadcasting, 1985b, Washington, DC.

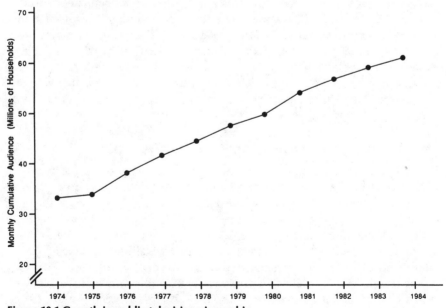

Figure 10.1 Growth in public television viewership.
Based on data reported in *Statistics in Brief* by Corporation for Public Broadcasting, 1985b, Washington, DC.

Despite the impressive sound to these statistics, today's PBS audience at any given moment remains miniscule by commercial network standards. On the average, the percentage of sets tuned to PBS during prime time is only 3%, whereas each of the major network's comparable ratings are between 15% and 25% (Fuller, 1985). Even the most watched PBS programs have attained less than a 20% rating. The highest rating ever for a PBS program went to the National Geographic program "The Sharks" in 1982, which was tuned in by 17.4% of U.S. TV households for at least 6 consecutive minutes.

Who is most likely to watch PBS shows? Consistently, PBS viewers tend to be those with higher incomes and more education (Corporation for Public Broadcasting, 1985a). This fact has profound importance, because it means that today's educational television is most likely to reach children who are from homes that are already advantaged in other ways.

Funding for Educational/Public Television

Historically, the single most important funding for PBS has been money channeled through the CPB from federal appropriations. Table 10.2 shows the level of CPB federal funding from 1969 to 1986. Note that funding levels increased steadily over the 1970s but, taking inflation into account, remained constant during the early 1980s and now seem to be dropping. The trend toward decreased federal funding for public television is likely to continue. In 1984, President Reagan vetoed a Public Broadcasting authorization bill that would have provided public television and radio with $238 million in 1987, $253 million in 1988, and $270 million in 1989.

Table 10.2 Federal Appropriations to the
Corporation for Public Broadcasting 1969–1986

YEAR	APPROPRIATION (MILLION DOLLARS)
1969	5.0
1970	15.0
1972	35.0
1974	47.7
1976	96.0
1978	119.2
1980	152.0
1982	172.0
1984	137.5
1986	159.5

Note. Based on data reported in *Summary of Corporation for Public Broadcasting Authorizations, Appropriations, and Public Broadcasting Income, Fiscal Years 1969–1990*, CPB Legislative Affairs Office, May 1986.

Although the federal government has provided a substantial share of public broadcasting funds, it is not the only source. State and local governments, individual memberships and subscriptions, business and industry, and philanthropic foundations all make significant contributions as well (Corporation for Public Broadcasting, 1985b). But these contributions, too, may be on the decline because the Reagan administration has also been reducing funds available to state and local public service and social/cultural agencies, and the 1986 Tax Reform Act has made it more difficult to use charitable contributions as tax deductions.

Programming for Educational Television

Funding is only a means to an end. In the matter of educational television, the end is to produce and broadcast quality programming that educates and entertains. So, our discussion now turns to programming for educational television.

"Sesame Street": Anatomy of a success

There can be no doubt that "Sesame Street" is the world's most famous and popular children's educational television program. It has been broadcast continuously in the United States for almost 20 years, which may make it the longest running television series of all time. It is broadcast by almost all of the PBS stations and the majority of these air the series year-round in both morning and afternoon, and many rerun shows on weekends. Recent audience statistics reveal that "Sesame Street" is viewed by almost half of all preschoolers on a weekly basis—that is, over 5.8 million children between the ages of 2 and 5 years view an average of three episodes per week. Internationally, it has been broadcast in English in more than 40 countries and there are at least eight foreign-language versions. Children in Mexico watch "Plaza Sésamo"; in Brazil, "Vila Sésamo"; in Germany, "Sesamstrasse"; and in France, "Bonjour Sesame."

"Sesame Street" is a production of the Children's Television Workshop (CTW). CTW was created in 1968, with funds from both public and private agencies. (The Carnegie Corporation, Ford Foundation, U.S. Office of Education, U.S. Office of Economic Opportunity, and the National Institute of Child Health and Human Development were all involved.) CTW's first mission, and the reason for its being brought into existence, was to produce and telecast a daily program that would both entertain young children and foster intellectual and cultural development (Ball & Bogatz, 1970).

Joan Ganz Cooney and Lloyd Morrisett, planners and parents of Children's Television Workshop and "Sesame Street," obtained $8 million in initial funding and 2 years in lead time. Cooney and Morrisett then brought in Harvard's prominent educational psychologist, Professor Gerald Lesser, to chair a top-notch, hard-working advisory panel. Dr. Edward Palmer was given a fully equipped lab in New York and a free hand to research and criticize production efforts, and regulars such as Jim Henson's muppets, Kermit the Frog, Big Bird, and the infamous Cookie Monster, were accompanied by guests of the stature of James Earl Jones and the popularity of Batman and Robin. At the business and technical level, a prestigious public relations firm was retained, and hard-headed executives were drawn in to criticize, counsel and sell "Sesame Street" even before the first show was produced. To satisfy the requirements of the Office of Education and various foundations who footed the bill, the Educational Testing Services (ETS) was commissioned to do evaluations of how well the program worked.

A series of planning seminars was held by experts in child development, preschool education, and television production. Out of these meetings came ideas for many of the basic instructional methods and ways of presenting materials. The planning phase went even further. Viewing preferences of youngsters were examined, and the attention-holding power of videotaped materials was assessed by playing them in competition with potential distractors. In 1969, "Sesame Street" was on the air, combining attention-holding tactics (e.g., fast movement, humor, slapstick, and animation) with a carefully planned educational curriculum designed to foster skills such as recognition of the letters of the alphabet, recognition of the numbers 1 through 10, simple counting ability, vocabulary, and the like.

A major question about a venture like "Sesame Street" was whether it succeeded as a teacher. Thus, during the first year of broadcast, the effects of "Sesame Street" were assessed in studies across five widely separated areas of the country. Children were assigned either to a control condition or a viewing condition, involving home or nursery school viewing. In the case of home viewers, parents were told about "Sesame Street," given publicity material about the program, and visited each week by members of the research team. The control subjects did not receive these treatments. In the school situation, the experimental classrooms received two television sets, while control classes did not. According to Ball and Bogatz (1970):

> It was generally understood that the teachers of the viewing classes would use the sets to have their pupils view "Sesame Street" but that the degree to which they did so, and the way "Sesame Street" was used in the classroom, was their prerogative (p. 19).

In both school and home samples, the experimental treatment lasted about 6 months. Altogether, about 950 children participated in all phases of the study.

Each child was both pretested and posttested. The tests were designed to measure the specific learning goals; thus, there were subtests on body parts, letters, numbers, forms, matching, relationships, sorting, and classification. An example is shown in Figure 10.2.

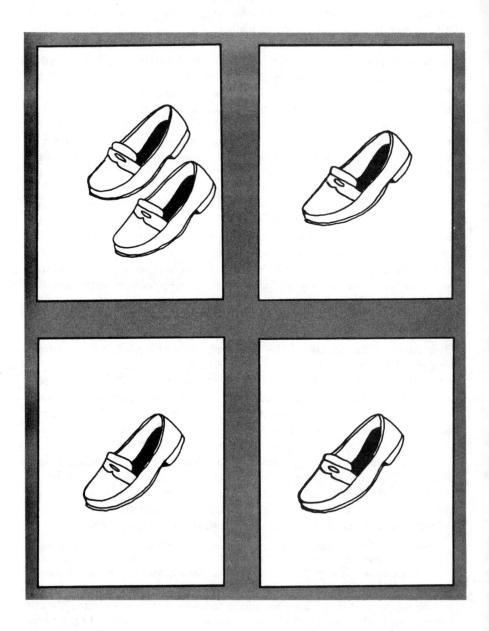

Figure 10.2 Sample item from the tests given to children to assess the effects of "Sesame Street."
From Ball and Bogatz (1970), courtesy of Children's Television Workshop.

Parents were also interviewed, both before and after the study, about their attitudes toward education, the child's viewing habits, and the "intellectual climate" in the home (e.g., how many books does the family own?).

Ball and Bogatz analyzed their data in several ways. Besides examining a total score and then separate subtest scores, they also looked at the whole sample and then subsets of children.

The original plan to compare viewers to nonviewers turned out to be infeasible because most of the subjects watched at least occasionally. Instead, the sample was divided into quartiles (a quartile contains 25% of the sample) on the basis of amount of viewing. Q_1 rarely watched "Sesame Street"; Q_2 watched two or three times a week; Q_3 about four or five times a week; and Q_4 more than five times. Because the different quartiles differed in original levels of proficiency on the pretest, the investigators decided to assess change scores, that is, the average differences between pretests and posttests. As Figure 10.3a indicates, the more that children watched the program, the more they tended to improve on the total score.

When the total score was broken down, it was clear that the effects of viewing held for all eight major subtests. The gains on some items were quite impressive; alphabet recitation, for example, on which the various groups were about equal at the beginning, had improved dramatically among children who watched "Sesame Street" regularly. (See Figure 10.3b.)

Of particular interest in considering the gains in specific subtests were scores on items and skills not directly taught on "Sesame Street." For example, "Sesame Street" apparently had some effect on reading skill and ability to write one's first name, both of which are important for school performance. (See Figure 10.3c.) For disadvantaged children, the six items in the reading subscale were significantly affected by amount of viewing despite the fact that reading words was not a "Sesame Street" goal, nor was it directly taught on the show.

A later investigation provided some additional information (Bogatz & Ball, 1972). By this time, "Sesame Street" itself had changed somewhat; for example, practice in sight-reading a 20-word vocabulary of common words and simple skills in Spanish had been introduced. Evaluation changed to incorporate these expanded goals, but the major focus of the tests was the same. Two other types of measures were also added: questions designed to examine attitudes toward race, school, and other people, and teacher rankings of school readiness at the beginning and end of the school year.

A new sample of children was selected in cities where "Sesame Street" had not been available the first year. This sample was restricted to urban disadvantaged children. The investigators also followed up 283 of the disadvantaged children studied during the first year. About half of these children had started in nursery school, kindergarten, or first grade.

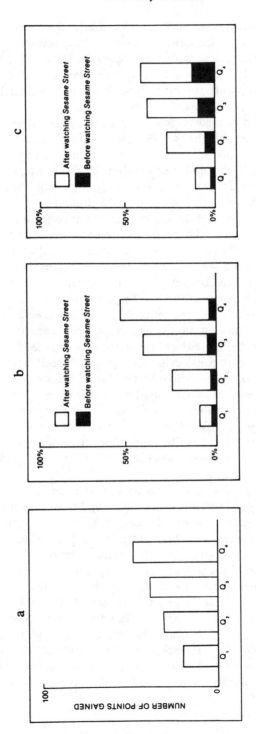

Figure 10.3 The relationship between amount of viewing of "Sesame Street" and children's abilities.
a. Improvement in total test scores for children grouped into different quartiles according to amount of viewing.
b. Percentage of children who recited the alphabet correctly, grouped according to quartiles of amount of viewing.
c. Percentage of children who wrote their first names correctly, grouped according to quartiles of amount of viewing.

From Ball and Bogatz, 1970, courtesy of Children' Workshop.

The results essentially replicated those of the first-year study—children who viewed "Sesame Street" improved more than children who did not. The follow-up study also revealed that heavy viewers were rated by teachers as better prepared for school than light viewers and adapted well to the school situation. The children who viewed frequently continued to outgain low viewers, particularly on the items introduced during the second year of the program. The show influenced other behaviors as well; viewers scored significantly higher on measures of attitudes toward school and toward people of other races.

"Sesame Street" revisited

Unfortunately, subsequent work casts some doubt as to whether "Sesame Street" was as effective as had been initially supposed. In the book *Sesame Street Revisited*, Thomas Cook and his associates (1975) claim that in reality rather slight (though statistically significant) increases were actually produced by "Sesame Street," and note that an equal amount of money spent in other ways might have greater educational impact on children. Even more critical, Cook and his associates suggest the possibility that broadcasting "Sesame Street" may widen rather than narrow the gap between the advantaged and the disadvantaged child. In the research conducted by ETS (described earlier) participating families were stimulated to watch "Sesame Street" by a variety of incentives provided by the experimenters. In naturally occurring situations with the absence of such incentives, it appears that children in advantaged families will be considerably more likely to watch "Sesame Street" than those in disadvantaged familes, and as a result any gap between the groups could be widened. This is both unfortunate and ironic because an apparent goal of "Sesame Street" was to narrow the gap. Joan Cooney had said in her original proposal that the general aim of "Sesame Street" was "to promote the intellectual and cultural growth of preschoolers, particularly disadvantaged preschoolers," and in her conclusion she referred to "the national demand that we give the disadvantaged a fair chance at the beginning."

"Electric Company"

In 1970, a team from the Children's Television Workshop began planning a program aimed specifically at reading skills. As with "Sesame Street," "Electric Company" grew out of a series of consultations with experts, this time in the area of reading. Prior to the first appearance of one of the shows, various reading curricula had been evaluated and experimental programs pretested (Fowles, 1971).

In the fall of 1971 the series began with a snappy format. Well-known personalities such as Bill Cosby frequented the show and heavy use was made of animation. The curriculum, directed primarily at second graders,

Figure 10.4 Learning to position adverbs. *"The Electric Company"* method.
Source: Courtesy of Children's Television Workshop.

involved what is termed sound-symbol analysis of the printed word. Children were taught the correspondence between letters (and combinations of letters) and sounds to enable them to decode words. Reading for meaning, using the context of the material, and syntax were also taught. (See Figure 10.4.)

The degree of "Electric Company's" success was evaluated using the same research design and researchers as that for "Sesame Street" (Ball & Bogatz, 1973). On a reading test battery designed specifically for the program by the Educational Testing Service, it was found that the first- through fourth-grade children who viewed "Electric Company" in school attained significantly higher scores than the nonviewers. However, the effect of home viewing seemed to be negligible. No significant effects were found, nor did the experimental group, which was encouraged to watch the program, watch significantly more than did the controls. Subsequent research has confirmed that, without direct teacher input and support, children gain little from watching "Electric Company" (Corder-Bolz, 1980).

In 1985, "Electric Company" went off the air after 14 years. In its final season, it reached about 11% of TV households on a cumulative monthly basis. Units of "Electric Company" programs are available to schools on videocassette for classroom use.

"3-2-1 Contact"

In 1977, the Children's Television Workshop began to explore the potential of television to motivate children's interest in science and technology. Funded by the National Science Foundation, Department of Education, United Technologies Corporation, Corporation for Public Broadcasting, and CTW, the series of 65 half-hour programs was broadcast beginning in January 1980. Like "Sesame Street" and "Electric Company," "3-2-1 Contact" was developed out of a collaboration between producers, formative researchers, and content experts. The series was geared toward 8- to 12-year-olds, and its goals were (a) "to help children experience the joy of scientific exploration," (b) "to help children become familiar with various styles of scientific thinking," and (c) "to help children, with a special appeal to girls and minorities, to recognize science and technology as open to their participation" (Children's Television Workshop, 1980). The series employs a magazine format featuring three young people, The Bloodhound Gang, who solve mysteries using scientific thinking. Animation and graphics are used to add to the appeal. There are almost 200 episodes produced to date on such diverse themes as oceans, tropics, space, water, measurement, electricity, flight, babies, senses, and communication. In its fifth broadcast season, "3-2-1 Contact" reached 4.6% of all US. TV households at least once on a weekly basis. The original series has been broadcast in 32 countries, and Germany, Spain, and France have produced their own versions in cooperation with CTW.

How effective is "3-2-1 Contact" in achieving its teaching objectives? A major study has just been completed, but the results have not yet been made public.

"Square One TV"

CTW's most recent production, "Square One TV," premiered in 1987 on close to 300 PBS stations with 75 half-hour shows. The series objectives are: "to promote a greater interest and enthusiasm for mathematics among the nation's 8- to 12-year-olds; to encourage children to use mathematics to solve problems they encounter every day; and to introduce important mathematical topics" (Children's Television Workshop, 1986). As with all other CTW projects, formative research was at the heart of the program development. More than 3,500 children and teachers throughout the country participated in the initial research to determine the most appropriate topics and format for the program and the appeal and effectiveness of early test programs. The results of the research helped the producers to shape the series, which ultimately employed a variety of television formats (for example, game show, music video, soap opera, detective drama) and covered many topics (for example, measurement, graphic representation, probability and statistics, and geometry). In the course of its first season, "Square One TV" reached 20 million households (approximately 23% of U.S. TV households) an average of five times. Summative research has yet to determine the series' effectiveness in attaining its stated goals.

RESEARCH AIMED AT INCREASING TV'S EFFECTIVENESS

Although programs designed to use television as a teacher appear to have some educational impact, they are plainly less effective than enthusiasts had initially hoped or anticipated. This fact has led researchers to ask how to increase TV's effectiveness. With this general aim in mind, three specific lines of research have been pursued.

Identifying Age Differences in Comprehension Abilities

A television program may fail to have the desired effect on children because they do not comprehend its messages. Comprehension is an active process requiring appropriate cognitive skills, familiarity with the codes and conventions of television, and the expenditure of effort (Salomon, 1976, 1979, 1983).

Much of the research on children's comprehension of television has been spearheaded by W. Andrew Collins, of the University of Minnesota (Collins, 1970, 1982, 1983; Collins, Wellman, Keniston, & Westby, 1978; Newcomb & Collins, 1979). Collins and his associates have documented that preschool children retain surprisingly little information about the plots of the stories they have seen on television. It is not until about age 11 or so that most children can really "follow" the typical prime-time show as an adult would. In addition, preschool and younger elementary school children have difficulty discriminating between plot-important (central) and plot-irrelevant (peripheral) content. As children grow older, central content accounts for an increasing proportion of what they recall. For example, in one study Collins and his associates found that second and third graders remembered only about 65% of the central content, whereas eight graders were able to recall 90% or more of this material. There is also an age-related improvement in ability to correctly infer TV events and relationships that are only implied.

What are the behavioral implications of children's poor comprehension of television? One aspect of this question was addressed by Collins as an outgrowth of earlier modeling studies (see chapter 4). The earlier studies showed that observers of aggressive behavior are less likely to exhibit post-exposure aggression if the model's aggressive behavior is unjustified and punished. Collins reasoned that if young viewers have difficulty integrating program information, then the separation of information about motives, aggressive action, and negative consequences by commercial interruptions should further reduce their comprehension of the aggression-inhibiting content and hence increase the likelihood of postexposure aggression. In one study (Collins, 1973) he found that whereas 6th and 10th graders showed virtually no difference in aggressive responding under interrupted and non-interrupted conditions, third graders were significantly more likely to respond aggressively in the interrupted condition. A subsequent study from another laboratory (Hayes & Kelly, 1984) confirmed that young children have more difficulty than older ones in understanding programs in which there has been a temporal separation of critical plot elements.

There have been several attempts to improve children's comprehension of television through the addition of adult commentary during viewing. For example, Collins, Sobol, and Westby (1981) showed second graders an edited action/adventure program in groups of two or three children plus an adult. For half of the groups, the adult made nonchalant facilitating comments that explained the essential motives and inferences in each of three scenes. At the same points in the program, the adult in the other condition made neutral comments that merely described the action in the scene. The children who heard the facilitating comments performed sig-nificantly better than those in the neutral comments group on questions both directly and indirectly related to the implicit program content explained by the adult co-viewer. This difference in comprehension suggests that the effective component of the intervention was the explanation rather than the attention-directing aspect of the adult's comments. Similarly, Watkins, Calvert, Huston-Stein, and Wright (1980) found that children from preschool, kindergarten, and third and fourth grades recalled significantly more central content from a prosocial cartoon when an adult co-viewer explained the importance and temporal relationships of several scenes during the viewing. Thus adults can enhance children's comprehension and recall of television by providing a structure that aids in the encoding and storage of the important content.

Learning How to Attract and Hold Children's Attention

Educational television is plagued by the risk of a popularity problem. Whereas commercial television need only entertain, educational television must entertain *and* teach. So it comes as no surprise that most children prefer to watch commercial television most of the time. What, if anything, can be done to make a program with intentional lessons more appealing to children?

Formal features research

During the formative stages of "Sesame Street," CTW was very concerned about holding the attention of young viewers. The "Sesame Street" research team therefore showed children tentative program segments while flashing a series of attractive slides on a screen to the side of the television set as distractors. The children were watched to see how often and for how long they turned their attention away from the TV set and toward the slides. Segments were retained for broadcast, modified, or eliminated based on their ability to hold children's attention in this way (Lesser, 1974).

With the original "Sesame Street" method, researchers focused on evaluating segments that had already been created. A more general research strategy is to try to identify in advance of production the abstract qualities or *formal features* of television content that increase or decrease its attention-holding power. The ultimate practical aim of such research is to be able to use these basic attention-holding ingredients in creating new programs tailored for a variety of educational or social purposes.

Formal features research was pioneered by Daniel Anderson and Stephen Levin, of the University of Massachusetts at Amherst. In an extensive research project, Anderson and Levin (1976; Levin and Anderson, 1976) had preschool children, one to four years of age, view segments from a wide variety of educational and commercial children's shows. The most consistent finding was that *action* played a major role in holding children's attention. The segments getting the most attention involved characters that moved around frequently and quickly, coupled with a lot of fast camera work (such as zooming in and out rapidly). Children were least attentive to segments displaying still drawings or characters that were inactive. Auditory as well as visual action affected attention. The more closely watched segments tended to have one or more of the following: lively music, applause, laughing, rhyming, alliteration, and peculiar voices or sounds. Finally, the characters themselves mattered. Children were more likely to pay attention to segments when the characters were women or children than when they were men.

One additional observation by Anderson and his colleagues (Anderson, 1977, 1985; Anderson, Alwitt, Lorch, & Levin, 1979) is of interest. These researchers have reported that preschool children typically display a pattern called *attentional inertia*. That is, the longer a young child has been looking at the screen, the longer he or she will continue to look; conversely, the longer the child has been sitting in front of the television but ignoring the screen, the less likely the child is to start looking.

Anderson and Levin's finding about the attention-drawing power of action was confirmed by Calvert, Huston, Watkins, and Wright (1982) with older children. These researchers found that kindergarten through fourth grade children attended most closely to programming that contained such "perceptually salient features" as rapid character action and special camera and sound effects. The same research team noted that these features are more often present in commercial than in educational public television programs (Huston et al., 1981).

The action-aggression dilemma

Formal features research has made it clear that action, broadly defined, is the most potent ingredient for holding young children's attention. This fact struck researchers as very significant because they suspected that producers of commercial children's programs used violence to try to attract and hold young viewers. (Recall from Gerbner's violence index that children's programs have far higher levels of violence than prime-time programs.)

Picking up on this issue, Huston-Stein, Fox, Greer, Watkins, and Whitaker (1981) proposed that high action might be as effective as violent content for attracting children's attention. These researchers compared preschoolers' attention to cartoons that were (a) high in action and violence, (b) high in action but low in violence, and (c) low in both action and violence. They found that youngsters were as attentive to the high action/low violent cartoon as they were to the high action/high violence one. However, the cartoon high in action but low in violence also stimulated as much aggressive behavior in a subsequent free-play situation as the high action/high violence program. This supports an instigation-arousal theory of aggression (see chapter 4), and unfortunately casts doubt on the value of developing high action/low violence fare.

The Attention-Comprehension Link

So far we have discussed attention and comprehension as if they were completely separate processes. In fact, however, there is reason to believe they are closely linked.

Anderson and his colleagues (Anderson & Lorch, 1983; Anderson, Lorch, Field, & Sanders, 1981) propose that the relationship between children's attention and comprehension is reciprocal: Attention affects comprehension which, in turn, affects attention. Consistent with this theory, there is evidence that the more attention-getting features a program has, the higher will be the level of attention it receives *and* the better it will be recalled and understood (Calvert, Huston, Watkins, & Wright, 1982). In addition, when a program contains features that suggest that it will not be comprehensible (such as dialogue in a foreign language), children will show reduced visual attention to it even when it is rich in action or other perceptually salient visual features (Anderson et al., 1981). Finally, as children grow older they become increasingly likely to deploy their attention on the basis of the informational complexity of a program rather than on the basis of the number of perceptually salient features it displays (Wright et al., 1984).

Teaching Children Critical Viewing Skills

A final way in which social scientists have tried to increase television's effectiveness (and reduce possible adverse or unwanted effects) is by developing curricula to teach children about television.

Dorr, Graves, and Phelps (1980) were pioneers in developing a critical viewing curriculum. Based on extensive interviewing of children, these researchers identified four critical evaluation skills that would be the objectives of the curricula: (a) decrease children's belief that TV programs are real, (b) increase children's tendencies to compare what they see on TV with other information sources, (c) decrease television's credibility by teaching children about economic and production aspects of television, and (d) teach children to evaluate television content by making use of the outlined skills.

Two different curricula were developed. The "industry curriculum" was designed to teach children about television's economic structure and production techniques, and how to use this knowledge to evaluate programming as real or fantasy. The training revolved around eight facts (Dorr et al., 1980):

1. Plots are made up.
2. Characters are actors.
3. Incidents are fabricated.
4. Settings are often constructed.
5. Programs are broadcast to make money.
6. Money for programs comes from advertisers purchasing air time.
7. Ads are to sell products to the viewer.
8. Audience size determines broadcaster income. (p. 73)

The "process curriculum" was designed to teach children processes and sources for evaluating TV content. The facts around which this curriculum was developed are:

1. Entertainment programs are made up.
2. Entertainment programs vary in how realistic they are.
3. Viewers can decide how realistic they find entertainment programs.
4. Television content may be evaluated by comparing it to one's own experience, asking other people, and consulting other media sources. (p. 73)

The effectiveness of these curricula was compared with a control curriculum on "social reasoning" which developed children's role-taking skills by teaching them how to take other people's feelings and perspectives into account.

All three curricula were taught during the school day in six 1-hour sessions to small groups of between four to seven children in kindergarten and second/third grades. The curricula, taught by research personnel with previous teaching experience, used similar methods of instruction: audio-visual materials, role playing, discussion, games, and drawing. In subsequent paper and pencil tests and interviews, the researchers demonstrated that the 6-hour curricula successfully taught children much about television and alternative information sources and how to use that knowledge in reasoning about the reality of television content. The researchers concluded that each of the critical viewing curricula contributed unique skills and should be combined into one program.

In a study funded by the American Broadcasting Company, Singer, Zuckerman, and Singer (1980) developed an eight-lesson critical viewing curriculum for third through fifth graders. The lessons were entitled: Introduction to Television, Reality and Fantasy on Television, Camera Effects and Special Effects, Commercials and the Television Business, Identification with Television Characters, Stereotypes on Television, Violence and Aggression, and How Viewers Can Influence Television. The lessons, taught by the regular classroom teachers after rather brief training, lasted about 40 minutes each and involved presentation of audio-visual materials (e.g., clips from TV programs), discussions, teaching of lesson-related vocabulary, and engaging in guided activities (e.g., practicing special effects on video equipment in the classroom). Testing of information learned (with a pretest-posttest method) revealed that the program was effective in conveying new information, especially about special effects, commercials, and advertising and in enhancing facility with TV-related vocabulary. A subsequent field test of the curriculum in nine elementary schools in several states showed similar pre- to posttest improvements in knowledge about television (Singer & Singer, 1983). The curriculum has also proven to be quite adaptable in that a simplified version of it was shown to be effective in teaching selected concepts to children in kindergarten through second grade (Rapaczynski, Singer, & Singer, 1982).

An exciting project by Huesmann, Eron, Klein, Brice, and Fischer (1983) shows that teaching children critical viewing skills may even be a means to counter some of the adverse effects of TV violence. In this investigation, a total of 169 first- and third-grade children were selected on the basis of their frequent exposure to television violence and were randomly assigned to an experimental or a control group. Over a 2-year period, the experimental group experienced two treatments designed to reduce the likelihood of their imitating aggressive behavior from television. The first intervention was comprised of three training sessions that emphasized the unreality of television portrayals, special effects, and how real people solve problems in ways different from TV characters. The second intervention, which took place 9 months later, involved two sessions in which the youngsters assisted in making a film to help children who had been fooled or harmed by television. In the first session, the subjects composed essays that addressed how television is not like real life and why it is bad to imitate TV violence or to watch too much television. During the second session, the children were videotaped while they read their essays and then viewed the final videotapes of themselves and their classmates. The control group met in parallel contexts, but the discussions were not television-related. The results indicated that the first intervention did not significantly affect the youngsters' judgment of TV realism, aggressive behavior, or violence viewing. However, the second intervention (which took place after the assessment of the first intervention's effects) altered the experimental group's attitudes about TV violence, reduced their (peer-rated) aggressive behavior, and reduced the relation between violence viewing and aggression. In other words, even though the experimental group watched the same amount of TV violence as the control after the second intervention, observing violence on TV was less likely to be followed by aggression for youngsters in the experimental than those in the control group. The results of this study suggest that attitude change exercises hold much promise as adjuncts to traditional critical viewing skills curricula and that important behavioral effects can be produced by such procedures.

PROSOCIAL TELEVISION

We now come to the last and most difficult question to be raised in this book. Can—and should—television be used purposely to cultivate and foster "prosocial" ways of thinking and acting?

The possibility that entertainment television could be harnessed to intentionally influence children's social attitudes and behavior has always been the opposite side of the coin to the TV violence issue. As early as 1969, when the Surgeon General's Committee was just getting under way, Surgeon General William Stewart declared to Congress:

The knowledge that should emerge from this kind of scientific endeavor will be knowledge aimed at understanding. If television can have a negative effect on children, it can also be a positive stimulus.... We must learn more about how to promote this latter capacity while we learn how to avoid the hazards of the former. (U.S. Senate Subcommittee, 1969, p. 339)

The Ten-Year Update to the Surgeon General's Report echoed the same sentiment, and went on to declare that "research on television's influence on prosocial behavior burgeoned into one of the most significant developments in the decade after the report of the Surgeon General's committee (Pearl, et al., 1982a, p. 48).

In this section we describe the concept of prosocial behavior, review the relevant background and research, and conclude with a discussion of the political and moral questions that arise when one tries to indoctrinate a whole nation of children.

What is "Prosocial Behavior"?

J.P. Rushton (1979, 1982), prominent for his work in this area, defines prosocial behavior as "that which is socially desirable and which in some way benefits another person or society at large" (Rushton, 1979, p. 323). The two broad categories of prosocial behavior are *altruism* and *self-control*. Each of these categories encompasses a number of specific kinds of action. Thus altruism includes generosity, helping, and cooperation; and self-control includes a willingness to work and wait for long-term goals as well as the ability to resist the temptation to cheat, steal, or lie.

Measuring Prosocial Television Content

We saw in our discussion of the effects of TV violence that measurement of the amount and type of aggressive and antisocial content of television played an important role for both research and public policy discussions. Similarly, the new interest in prosocial effects created the need to identify and measure prosocial content.

The first step was accomplished in 1972 with the development of a coding and scoring system (Davidson & Neale, 1974; Rubinstein, Liebert, Neale, & Poulos, 1974). Drawing largely on the previous psychological investigations of prosocial behavior, the authors named and explicitly defined seven categories of behavior that are generally socially valued (altruism, control of aggressive impulses, delay of gratification, explaining the feelings of self and others, reparation for bad behavior, resistance to temptation, and sympathy). Each of these behaviors is defined in Table 10.3. The system has been used in several investigations of prosocial content in American programming.

Table 10.3 Definitions of Prosocial Behaviors

Altruism—consists of sharing, helping, and cooperation involving humans or animals.

Control of aggressive impulses—involves nonaggressive acts or statements that serve to eliminate or prevent aggression by self or others toward humans or animals.

Delay of gratification/task persistence—consists of the related acts of delay of gratification and task persistence, expressed either nonverbally or verbally.

Explaining feelings of self or others—consists of statements to another person(s) explaining the feelings, thinking, or action of self or others with the intent of effective positive outcome, including increasing the understanding of others, resolving strife, smoothing out difficulties, or reassuring someone.

Reparation for bad behavior—refers to behavior that is clearly intended as reparation for an act seen as a wrongdoing committed by the person himself/herself.

Resistance to temptation—refers to withstanding the temptation to engage in behaviors generally prohibited by society (e.g., stealing), which may be prohibited in the program explicitly or implicitly.

Sympathy—is a verbal or behavioral expression of concern for others and their problems.

Note. Assessing Television's Influence on Children's Prosocial Behavior by E.A. Rubinstein, R.M. Liebert, J.M. Neale, and R.W. Poulos, 1974, New York: Brookdale International Institute.

In the most extensive analysis, 300 prime-time, afternoon, and cartoon programs broadcast during 1974 were analyzed for prosocial content (Liebert & Poulos, 1975). The researchers found considerable variability in the frequency of the various prosocial categories. For instance, whereas there was an average of about 11 altruistic acts and 6 sympathetic behaviors per hour of programming, control of aggressive impulses and resistance to temptation appeared less than once an hour. These frequencies of prosocial behavior are similar to those obtained in an independent analysis of 1974 children's Saturday morning programming. Here, Poulos, Harvey, and Liebert (1976) found about 13 altruistic acts and five sympathetic responses per hour, but almost a complete absence of control of aggressive impulses. Examining the 1975 to 1978 broadcast seasons, Greenberg and his colleagues (Greenberg, Edison, Korzenny, Fernandez-Collado, & Atkin, 1980) also found that altruism was the most frequently portrayed prosocial behavior on Saturday morning programs, occurring at an average rate of 19.6 acts per hour. During prime time, however, they found the most prevalent prosocial behaviors were explaining the feelings of self or others, which had an hourly rate of approximately 22 acts. Overall, it is clear that in both adult- and child-oriented programs, viewers are exposed to a fair number of prosocial interpersonal behaviors, but only infrequent displays of self-control behaviors.

Aside from knowing the amount of socially desirable behavior shown on TV, it is important to know where these behaviors are performed. Certainly context factors should influence the impact of prosocial actions on the viewer. In a study of 100 diverse entertainment programs, Sprafkin, Rubinstein, and Stone (1977) found that prosocial behaviors appeared most frequently in situation comedies and dramas and least often in crime adventures. This same pattern has been found in two subsequent studies (Greenberg, Edison, et al., 1980; Harvey, Sprafkin, & Rubinstein, 1979).

Prosocial TV Effects: Early Simulation Studies

Paralleling developments in research on antisocial TV effects, research on the prosocial effects of television has its roots in early modeling studies inspired by social learning theory. All these studies used "home-made" videotapes shown to children on a television screen.

Sharing

The value placed by society on sharing is clearly shown in the adage that it is more blessed to give than to receive. But sharing is not innately built into the human organism, as any parent of a 2-year-old can testify. It must be taught in the same manner in which society attempts to teach all its values, by providing direct instruction and appropriate examples.

Bryan and Walbek (1970) investigated the effects of both these teaching techniques through simulated television programs on children's sharing. In one study, third- and fourth-grade youngsters were taken individually to a research trailer and permitted to play a bowling game for 10 trials. The game was rigged so that all the children obtained high scores and thus "won" a gift certificate which could be exchanged for money or prizes. The children were informed that they could donate their winnings to the March of Dimes if they wished. After each child played the game for a while, he or she saw a TV program of another child of the same sex playing the game. The other child served as a model who was either generous, donating one third of his/her winnings; or selfish, donating none. For two groups, the model also made statements about sharing, preaching either greed or generosity; while in the third no such statements were made. After viewing the program, each child played the game again and was given the opportunity to share in private. This test of prosocial behavior revealed that children who saw a charitable television model were significantly more likely to share than those who saw a greedy one, regardless of the nature of the preaching.

Resistance to temptation

In another early study using simulated television, Stein and Bryan (1972) demonstrated that a televised model also can influence children's resistance to temptation. Third- and fourth-grade girls viewed a sequence that showed a peer model playing a bowling game; half of the subjects saw a skilled model who won often, while the other half saw an unskilled model who won less frequently. In either case, the model was instructed to reward herself, according to a stringent rule, by taking a stack of nickels each time she obtained a certain high score.

The children were subdivided into four groups according to the model's preaching and practicing of the rule. Either she preached and practiced rule adherence, preached and practiced rule breaking, or was inconsistent in what she said and did. Then each child played the game herself. The measure of rule adherence was the number of nickels the child took on non winning trials. Those who viewed a model who both preached and practiced rule adherence closely followed the stringent self-reward rule themselves and thus successfully resisted temptation more than those who saw a model who preached and practiced transgression.

Prosocial Effects of Real TV Shows

A major limitation of the early laboratory studies we have considered so far is that very few children would choose to watch any of the television sequences they employed, if given a choice between these sequences and "real television." So the next step was to determine whether existing shows had prosocial effects.

"Mister Rogers' Neighborhood"

The first series tested was "Mister Rogers' Neighborhood," a program that deliberately contains social lessons. In an investigation described in chapter 5, Stein and Friedrich (1972) observed preschoolers' naturally occurring behavior during a 4-week period in a nursery school setting both before and after exposing them to one of three conditions—"Mister Rogers' Neighborhood," which was the prosocial condition; "Batman and Superman," which was the aggressive condition, or neutral films. Children who watched the prosocial programs generally showed increases in self-control relative to those exposed to the aggressive or neutral fare. Further, lower socioeconomic children who saw "Mister Rogers' Neighborhood" also showed an increase in prosocial interpersonal behaviors.

In a later study, Friedrich and Stein (1975) examined the effect of providing verbal labeling and role-playing training after showing episodes from "Mister Rogers' Neighborhood" to kindergarten youngsters. They found that subsequent to viewing, children exposed to "Mister Rogers' Neighborhood" could correctly answer more questions about prosocial behavior and spontaneously verbalized more prosocial phrases than children who saw neutral films. Furthermore, children who had watched "Mister Rogers' Neighborhood" and had been given role-playing training were also more likely to help another child. Similarly, Friedrich-Cofer, Huston-Stein, Kipnis, Susman, and Clewett (1979) found that exposure to 20 episodes of "Mister Rogers' Neighborhood" over an 8-week period significantly enhanced the prosocial interpersonal behavior of urban poor preschoolers, but only if they had also been provided with play materials relevant to the prosocial content.

Like "Sesame Street," "Mister Rogers' Neighborhood" was designed for public television. Though millions of children may watch one or another public television show in a given week, public television reaches quite a small audience, composed mainly of the children of professional and upper managerial class parents.

So the next question was to ask whether *commercial* series, as broadcast, can have measurable prosocial effects. Several studies done over the past decade suggest that the answer is yes.

Commercial shows

A simple survey conducted by CBS of over 700 children showed that about 90% were able to verbalize at least one prosocial message from specific episodes of the animated series "Fat Albert and the Cosby Kids;" widely cited messages were the importance of being kind to friends in trouble, being honest, and valuing property (CBS, 1974). Similar results were later reported for four other CBS Saturday morning programs: "The Harlem Globetrotters Popcorn Machine," "U.S. of Archie," "Shazam," and "Isis" (CBS, 1977).

Squire D. Rushnell, vice president of children's and early-morning programs for ABC, points out that since the early 1970s, each of the networks named vice presidents in charge of children's programming exclusively and introduced inserts and programs with prosocial themes (Rushnell, 1981). For example, CBS consulted with educators and child psychologists to develop "Fat Albert and the Cosby Kids." In addition, it created "Festival of Lively Arts for Young People" (specials on aspects of the arts), "In the News" (2-minute news stories written for children and inserted during program breaks), and "30 Minutes" (based on "60 Minutes"). ABC introduced high quality drama for children in "ABC Afterschool Specials" and educational messages in "Schoolhouse Rock," "Grammar Rock," "America Rock," "Science Rock," and "Body Rock." NBC introduced "GO," an informative live action Saturday morning program and "Special Treats," after-school dramas for children. Unfortunately, there has been no systematic research by the networks to determine the extent to which any of these programs actually influence children's behaviors and attitudes. However, there have been several studies by academic researchers that have demonstrated clear effects for some network shows.

In a study of our own (Sprafkin, Liebert, & Poulos, 1975), we selected for our principal treatments two programs from the "Lassie" series that were similar in many ways (characters, setting, written for the same audience). The critical difference was that one had a highly dramatic scene in which Jeff, the lead child character, risks his life to save a puppy. We also picked a noncanine family comedy episode from the "The Brady Bunch." We wanted to see whether children exposed to the prosocial "Lassie" program would be more willing to help than those shown either of two control programs. As a first assessment of prosocial influences from entertainment programs, we wanted to create the most sensitive or conservative assessment situation, and therefore employed a behavioral test that approximated that presented in the program. Because we couldn't have the children show their willingness to help a puppy in distress by risking their lives like Jeff did in the film, we constructed a situation in which they would have to make a choice between alerting adults that animals needed help or earning points toward prizes. We showed first grade children one of the three programs and then put them in the situation of having to choose between sacrifice and self-interest in the absence of any adults. As Figure 10.5 shows, children in the prosocial "Lassie" condition were more willing to help than those in either the neutral "Lassie" or "Brady Bunch" control conditions, which did not differ from each other. So, after seeing a boy sacrifice for an animal, the children were likely to do the same.

Collins and Getz (1976) tested the effects of prosocial and antisocial versions of an action-adventure program. The half-hour program that had appeared on TV ("Mod Squad") was edited for the study so that in one version the protagonist constructively coped with an interpersonal conflict, and in the other version he responded aggressively. Fourth, seventh, and tenth graders who saw one of these programs or a neutral program were subsequently faced with an adaptation of the "Help-Hurt game" which was previously used by Liebert and Baron (1972) and described in chapter 5. It was found that the children who viewed the constructive coping model responded in a more helpful manner to a peer who was working on a task in another room than children in the other two conditions.

Baran, Chase, and Courtright (1979) demonstrated prosocial effects with a "Waltons" episode that modeled a cooperative problem-solving solution to a conflict situation. Second and third grade children who viewed the cooperative program subsequently behaved more cooperatively in a game situation than those who saw either a control "program" (a videotape that presented noncooperative behavior) or no program at all.

Liss, Reinhardt, and Fredriksen (1983) examined the effects of programs that deliver prosocial or moral messages via characters that behave aggressively. This is a frequent occurrence in both superhero and crime/adventure programs. Liss and her associates selected an excerpt from the cartoon series "Superfriends," in which the superheroes use aggression in the context of teaching the lesson not to take others' property. This "prosocial/aggressive" condition was compared to a purely prosocial condition comprised of a totally nonaggressive excerpt from another "Superfriends" program that taught the same moral. Kindergarten, second, and fourth grade children were shown one of the three cartoons and then were put in a situation in which they could hurt or help another child in the context of the "Help-Hurt game." Children in the purely prosocial condition helped more than they hurt, and helped more and tended to hurt less than those in the prosocial/ aggressive condition. In a subsequent interview, it was found that the children in the purely prosocial condition understood the program's plot and moral lesson significantly better than those in the prosocial/aggressive condition. The results further demonstrate the potential of television to inculcate prosocial behavior and also convey the warning that prosocial behavior should *not* be presented in an aggressive context.

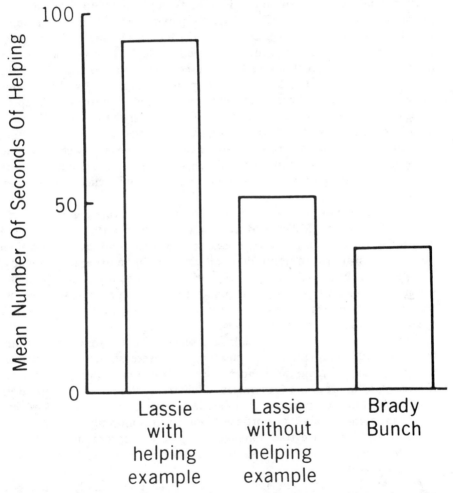

Figure 10.5 Duration of children's helping in the Sprafkin, Liebert, and Poulos (1985) study. From "Effects of a Prosocial Televised Example on Children's Helping" by J.N. Sprafkin, R.M. Liebert, and R.W. Poulos, 1975, *Journal of Experimental Child Psychology*, 20, 119—126.

Countering stereotypes and fostering goodwill

A major aim of many consciously "prosocial" programs for children is to counter stereotypes and foster intergroup goodwill. "Sesame Street" pioneered this type of social education in American television, especially by its systematic portrayal of blacks and Hispanics in an almost exclusively positive light. Bogatz and Ball's (1972) findings suggest that exposure to "Sesame Street" makes children's attitudes toward these groups more favorable. Similarly, "Sesame Street" segments that depicted multiracial themes significantly enhanced the desirability of playing with nonwhite (i.e., Oriental and North American Indian) playmates for white Canadian preschool children (Goldberg & Gorn, 1979; Gorn, Goldberg, & Kanungo, 1976). Likewise, exposure to the "Big Blue Marble," which was designed to encourage international awareness, caused American youngsters in the fourth through sixth grades to perceive people around the world as being more similar to one another and children in other countries as happier, healthier, and better off than they had before viewing the program (Roberts et al., 1974). Finally, "Vegetable Soup," which presents a favorable picture of many ethnic groups, was found to make child viewers between 6 and 10 years of age more accepting of children of different races and to more strongly identify with their own racial/ethnic group (Mays, Henderson, Seidman, & Steiner, 1975).

There is also evidence that television can counter sex-role stereotypes. In a correlational study, Miller and Reeves (1976) found that grade school children who view more non–sex stereotyped programs are more likely than other children to accept nontraditional sex roles. In an experimental study, Davidson, Yasuna, and Tower (1979) found that 5- to 6-year-old girls who saw a cartoon showing females as competent athletes subsequently gave less stereotyped responses on a sex-role attitude measure than those who saw a neutral or sex-role stereotyped cartoon.

Counter-stereotyped commercials also seem to have an impact. A study by Atkin (1975b) revealed that children who were shown a commercial featuring a female judge were more likely than a control group to rate the profession as appropriate for females. Similarly, O'Bryant and Corder-Bolz (1978) found that elementary school students exposed over a 4-week period to several commercials that portrayed women in nontraditional roles were more likely to perceive traditionally male jobs as appropriate for women than youngsters who were shown commercials featuring women in traditional roles.

An example of how television has been used intentionally to improve children's sex-role attitudes is the "Freestyle" TV series. The program was funded in 1975 by the National Institute of Education ($4 million) in response to statistics indicating that only a small proportion of females were training for careers outside the home (Johnston, Ettema, & Davidson, 1980):

The Career Awareness Division of NIE saw a partial remedy for this problem in a television intervention aimed at 9–12 year olds. Called the TV Career Awareness Project, the product would be a carefully articulated package designed to influence the attitudes and behaviors of this age group in a way that would reduce sex-role stereotypes and expand the "career awareness" of children, especially girls, in non-traditional ways. The task was to be accomplished by focusing on non-traditional possibilities in the 9–12 year old's own world, an approach that would distinguish it from more typical career education programs that focus on adult occupations. Its purpose would be to have children relate non-traditional childhood interests to educational, and ultimately to occupational choices. (p. 159)

Based on attitude questionnaires administered before and after viewing the 13 episodes, "Freestyle" was shown to be successful in making boys more accepting of girls engaging in mechanical activities, football, and basketball; girls increased their interest in mechanical activities, football, and basketball (see Figure 10.6); boys and girls became more accepting of boys doing traditional female activities (caring for children, helping around the house, and assisting sick and old people); boys and girls became more approving of men and women having nontraditional jobs (e.g., women as mechanics, truck drivers, or engineers; men as nurses or secretaries); and boys' and girls' perceptions of appropriate male and female family roles (e.g., child care, cooking, home repair) became less traditional.

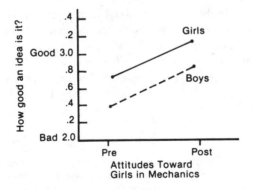

Figure 10.6 "Freestyle" effects on children's attitudes toward girls in mechanics.
Based on the responses to three questions: How do you feel about girls your age (1) fixing a broken bike, (2) working with an adult on a car motor, and (3) building a radio or something else that runs on electricity?
Based on data reported in *An Evaluation of "Freestyle": A Television Series Designed to Reduce Stereotypes* by J. Johnston, J. Ettema, and T. Davidson, 1980, Ann Arbor, MI: Institute for Social Research.

Countering TV violence effects
Corder-Bolz (1980) developed two 60-second messages that related to the content of an aggression-laden "Batman" program. One spot explained that

"Batman" was not real and the other that in real life it is illegal to hit and hurt others and that people should handle problems in a different manner than Batman. The spots were inserted in the commercial breaks of a "Batman" program and shown to a sample of 5- to 7-year-olds. Compared to a control group who saw the "Batman" program without the inserts, the children who saw the spots were subsequently less likely to think that the behaviors of hitting, hurting, and stealing from people were acceptable.

Meta-analysis of prosocial television effects

In our discussion of TV violence, we mentioned Hearold's (1986) meta-analysis of studies of TV's effects on children. (Recall that this procedure involves coding various characteristics of a body of research and then calculating summary statistics that represent a general conclusion which can be drawn across the studies.) Hearold found 190 tests of the effects of prosocial TV in the literature through 1978. She coded each test on such details as subjects (e.g., number, mean age, gender, ethnicity); treatment (e.g., program type, animated/live, length); outcome (including type of behaviors, such as cooperation, and type of measure, such as observation or questionnaire); design (e.g., how subjects are assigned to treatments); and effect size. (Recall from p. 157 that effect size is a measure of the strength of a relationship or effect.)

The analysis left no doubt that prosocial TV can have prosocial effects. In fact, the average effect size for prosocial television on prosocial behavior (.63) was far higher than that for the effects of antisocial television on antisocial behavior (.30). The effect size for prosocial effects continued to maintain its lead over that for antisocial effects when only the most ecologically valid studies were considered (.36 and .23, respectively).*

Hearold (1986) believes that the policy implications of her analysis are far-reaching:

> Many organizations and groups have chosen to work for the removal of sex and violence in television programs. It is a defensive position: eliminate the negative. Alternately, I would recommend accentuating the positive: apply money and effort to creating new entertainment programs with prosocial themes, especially for children (to whom the empirical evidence most clearly applies). Although fewer studies exist on prosocial effects, the effect size is so much larger, holds up better under more stringent experimental conditions,

---

*Ecological validity refers to the degree of authenticity or real world naturalness of the treatment, viewing and measurement setting, and outcome behavior.

and is consistently higher for boys and girls, that the potential for prosocial effects overrides the smaller but persistent negative effects of antisocial programs. (p. 116)

LIMITATIONS AND RESERVATIONS

Evidence reviewed in this chapter shows quite clearly that television entertainment has great potential power to socialize in any direction in which carefully designed, systematic programming is offered. As the NIMH Ten-Year Update report concluded about prosocial television (Pearl et al., 1982a, p. 51):

> The clear and simple message derived from the research on prosocial behavior is that children learn from watching television and what they learn depends on what they watch... if they look at prosocial programs, they will more likely become more generous, friendly, and self-controlled. Television can have beneficial effects; it is a potential force for good.

Despite this potential, there are some very important limitations and reservations that must be considered by anyone who would harness TV for the benefit of children.

Limits of Current Knowledge

Although most studies suggest that prosocial television can have desired effects, our ability to magnify these effects and minimize undesired ones is in its infancy. Also, it is evident that the entire process of socialization is highly complex. For example, there are a number of studies indicating that "Mister Rogers' Neighborhood" and "Sesame Street's" prosocial episodes can have prosocial effects, but that the influence is limited to situations that are quite similar to those presented on the program (Friedrich & Stein, 1975; Gorn, Goldberg, & Kanungo, 1976; Leifer, 1975; Paulson, McDonald, & Whittlemore, 1972) or to cases in which the television program exposure is supplemented by reinforcement of key concepts through classroom activities (e.g., Friedrich & Stein, 1975; Friedrich-Cofer, et al., 1979). In addition, while a single exposure to a prosocial segment of "Sesame Street" apparentiy produces immediate effects, these do not even last for a day (Goldberg & Gorn, 1979).

Finally, two studies suggest that televised messages designed to teach children how to deal with interpersonal conflict may backfire with very young children. Silverman (1976) found that 3-year-old children exposed to episodes from "Sesame Street" that contained conflict followed by a prosocial resolution became *less* cooperative in a subsequent task. In a follow-up study, Silverman and Sprafkin (1980) examined the independent effects of the conflict and resolution portions of four of these problematic spots. It was found that while exposure to the resolution-only spots did not increase cooperation, the children who saw the conflict-only spots were actually less cooperative relative to a control group. This suggests that the decrement in cooperative behavior shown in the original study was due to the conflict portions of the "Sesame Street" spots. These findings may help to explain why previous studies found increases in physical and verbal aggression (e.g., Coates, Pusser, & Goodman, 1976) and decreases in cooperation (e.g., Tower, Singer, Singer, & Biggs, 1979) in the free-play social interactions of preschoolers following exposure to "Sesame Street." Clearly, even the best intentions for prosocial effects may be undermined, and extreme care should be used when attempting to teach very young children how to deal with interpersonal conflict through TV.

Practical Matters

In assessing the potential of prosocial television content to have important social effects, Cook et al., (1983) raise several practical issues that highlight the factors that stand in the way of harnessing television's potential. First, there is the question of the degree to which children would select to watch prosocial programs when alternative programs and activities are available. The children who participated in the research examining prosocial television effects did not have these alternatives, whereas viewers at home clearly do. Second, why should the networks broadcast prosocial programs? The networks are aware of the process involved in creating prosocial programming such as "Sesame Street" or "Mister Rogers' Neighborhood," and apparently choose the wider appeal cartoons over such programming. The financial incentive for capturing a larger audience is obvious, and there are no particularly compelling incentives to the broadcasters to improve the quality of children's programming. Finally, it is difficult to fully assess the potential of television to encourage socially desirable behaviors and values in the absence of longitudinal studies that examine the effects of spontaneous exposure to prosocial content over prolonged periods.

Moral Opposition to Prosocial Television

Our most serious reservation about prosocial television is that there are legitimate moral objections to using a public medium to socially indoctrinate a whole nation of children. This reservation derives in large measure from our own experience with an extensive prosocial television project.

Selling cooperation to children: A personal experience
In 1975 we (Liebert, Sprafkin, & Poulos) published an article entitled, "Selling Cooperation to Children" which reported our involvement in an effort to use 30-second TV spot messages as "commercials" for cooperation. The project was conceived by Ben Logan, who worked with an agency of The United Methodist Church concerned with media. The agency was originally called the Television, Radio and Film Commission (TRAFCO) and then became United Methodist Communications. Logan and his associates had taken note of the Surgeon General's Report and specifically wanted to direct their efforts and those of other church groups toward doing something positive about television.

The decision was made to capitalize on the availability of free air time on the commercial networks through the vehicle of public service announcements (*PSAs*). PSAs are typically 15 or 30 seconds long and are interspersed with regular commercials. They are offered to networks or individual broadcasters on a gratis basis by nonprofit charitable, public service, and religious organizations. The broadcaster does not pay for the production and costsreceives a copy of the PSA free; the sponsoring agency does not pay for the air time.

Collaborating with our research team at the State University of New York at Stony Brook, Logan decided to build PSAs around the theme of cooperation, a type of prosocial behavior that commended itself for three reasons. First, cooperation is pragmatic as well as prosocial. Unlike sharing, in which one's own material resources are diminished, cooperation provides an opportunity for both parties to be nice *and* to benefit. Second, cooperation is often an alternative to aggression, as when a fight may break out over competition for resources. Third, cooperation can be taught and must be learned. Thus modeling of successful cooperation on TV might well influence children's cooperation with one another in real life.

The United Methodist Church and other church groups provided the money for developing, producing, and distributing three 30-second spots designed to make children more cooperative. Development involved ongoing consultation with our team on the application of psychological principles in writing the story lines. More important, the spots were subjected to an intensive formative research effort as they developed. Each spot was tested by positioning it next to regular commercials, which in turn were inserted into actual entertainment programming so that the format was identical to what would finally appear on the air. Children of the target age range (4 to 10 years) watched from a comfortable sofa in a relaxed, den-like atmosphere furnished with such natural distractors as toys, books, and wall decorations. As the children watched, video recordings of their facial expressions and reactions were made and later analyzed in detail. Tests of comprehension of the content and meaning of each element in the spots were also performed.

Figure 10.7 Scenes from "The Swing."

As a final test, children were observed in an actual play situation after seeing either the cooperative spot or a commercial of the same length to obtain an actual behavioral measure of cooperation. This research procedure continued with each spot until a highly effective message, produced by a well-known Hollywood studio, was "in the can" and ready to go on the air.

As might be expected, the spots that ultimately emerged were simple and graphic. For example, the first and best known spot, "The Swing," opens with a boy and girl, 8 to 10 years of age, running across a field to reach a swing on a playground. They begin to struggle over the swing, and each claims first rights. After a moment during which battle seems inevitable, with each youngster scowling at the other, one of them produces the insight that they should take turns and *suggests that the other child should go first*. Each of the children is finally shown taking a turn, joyfully swinging through the air with the help of the other. Over all of this, an announcer's voice concludes: "There are lots of things you can do when two people want the same thing. One of them is to take turns. And that is a good one." The spot ends with an upbeat musical flourish. (See Figure 10.7.)

"The Swing" was first broadcast in May 1974 and soon had been shown by all three networks and numerous independent stations at favorable air times. It was also distributed internationally and had been seen within a few months by tens of millions of children all over the world. Then, on August 18, 1974, a new twist was introduced. Caryl Rivers, in a freelance article for the *New York Times* based on a then recent conference on "Behavioral Control through the Media," pointed out that the entire effort could be seen as a highly objectionable form of psychological behavior control. Here is an excerpt from Rivers' report of the conference:

Dr. Liebert is so convinced of the harmful effects of televised violence on children that he is now making 30-second spots for TV to demonstrate to children that there are non-violent, non-aggressive alternatives for solving problems. For example, in one spot (distributed as a public service by the Broadcasting and Film Commission of the National Council of Churches and already shown on all three networks) two children are running toward the one empty swing in a playground. They arrive at the same time, and each child grabs an end of the swing. Impasse. The kids must either fight or find some other way to resolve the situation. Finally they decide to take turns. Both kids are winners, nobody loses.

The outburst that followed Liebert's presentation flashed around the conference table. Did he believe he had a right to deliberately try to impose values on children? Whose values were they? Should children indeed be taught cooperation? Did ghetto kids perhaps need to be taught to slug it out in order to survive in this society? Was it not, in fact, immoral to create a TV advertisement the prime function of which was to influence kids' behavior? Liebert was accused of hubris, manipulation and even brainwashing. One would have thought he had proposed setting up Hitler Youth Camps on Sesame Street. He was nonplussed. He had not expected that a 30-second spot about cooperativeness in sharing a swing would have raised such a furor.

However, I understood why the hackles had gone up around that conference table. I am one of those people who is terrified of manipulation. A Skinnerian world filled with conditioned people scares the daylights out of me—even if those people do hate war and do love their fellow man. I agree with Nobel Prize-winner George Wald that we reduce our unpredictability at our grave risk. "Our technology," he says, "has given us dependable machines and livestock. We shall now have to choose whether to turn it to giving us more reliable, convenient and efficient men, at the cost of our freedom."*

Is "prosocial" the same as "ultimate good"? The most vociferous critics of intentional prosocial television takes an even harder line than Caryl Rivers. They argue that the values underlying prosocial television are *un*desirable values and hint that the whole concept of prosocial behavior is morally pretentious and dangerous. Representative of this viewpoint is Walter Karp, a contributing editor of *Channels*, a popular magazine about television and society. Karp disagrees with the idea, implicit in programs such as "The Swing," that cooperation and other forms of prosocial behavior are "good" at all. Karp favors building a society of tough, vigorous, independent individuals and sees prosocial television as cultivating a namby-pamby kind of child who lacks these qualities. He wrote:

[Prosocial television] is systematic training for personal weakness and social subservience. It promotes conformity and saps inner strength. It teaches children to look to the group for their opinions and to despise those who do not do the same. Out of a pretended fear of "aggressiveness," it would deprive a free people of the very inner force and self-assurance they need to stand up and fight for their rights. Is this not a little sinister? (1984, p. 5)

A Final Word

The concerns of Rivers and Karp reflect the basic dilemma that television has created. As we saw in chapter 1, there is every indication that TV viewing will continue to be *the* major pastime of children, and that this is becoming true all over the world. In addition, research evidence demonstrates conclusively that entertainment television does influence children's values, beliefs, attitudes, and actions to some extent, although in an unsystematic, willy-nilly fashion. Most important, perhaps, the accumulated evidence (as well as our own experience) suggests that it would

---

*Copyright © by The New York Times Company. Reprinted by permission.

be possible to design TV entertainment for children on a conscious basis that, given their level of viewing (15 to 20 hours per week, every week, from infancy to adulthood) would exert great influence. This, apparently, is the strategy for socializing the young employed in some dictatorships. Such systematic use of television entertainment to influence children is undoubtedly a subtle but effective form of brainwashing. Now that we *can* harness the potential power of television to influence children, the question of whether we *will* remains.

Appendix A

ANSWERING QUESTIONS ABOUT TELEVISION
The Experimental Method

The experimental method involves the manipulation of some experience (called the *independent* variable) and then the measurement of some aspect of behavior (the *dependent* variable). The major purpose is to determine if the changes in the independent variable produce changes in the dependent variable; that is, to determine whether there is a causal relationship between the two. An additional goal is to insure that *only* the independent variable could have caused the differences—to eliminate alternative interpretations of the results. For example, an investigator may be interested in the effects of praise on children's friendliness. Suppose the investigator asks a teacher to enthusiastically praise children in his or her class for a week, and finds that on the last day all are friendly. Can the investigator now say that praise increases friendliness? No. Several so-called rival hypotheses can explain these data; for example, the weather may have been nicer on the day of testing, the class lessons may have been easier, or the weekend may have been nearer. Any of these factors might have put everyone in a good mood, thereby making them friendlier. The experimenter must try to eliminate these rival hypotheses, and usually does so by employing a *control group*.

The simplest kind of experiment, then, involves two groups: one, the experimental group, receives the experience (or "treatment") of interest while the other, the control group, does not. When the experiment is concluded, the investigator will have one or more scores for each participant—measures of the dependent variable. He or she will then compare the average scores of the two groups. If the children who received praise are friendlier than those who did not, nice weather presumably had nothing to do with it, because everyone benefited from the sunshine.

But the researcher wants to go yet a step further and ask: can I *infer* from the experiment that other children who did not actually participate in this research will also be similarly affected by praise? Or could my results have appeared, with the particular children who did participate, simply by chance? It is this pair of questions, regarding inference to the larger *population* of children who were not studied directly, that is critical.

Obtaining the answer involves performing an appropriate statistical test that tells us the probability that the difference between the experimental and control groups is due only to chance. If—and only if—the probability is low do we infer that the results hold in the larger population of untested individuals. In behavioral research, the probability level is acceptably low when the likelihood is 5 or less in 100 that the obtained results would have occurred by chance. This level is called the .05 level of significance and is commonly written, "$p < .05$" and read "probability less than five percent."

All of the findings put forth as "significant" in this book have met this stringent criterion.

The Correlational Method

The correlational method is employed to determine if two (or more) variables are related; that is, to see if they change or co-vary together. Many social scientific research questions have been answered using this method. For example, "Is mental illness related to social class?" or, "Are grades related to IQ test scores?" The first step in applying the correlational method involves obtaining pairs of observations on a group of people. Next, the degree of relationship between the two sets of scores is assessed. A statistic called the *Pearson product moment correlation coefficient*, usually abbreviated r, is used for this purpose. This statistic may range in value from -1.00 to $+1.00$; the larger the absolute value of r, the stronger the relationship. An r of 1.00 (either plus or minus) indicates a perfect relationship. An r of 0.00 indicates no relationship. The sign of the correlation coefficient indicates the direction of the relationship. When the sign is positive, then the variables are *directly related*; as scores on one measure increase or decrease, the scores on the other tend to move in the same direction. When the sign is negative, the variables are *inversely related*; scores on one measure increase as scores on the other decrease.

Finally, the correlational study, like the experiment, usually requires an inference. When the investigator computes the correlation between two measures for some sample of individuals, this alone does not permit him or her to generalize the relationship and assume that it would hold for other people as well. To make such a determination, tests of statistical significance are employed in correlational studies just as they are employed in experiments.

As with any type of research, there are problems accompanying the correlational method. The most serious one concerns establishing causality; usually we cannot infer, when A and B are related, whether A causes B, or B causes A. For example, the question of primary interest for our purpose is, "Is viewing television violence related to violent or aggressive behavior?" The investigator collects data from many youngsters on the amount of viewing of violent TV and the amount of aggression they engage in at school, and then determines the degree of correlation. But in most instances—and without further special computation—it cannot be said that violence viewing *causes* violent behavior. For example, an equally plausible hypothesis is that children who are already aggressive *choose* to watch violence on TV.

Appendix B

ANNOTATED BIBLIOGRAPHY OF PAPERS IN SURGEON GENERAL'S REPORT

The list that follows* describes each of the research reports and related publications of the NIMH Surgeon General's inquiry. The papers themselves are available in seven volumes:

Television and Social Behavior: Media Content and Control (Reports and Papers, Volume 1)

Television and Social Behavior: Television and Social Learning (Reports and Papers, Volume 2)

Television and Social Behavior: Television and Adolescent Aggressiveness (Reports and Papers, Volume 3)

Television and Social Behavior: Television in Day-to-Day Life: Patterns of Use (Reports and Papers, Volume 4)

Television and Social Behavior: Television's Effects: Further Explorations (Reports and Papers, Volume 5)

Television and Growing Up: The Impact of Televised Violence (Report of the Surgeon General's Scientific Advisory Committee on Television and Social Behavior)

Television and Social Behavior: An Annotated Bibliography of Research Focusing on Television's Impact on Children

*Reprinted, with minor modifications, from *Television and Growing Up: The Impact of Televised Violence* from the Surgeon General's Scientific Advisory Committee on Television and Social Behavior, 1972, Washington, DC: United States Government Printing Office.

Any of these volumes can be purchased from the Superintendent of Documents, U.S. Government Printing Office, Washington, D.C. 20402

AUTHOR AND TITLE	SUBJECTS	DESCRIPTION
1. Baldwin & Lewis Violence in Television: The Industry Looks at Itself (Volume 1)	48 producers, writers, and directors	Interviews were conducted with the writers, producers, and directors of network action-adventure programming. The respondents were asked to describe the role of violence in such programs and how the inustry handles this aspect (i.e., censorship activities). In addition, the subjects were asked to respond to the critics of television violence and to comment on their beliefs about the possible effects of viewing televised violence.
2. Bechtel, Achelpohl, & Akers Correlates Between Observed Behavior and Questionnaire Responses on Television Viewing (Volume 4)	20 families Total N =82	Videotape cameras were installed in the homes of participating families. Observations of viewing behavior were continuously recorded for 5 days. The videotape records were coded, in $2\frac{1}{2}$-minute intervals for attention to the set (e.g., watching/not watching), and types of simultaneous activity (e.g., eating, reading). These behavior records were compared with the viewer's responses to questionnaire measures of viewing behavior.
3. Blatt, Spencer, & Ward A Cognitive Develop- mental Study of Children's Reactions to Television Advertising (Volume 4)	20 children 5 kindergarten 5 second grade 5 fourth grade 5 sixth grade	Children were shown a 1-hour videotape of "Saturday morning" television programming which included cartoons and other children's programs, plus 15 minutes of commercials. On the following day, the children were interviewed, in groups of five, concerning their reactions to the commercials (e.g., recall and understanding of the commercial message) and general attitudes toward advertising.
4. Cantor The Role of the Producer in Choosing Children's Television Content (Volume 1)	24 producers and writers	Twenty producers and four writers of children's programs were interviewed. Respondents were asked to describe the manner in which shows are selected by the networks and sponsors; the relationship between the producers and network; and the producer's conception of the audience for his program.

AUTHOR AND TITLE	SUBJECTS	DESCRIPTION
5. Chaffee Television and Adolescent Aggressiveness (Volume 3)		A summary of current research on the relationship between viewing televised violence and the aggressive behavior of adolescents.
6. Chaffee & McLeod Adolescent Television Use in the Family Context (Volume 3)	1,292 junior and senior high school 641 8th grade 651 10th grade	This survey related adolescent's television viewing (e.g. viewing televised violence) to factors such as: IQ, parent's television use, SES, and family communication patterns. The latter factor was defined by the parent's relative emphasis on either socio— (i.e., maintaining interpersonal harmony/repression of conflicts) or concept—(i.e., free discussion and mutual understanding of conflicts) orientations.
7. Clark Race Identification, and Television Violence Experiment I (Volume 5)	71 teenagers 38 white 33 black	Adolescents were shown a videotape of a "Dragnet" episode which featured three main characters: "Black Militant," "Black Policeman," and "White Policeman." The subjects viewed the program in either racially "mixed" or "homogeneous" groups. Postviewing questionnaires assessed the viewer's identification with the various characters and the role of black consciousness in such identification.
Experiment II (Volume 5)	45 white, college students	Subjects viewed the "Dragnet" program in dyads composed of either a black or white confederate who either engaged in social communication (i.e., friendly conversation) or remained silent during the viewing period.
8. Clark & Blankenburg Trends in Violent Content in Selected Mass Media (Volume 1)		Several forms of mass media (e.g., front page newspaper stories, a weekly magazine, and television entertainment programming) were inspected for the presence of violent content and their treatment of violent themes. Comparisons were obtained between media violence and environmental or real volence (i.e., FBI Uniform Crime Reports).
9. Comstock Media Control and Content: An Overview (Volume 1)		A review of this program's research on decision-making in television production and violence in television content.

AUTHOR AND TITLE	SUBJECTS	DESCRIPTION
10. Dahlgren Television in the Socialization Process: Structures and Pro- gramming of the Swedish Broadcasting Corporation (Volume 1)		A description of the broadcast policies of Sveriges Radio.
11. Dominick & Greenberg Attitudes Toward Vio- lence: The Interaction of TV Exposure, Family Attitudes, and Social Class (Volume 3)	838 children 434 fourth-, fifth-, and sixth-grade boys 404 fourth,- fifth-, and sixth-grade girls	Each child's prior exposure to televised violence, his perception of his parents' attitudes concerning the appropriateness of violence, and his family's socioeconomic level were related to various measures of the child's attitudes toward violence (e.g., willingness to use violence, perceived effectiveness of violence, and approval of aggression).
12. Ekman, Liebert, Friesen, Harrison, Zlatchin, Malmstrom, & Baron Facial Expressions of Emotion While Watching Televised Violence as Predictors of Subsequent Aggression (Volume 5)	65 5- to 6-year- old children (30 boys and 35 girls)	Children's facial expression while viewing televised violence were used as an index of the child's emotional reaction to such fare. This index was then used to assess the relationship between the child's emotional response to observing violent acts and his subsequent willingness to engage in interpersonal aggression.
13. Feshbach Reality and Fantasy in Filmed Violence Experiment I (Volume 2)	129, 9- to 11- year-old children	Children viewed either real (i.e., newsreel), fantasy (i.e., Hollywood movie), or control (e.g., circus movie) films and were then allowed to play a game in which they could engage in aggressive acts against an ostensible victim.
Experiment II (Volume 2)	40, 9- to 11- year-old children	In this study, each child was informed that the movie he or she was about to view was either real ("NBC newsreel") or fantasy ("Hollywood movie"). Measures of the child's subsequent aggressive behavior were identical to the first study.
Experiment III (Volume 2)	30, 9- to 11- year-old children	This study was similar to the second except that each child was informed that his aggressive behavior in the "guessing game" was only make believe. Results of this study were compared with the results of the previous experiment.

AUTHOR AND TITLE	SUBJECTS	DESCRIPTION
14. Feshbach & Singer Television and Aggression: Some Reactions to the Liebert, Sobol, and Davidson Review and Response (Volume 5)		A response to a comment on a reply to a critique of the catharsis thesis (see items 14, 35, and 36).
15. Feshbach & Singer Television and Aggression: A Reply to Liebert, Sobol, and Davidson. (Volume 5)		A reply to a critique of the catharsis thesis (see items 15, 35, and 36).
16. Foulkes, Belvedere, & Brubaker Televised Violence and Dream Content (Volume 5)	40, 10- to 12-year-old boys	This study was designed to assess the relationship between viewing televised violence and the subsequent content of the child's dreams. Children viewed either a violent or nonviolent program immediately prior to bedtime. Their dreams were monitored during the sleep period and scored on a variety of dimensions (e.g., hostility, vividness, and hedonic tone).
17. Friedman & Johnson Mass Media Use and Aggression: A Pilot Study (Volume 3)	80 preado-lescent boys 40 "aggressive" 40 "nonaggres-ive"	Adolescent's attitudes toward aggression (e.g., tendency to engage in overt physical aggression) and his patterns of television use (e.g., amount of time spent viewing, program preferences) were studied in an attempt to assess the relationship between viewing televised violence and engaging in antisocial acts.
18. Gerbner The Structure and Process of Television Program Content Regulation in the United States (Volume 1)		A description of broadcast and content control structures operative in American television programming.
19. Gerbner Violence in Television Drama: Trends and Symbolic Functions (Volume 1)		This study provided an analysis of a one week sample of prime time entertainment programming. It described various factors relating to the frequency and symbolic character-istics of televised violence.
20. Greenberg Television's Effects: Further Explorations (Volume 5)		An overview of several current research projects that provide a diversity of theoretical and methodological approaches to research on the effects of television.

AUTHOR AND TITLE	SUBJECTS	DESCRIPTION
21. Greenberg, Ericson, & Vlahos Children's Television Behaviors as Perceived by Mother and Child (Volume 4)	85, fourth- and fifth-grade children and their mothers	Mothers, interviewed at home, were asked to describe their child's viewing patterns (e.g. program preferences, rules about viewing) while each child answered similar questions in the classroom. The child's self reported viewing behavior was compared with the mother's description.
22. Greenberg & Gordon Perceptions of Violence in Television Programs: Critics and the Public (Volume 1)	53 critics 303 men and women	A telephone survey (public) and mail questionnaires (critics) asked the respondents to rate the amount of violence contained in various television entertainment programs.
23. Greenberg & Gordon Social Class and Racial Differences in Children's Perception of Televised Violence (Volume 5)	325 fifth-grade boys 89 low SES white 89 low SES black 90 middle SES white 57 upper SES white	This study assessed boys' evaluation of violence portrayed on television in terms of the degree of perceived violence, acceptibility of violence, liking, degree of arousal, and perceived reality of the violent act.
24. Greenberg & Gordon Children's Perceptions of Television Violence: A Replication (Volume 5)	263 eighth-grade boys 66 low SES black 78 low SES white 37 middle SES white 82 upper-middle SES white	A replication of the prior study conducted with younger boys (see item 23).
25. Gurevitch The Structure and Content of Television Broadcasting in Four Countries: An Overview (Volume 1)		An introduction to a review of the broadcasting policies of Great Britain, Israel, Sweden, and the United States.
26. Halloran & Croll Television Programmes in Great Britain: Content and Control (Volume 1)		A discussion of television broadcasting in Great Britain.
27. Israel & Robinson Demographic Characteristics of Viewers of Television Violence and News Programs (Volume 4)	6,834 adults	Information on preferences and viewing patterns of a nationwide survey of adult television viewers were related to various demographic characteristics (e.g., age, education, income, sex).

AUTHOR AND TITLE	SUBJECTS	DESCRIPTION
28. Johnson, Friedman, & Gross Four Masculine Styles in Television Programming: A Study of the Viewing Preferences of Adolescent Males (Volume 3)	80 eighth-grade boys 39 "aggressive" 41 "nonaggressive"	This study compared the program preference patterns of boys with a history of "social aggressiveness" with their nonaggressive peers in an attempt to construct a program classification scheme based on the masculine role concept portrayed in each program.
29. Katzman Violence and Color Television: What Children of Different Ages Learn (Volume 5)	240 fourth-, sixth-, and ninth-grade boys	Children viewed (in either color or black-and-white format) a color television program which had been edited into either "high-violence" or "low-violence" versions. Postviewing measures tested the child's recall of central and peripheral details and related this recall to the color/violence variations.
30. Kenny Threats to the Internal Validity of Cross-Lagged Panel Inference, as related to "Television Violence and Child Aggression: A Follow-up Study" (Volume 3)		A methodological note on the research design employed in a study by Lefkowitz, Eron, Walder, and Huesmann (see item 31).
31. Lefkowitz, Eron, Walder, & Huesmann Television Violence and Child Aggression: A Follow-up Study (Volume 3)	875 children—third-grade sample 382 adolescent—eighth-grade sample 427 19-year-olds	As part of a longitudinal study of childhood aggression, the investigators queried the child and/or his parents about his television viewing patterns (e.g., program preferences). Cross-lagged correlations between television viewing at age three and adolescent aggressiveness at age 19 were obtained to provide causal inferences regarding television's role in the development of aggressive behavior.
32. Leifer & Roberts Children's Responses to Television Violence Experiment I (Volume 2)	271 children 40 kindergarten 54 3rd grade 56 6th grade 51 9th grade 70 12th grade	Subsequent to viewing a television program which contained a number of violent acts each child was asked to evaluate the motivations and consequences surrounding each depicted act of violence. The child's understanding of these characteristics of violent act was then assessed in terms of the child's willingness to engage in aggressive behavior.

AUTHOR AND TITLE	SUBJECTS	DESCRIPTION
Experiment II (Volume 2)	132 children 62 preschool 40 5th grade 30 12th grade	Each child viewed a television program which was edited to provide one of four combinations of motivations/consequences for the portrayed violent acts: good-good, good-bad, bad-good, bad-bad. Post-viewing measures were similar to the prior study.
Experiment III (Volume 2)	160 children 51 4th grade 56 7th grade 53 10th grade	Children viewed one of two versions of a movie in which the justifications for aggression had been edited to provide for an "aggression-less justified" version. Post-viewing measures of aggressive behavior were similar to those employed in the first experiment.
Experiment IV (Volume 2)	349 children 99 3rd grade 138 6th grade 112 10th grade	The temporal separation of the motivations for an aggressive act and consequences accruing to the aggressor on the child's postviewing aggressive behavior, was explored in this present study. Measures of aggressive behavior were similar to previous studies.
33. Liebert Some Relationships Between Viewing Violence and Behaving Aggressively (Volume 2)		A review of current research on television's role in the imitation and/or disinhibition of aggressive behavior (with an additional report: Strauss & Poulos, "Television and Social Learning: A Summary of the Experimental Effects of Observed Filmed Aggression").
34. Liebert & Baron Short-Term Effects of Televised Aggression on Children's Aggressive Behavior (Volume 2)	136 children (68 boys and 68 girls) (65, 5- to 6-year-olds) (71, 8- to 9-year-olds)	In this study the child-viewer's willingness to engage in interpersonal aggression was assessed subsequent to viewing either aggressive or neutral television programming.
35. Liebert, Davidson, & Sobol Catharsis of Aggression Among Institutionalized Boys: Further Comments (Volume 5)		A comment on a reply to a critique of the catharsis thesis (see item 14, 15, and 36).
36. Liebert, Sobol & Davidson Catharsis of Aggression Among Institutionalized Boys: Fact or Artifact? (Volume 5)		A commentary on a study of the role of catharsis in evaluating the effects of viewing televised violence (see items 14, 15, and 35).

AUTHOR AND TITLE	SUBJECTS	DESCRIPTION
37. LoSciuto A National Inventory of Television Viewing Behavior (Volume 4)	252 families	A nationwide sample of American families were interviewed concerning various aspects of television viewing such as: why people watch television, what they learn from programs, extent of viewing, and program preferences.
38. Lyle Television in Day-to-Day Life: Patterns of Use (Volume 4)		A review of current research on the role of television in some aspects of daily life.
39. Lyle & Hoffman Children's Use of Television and Other Media (Volume 4)	1,682 children 300 1st grade 793–877, 6th grade 469–505, 10th grade	Children were interviewed about the role television plays in their daily life (e.g., extent and duration of viewing, program preferences, attitudes toward television, use of other forms of mass media). In addition, the mothers of first-graders were also interviewed concerning their perceptions of the role of television viewing patterns and perceived extent of learning from television.
40. Lyle & Hoffman Explorations in patterns of television viewing by preschool children (Volume 4)	158 children 40 3-year-olds 82 4-year-olds 35 5-year-olds 1 6-year-old	A selected sample of Caucasian, Black, and Mexican-American preschool boys and girls were interviewed concerning their television viewing (e.g., program preferences, extent of viewing, recognition of television characters). In addition, mothers were interviewed concerning their child's television viewing patterns and perceived extent of learning from television.
41. McIntyre & Teevan Television and Deviant Behavior (Volume 3)	2,270 junior and senior high school students	Questionnaire responses were used to provide an estimate of the relationship between television viewing patterns (e.g. program preferences) and self-reported aggressive and delinquent behavior.
42. McLeod, Atkin, & Chaffee Adolescents, Parents and Television Use: Self- Report and Other- Report Measures from the Wisconsin Sample (Volume 3)	648 students Maryland Sample 229 7th grade 244 10th grade Wisconsin Sample 68 7th grade 83 10th grade	Self-report, peer, and "other" rated indices of aggressive behavior were related to various aspects of the adolescent's pattern of television use (e.g., extent of viewing, program preferences, cognitive reactions to televised violence).
43. McLeod, Atkin, & Chaffee Adolescents, Parents and Television Use: Adoles- cent Self-Report and Other-Report Measures from the Maryland and Wisconsin Sample (Volume 3)		See item 42: A comparison between adolescent television viewing and self reported aggressive or delinquent behavior.

AUTHOR AND TITLE	SUBJECTS	DESCRIPTION
44. Murray 　　Television in Inner-City 　　Homes: Viewing 　　Behavior of Young 　　Boys 　　(Volume 4)	27 5- to 6-year- old boys	Observation of in-home television viewing, parent-child interviews, diary records of 1 week's television viewing and measures of cognitive and social development were used to provide a description of the role television plays in the daily lives of a selected sample of young boys (with an additional report: Furfey, "First Graders Watching Television").
45. Neale 　　Comment on: Television 　　Violence and Child 　　Aggression: A Follow- 　　up Study 　　(Volume 3)		A methodological note on the Lefkowitz, Eron, Walder, & Huesmann study (see item 31).
46. Rabinovitch, MacLean, 　　Markham, & Talbott 　　Children's Violence 　　Perception as a 　　Function of Television 　　Violence 　　(Volume 5)	57 sixth-grade children 24 girls 33 boys	This study was designed to assess changes in the child's perception of violence as a result of viewing televised violence. Children viewed either an aggressive or nonaggressive television program and were then presented with a discrimination task (i.e., identifying a tachistoscopically presented slide as either "violent" or "nonviolent").
47. Robinson 　　Television's Impact on 　　Everyday Life: Some 　　Cross-National 　　Evidence 　　(Volume 4)		This study was focused on the respondent's allocation of time ("time-budgets") to various activities (e.g., work, child care, leisure, mass media use) in his daily life. Time budgets were sampled in 15 cities in 11 counties.
48. Robinson 　　Toward Defining the 　　Functions of Television 　　(Volume 4)		A review of current research on the role of television in relation to other daily activities.
49. Robinson & Bachman 　　Television Viewing 　　Habits and Aggression 　　(Volume 3)	1,559 19-year- old males	As part of a nationwide survey of the changing characteristics of youth, respondents were asked to indicate the extent of their television viewing, program preferences, and the locus of "greatest-learning-about-life"— television vs. school. These findings were then related to the respondents' self-reported incidence of aggressive and delinquent behaviors.
50. Shinar 　　Structure and Content of 　　Television Broadcasting 　　in Israel 　　(Volume 1)		A review of television broadcasting policies in Israel.

AUTHOR AND TITLE	SUBJECTS	DESCRIPTION
51. Stein & Friedrich Television Content and Young Children's Behavior (Volume 2) (with Vondracek)	97 3½- to 5½- year-olds 52 boys 45 girls	Preschool children were exposed to either an "aggressive, neutral, or prosocial" television diet and then observed during the course of their daily interaction with other children in their classroom. The observations were conducted over a 9-week period including 3-week baseline, 4-week controlled viewing, and 2-week follow-up periods. Changes (over baseline) in either aggressive or prosocial behaviors were used to provide a measure of the impact of television programming.
52. Stevenson Television and the Behavior of Preschool Children (Volume 2)		A discussion of research findings on the impact of television in early childhood and suggestions for future research.
53. Tannenbaum Studies in Film- and TV-Mediated Arousal and Aggression (Volume 5)		A review of research and theory on mediating factors (e.g., emotional arousal) in the relationships between viewing televised violence and subsequent aggressive behavior.
54. Wackman, Reale, & Ward Racial Differences in Responses to Advertising Among Adolescents (Volume 4)	1,149 8th–12th grade 1,049 whites 100 blacks	This study was focused on a comparison of the responses of black and white adolescents to television advertising in terms of their favorite ads, extent of "learning consumer roles," and reasons offered for viewing commercials.
55. Ward Effects of Television Advertising on Children and Adolescents (Volume 4)		A review and discussion of research, in the current program, on the impact of television advertising.
56. Ward, Levinson, & Wackman Children's Attention to Television Advertising (Volume 4)	134 mothers of 5- to 12-year- old children	Interviews were conducted with the mothers of young children in order to determine the short-term consequences of watching television advertising.
57. Ward, Reale, & Levinson Children's Perceptions, Explanations, and Judgments of Television Advertising: A Further Exploration. (Volume 4)		An elaboration of the Blatt, Spencer, & Ward study (see item 3).
58. Ward & Robertson Adolescent Attitudes Toward Television Advertising (Volume 4)	1,094 8th–12th grades	This study was designed to relate adolescent's attitudes toward television advertising to demographic characteristics, family communication patterns, and television use.

AUTHOR AND TITLE	SUBJECTS	DESCRIPTION
59. Ward & Wackman Family Media Influences on Adolescent Consumer Learning (Volume 4)	1,094 8th–12th grades	This survey assessed the adolescent's "consumer skills" (i.e., recall of advertising content, attitudes toward commercials, materialistic attitudes, and buying behavior) and related these skills to various demographic characteristics.
60. Ward & Wackman Television Advertising and Intra-Family Influence: Children's Purchase Influence Attempts and Parental Yielding (Volume 4)	109 mothers of 5- to 12-year-old children	Interviewers asked the mothers of young children to describe the "effects of television advertising" in terms of the frequency and intensity of their child's "requests" for advertised products.

Appendix C

TELEVISION AND THE EMOTIONALLY DISTURBED CHILD
Joyce Sprafkin

With few exceptions, the literature on the effects of television on children has focused on normal (i.e., nonhandicapped) populations. It has been the intention of this book to present what is known about the effects of television on the broad range of normal children. However, it is also important to explore the impact of the medium on handicapped children because their use of and reactions to TV may differ from that of the larger population.

For the past several years I have been involved in a program of research with Dr. Kenneth Gadow, a specialist in handicapped children, to assess the effects of television on children who have been labeled emotionally disturbed (ED).* This population was selected for study because it has several characteristics that are associated with frequent TV use and reactivity to TV violence. Studies on normal children have shown that children who are heavy TV viewers tend to have major difficulties getting along with peers or parents and are low academic achievers (e.g., Himmelweit et al., 1958; Huesmann, Eron, & Lefkowitz, 1984). Those who are most affected by TV violence portrayals tend to be somewhat more aggressive initially (Dorr & Kovaric, 1980). These characteristics (interpersonal and academic difficulties and aggressivity) are prevalent in the ED population (Cullinan, Epstein, & Kauffman, 1984; McCarthy & Paraskevopoulos, 1969).

In this section I will provide an overview of the research that has examined television and the ED child. The organization of the presentation has been shaped largely by social learning theory, which assumes that in order for television content to affect a viewer, the viewer must (a) be exposed to the content, (b) comprehend it to some degree, and (c) accept the message and adopt the behaviors or attitudes portrayed (see chapter 4). Ac-

---

*The definition of "emotionally disturbed" varies with geographic locale and professional discipline. The youngsters involved in the program of research attended a public elementary school that served the behavior disordered youngsters from 27 school districts in the surrounding communities on Long Island, New York. The most common reasons for referral to the school are oppositional behavior, overactivity, aggressivity, and emotional lability.

cordingly, ED children's exposure to television (i.e., how much and what kinds of programs they watch), the extent to which they comprehend media content, and the effects of various types of television content will be considered successively. Finally, I discuss therapeutic uses of TV for institutionalized ED children.

Television Viewing Habits

A literature review by Sprafkin, Gadow, and Grayson (1984) located only two studies that examined the television viewing habits of ED children. Surveys (Donohue, 1978; Rubinstein, Fracchia, Kochnower, & Sprafkin, 1977) show that institutionalized ED children watch a heavy diet of aggressive programs and prefer aggressive over nonaggressive television characters. Child care workers in institutions for ED children report that they observe frequent instances of imitative aggression in response to viewing television (Rubinstein et al., 1977).

We (Sprafkin & Gadow, 1986) conducted a study of the television viewing habits of ED children in which 42 ED boys and 42 normal boys completed a television viewing diary of the programs they typically watch. The viewing habits comparisons revealed that the ED children watched more hours of television than the normal children. Of greater importance is the finding that the ED children watched significantly more crime dramas and named significantly more crime dramas as favorite programs than did the normals. Furthermore, cartoons were viewed for significantly more hours by the ED students. Content analyses clearly indicate that both crime dramas and cartoons contain high levels of aggressive behavior (see chapter 7).

Comprehension of Television Content

Children's perceptions of the reality of television content have been identified as an important cognitive mediator of reactivity. In the case of aggressive television content, research has shown that the belief that the TV aggression is real (not staged) enhances the likelihood of post-exposure aggression (Atkin, 1983; Feshbach, 1976; Sawin, 1981).

To examine ED children's perceptions of the reality versus fantasy content of television, we (Sprafkin, Gadow, & Dussault, 1986) compared the performance of 41 ED boys with that of 41 normal boys on a specially developed test that involved viewing and answering questions about actual TV excerpts. The Videotest, as it came to be called, was constructed to assess, with minimal reliance on the test taker's reading ability, children's knowledge about the realism of people and situations shown on television and the truthfulness of commercials. The findings of this study, as well as those from a second study on another sample of ED and normal children

(Sprafkin, Kelly, & Gadow, 1987), indicated that ED children were more likely than their normal peers to perceive television programs as accurate depictions of the real world and commercials as truthful. It is reasonable to speculate that these perceptions may render ED children more susceptible than normal peers to the influences of TV programs and commercials.

Effects of Television Aggression on Behavior

Despite the seeming vulnerability of ED children to television's adverse effects, there has been little research bearing on this issue. A review of the literature (Sprafkin et al., 1984) located only one investigation that was relevant to this topic, an early study by Walters and Willows (1968) which showed that institutionalized ED children became more aggressive toward toys after viewing a videotape of an aggressive model.

We (Sprafkin & Gadow, in press) conducted the first laboratory study on the effects of television aggression on noninstitutionalized ED children. As an attempt to parallel previous research, we employed the "Help-Hurt game," a measure of aggression that had been used repeatedly in laboratory studies of nonhandicapped children (Collins & Getz, 1976; Liebert & Baron, 1972; Liss, et al., 1983; see chapters 10, 5, and 7, respectively). Fifteen ED and 23 learning disabled (LD) children (average age: 7 years) viewed either an aggressive or control cartoon and then played the game. The children who watched the aggressive cartoon pressed the Hurt button for significantly more time than those who were exposed to the control cartoon. These findings are consistent with prior research on normal children.

To help clarify the clinical relevance of media aggression for ED youngsters, four field experiments using cartoons as media stimuli were then conducted. While the studies varied with regard to specific details, they all followed the same general protocol. Prior to and following media exposure periods were baseline conditions that allowed us to evaluate the children's normal levels of social interaction. During a media exposure period, children watched either aggressive or nonaggressive cartoons prior to going to lunch. A within-subject design was employed such that all children viewed aggressive and nonaggressive cartoons, but on different days.* Direct observations of social interactions during lunch and recess were completed by trained observers who were unaware of the treatment conditions. The

---

*This design was employed because the ED population is heterogeneous, which often results in problems of initial differences between groups that are assigned to contrasting TV conditions. Studies in which all participants are rotated through the various television exposure conditions is an uncommon design, but one that can be useful in eliminating the issue of preexisting differences between groups.

data were analyzed by comparing baseline and aggressive and control cartoon conditions.

For our first study, we (Gadow & Sprafkin, 1987) examined two classes of ED children, one younger (average age: 6.6 years) and one older (average age: 10.1 years). The findings indicated that the older ED class exhibited a significant increase in both physical aggression and appropriate social interaction following the aggressive cartoons compared with baseline levels, with a similar trend for nonphysical aggression. This is consistent with predictions made by the arousal hypothesis. The younger group, however, showed a different pattern of reactivity. They became significantly more noncompliant following exposure to aggressive cartoons, but their aggressive behavior did not change from baseline. By contrast, their level of physical and nonphysical aggression decreased following the control cartoons.

Our second field experiment (Sprafkin, Gadow, & Grayson, in press) employed four classes of ED children (20 boys and 6 girls, average age: 8.1 years). The results revealed a significant media effect for two behavior categories, nonphysical and physical aggression. However, contrary to prediction, there were significantly more instances of nonphysical aggression on days that the children were shown control cartoons than on baseline days, and significantly more acts of physical aggression following the control cartoons relative to the aggressive cartoon and baseline conditions in the recess setting. *Post hoc* consideration of the qualities of the control programs that may account for this effect led us to suspect that the control programs (which, while nonaggressive, were suspenseful and danger-laden) were arousing for this group of children.

Our third field experiment (Sprafkin, Gadow, & Grayson, 1987) used the identical methods as the preceding study but involved LD children. The LD children were much less reactive to the cartoons than the ED children; however, there was evidence for media reactivity with the lower IQ youngsters, who became significantly more physically aggressive following control compared with aggressive cartoons.

In our fourth field experiment, the same design was employed with preschool ED children (Gadow, Sprafkin, & Ficarrotto, 1987). Two classes showed a clear pattern of media reactivity. Their level of nonphysical aggression increased above baseline following both aggressive (marginally significant) and control (significant) cartoons, but the two cartoon conditions generated comparable levels of aggression.*

---

*It is important to note that the programs shown in the control condition varied somewhat between the studies. The programs were, however, the least aggressive cartoons in a videotape library of several hundred broadcasted children's programs. The series (and the number of episodes) used were as follows: Gadow & Sprafkin (1987), older class = "Fat Albert" (2), "Devlin" (2), younger class = "Fat Albert" (2), "Devlin" (2), "Lassie's Rescue Rangers" (2); Sprafkin et al. (in press, 1987) = "Lassie's Rescue Rangers" (6); Gadow et al. (1987) = "Fat Albert" (1), "Devlin" (1), "Lassie's Rescue Rangers" (2). The series represented in the aggressive TV condition include "Tom and Jerry," "Woody Woodpecker," "Bugs Bunny," and "Pink Panther."

These field experiments suggest that the reactions of ED children to aggressive and nonaggressive cartoons are far from predictable. Two groups of children (Gadow & Sprafkin, 1987, older class; Gadow et al., 1987) became more aggressive following exposure to aggressive cartoons, but in the latter instance the control cartoons produced the same effect. None of the other studies showed significant increases in aggressive behavior following the aggressive cartoons. With regard to reactions to the control programs, one group of children (Gadow & Sprafkin, 1987, younger class) became significantly less aggressive and two groups (Sprafkin et al., 1987; in press) became significantly more aggressive. It appears that ED children *do* become more aggressive or noncompliant following cartoons; however, the problematic content is not at all clear from the existing data. Arousal rather than modeling mechanisms seem to be involved, but further research is needed to clarify what TV stimulus, child, and setting characteristics determine the impact.

Therapeutic Uses of TV

There have been isolated attempts to use TV programs that contain prosocial content to enhance the social functioning of ED children in institutional settings. Two of these endeavors will be described.

Elias (1979, 1983) excerpted segments from the "Inside/Out" TV series (developed by the Agency for Instructional Television) dealing with such topics as peer pressure, teasing, and expressing one's feelings. Fifty-two boys between 7 and 15 years old living in a residential treatment center for ED children were shown the "Inside/Out" segments twice weekly for five consecutive weeks. Each showing was followed by a group discussion which highlighted problem-solving strategies and focused on aspects of the program content. A control group of 57 boys did not see any special programs. Based on a sociometric measure and unobtrusive behavioral observations of boys in the two groups, it was found that the boys who saw the "Inside/Out" segments showed increased positive behaviors, decreased social isolation, and greater popularity relative to the control group.

Sprafkin and Rubinstein (1982) studied 132 youngsters in four high functioning wards (average age: 14 years) in a state residential facility for ED children. A prosocial television diet was constructed containing 10 programs with frequent instances of prosocial behavior, and its influence relative to a control TV diet was assessed. The study also compared the effects of the two viewing regimens with and without a postviewing discussion, which evaluated the pro- and antisocial behaviors contained in the programs, encouraging the former and discouraging the latter. The four treatments (prosocial with and without discussion, control TV diet with and without discussion) were rotated through the four wards over a period of approximately 1 year. Each treatment phase involved: (a) 1 week of observing the youngsters' social behavior, (b) 2 weeks of watching the 10 programs (either prosocial or control) with or without the discussion, and (c) 1 week of follow-up behavioral observations. The programs in the prosocial diet were previously broadcast on commercial television and dealt with the benefits of helping others, compromising when there is a conflict, considering other peoples' feelings, cooperating with teachers, and problems with stealing and playing practical jokes. They include situation comedies ("Brady Bunch"), dramas ("Room 222"), and cartoons ("Fat Albert and the Cosby Kids"). The control programs were selected on the basis of a survey of the television viewing habits and preferences of the youngsters on the four wards and was composed of the 10 most popular series, which included cartoons ("The Flintstones") and situation comedies ("Sanford and Son").

The results showed that altruistic behaviors increased for the children exposed to the prosocial television relative to those who saw the standard fare. This facilitation of altruism was more pronounced for those youngsters who were above average on baseline measures of physical aggression. Verbal aggression (e.g., threats, teases, name-calling) and aggression toward objects decreased for youngsters exposed to the prosocial shows without group discussion, while both behaviors increased if the TV show was followed by a discussion. Symbolic aggression (use of noncontact and nonverbal aggressive behaviors, including chasing and threatening gestures) decreased in the physically aggressive subjects who were exposed to the prosocial programming compared with the other groups. For reasons perhaps unique to this population, discussion following prosocial viewing appears to be at best ineffective and at worst detrimental in facilitating prosocial and reducing antisocial behavior, perhaps because the rather "tough" image youths reacted against the moralistic tone of the prosocial discussion. Nevertheless, the study shows that prosocial commercial television can be used as a therapeutic tool for shaping positive social behavior in the institutionalized ED child.

Teaching Critical Viewing Skills

One possible approach to diminish the adverse and enhance the positive effects of the medium is the development of school-based critical television viewing skills (or television literacy) curricula. As we discussed in chapter 10, one of the assumptions underlying this approach is that if children understand how television programs are made, what is real versus pretend, and how special effects make the impossible appear real, they will be less vulnerable to the medium's negative consequences.

We (Sprafkin, Gadow, & Kant, 1988) assessed the effects of a viewing skills curriculum on the television-related knowledge and attitudes of elementary school–aged ED children. Three classes received the 12-lesson curriculum over a 4-week period and three classes served as a control group. The children who received the curriculum made significantly more accurate reality-fantasy discriminations concerning television program content than those in the control group. Whether or not this greater media awareness leads to changed viewing habits or less media reactivity is unknown at this point, but is currently being investigated with a larger sample of ED youngsters.

Conclusion

In summary, research has shown that ED children watch more TV overall and more aggressive programs (i.e., crime dramas and cartoons) than their normal peers. They are more likely to believe in the accuracy of TV drama and advertising claims, although there is preliminary evidence indicating that these children can be taught to be more critical of what they see, potentially defusing some of TV's impact. Like their normal peers, watching aggressive programming is related to greater willingness to hurt another child when these children are tested in a laboratory setting. Moreover, most ED children become more aggresive in naturalistic settings after watching cartoons, although it is sometimes the case that nonaggressive but suspenseful cartoons produce more aggressive behavior than aggressive cartoons. It is also possible to enhance the social functioning of institutionalized ED children with selected programs that emphasize prosocial themes.

It is important to bear in mind that the findings from these studies should not be generalized to other populatons, settings, or media materials, nor should they be used to make statements about the *long-term* effects of exposure to television. These studies do, however, emphasize the point that special populations of children often react to television in ways that are different than nonhandicapped children. There is a need for further research on how television is used, comprehended, and reacted to by ED children as well as by children with other handicaps, such as learning disabilities and mental retardation.

References

Abeles, N. (1986). Proceedings of the American Psychological Association, Incorporated, for the year 1985. *American Psychologist, 41*(6), 633–647.

Absence of NAB code not expected to have major impact; NAD pre-screening of kids' ads increases. (1983, February 14). *Television/Radio Age*, pp. 54–56.

Action for Children's Television. (1972, Spring/Summer). ACT petitions Federal Trade Commission. *ACT NEWSLETTER*.

Action for Children's Television. (1980). *FTC Children's advertising rulemaking fact sheet*. Newtonville, MA: ACT.

Actor Savalas won't testify. (1977, October 5). *Sarasota Journal*.

Alsop, R. (1985, September 5). Watchdogs zealously censor advertising targeted to kids. *The Wall Street Journal*, Section 2, p. 35.

American Academy of Child Psychiatry. (1984, November 28). *Draft of Final Report of The Task Force on Violence and the Media*. Washington, DC: Author.

American Academy of Pediatrics. (1986). *Television and the family*. ELK Grove Village, IL: Author.

American Broadcasting Companies. (1983). A research perspective on television and violence. Report by Social Research Unit and the Broadcast Standards and Practices Department. New York: Author.

American Medical Association. (1976). Policy no. 38. *Violence on TV: An environmental hazard*. Reference Committee E, 367.

American Psychological Association. (1985, February 22). Resolution passed by the APA Council of Representatives. Washington, DC: Public Information Office.

Anderson, D.R. (1977, March). *Children's attention to television*. Paper presented at the Biennial Meeting of the Society for Research in Child Development, New Orleans.

Anderson, D.R. (1985). On-line cognitive processing of television. In A. Mitchell & L. Alwitt (Eds.), *Psychological processes and advertising effects: Theory, research, and application* (pp. 177–199). Hillsdale, NJ: Lawrence Erlbaum Associates.

Anderson, D.R., Alwitt, L.F., Lorch, E.P., & Levin, S.R. (1979). Watching children watch television. In G. Hale & M. Lewis (Eds.), *Attention and the development of cognitive skills*. New York: Plenum.

Anderson, D.R., Field, D.E., Collins, P.A., Lorch, E.P., & Nathan, J.G. (1985). Estimates of young children's time with television: A methodological comparison of parent reports with time-lapse video home observation. *Child Development, 56*, 1345–1357.

Anderson, D.R., & Levin, S.R. (1976). Young children's attention to "Sesame Street." *Child Development, 47*(3), 806–811.

Anderson, D.R., & Lorch, E.P. (1983). Looking at television: Action or reaction? In J. Bryant & D.R. Anderson (Eds.), *Children's understanding of television: Research on attention and comprehension* (pp. 1–33). New York: Academic Press.

Anderson, D.R., Lorch, E.P., Field, D.E., Collins, P.A., & Nathan, J.G. (1986). *Television viewing at home: Age trends in visual attention and time with TV*. Unpublished manuscript, University of Massachusetts, Amherst.

Anderson, D.R., Lorch, E.P., Field, D.E., & Sanders, J. (1981). The effects of TV program comprehensibility on preschool children's visual attention to television. *Child Development, 52*, 151–157.

Andison, F.S. (1977). TV violence and viewer aggression: A cumulation of study results 1956–1976. *Public Opinion Quarterly, 41*, 314–331.

Another kind of ratings war: The campaign to take the sex and violence out of television. (1981, July 6). *Time*, pp. 17–19.

Aronoff, C. (1974). Old age in prime time. *Journal of Communication, 24*, 86–87.

Atkin, C. (1975a). *Effects of television advertising on children–First year experimental evidence* (Report 1). East Lansing: Michigan State University.

Atkin, C. (1975b). *Effects of television advertising on children–Second year experimental evidence* (Report 2). East Lansing: Michigan State University.

Atkin, C. (1975c). *Effects of television advertising on children–Survey of pre-adolescent's response to television commercials* (Report 6). East Lansing: Michigan State University.

Atkin, C. (1975d). *Effects of television advertising on children–Parent child communication in supermarket breakfast selection* (Report 7). East Lansing: Michigan State University.

Atkin, C. (1975e). *Effects of television advertising on children–Survey of children's and mother's responses to television commercials* (Report 8). East Lansing: Michigan State University.

Atkin, C. (1978). Observation of parent-child interaction in supermarket decision making. *Journal of Marketing, 42*, 41–45.

Atkin, C.K. (1978b). Effects of drug commercials on young viewers. *Journal of Communication, 28,* 71–79.

Atkin, C.K. (1982). Television advertising and socialization to consumer roles. In D. Pearl, L. Bouthilet, & J. Lazar (Eds.), *Television and behavior: Ten years of scientific progress and implications for the eighties, Vol. 2, Technical Reviews* (pp. 191–200). Washington, DC: U.S. Government Printing Office.

Atkin, C. (1983). Effects of realistic TV violence vs. fictional violence on aggression. *Journalism Quarterly. 60*(4), 615–621.

Atkin, C., & Gibson, W. (1978). *Children's nutrition learning from television advertising.* Unpublished manuscript, Michigan State University, East Lansing.

Atkin, C.K., & Heald, G. (1977). The content of children's toy and food commercials. *Journal of Communication, 27*(1), 107–114.

Atkin, C.K., Murray, J.P., & Nayman, O.B. (1971). *Television and social behavior: An annotated bibliography of research focusing on television's impact on children.* Washington: U.S. Public Health Service.

Atkin, C., Reeves, B., & Gibson, W. (1979). *Effects of television food advertising on children.* Paper presented at the meeting of the Association for Education in Journalism, Houston, TX.

Baker, R.K. (1969). The views, standards, and practices of the television industry. In R.K. Baker & S.J. Ball (Eds.), *Violence and the media* (pp. 593–614). Washington, DC: U.S. Government Printing Office.

Baker, R.K., & Ball, S.J. (1969). *Mass media and violence. Staff report to the National Commission on the causes and prevention of violence, Volume 9.* Washington, DC: U.S. Government Printing Office.

Baldwin, T.F., & Lewis, C. (1972). Violence in television: The industry looks at itself. In G.A. Comstock & E.A. Rubinstein (Eds.), *Television and social behavior. Vol. 1. Media content and control.* (pp. 290–373). Washington, DC: U.S. Government Printing Office.

Ball, S., & Bogatz, G. (1970). *The first year of Sesame Street: An evaluation.* Princeton, NJ: Educational Testing Service.

Ball, S., & Bogatz, G. (1973). *Reading with television: An evaluation of the Electric Company.* Princeton, NJ: Educational Testing Service.

Bandura, A. (1963, October 22). What TV violence can do to your child. *Look,* pp. 46–52.

Bandura, A. (1965). Influence of models' reinforcement contingencies on the acquisition of imitative responses. *Journal of Personality and Social Psychology, 1*, 589–595.

Bandura, A., Ross, D., & Ross, S.A. (1961). Transmission of aggression through imitation of aggressive models. *Journal of Abnormal and Social Psychology, 63*, 575–582.

Bandura, A., Ross, D., & Ross, S.A. (1963). Imitation of film-mediated aggressive models. *Journal of Abnormal and Social Psychology, 66*, 3–11.

Bandura, A., & Walters, R.H. (1963). *Social learning and personality development.* New York: Holt, Rinehart & Winston.

Baptista-Fernandez, P, Greenberg, B.S., & Atkin, C. (1980). The context, characteristics and communication behaviors of blacks on television. In B.S. Greenberg (Ed.), *Life on television: Content analyses of U.S. TV drama* (pp. 13–21). Norwood, NJ: Ablex Publishing.

Baran, S.J. (1976). Sex on TV and adolescent sexual self-image. *Journal of Broadcasting, 20,* 61–68.

Baran, S.J., Chase, L.J., & Courtright, J.A. (1979). Television drama as a facilitator of prosocial behavior: "The Waltons." *Journal of Broadcasting, 23*(3), 277–284.

Barcus, F.E. (1971). *Saturday children's television: A report on TV programming and advertising on Boston commercial television.* Newtonville, MA: Action for Children's Television.

Barcus, F.E. (1977). *Children's television: An analysis of programming and advertising.* New York: Praeger Publishing.

Barcus, F.E. (1978a). *Commercial children's television on weekends and weekday afternoons.* Newtonville, MA: Action for Children's Television.

Barcus, F.E. (1978b). *Food advertising on children's television: An analysis of appeals and nutritional content.* Newtonville, MA: Action for Children's Television.

Barcus, F.E. (1983). *Images of life on children's television.* New York: Praeger Publishers.

Barnouw, E. (1972). *A history of broadcasting in the United States. Vol. III–from 1953: The image empire.* New York: Oxford University Press.

Baxter, R.L., De Riemer, C., Landini, A., Leslie, L., & Singletary, M.W. (1985). A content analysis of music videos. *Journal of Broadcasting & Electronic Media, 29*(3), 333–340.

Bechtel, R.B., Achelpohl, C., & Akers, R. (1972). Correlates between observed behavior and questionnaire responses on television viewing. In E.A. Rubinstein, G.A. Comstock, & J.P. Murray (Eds.), *Television and social behavior. Vol. 4, Television in day-to-day life: Patterns of use* (pp. 274–344). Washington, DC: U.S. Government Printing Office.

Beer and wine ads: The gathering storm. (1985, January 28). *Broadcasting,* pp. 31–33.

Belson, W.A. (1978). *Television violence and the adolescent boy.* Hampshire, England: Saxon House.

Berkowitz, L. (1962). *Aggression: A social psychological analysis.* New York: McGraw-Hill.

Berkowitz, L. (1965). Some aspects of observed aggression. *Journal of Personality and Social Psychology, 2,* 359–369.

Berkowitz, L. (1969). The frustration-aggression hypothesis revisited. In L. Berkowitz (Ed.), *Roots of aggression: A re-examination of the frustration-aggression hypothesis.* New York: Atherton Press.

Berkowitz, L., & Geen, R.G. (1966). Film violence and the cue properties of available targets. *Journal of Personality and Social Psychology, 3,* 525–530.

Berkowitz, L., & Geen, R.G. (1967). Stimulus qualities of the target of aggression: A further study. *Journal of Personality and Social Psychology, 5,* 364–368.

Beuf, A. (1974). Doctor, lawyer, household drudge. *Journal of Communication, 24*(2), 142–145.

Bever, T., Smith, M., Bengen, B., & Johnson, T. (1975). Young viewers' troubling responses to TV ads. *Harvard Business Review, 53*(6), 109–120.

Bishop, J.M., & Krause, J.M. (1984). Depictions of aging and old age on Saturday morning television. *The Gerontologist, 24*(1), 91–94.

Blatt, J., Spencer, L., & Ward, S. (1972). A cognitive developmental study of children's reactions to television advertising. In E.A. Rubinstein, G.A. Comstock, & J.P. Murray (Eds.), *Television and social behavior. Vol. IV: Television in day-to-day life: Patterns of use* (pp. 452–467). Washington, DC: U.S. Government Printing Office.

Boffey, P.M., & Walsh, J. (1970, May 22). Study of TV violence. Seven top researchers blackballed from panel. *Science, 168,* 949–952.

Bogatz, G.A., & Ball, S. (1972). *The second year of Sesame Street: A continuing evaluation.* Princeton, NJ: Educational Testing Service.

Boyd, D.A. & Straubhaar, J.D. (1985). Developmental impact of the home video cassette recorder on third world countries. *Journal of Broadcasting & Electronic Media, 29*(1), 5–21.

Boyer, P.J. (1986 February 3). Ethics of toy-based TV shows are disputed. *The New York Times,* p. 1.

Branscomb, A.W., & Savage, M. (1978). The broadcast reform movement: At the crossroads. *Journal of Communication, 28*(4), 25–34.

Brown, L. (1971). *Television: The business behind the box.* New York: Harcourt Brace Jovanovich.

Brown, L. (1976, July 30). Study assails sponsors on TV violence. *New York Times.*

Brown, L. (1977). *The New York Times encyclopedia of television.* New York: Times Books.

Bryan, J.H., & Walbek, N.B. (1970). Preaching and practicing generosity: Children's actions and reactions. *Child Development, 41,* 329–353.

Bryant, J. (1985, October 28). Testimony at hearings before the U.S. House of Representatives' Subcommittee on Telecommunications, Consumer Protection, and Finance.

Bryant, J., Carveth, R.A., & Brown, D. (1981). Television viewing and anxiety: An experimental examination. *Journal of Communication, 31,* 106–119.

Buchanan, J. (1977a, October 6). Zamora didn't mean to shoot, doctor says. *Miami Herald.*

Buchanan, J. (1977b, October 7). Zamora guilty of murder. *Miami Herald.*

Buerkel-Rothfuss, N.L., & Mayes, S. (1981). Soap opera viewing: The cultivation effect. *Journal of Communication, 31*(3), 108–115.

Bureau of the Census (1985). *Statistical abstract of the United States – 1986.* Washington, DC: U.S. Department of Commerce.

Busby, L. (1974). Defining the sex role standard in commercial network television programs directed toward children. *Journalism Quarterly, 51,* 690–696.

Calvert, S.L., Huston, A.C., Watkins, B.A., & Wright, J.C. (1982). The relation between selective attention to television forms and children's comprehension of content. *Child Development, 53,* 601–610.

Cantor, M.G. (1972). The role of the producer in choosing children's television content. In G.A. Comstock & E.A. Rubinstein (Eds.), *Television and social behavior. Vol. 1: Media content and control* (pp. 259–289). Washington, DC: U.S. Government Printing Office.

Cantor, M.G. (1982). The organization and production of prime time television. In D. Pearl, L. Bouthilet, & J. Lazar (Eds.), *Television and behavior: Ten years of scientific progress and implications for the eighties* (Vol. 2, pp. 349–362). Washington, DC: U.S. Government Printing Office.

Carnegie Commission. (1967). *Public television: A program for action.* New York: Harper & Row.

Cater, D., & Strickland, S. (1975). *TV violence and the child: The evolution and fate of the Surgeon General's Report.* New York: Russell Sage.

Chaffee, S.H., & McLeod, J.M. (1971, September). *Adolescents, parents, and television violence.* Paper presented at American Psychological Association meeting. Washington, DC.

Charren, P. (1974). The selling game. *Madison Avenue, 17,* 4–5.

Children's Advertising Review Unit (1983). *Self-regulatory guidelines for children's advertising.* New York: National Advetising Division, Council of Better Business Bureaus.

Children's Television Workshop. (1980). *International research notes.* New York: Author.

Children's Television Workshop. (1986). *Square One Television: A new television series about mathematics.* New York: Author.

Christenson, P.G. (1982). Children's perceptions of TV commercials and products: The effects of PSAs. *Communication Research, 9*(4), 491–524.

Cisin, I.H., Coffin, T.E., Janis, I.L., Klapper, J.T., Mendelsohn, H., Omwake, E., Pinderhughes, C.A., Pool, I. de Sola, Siegel, A.E., Wallace, A.F.C., Watson, A.S., & Wiebe, G.D. (1972). *Television and growing up: The impact of televised violence.* Washington, DC: U.S. Government Printing Office.

Clancy-Hepburn, K., Hickey, A., & Nevill, G. (1974). Children's behavior responses to TV food advertisements. *Journal of Nutrition Education, 6*(3), 93–96.

Clark, C.C. (1972). Race, identification, and television violence. In G.A. Comstock, E.A. Rubinstein & J.P. Murray (Eds.), *Television and social behavior, Vol. 5, Television's effects: Further explorations.* Washington, DC: U.S. Government Printing Office.

Cline, V.B. (Ed.) (1974a). *Where do you draw the line? An exploration into media violence, pornography and censorship.* Provo, UT: Brigham Young University Press.

Cline, V.B. (1974b). Another view: Pornography effects, the state of the art. In V.B. Cline (Ed.), *Where do you draw the line?* (pp. 203–244). Provo, UT: Brigham Young University Press.

Coates, B., Pusser, H.E. & Goodman, I. (1976). The influence of *Sesame Street* and *Mister Rogers' Neighborhood* on children's social behavior in the preschool. *Child Development, 47,* 138–144.

Coffin, T.E., & Tuchman, S. (1973). Rating television programs for violence: Comparison of five surveys. *Journal of Broadcasting, 17*(1), 3–20.

Cole, B., & Oettinger, M. (1978). *Reluctant regulators: The FCC and the broadcast audience.* Reading, MA: Addison-Wesley.

Collins, W.A. (1970). Learning of media content: A developmental study. *Child Development, 41,* 1133–1142.

Collins, W.A. (1973). Effect of temporal separation between motivation, aggression, and consequences: A developmental study. *Developmental Psychology, 8*(2), 215–221.

Collins, W.A. (1982). Cognitive processing in television viewing. In D. Pearl, L. Bouthilet, & J. Lazar (Eds.), *Television and behavior: Ten years of scientific progress and implications for the eighties* (Vol. 2 pp. 9–23). Washington, DC: U.S. Government Printing Office.

Collins, W.A. (1983). Interpretation and inference in children's television viewing. In J. Bryant & D.R. Anderson (Eds.), *Children's understanding of television: Research on attention and comprehension* (pp. 125–150). New York: Academic Press.

Collins, W.A., & Getz, S.K. (1976). Children's social responses following modeled reactions to provocation: Prosocial effects of a television drama. *Journal of Personality, 44,* 488–500.

Collins, W.A., Sobol, B.L., & Westby, S. (1981). Effects of adult commentary on children's comprehension and inferences about a televised aggressive portrayal. *Child Development, 52,* 158–163.

Collins, W.A., Wellman, H., Keniston, A.H., & Westby, S.D. (1978). Age-related aspects of comprehension and inference from a televised dramatic narrative. *Child Development, 49*(2), 389–399.

Columbia Broadcasting System. (1974). A study of messages received by children who viewed an episode of *Fat Albert and the Cosby Kids.* New York: CBS Broadcast Group.

Columbia Broadcasting System. (1977). *Communicating with children through television.* New York: Author.

Commission on Obscenity and Pornography. (1970). *Report of the Commission on Obscenity and Pornography.* New York: Bantam Books.

Comstock, G. (1974, Summer). Review of television and antisocial behavior: Field experiments (by S. Milgram & R.L. Shotland). *Journal of Communication,* 155–158.

Comstock, G. (1975). *Television and human behavior: The key studies.* Santa Monica, CA: The Rand Corporation.

Comstock, G., Chaffee, S., Katzman, N., McCombs, M., & Roberts, D. (1978). *Television and human behavior.* New York: Columbia University Press.

Cook, T.D., Appleton, H., Conner, R.F., Shaffer, A., Tabkin, G., & Weber, J.S. (1975). *Sesame Street revisited.* New York: Russell Sage.

Cook, T.D., Kendzierski, D.A., & Thomas, S.V. (1983). The implicit assumptions of television research: An analysis of the 1982 NIMH report on *Television and behavior. Public Opinion Quarterly, 47,* 161–201.

Corder-Bolz, C.R. (1980). Mediation: The role of significant others. *Journal of Communication, 30,* 106–118.

Corder-Bolz, C.R. (1982). Television literary and critical television viewing skills. In D. Pearl, L. Bouthilet, & J. Lazar (Eds.), *Television and behavior: Ten years of scientific progress and implications for the eighties* (Vol. 2, pp. 91–101). Washington, DC: U.S. Government Printing Office.

Corporation for Public Broadcasting. (1985a). *Demographic composition of public television audiences.* In-house report.

Corporation for Public Broadcasting. (1985b). *Statistics in brief.* Washington, DC: Author.

Corporation for Public Broadcasting. (1986, May). *Summary of Corporation for Public Broadcasting authorizations, appropriations, and public broadcasting income, fiscal years 1969–*1990. Legislative Affairs Office.

Corteen, R.S., & Williams, T. (1986). Television and reading skills. In T. Williams (Ed.), *The impact of television: A natural experiment in three communities* (pp. 39–84). Orlando, FL: Academic Press.

Courtney, A.E., & Whipple, T.W. (1974). Women in TV commercials. *Journal of Communication, 24,* 110–118.

Courtney, A.E., & Whipple, T.W. (1983). *Sex stereotyping in advertising.* Lexington, MA: Lexington Books.

Cowan, G. (1978). *See no evil: The backstage battle over sex and violence in television.* New York: Simon and Schuster.

Cray, E. (1986, December 29). Sex and the network censors: Relaxed rules make it tough to separate sleaze from tease. *Electronic Media,* p. 1.

Crook, D. (1986, November 12). '86 elections signal a broadcasting change. *Los Angeles Times,* Part VI. p. 1.

Cullinan, D., Eptein, M.H., & Kauffman, J.M. (1984). Teachers' ratings of students' behaviors: What constitutes behavior disorder in school? *Behavioral Disorders, 10,* 9–19.

Dad confiscates television; teenager kills himself. (1983, February 11). *The Times Record,* p. 3.

Daltry, L. (1978, March 3). Television on trial: The tube made me do it. *New West,* pp. 69–70.

Davidson, E.S., & Neale, J.M. (1984, September). *Analyzing prosocial content on entertainment television.* Paper presented at the 82nd Annual Convention of the American Psychological Association, New Orleans.

Davidson, E.S., Yasuna, A., & Tower, A. (1979). The effects of television cartoons on sex-role stereotyping in young girls. *Child Development, 50,* 597–600.

DeFleur, M.L. (1964). Occupational roles as portrayed on television. *Public Opinion Quarterly, 28,* 57–74.

Did TV make him do it? A young killer and television go to trial for murder, (1977, October 10). *Time,* pp. 87–88.

Dominick, J.R., & Greenberg, B.S. (1970). Three seasons of blacks on television. *Journal of Advertising Research, 10,* 21–27.

Dominick, J.R., & Greenberg, B.S. (1972). Attitudes toward violence: The interaction of television exposure, family attitudes, and social class. In G.A. Comstock & E.A. Rubinstein (Eds.), *Television and social behavior. Vol. III: Television and adolescent aggressiveness* (pp. 314–335). Washington, DC: U.S. Government Printing Office.

Donagher, P.C., Poulos, R.W., Liebert, R.M., & Davidson, E.S. (1975). Race, sex, and social example: An analysis of character portrayals on interracial television entertainment. *Psychological Reports, 37,* 1023–1034.

Donnerstein, E. (1984). Pornography: Its effect on violence against women. In N.M. Malamuth & E. Donnerstein (Eds.), *Pornography and sexual aggression* (pp. 53–81). New York: Academic Press.

Donohue, T.R. (1978). Television's impact on emotionally disturbed children's value systems. *Child Study Journal, 8,* 187–201.

Donohue, T.R., Henke, L.L., & Donohue, W.A. (1980). Do kids know what TV commercials intend? *Journal of Advertising Research, 20*(5), 51–57.

Donohue, T.R., Henke, L.L. & Meyer, T.P. (1983). Learning about television commercials: The impact of instructional units on children's perceptions of motive and intent. *Journal of Broadcasting, 27*(3), 251–261.

Doolittle, J., & Pepper, R. (1975). Children's TV ad content. *Journal of Broadcasting, 19*(3), 131–142.

Dorr, A., Graves, S.B., & Phelps, E. (1980). Television literacy for young children. *Journal of Communication, 30*(3), 71–83.

Dorr, A., & Kovaric, P. (1980). Some of the people some of the time–But which people? Televised violence and its effects. In E.L. Palmer & A. Dorr (Eds.), *Children and the faces of television: Teaching, violence, selling* (pp. 183–199). New York: Academic Press.

Dougherty, P.H. (1976, June 9). Thompson scores TV violence. *New York Times.*

Downs, A.C., & Gowan, D.C. (1980). Sex differences in reinforcement and punishment on prime-time television. *Sex Roles, 6*(5), 683–694.

Drabman, R.S., & Thomas, M.H. (1974). Does media violence increase children's toleration of real-life aggression? *Developmental Psychology, 10,* 418–421.

Drabman, R.S., & Thomas, M.H. (1976). Does watching violence on television cause apathy? *Pediatrics, 57,* 329–331.

Dussere, S. (1976). *The effects of television advertising on children's eating habits.* Unpublished doctoral dissertation, University of Massachusetts at Amherst.

Elias, M.J. (1979, November). Helping emotionally disturbed children through prosocial television. *Exceptional Children,* pp. 217–218.

Elias, M.J. (1983). Improving coping skills of emotionally disturbed boys through television-based social problem solving. *American Journal of Orthopsychiatry, 53,* 61–72.

Eron, L.D. (1963). Relationship of TV viewing habits and aggressve behavior in children. *Journal of Abnormal and Social Psychology, 67,* 193–196.

FCC delays decision on children's TV programs. (1980, December 3). *Los Angeles Times.*

Federal Communications Commission. (1971). *Adding the equal employment program filing requirement to commission rules,* p. 709.

Federal Communication Commission. (1983, December 22). Children's television programming and advertising practices. *Federal Register, 49,* 1704–1727.

Federal Communication Commission. (1984, August 23). Revision of programming and commercialization policies, ascertainment requirements, and program log requirements for commercial television stations. *Federal Register, 49,* 33588–33620.

Federal Communication Commission (1985, April 12). FCC denies ACT's request to prohibit profit-sharing arrangements in broadcasting children's programming. *FCC News,* Report No. MM–14.

Federal Trade Commission. (1978). *Staff report on television advertising to children.* Washington, DC: U.S. Government Printing Office.

Federal Trade Commission. (1979). *Presiding Officer's Order No. 78: Certification to the commission of recommended disputed issues of fact.* Washington, DC: Author.

Federal Trade Commission. (1981a, February). *Citizen's guide to the Federal Trade Commission.* Washington, DC: Author.

Federal Trade Commission. (1981b, March 31). *FTC final staff report and recommendation.* Washington, DC: Author.

Federal Trade Commission. (1981c, September). *1980 Annual report of the Federal Trade Commission.* Washington, DC: Author.

Feshbach, S. (1955). The drive-reducing function of fantasy behavior. *Journal of Abnormal and Social Psychology, 50,* 3–11.

Feshbach, S. (1976). The role of fantasy in the response to television. *Journal of Social Issues, 32*(4), 71–85.

Feshbach, S., Feshbach, N.D., & Cohen, S.E. (1982). Enhancing children's discrimination in response to television advertising: The effects of psychoeducational training in two elementary school-age groups. *Developmental Review, 2,* 385–403.

Feshbach, S., & Singer, R. (1971). *Television and aggression.* San Francisco: Jossey-Bass.

Financial figures, finally. (1986, May 19). *Broadcasting,* p. 39.

Fizzled boycott: Sponsors still face threat. (1981, July 31). *Time,* p. 63.

Fowler, M.S. (1982, December 15). Regulating TV; It's like opening Pandora's box. *Newsday,* p. 71.

Fowles, B. (1971). Building a curriculum for "The Electric Company." In *The Electric Company: An introduction to the new television program designed to help teach reading to children.* New York: Children's Television Workshop.

Freedman, J.L. (1984). Effect of television violence on aggressiveness. *Psychological Bulletin, 96*(2), 227–246.

Friedrich, L.K., & Stein, A.H. (1975). Prosocial television and young children: The effects of verbal labeling and role playing on learning and behavior. *Child Development, 46,* 27–38.

Friedrich-Cofer, L.K., Huston-Stein, A., Kipnis, D.M., Susman, E.J., & Clewett, A.S. (1979). Environmental enhancement of prosocial television content: Effects on interpersonal behavior, imaginative play, and self-regulation in a natural setting. *Developmental Psychology, 15,* 637–646.

Friedrich-Cofer, L., & Huston, A.C. (1986). Television violence and aggression: The debate continues. *Psychological Bulletin,* pp. 1–20.

Frueh, T., & McGhee, P.E. (1975). Traditional sex role development and amount of time spent watching television. *Developmental Psychology, 11*(1), 109.

FTC gets off kiddie bandwagon. (1981, October 1). *Daily News,* p.40.

Fuller, J.W. (1985). National public television. In S.T. Eastman, S.W. Head, & L. Klein (Eds.), *Broadcast/cable programming* (pp. 403–418). Belmont, CA: Wadsworth Publishing Company.

Gadow, K.D., & Sprafkin, J. (1987). Effects of viewing high versus low aggresison cartoons on emotionally disturbed children. *Journal of Pediatric Psychology, 12*(3), 413–427.

Gadow, K.D., Sprafkin, J., & Ficarrotto, T. (1987). Effects of viewing aggression-laden cartoons on preschool-aged emotionally disturbed children. *Child Psychiatry and Human Development, 17*(4), 257–274.

Gaines, L., & Esserman, J. (1981). A quantitative study of young children's comprehension of televsion programs and commercials. In J.F. Esserman (Ed.), *Television advertising and children: Issues, research and findings* (pp. 96–105). New York: Child Research Service.

Galst, J.P. (1980). Television food commercials and pro-nutritional public service announcements as determinants of young children's snack choices. *Child Development, 51,* 935–938.

Geen, R.G., & Berkowitz, L. (1966). Name-mediating aggressive cue properties. *Journal of Personality, 34,* 456–465.

Geen, R.G., & Berkowitz, L. (1967). Some conditions facilitating the occurrence of aggression after the observation of violence. *Journal of Personality, 35,* 666–676.

Gerbner, G. (1969). The television world of violence. In D.L. Lange, R.K. Baker, & S.J. Ball (Eds.), *Mass media and violence* (Vol. XI, pp. 311–339). Washington, DC: U.S. Government Printing Office.

Gerbner, G. (1972). Violence in television drama: Trends in symbolic functions. In G.A. Comstock & E.A. Rubinstein (Eds.), *Television and social behavior (Vol. 1): Media content and control* (pp. 28–187). Washington, DC: U.S. Government Printing Office.

Gerbner, G., Gross, L., Morgan, M., & Signorielli, N. (1980). The 'mainstreaming' of America: Violence Profile No. 11. *Journal of Communication, 30*(3), 10–29.

Gerbner, G., Gross, L., Morgan, M., & Signorielli, N. (1982). Charting the mainstream: Television's contributions to political orientations. *Journal of Communication, 32*(2), 100–127.

Gerbner, G., Gross, L., Signorielli, N., & Morgan, M. (1980a). Aging with television: Images on television drama and conceptions of social reality. *Journal of Communication, 30*(1), 37–47.

Gerbner, G., Gross, L., Signorielli, N., Morgan, M. (1986). *Television's mean world: Violence Profile No. 14–15.* University of Pennsylvania, Annenberg School of Communications, Philadelphia, PA.

Gerbner, G., Gross, L., Signorielli, N., Morgan, M., & Jackson-Beeck, M. (1979). The demonstration of power: Violence Profile No. 10. *Journal of Communication, 29*(3), 177–195.

Goldberg, M.E., & Gorn, G.J. (1977, March). *Material vs. social preferences, parent-child relations, and the child's emotional responses.* Paper presented at the Telecommunications Policy Research Conference, Airlie House, VA.

Goldberg, M.E., & Gorn, G.J. (1979). Television's impact on preferences for non-white playmates: Canadian "Sesame Street" inserts. *Journal of Broadcasting, 23*(1), 27–32.

Gorn, G.J., & Goldberg, M.E. (1982). Behavioral evidence of the effects of televised food messages on children. *Journal of Consumer Research, 9,* 200–205.

Gorn, G.J., Goldberg, M.E., & Kanungo, R.N. (1976). The role of educational television in changing the intergroup attitudes of children. *Child Development, 47*(1), 227–280.

Gould, J. (1972, January, 11). TV violence held unharmful to youth. *The New York Times.*

Gould, M.S., & Shaffer, D. (1986). The impact of suicide in television movies. *New England Journal of Medicine, 315*(11), 690–694.

Graves, S.N. (1975). *How to encourage positive racial attitudes.* Paper presented at the Society for Research in Child Development, Denver CO.

Greenberg, B.S., & Baptista-Fernandez, P. (1980). Hispanic Americans: The new minority on television. In B.S. Greenberg (Ed.), *Life on television: Content analyses of U.S. TV drama* (pp. 3–12). Norwood, NJ: Ablex Publishing.

Greenberg, B.S., Edison, N., Korzenny, F., Fernandez-Collado, C., & Atkin, C.K. (1980). Antisocial and prosocial behaviors on television. In B.S. Greenberg (Ed.), *Life on television: Content analysis of U.S. TV drama* (pp. 99–128). Norwood, NJ: Ablex Publishing Corporation.

Greenberg, B.S., & Gordon, T.F. (1972a). Children's perceptions of television violence: A replication. In G.A. Comstock, E.A. Rubinstein, & J.P. Murray (Eds.), *Television and social behavior. Vol. V: Television's effects: Further explorations* (pp. 211–230). Washington, DC: U.S. Government Printing Office.

Greenberg, B.S., & Gordon, T.F. (1972b). Perceptions of violence in TV programs: Critics and the public. In G.A. Comstock & E.A. Rubinstein (Eds.), *Television and social behavior, Vol. I, Media content and control* (pp. 244–258). Washington, DC: U.S. Government Printing Office.

Greenberg, B.S., Korzenny, F., & Atkin, C.K. (1979). The portrayal of aging: Trends on commercial television. *Research on Aging, 1*(3), 319–334.

Greenberg, B.S., Richards, M., & Henderson, L. (1980). Trends in sex-role portrayals on television. In B.S. Greenberg (Ed.), *Life on television: Content analyses of U.S. TV drama* (pp. 65–87). Norwood, NJ: Ablex Publishing.

Greenberg, B.S., Stanley, C., Siemicki, M., Heeter, C., Soderman, A., & Linsangan, R. (1986). *Sex content on soaps and primetime television series most viewed by adolescents.* Unpublished manuscript, Department of Telecommunication, Michigan State University, East Lansing.

Gross, L., & Morgan, M. (1985). Television and enculturation. In J. Dominick & J. Fletcher (Eds.), *Broadcasting research methods* (pp. 221–234). Boston: Allyn and Bacon.

Group for the Advancement of Psychiatry, Committee on Social Issues. (1982). *The child and television drama: The psychosocial impact of cumulative viewing.* New York: Mental Health Materials Center.

Growing avenues for children's TV programming. (1985, December 30). *Broadcasting,* p. 27.

Hanratty, M.A., Liebert, R.M., Morris, L.W., & Fernandez, L.E. (1969). Imitation of film-mediated aggression against live and inanimate victims. *Proceedings for the 77th Annual Convention of the American Psychological Association,* pp. 457–458.

Hanratty, M.A., O'Neal, E., & Sulzer, J.L. (1972). The effect of frustration upon imitation of aggression. *Journal of Personality and Social Psychology, 21,* 30–34.

Harris, A., & Feinberg, J. (1977). Television and aging: Is what you see what you get? *The Gerontologist, 17,* 464–468.

Harrison, L.F., & Williams, T. (1986). Television and cognitive development. In T. Williams (Ed.), *The impact of television: A natural experiment in three communities* (pp. 87–138). Orlando, FL: Academic Press.

Hartley, R.L. (1964). *The impact of viewing "aggression": Studies and problems of extrapolation.* New York: Columbia Broadcasting System. Office of Social Research.

Hartmann, D.P. (1969). Influence of symbolically modelled instrumental aggression and pain cues on aggressive behavior. *Journal of Personality and Social Psychology, 11,* 280–288.

Hartmann, D.P., & Gelfand, D.M. (1969, June). *Motivational variables affecting performance of vicariously learned responses.* Paper presented at Western Psychological Associatioon Meeting, Vancouver, British Columbia.

Harvey, S.E., Sprafkin, J.N., & Rubinstein, E. (1979). Prime time television: A profile of aggressive and prosocial behaviors. *Journal of Broadcasting, 23*(2), 179–189.

Hawkins, R.P., & Pingree, S. (1982). Television's influence on social reality. In D. Pearl, L. Bouthilet, & J. Lazar (Eds.), *Television and behavior: Ten years of scientific progress and implications for the eighties* (Vol. 2, pp. 224–247), Washington, DC: U.S. Government Printing Office.

Hayes, D.S., & Kelly, S.B. (1984). Young children's processing of television: Modality differences in the retention of temporal relations. *Journal of Experimental Child Psychology, 38,* 505–514.

Head, S.W. (1954). Content analysis of television drama programs. *Quarterly of Film, Radio and Television, 9,* 175–194.

Hearold, S. (1986). A synthesis of 1043 effects of television on social behavior. In G. Comstock (Ed.), *Public communications and behavior: Volume I* (pp. 65–133). New York: Academic Press.

Heller, M.S. (1978). *Broadcast standards editing.* New York: American Broadcasting Companies.

Heller, M.S., & Polsky, S. (1976). *Studies in violence and television.* New York: American Broadcasting Companies.

Hellman, H. & Soramäki, M. (1985). Economic concentration in the videocassette industry: A cultural comparison. *Journal of Communication, 35*(3), 122–134.

Hennessee, J.A., & Nicholson, J. (1972, May 28). N.O.W. says: TV commercials insult women. *New York Times magazine,* pp. 12–13.

Hennigan, K.M., Del Rosario, M.L., Heath, L., Cook, T.D., Wharton, J.D., & Calder, B.J. (1982). Impact of the introduction of television on crime in the United States: Empirical findings and theoretical implications. *Journal of Personality and Social Psychology, 42,* 461–477.

Hickey, N. (1975, December 6). Does America want family viewing time? *TV Guide.*

Hicks, D.J. (1965). Imitation and retention of film-mediated aggressive peer and adult models. *Journal of Personality and Social Psychology, 2,* 97–100.

Hicks, D.J. (1968). Short- and long-term retention of affectively varied modeled behavior. *Psychonomic Science, 11,* 369–370.

Himmelweit, H., Oppenheim, A.N., & Vince, P. (1958). *Television and the child: An empirical study of the effects of television on the young.* London: Oxford University Press.

Hinton, J., Seggar, J., Northcott, H., & Fontes, B. (1973). Tokenism and improving the imagery of blacks in TV drama and comedy. *Journal of Broadcasting, 18,* 423–432.

Hollenbeck, A.R., & Slaby, R.G. (1979). Infant visual and vocal responses to television. *Child Development, 50,* 41–45.

Holtzman, J.M., & Akiyama, H. (1985). What children see: The aged on television in Japan and the United States. *The Gerontologists, 25*(1), 62–68.

How cable works. (1981, July 5). *New York Times,* Sec. 2, p. 22.

Hoyt, J.L. (1970). Effect of media violence "justification" on aggression. *Journal of Broadcasting, 14,* 455–465.

Huesmann, L.R. (1982). Television violence and aggressive behavior. In D. Pearl, L. Bouthilet, & J. Lazar (Eds.), *Television and behavior: Ten years of scientific progress and implications for the eighties* (Vol. 2, pp. 126–137). Washington, DC: U.S. Government Printing Office.

Huesmann, L.R. (1986). Psychological processes promoting the relation between exposure to media violence and aggressive behavior by the viewer. *Journal of Social Issues, 42,* 125–139.

Huesmann, L.R., Eron, L.D., Berkowitz, L., & Chaffee, S. (1987). *Effects of television violence on aggression: A reply to Freedman,* Unpublished manuscript, Department of Psychology, University of Illinois at Chicago.

Huesmann, L.R., Eron, L.D., Klein, R., Brice, P. & Fischer, P. (1983). Mitigating the imitation of aggressive behaviors by changing children's attitudes about media violence. *Journal of Personality and Social Psychology, 44*(5), 899–910.

Huesmann, L.R., Eron, L.D., Lefkowitz, M.M., & Walder, L.O. (1984). Stability of aggression over time and generations. *Developmental Psychology, 20*(6), 1120–1134.

Huesmann, L.R., Lagerspetz, K., & Eron, L.D. (1984). Intervening variables in the TV violence-aggression relation: Evidence from two countries. *Developmental Psychology, 20*(5), 746–775.

Huston, A.C. (1985, October 25). *Improving children's television programming.* Testimony before the U.S. House of Representatives Subcommittee on Telecommunications, Consumer Protection and Finance.

Huston, A.C., Greer, D., Wright, J.C., Welch, R., & Ross, R. (1984). Children's comprehension of televised formal features with masculine and feminine connotations. *Developmental Psychology, 20*(4), 707–716.

Huston, A.C., Wright, J.C., Wartella, E., Rice, M.L., Watkins, B.A., Campbell, T., & Potts, R. (1981). Communicating more than content: Formal features of children's television programs. *Journal of Communication, 31*(3), 32–48.

Huston-Stein, A., Fox, S., Greer, D., Watkins, B.A., & Whitaker, J. (1981). The effects of TV action and violence on children's social behavior. *The Journal of Genetic Psychology, 138,* 183–191.

If the eye offend thee. (1977, September 26). *Time,* p. 53.

Ingelfinger, F.J. (1976, April 8). Violence on TV: "An unchecked environmental hazard." *The New England Journal of Medicine,* pp. 837–838.

Iskoe, A. (1976). *Advertising via famous personalities and the effects on children.* Unpublished manuscript, The Wharton School, University of Pennsylvania, Philadelphia.

Jeffrey, D.B., McLellarn, R.W., & Fox, D.T. (1982). The development of children's eating habits: The role of television commercials. *Health Education Quarterly, 9*(2 & 3), 78–93.

Jennings, R. (1970). *Programming and advertising practices in television directed to children.* Boston: Action for Children's Television.

Johnson, N. (1967). *How to talk back to your television set.* Boston: Little, Brown, & Co.

Johnston, J., Ettema, J., & Davidson, T. (1980). *An evaluation of "Freestyle": A television series designed to reduce sex role stereotypes.* Ann Arbor, MI: Institute for Social Research.

Joy, L.A., Kimball, M.M., & Zabrack, M.L. (1986). Television and children's aggressive behavior. In T.M. Williams (Ed.), *The impact of television: A natural experiment in three communities* (pp. 303–360). Orlando, FL: Academic Press, Inc.

Kaplan, R.M., & Singer, R.D. (1976). Television violence and viewer aggression: A reexamination of the evidence. *Journal of Social Issues, 32*(4), 35–70.

Karp, W. (1984, April 22). TV reformers screen out children's real needs. *Newsday,* p. 5.

Kimball, M.M. (1986). Television and sex-role attitudes. In T.M. Williams (Ed.), *The impact of television* (pp. 265–301). New York: Academic Press.

Kunkel, D. (1986). *Children and host-selling television commercials.* Unpublished manuscript, Department of Human Development, University of Kansas, Lawrence.

Kunkel, D., & Watkins, B. (1986). *Children's television regulatory policy: Where we are and how we got there.* Paper presented at the meeting of the International Communication Association, Chicago.

Lange, D.L., Baker, R.K., & Ball, S.J. (1969). *Mass media and violence, Vol. XI: A report to the National Commission on the Causes and Prevention of Violence.* Washington, DC: U.S. Government Printing Office.

Larsen, D.N. (1968). *Violence and the mass media.* New York: Harper & Row.

The last drag. (1971, January 4). *Newsweek,* p. 65.

Lefkowitz, M.M., Eron, L.D., Walder, L.O., & Huesmann, L.R. (1972). Television violence and child aggression: A followup study. In G.A. Comstock & E.A. Rubinstein (Eds.), *Television and social behavior, Vol. III: Television and adolescent aggressiveness* (pp. 35–135). Washington, DC: U.S. Government Printing Office.

Leifer, A.D. (1975). Research on the socialization influence of television in the United States. In *Television and socialization processes in the family,* A documentation of the Prix Jeunesse Seminar. Munich: Verlag Dokumentation.

Leifer, A.D., & Roberts, D.F. (1972). Children's response to television violence. In J.P. Murray, E.A. Rubinstein, & G.A. Comstock (Eds.), *Television and social behavior Vol. 2: Television and social learning.* Washington, DC: U.S. Government Printing Office.

Lemon, J. (1977). Women and blacks on prime-time television, *Journal of Communication, 27*(4), 70–79.

Lesser, G. (1974). *Children and television: Lessons from "Sesame Street."* New York: Vintage Books.

Levering, R. (1978, August 3). TV on trial. *San Francisco Bay Guardian,* p. 5.

Levin, E. (1981). Censors in action. In B. Cole (Ed.), *Television today: A close-up view* (pp. 322–329). New York: Oxford University Press.

Levin, S.R., & Anderson, D.R. (1976). The development of attention. *Journal of Communication, 26*(2), 126–135.

Levin, S.R., Petros, T.V., & Petrella, F.W. (1982). Preschoolers' awareness of television advertising. *Child Development, 53,* 933–937.

Levinson, R.M. (1975). From Olive Oyl to Sweet Polly Purebread: Sex role stereotypes and televised cartoons. *Journal of Popular Culture, 9*(3), 561–572.

Levy, M.R. (1983). The time-shifting use of home video recorders. *Journal of Broadcasting, 27*(3). 263–268.

Lewine, R.F., Eastman, S.T., & Adams, W.J. (1985). Prime-time network television programming. In S.T. Eastman, S.W. Head, & L. Klein (Ed.), *Broadcast/cable programming: Strategies and practices* (pp. 119–165). Belmont, CA: Wadsworth Publishing Company.

Liebert, D.E., Sprafkin, J.N., Liebert, R.M., & Rubinstein, E.A. (1977). Effects of television commercial disclaimers on the product expectations of children. *Journal of Communication, 27*(1), 118–124.

Liebert, R.M. (1982). Review of television, imagination, and aggression: A study of preschoolers. *Contemporary Psychology, 27*(11), 896–897.

Liebert, R.M., & Baron, R.A. (1972). Short-term effects of televised aggression on children's aggressive behavior. In J.P. Murray, E.A. Rubinstein, & G.A. Comstock (Eds.), *Television and social behavior (Vol. 2): Television and social learning* (pp. 181–201). Washington, DC: U.S. Government Printing Office.

Liebert, R.M., Cohen, L.A., Joyce, C., Murrel, S., Nisonoff, L., & Sonnenschein, S. (1977, Summer). Predispositions revisited. *Journal of Communication,* 217–221.

Liebert, R.M., & Poulos, R.W. (1975). Television and personality development: The socializing effects of an entertainment medium. In A. Davids (Ed.), *Child personality and psychopathology: Current topics, Vol. 2* (pp. 61–97). New York: John Wiley & Sons.

Liebert, R.M., & Schwartzberg, N.S. (1977). Effects of mass media. *Annual Review of Psychology, 28,* 141–173.

Liebert, R.M., Sobol, M.P., & Davidson, E.S. (1972). Catharsis of aggression among institutionalized boys: Fact or artifact? In G.A. Comstock, E.A. Rubistein, & J.P. Murray (Eds.), *Television and social behavior, Vol. V: Television's effects: Further explorations* (pp. 351–358). Washington, DC: U.S. Government Printing Office.

Liebert, R.M., Sprafkin, J.N., & Poulos, R.W. (1975). Selling cooperation to children. In *Proceedings of the 20th Annual Conference of the Advertising Conference of the Advertising Research Foundation,* New York.

Liss, M.A., Reinhardt, L.C., & Fredriksen, S. (1983). TV heroes: The impact of rhetoric and deeds. *Journal of Applied Developmental Psychology, 4*(2), 175–187.

Locker, A. (1975, July 14–17). Testimony at the Hearings on Broadcast Advertising and Children before the Subcommittee on Communications of the Committee on Interstate and Foreign Commerce, House of Representatives (pp. 345–362). Washington, DC: U.S. Government Printing Office.

Logan, B., & Moody, K. (Eds.) (1979). *Television awareness training: The viewer's guide.* New York: Media Action Research Center.

Long, M.L., & Simon, R.J. (1974). The roles and statuses of women on children and family TV programs. *Journalism Quarterly, 51*(1), 107–110.

Louis Harris and Associates. (1986). *American teens speak: Sex, myths, TV, and birth control.* New York: Planned Parenthood Federation of America.

Lovaas, O.I. (1961). Effect of exposure to symbolic aggression on aggressive behavior. *Child Development, 32,* 37–44.

Lyle, J., & Hoffman, H.R. (1972). Children's use of television and other media. In E.A. Rubinstein, G.A. Comstock, & J.P. Murray (Eds.), *Television in day-to-day life: Patterns of use* (pp. 129–256). Washington, DC: U.S. Government Printing Office.

Macklin, M.C., & Kolbe, R.H. (1984). Sex role stereotyping in childen's advertising: Current and past trends. *Journal of Advertising, 13*(2), 34–42.

Maddox, L.M., & Zanot, E.J. (1984, Spring). Suspension of the NAB Code and its effect on regulation of advertising. *Journalism Quarterly*, pp. 125–130.

Mandel, B. (1978, August 10). Was TV born guilty? *San Francisco Examiner*, p. 35.

Mannes, M. (1970, November 14). Television: The splitting image. *Saturday Review.*

Marecek, J., Piliavin, J.A., Fitzsimmons, E., Krogh, E.C., Leader, E., & Trudell, B. (1978). Women as TV experts: The voice of authority. *Journal of Communication, 28*(1), 159–168.

Mark, N. (1972, February 7). Scientists say TV violence DOES influence children. *Birmingham News.*

Mayer, M. (1972). *About television.* New York: Harper & Row.

Mays, L., Henderson, E.H., Seidman, S.K., & Steiner, V.S. (1975). *On meeting real people: An evaluation report on Vegetable Soup: The effects of a multiethnic children's television series on intergroup attitudes of children.* Albany, NY: New York State Education Department. (ERIC Document Reproduction Service No. ED 123 319).

McCarthy, J.M., & Paraskevopoulos, J. (1969). Behavior patterns of learning disabled, emotionally disturbed, and average children. *Exceptional Children, 36,* 69–74.

McIntyre, J.J., & Teevan, J.J., Jr. (1972). Television violence and deviant behavior. In G.A. Comstock & E.A. Rubinstein (Eds.), *Television and social behavior. Vol. III: Television and adolescent aggressiveness* (pp. 383–435). Washington, DC: U.S. Government Printing Office.

McLeod, J.M., Atkin, C.K., & Chaffee, S.H. (1972a). Adolescents, parents and television use: Adolescent self-report measures from Maryland and Wisconsin samples. In G.A. Comstock & E.A. Rubinstein (Eds.), *Television and social behavior, Vol. III: Television and adolescent aggressiveness* (pp. 173–238). Washington, DC: U.S. Government Printing Office.

McLeod, J.M., Atkin, C.K., & Chaffee, S.H. (1972b). Adolescents, parents and television use: Self-report and other-report measures from the Wisconsin sample. In G.A. Comstock & E.A. Rubinstein (Eds.), *Television and social behavior, Vol. III: Television and adolescent aggressiveness* (pp. 239–313). Washington, DC: U.S. Government Printing Office.

Media Commentary Council, Inc. (1986). *Channels: 1986 Field guide to the electronic media.* New York: Author.

Melody, W.H. (1973). *Children's television: The economics of exploitation.* New Haven, CT: Yale University Press.

Merriam, E. (1964, October). We're teaching our children that violence is fun. *Ladies Home Journal,* 44, 49, 52. Reprinted in O. Larsen (Ed.). (1968). *Violence in the mass media* (pp. 40–47). New York: Harper & Row.

Milavsky, J.R., Kessler, R., Stipp, H., Rubens, W.S. (1982). Television and aggression: Results of a panel study. In D. Pearl, L. Bouthilet, & J. Lazar (Eds.), *Television and behavior: Ten years of scientific progress and implications for the eighties* (Vol. 2, pp. 138–157). Washington, DC: U.S. Government Printing Office.

Milavsky, J.R., Pekowsky, B., & Stipp, H. (1975–1976). TV drug advertising and proprietary and illicit drug use among boys. *Public Opinion Quarterly, 39,* 457–481.

Milgram, S., & Shotland, R.L. (1973). *Television and antisocial behavior: Field experiments.* New York: Academic Press.

Miller, M.M., & Reeves, B. (1976). Linking dramatic TV content to children's occupational sex-role stereotypes. *Journal of Broadcasting, 20,* 35–50.

Minow, N.N. (1964). *Equal time: The private broadcaster and the public interest.* New York: Atheneum.

Morgan, M. (1982). Television and adolescents' sex role stereotypes: A longitudinal study. *Journal of Personality and Social Psychology, 43*(5), 947–955.

Morgan, M., & Gross, L. (1982). Television and educational achievement and aspiration. In D. Pearl, L. Bouthilet, & J. Lazar (Eds.), *Television and behavior: Ten years of scientific progress and implications for the eighties* (Vol. 2, pp. 78–90). Washington, DC: U.S. Government Printing Office.

Murray, J.P. (1980). *Television and youth: 25 years of research and controversy.* Boys Town, NE: Boys Town Center for the Study of Youth Development.

Murray, J.P. (1984, October 25). *Impact of televised violence on children.* Testimony before the U.S. Senate Subcommittee on Juvenile Justice, Committee on the Judiciary.

National Commission on the Causes and Prevention of Violence. (1969, September 23). *Commission statement on violence in television entertainment programs.*

National Federation for Decency. (1977). *Sex on television.* Tupelo, MS.

National PTA. (1978, February 15). National PTA names best and worst TV shows with new program guide. (Press release). Chicago, IL.

National Science Foundation. (1977). *Research on the effects of television advertising on children: A review of the literature and recommendations for future research.* Washington, DC: Author.

Nelson, J.P., Gelfand, D.M., & Hartmann, D.P. (1969). Children's aggression following competition and exposure to an aggressive model. *Child Development, 40,* 1085–1097.

Networks lose their censors; more violence ahead? (1986, December 1). *View,* p. 14.

Newcomb, A.F., & Collins, W.A. (1979). Children's comprehension of family role portrayals in televised dramas: Effects of socioeconomic status, ethnicity, and age. *Developmental Psychology, 15*(4), 417–423.

News from NAACP. (1951, July 19). Cited in *Window dressing on the set: Women and minorities in television.* U.S. Commission on Civil Rights.

Nielsen Report. (1986). Television: 1986 Nielson Report. Northbrook, IL: A.C. Nielsen.

Northcott, H. (1975). Too young, too old—Age in the world of television. *The Gerontologist, 15,* 184–186.

O'Bryant, S.L., & Corder-Bolz, C.R. (1978). The effects of television on children's stereotyping of women's work roles. *Journal of Vocational Behavior, 12,* 233–244.

O'Donnell, W.J., & O'Donnell, K.J. (1978). Update: Sex-role messages in TV commercials. *Journal of Communication, 28*(1), 156–158.

An "overwhelming" violence—TV tie. (1982, May 6). *New York Times,* p. C27.

Paisley, M.B. (1972). *Social policy research and the realities of the system: Violence done to TV research.* Stanford University: Institute of Communication Research.

Parke, R.D., Berkowitz, L., Leyens, J.P., West, S.G., & Sebastian, R.J. (1977). Some effects of violent and non-violent movies on the behavior of juvenile delinquents. In *Advances in Experimental Social Psychology, Vol. 10.* New York: Academic Press.

Paskowski, M. (1986, April). See Spot jump. *Marketing and Media Decisions,* pp. 65–70.

Paulson, F.L., McDonald, D.L., & Whittlemore, S.L. (1972). An evaluation of *Sesame Street* programming designed to teach cooperative behavior. Monmouth, OR: Teaching Research.

Pearl, D., Bouthilet, L., & Lazar, J. (1982a). *Television and behavior: Ten years of scientific progress and implications for the eighties* (Vol. 1). Washington, DC: U.S. Government Printing Office.

Pearl, D., Bouthilet, L., & Lazar, J. (1982b). *Television and behavior: Ten years of scientific progress and implications for the eighties* (Vol. 2). Washington, DC: U.S. Government Printing Office.

Peterson, P.E., Jeffrey, D.G., Bridgwater, C.A., & Dawson, B. (1984). How pronutrition television programming affects children's dietary habits. *Developmental Psychology, 20*(1), 55–63.

P & G's move in a "holy war." (1981, June 29). *Newsweek*, p. 60.

Phillips, D.P. & Carstensen, L.L. (1986). Clustering of teenage suicides after television news stories about suicide. *The New England Journal of Medicine, 315*(11), 685–689.

Pierce, C.M. (1984). Television and violence: Social psychiatric perspectives. *American Journal of Social Psychiatry, 3,* 41–44.

Pingree, S., & Hawkins, R. (1981). U.S. programs on Australian television: The cultivation effect. *Journal of Communication, 31*(1), 97–105.

Poulos, R.W., Harvey, S.E., & Liebert, R.M. (1976). Saturday morning television: A profile of the 1974–75 children's season. *Psychological Reports, 39,* 1047–1057.

Pull plug on TV violence: AMA asks 10 big firms. (1977, February 7). Newsday.

Rabinovitch, M.S., McLean, M.S., Jr., Markham, J.W., & Talbott, A.D. (1972). Children's violence perception as a function of television violence. In G.A. Comstock, E.A. Rubinstein, & J.P. Murray (Eds.), *Television and social behavior, Vol. 5, Television's effects: Further explorations.* Washington, DC: U.S. Government Printing Office.

Rapaczynski, W., Singer, D.G., & Singer, J.L. (1982). Teaching television: A curriculum for young children. *Journal of Communication, 32*(2), 46–55.

Remsberg, B. (1982, October 5). Jeremy's tragedy. *Family Circle Magazine*, pp. 40, 44–45, 158.

Rice, M.L., Huston, A.C., & Wright, J.C. (1982). The forms of television: Effects on children's attention, comprehension, and social behavior. In D. Pearl, L. Bouthilet, & J. Lazar (Eds.), *Television and behavior: Ten years of scientific progress and implications for the eighties* (Vol. 2, pp. 24–38). Washington, DC: U.S. Government Printing Office.

Rivers, C. (1974, August 18). What sort of behavior control should TV impose on children: Violence or harmony? *New York Times.*

Roberts, C. (1970). The portrayal of blacks on network television. *Journal of Broadcasting, 15,* 45–53,

Roberts, D.F., Christenson, P., Gibson, W.A., Mooser, L., & Goldberg, M.E. (1980). Developing discriminating consumers. *Journal of Communication, 30*(3), 94–105.

Roberts, D.F., Herold, C., Hornby, M., King, S., Sterne, D., Whiteley, S., & Silverman, T. (1974). *Earth's a big blue marble: A report on the impact of a children's television series on children's opinions.* Unpublished manuscript, Stanford University, Stanford, CA.

Roberts, E.J. (1982). Television and sexual learning in childhood. In D. Pearl, L. Bouthilet, & J. Lazar (Eds.), *Television and behavior: Ten years of scientific progress and implications for the eighties* (Vol 2, pp. 209–223). Washington, DC: U.S. Government Printing Office.

Roberts, E.J., Kline, D., & Gagnon, J. (1978). *Family life and sexual learning.* Cambridge, MA: Population Education.

Robertson, T.S., & Rossiter, J.R. (1974). Children and commercial persuasion: An attribution theory analysis. *Journal of Consumer Research, 1*(1), 13–20.

Robinson, J.P. (1972). Television's impact on everyday life: Some cross-national evidence. In E.A. Rubinstein, G.A. Comstock, & J.P. Murray (Eds.), *Television and social behavior, Vol. IV: Television in day-to-day life: Patterns of use* (pp. 410–431). Washington, DC: U.S. Government Printing Office.

Robinson, J.P. (1981). Television and leisure time: A new scenario. *Journal of Communication, 31*(1), 120–130.

Robinson, J.P., & Bachman, J.G. (1972). Television viewing habits and aggression. In G.A. Comstock & E.A. Rubinstein (Eds.), *Television and social behavior. Vol. III: Television and adolescent aggressiveness* (pp. 372–382). Washington, DC: U.S. Government Printing Office.

Roper, B.W. (1985). *Public attitudes toward television and other media in a time of change.* New York: Television Information Office.

Rosenkrans, M.A., & Hartup, W.W. (1967). Imitative influences of consistent and inconsistent response consequences to a model on aggressive behavior in children. *Journal of Personality and Social Psychology, 7,* 429–434.

Rosenthal, R. (1986). Media violence, antisocial behavior, and the social consequences of small effects. *Journal of Social Issues, 42,* 141–154.

Ross, R.P., Campbell, T., Huston-Stein, A., & Wright, J.C. (1981). Nutritional misinformation of children: A developmental and experimental analysis of the effects of televised food commercials. *Journal of Applied Developmental Psychology, 1,* 329–347.

Ross, R.P., Campbell, T., Wright, J.C., Huston, A.C., Rice, M.L., & Turk, P. (1984). When celebrities talk, children listen: An experimental analysis of children's responses to TV ads with celebrity endorsement. *Journal of Applied Developmental Psychology, 5,* 185–202.

Rossiter, J.R., & Robertson, T.S. (1980). Children's dispositions toward proprietary drugs and the role of television drug advertising. *Public Opinion Quarterly, 44*(3), 316–329.

Rothenberg, M. (1975). Effect of television violence on children and youth. *Journal of the American Medical Association, 234,* 1043–1046.

Rothenberg, M.B. (1985). Role of television in shaping the attitudes of children. *Children's Health Care, 13*(4), 148–149.

Rowland, W.D. (1983). *The politics of TV violence.* Beverly Hills, CA: Sage.

Rubinstein, E.A., Fracchia, J.F., Kochnower, J.M., & Sprafkin, J.N. (1977). *Television viewing behaviors of mental patients: A survey of psychiatric centers in New York State.* New York: Brookdale International Institute.

Rubinstein, E.A., Liebert, R.M., Neale, J.M., & Poulos, R.W. (1974). *Assessing television's influence on children's prosocial behavior.* New York: Brookdale International Institute.

Rushnell, S.D. (1981). Nonprime time programming. In S.T. Eastman, S.W. Head, & L. Klein (Eds.), *Strategies for winning television and radio audiences.* Belmont, CA: Wadsworth Publishing Company.

Rushnell, S.D. (1985). Nonprime-time network programming. In S.T. Eastman, S.W. Head, & L. Klein (Eds.), *Broadcast/cable programming: Strategies and practices* (pp. 146–165). Belmont, CA: Wadsworth Publishing Company.

Rushton, J.P. (1979). Effects of television and film material on the prosocial behavior of children. In L. Berkowitz (Ed.), *Advances in experimental social psychology*. New York: Academic Press.

Rushton, J.P. (1982). Television and prosocial behavior. In D. Pearl, L. Bouthilet, & J. Lazar (Eds.), *Television and behavior: Ten years of scientific progress and implications for the eighties* (Vol. 2, pp. 248–257). Washington, DC: U.S. Government Printing Office.

Salomon, G. (1976). Cognitive skill learning across cultures. *Journal of Communication, 26*(2), 138–144.

Salomon, G. (1979). *Interaction of media, cognition, and learning.* San Fransisco: Josey-Bass Publishers.

Salomon, G. (1983). Television watching and mental effort: A social psychological view. In J. Bryant & D.R. Anderson (Eds.), *Children's understanding of television: Research on attention and comprehension* (pp. 181–198). New York: Academic Press.

Saturday morning kiddie sweepstakes. (1983, August 22). *Home Furnishings Daily,* p. 46.

Savitsky, J.C., Rogers, R.W., Izard, C.E., & Liebert, R.M. (1971). Role of frustration and anger in the imitation of filmed aggression against a human victim. *Psychological Reports, 29,* 807–810.

Sawin, D.B. (1981). The fantasy-reality distinction in televised violence: Modifying influences on children's aggression. *Journal of Research in Personality, 15,* 323–330.

Schaer, S.C. (1982, April 11). Tuning out the big three: A big drop in prime-time viewing raises doubts about the networks' dominance. *Newsday,* Part II, p. 3.

Schramm, W. (1960). The audiences of educational television. In W. Schramm (Ed.), *The impact of educational television.* Urbana, IL: University of Illinois Press.

Schramm, W., Lyle, J., & Parker, E.B. (1961). *Television in the lives of our children.* Stanford, CA: Stanford University Press.

Seggar, J.F. (1975). Imagery of women in television drama: 1974. *Journal of Broadcasting, 19*(3), 273–282.

Sex and TV. (1978, February 20). *Newsweek,* pp. 54–61.

Sex busters: A Meese Commission and Supreme Court echo a new moral militancy. (1986, July 21). *Time,* pp. 12–21.

Sex on television: Networks feel heat from advertisers. (1978, June 3). *TV Guide,* p. A-1.

Sheehan, P.W. (1983). Age trends and the correlates of children's television viewing. *Australian Journal of Psychology, 35*(3), 417–431.

Sheikh, A.A., Prasad, V.K., & Rao, T.R. (1974). Children's TV commercials: A review of research. *Journal of Communication, 24*(4), 126–136.

Siegel, A.E. (1956). Film-mediated fantasy aggression and strength of aggressive drive. *Child Development, 27,* 365–378.

Signorielli, N. (1982). Marital status in television drama: A case of reduced options. *Journal of Broadcasting, 26*(2), 585–597.

Signorielli, N. (1986). *Television and conceptions about sex-roles: Maintaining conventionality and the status quo.* Unpublished manuscript, Annenberg School of Communications, Philadelphia, PA.

Signorielli, N., Gross, L., & Morgan, M. (1982). Violence in television programs: Ten years later. In D. Pearl, L. Bouthilet, & J. Lazar (Eds.), *Television and behavior: Ten years of scientific progress and implications for the eighties* (Vol. 2, pp. 158–173). Washington, DC: U.S. Government Printing Office.

Silverman, L.T. (1976). *The effects of television programming on the prosocial behavior of preschool children.* Research report to the National Association of Broadcasters.

Silverman, L.T., & Sprafkin, J.N. (1980). The effects of *Sesame Street's* prosocial spots on cooperative play between young children. *Journal of Broadcasting, 24,* 135–147.

Silverman-Watkins, L.T., & Sprafkin, J.N. (1983). Adolescents' comprehension of televised sexual innuendos. *Journal of Applied Developmental Psychology, 4,* 359–369.

Singer, D.G. (1982). Television and the developing imagination of the child. In D. Pearl, L. Bouthilet, & J. Lazar (Eds.), *Television and behavior: Ten years of scientific progress and implications for the eighties* (Vol. 2), pp. 39–52). Washington, DC: U.S. Government Printing Office.

Singer, D.G., & Singer, J.L. (1983). Learning how to be intelligent consumers of television. In M.J. Howe (Ed.), *Learning from television* (pp. 203–222). London: Academic Press.

Singer, D.G., Zuckerman, D.M., & Singer, J.L. (1980). Helping elementary school children learn about TV. *Journal of Communication, 30*(3), 84–93.

Singer, J.L., & Singer, D.G. (1981). Television, imagination, and aggression: A study of preschoolers. Hillsdale, NJ: Lawrence Erlbaum Associates.

Singer, J.L., & Singer, D.G. (1983a). Implications of childhood television viewing for cognition, imagination, and emotion. In J. Bryant & D.R. Anderson (Eds.), *Children's understanding of television* (pp. 265–295). New York: Academic Press.

Singer, J.L., & Singer, D.G. (1983b, July). Psychologists look at television: Cognitive, developmental, personality, and social policy implications. *American Psychologist,* 826–834.

Singer, J.L., Singer, D.G., & Rapaczynski, W. (1984a). Children's imagination as predicted by family patterns and television viewing: A longitudinal study. *Genetic Psychology Monographs, 110,* 43–69.

Singer, J.L., Singer, D.G., & Rapaczynski, W. (1984b, Spring). Family patterns and television viewing as predictors of children's beliefs and aggression. *Journal of Communication,* 73–89.

S*M*A*S*H: An all time ratings record. (1983, March 14). *Time,* p. 79.

Smythe, D. (1954). Reality as presented by television. *Public Opinion Quarterly, 18,* 143–156.

Somers, A. (1976). Violence, television and the health of American youth. *The New England Journal of Medicine, 294,* 811–817.

Sprafkin, J., & Gadow, K.D. (1986). Television viewing habits of emotionally disturbed, learning disabled, and mentally retarded children. *Journal of Applied Developmental Psychology, 7,* 45–59.

Sprafkin, J., & Gadow, K.D. (in press). The immediate impact of aggressive cartoons on emotionally disturbed and learning disabled children. *Journal of Genetic Psychology.*

Sprafkin, J., Gadow, K.D., & Dussault, M. (1986). Reality perceptions of television: A preliminary comparison of emotionally disturbed and nonhandicapped children. *American Journal of Orthopsychiatry, 56,* 147–152.

Sprafkin, J., Gadow, K.D., & Grayson, P. (1984). Television and the emotionally disturbed, learning disabled, and mentally retarded child: A review. In K.D. Gadow (Ed.), *Advances in learning and behavioral disabilities* (Vol. 3, pp. 151–213). Greenwich, CT: JAI Press.

Sprafkin, J., Gadow, K.D., & Grayson, P. (1987). Effects of viewing aggressive cartoons on the behavior of learning disabled children. *Journal of Child Psychology and Psychiatry, 28,* 387–398.

Sprafkin, J., Gadow, K.D., & Grayson, P. (in press). The effects of cartoons on emotionally disturbed children's social behavior in school settings. *Journal of Child Psychology and Psychiatry.*

Sprafkin, J., Gadow, K.D., & Kant, G. (1988). Teaching emotionally disturbed children to discriminate reality from fantasy on television. *Journal of Special Education, in press.*

Sprafkin, J., Kelly, E., & Gadow, K.D. (1987). Reality perceptions of television: A comparison of emotionally disturbed, learning disabled, and nonhandicapped children. *Journal of Developmental and Behavioral Pediatrics, 8,* 149–153.

Sprafkin, J.N., Liebert, R.M., & Poulos, R.W. (1975). Effects of a prosocial televised example on children's helping. *Journal of Experimental Child Psychology, 20,* 119–126.

Sprafkin, J.N., & Rubinstein, E.A. (1982). Using television to improve the social behavior of institutionalized children. *Prevention in Human Services, 2,* 107–114.

Sprafkin, J.N., Rubinstein, E.A., & Stone, A. (1977). *A content analysis of four television diets.* New York: Brookdale International Institute.

Sprafkin, J.N., Silverman, L.T., & Rubinstein, E.A. (1979). *Public reactions to sex on television.* New York: Brookdale International Institute.

Sprafkin, J.N., & Silverman, L.T. (1981). Update: Physically intimate and sexual behavior on prime-time television: 1978–79. *Journal of Communication, 31*(1), 34–40.

Sprafkin, J.N., Silverman, L.T., & Rubinstein, E.A. (1980). Reactions to sex on television: An exploratory study. *Public Opinion Quarterly, 44,* 303–315.

Stein, A.H., & Friedrich, L.K. (1972). Television content and young children's behavior. In J.P. Murray, E.A. Rubinstein, & G.A. Comstock (Eds.), *Television and social behavior. Vol. II: Television and social learning* (pp. 202–317). Washington, DC: U.S. Government Printing Office.

Stein, G.M., & Bryan, J.G. (1972). The effect of a television model upon rule adoption behavior of children. *Child Development, 43,* 268–273.

Steinberg, C.S. (1980). *TV Facts.* New York: Facts on File, Inc.

Steinberg, C. (1985). *TV Facts.* New York: Facts on File Publications.

Steiner, G.A. (1963). *The people look at television.* New York: Alfred A. Knopf.

Steinfeld, J.L. (1973). TV violence is harmful. *Readers Digest, 4,* 37–45.

Sterling, C.H., & Haight, T.R. (1978). *The mass media: Aspen Institute guide to communication industry trends.* New York: Praeger Publishers.

Sternglanz, S.H., & Serbin, L.A. (1974). Sex role stereotyping in children's television programs. *Developmental Psychology, 10*(5), 710–715.

Steuer, F.B., Applefield, J.M., & Smith, R. (1971). Televised aggression and the interpersonal aggression of preschool children. *Journal of Experimental Child Psychology, 11,* 442–447.

Stookey, A., & Waz, J. (1980, April 7). The NAB: Not for all broadcasters. *Access,* p. 1.

Study links TV youths' aggression. (1982, May 5). *Newsday,* p. 7.

Tan, A.S. (1979). TV beauty ads and role expectations of adolescent female viewers. *Journalism Quarterly, 56,* 283–288.

Tannenbaum, P.H. (1971). Emotional arousal as a mediator of communication effects. *Technical reports of the Commission on Obscenity and Pornography* (Vol. 8). Washington, DC: U.S. Government Printing Office.

Tannenbaum, P.H. (1980). Entertainment as vicarious emotional experience. In P.H. Tannenbaum (Ed.), *The entertainment functions of television.* Hillside, NJ: Lawrence Erlbaum Associates.

Taylor, J.A. (1953). A personality scale of manifest anxiety. *Journal of Abnormal and Social Psychology, 48,* 285–290.

Tedesco, N.S. (1974). Patterns in prime time. *Journal of Communication, 24,* 118–124.

Television Information Office. (1981). *ABC's of radio and television.* New York: Author.

Thomas, M.H., & Drabman, R.S. (1977, August). *Effects of television violence on expectations of others' aggression.* Paper presented at the Annual Convention of the American Psychological Association, San Fransisco, CA.

Tower, R.B., Singer, D.G., Singer, J.L., & Biggs, A. (1979). Differential effects of television programming on preschoolers' cognition, imagination, and social play. *American Journal of Orthopsychiatry, 49*(2), 265–281.

Toying with kid's TV. (1985, May 13). *Newsweek,* p. 85.

Turner, C.W., Hesse, B.W., & Peterson-Lewis, S. (1986). Naturalistic studies of the long-term effects of television violence. *Journal of Social Issues, 42,* 51–73.

United States Commission on Civil Rights. (1977). *Window dressing on the set: Women and minorities in television.* Washington, DC: U.S. Government Printing Office.

United States Commission on Civil Rights. (1979). *Window dressing on the set: An update.* Washington, DC: U.S. Government Printing Office.

United States Senate, Committee on the Judiciary. (1956, January 16). *Television and juvenile delinquency. Investigation of juvenile delinquency in the United States.* 84th Congress, 2nd session, Report No. 1466.

United States Senate. (1961). *Effects on young people of violence and crime portrayals on television.* Part 10, Hearings before the Subcommittee to Investigate Juvenile Delinquency, Committee on the Judiciary, 87th Congress.

United States Senate, Subcommittee to Investigate Juvenile Delinquency. (1965). *Hearings on juvenile delinquency. Part 16. Effects on young people of violence and crime portrayed on television.* 88th Congress, 2nd session, July 30, 1964. Washington, DC: U.S. Government Printing Office.

United States Senate, Subcommittee on Communication. (1969). *Federal Communications Commission policy matters and television programming (Part 2).* Washington, DC: U.S. Government Printing Office.

United States Senate. (1972, March). *Hearings before the Subcommittee on Communications of the Committee on Commerce.*

Violence revisited. (1972, March 6). *Newsweek,* pp. 55–56.

Wachtel, E. (1986, November). *Television hiring practices 1980–1985: A report on the status of minorities and women.* New York: United Church of Christ.

Walters, R.H. & Thomas, E.L. (1963). Enhancement of punitiveness by visual and audiovisual displays. *Canadian Journal of Psychology, 17,* 244–255.

Walters, R.H. & Willows, D.C. (1968). Imitative behavior of disturbed and nondisturbed children following exposure to aggressive and nonaggressive models. *Child Development, 39,* 79–89.

Ward, S., Levinson, D., & Wackman, D. (1972). Children's attention to television advertising. In E.A. Rubinstein, G.A. Comstock, & J.P. Murray (Eds.), *Television and social behavior. Vol. IV: Television in day-to-day life: Patterns of use* (pp. 491–515). Washington, DC: U.S. Government Printing Office.

Ward, S., Reale, G., & Levinson, D. (1972). Children's perceptions, explanations, and judgments of television advertising: A further exploration. In E.A. Rubinstein, G.A. Comstock, & J.P. Murray (Eds.), *Television and social behavior. Vol. IV: Television in day-to-day life: Patterns of use* (pp. 468–490). Washington, DC: U.S. Government Printing Office.

Ward, S., & Wackman, D. (1972). Television advertising and intrafamily influence: Children's purchase influence attempts and parental yielding. In E.A. Rubinstein, G.A. Comstock, & J.P. Murray (Eds.), *Television and social behavior. Vol. IV: Television in day-to-day life: Patterns of use* (pp. 516–525). Washington, DC: U.S. Government Printing Office.

Ward, S., & Wackman, D.B. (1973). Children's information processing of television advertising. In P. Clarke (Ed.), *New models for mass communication research.* Beverly Hills, CA: Sage Publications.

Ward, S., Wackman, D., & Wartella, E. (1977). *How children learn to buy: The development of consumer information-processing skills.* Beverly Hills, CA: Sage.

Warning from Washington: Violence on television is harmful to children. (1982, May 17). *Time,* p. 77.

Waterman, D. (1985). Prerecorded home video and the distribution of theatrical feature films. In E.M. Noam (Ed.), *Video media competition: Regulation, economics, and technology* (pp. 221–243). New York: Columbia University Press.

Watkins, B., Calvert, S., Huston-Stein, A., & Wright, J.C. (1980). Children's recall of television material: Effects of presentation mode and adult labeling. *Developmental Psychology, 16,* 672–679.

Webs focus on kids: Attack barter and erosion on 3 fronts. (1986, June 9). *Television/Radio Age,* pp. 35–37.

Weigel, R.H., Loomis, J.W., & Soja, M.J. (1980). Race relations on prime-time television. *Journal of Personality and Social Psychology, 39*(5), 884–893.

Welch, R.L., Huston-Stein, A., Wright, J.C., & Plehal, R. (1979). Subtle sex-role cues in children's commercials. *Journal of Communication, 29*(3), 202–209.

White, M.E. (1978, March 29). Mom, Why's the TV set sweating? *New York Times.*

Whiteside, T. (1970, December 19). Annals of advertising. The New Yorker, pp. 42–48ff.

Wiley feels heat from TV's screen. (1974, October 21). *Broadcasting,* p. 41.

Williams, T.H., & Handford, A.G. (1986). Television and other leisure activities. In T.H. Williams (Ed.), *The impact of television: A natural experiment in three communities* (pp. 143–213). Orlando, FL: Academic Press, Inc.

Wimmer, R.D., & Popowski, M.L. (1985). Program and audience research. In S.T. Eastman, S.W. Head, & L. Klein (Eds.), *Broadcast/cable programming: Strategies and practices* (pp. 39–80). Belmont, CA: Wadsworth Publishing Company.

Winick, M.P., & Winick, C. (1979). *The television experience: What children see.* Beverly Hills, CA: Sage Publications.

Wolf, T.M. (1972). A developmental investigation of televised modeled verbalizations of resistance to deviation. *Developmental Psychology, 6,* 537.

Wright, J.C., Huston, A.C., Ross, R.P., Calvert, S.L., Rolandelli, D., Weeks, L.A., Raeissi, P., & Potts, R. (1984). Pace and continuity of television programs: Effects on children's attention and comprehension. *Developmental Psychology, 20*(4), 653–666.

Zillmann, D. (1969). *Emotional arousal as a factor in communication–mediated aggressive behavior.* Unpublished doctoral dissertation, University of Pennsylvania, Philadelphia.

Zillmann, D., & Bryant, J. (1982). Pornography, sexual callousness, and the trivialization of rape. *Journal of Communication, 32*(4), 10–21.

Zuckerman, P., Ziegler, M., & Stevenson, H.W. (1978). Children's viewing of television and recognition memory of commercials. *Child Development. 49,* 96–104.

Author Index

Subject Index

About the Authors

ROBERT M. LIEBERT (Ph.D.) is Professor of Psychology, State University of New York at Stony Brook. A principal investigator and overview writer for the National Institute of Mental Health's program on Television and Social Behavior, Dr. Liebert has published numerous articles on children's social development. He has co-authored seven other books, including *The Child: Development from Birth through Adolescence, Personality: Strategies and Issues, Developmental Psychology,* and *Science and Behavior: An Introduction to Methods of Research.*

JOYCE SPRAFKIN (Ph.D.) is an Assistant Professor in the Department of Psychiatry and Behavioral Science, State University of New York at Stony Brook. She has published numerous articles about the effects of television on children and has specialized in TV and special populations for which she has received several NIMH research grants and coauthored a chapter in the NIMH Ten-Year Update. She is also the senior editor of a book, *Rx Television: Enhancing the Preventive Impact of TV.*

Pergamon General Psychology Series

Editors:
Arnold P. Goldstein, Syracuse University
Leonard Krasner, Stanford University & SUNY at Stony Brook

*Out of print in original format. Available in custom reprint edition.